BEFORE
MANDELA'S
RAINBOW

FOR MY FAVOURITE HUSH PUPPY...
SKIP THE RUDE BITS AND YOU'LL
·HAVE A LOT LESS TO
DIGEST!
ORRA BEST...

Eddie Joffe

EDWARD JOFFE

authorHOUSE®

AuthorHouse™ UK
1663 Liberty Drive
Bloomington, IN 47403 USA
www.authorhouse.co.uk
Phone: 0800.197.4150

This edition published by AuthorHouse   12/01/2015

ISBN: 978-1-4772-4170-7 (sc)
ISBN: 978-1-4817-8497-9 (hc)
ISBN: 978-1-4918-9208-4 (e)

Print information available on the last page.

Certain stock imagery © Thinkstock.

This book is printed on acid-free paper.

Dedications

This book is dedicated to my beloved wifie Sheena, not only for the plethora of creature comforts she has constantly afforded me but for the love, the patience, the encouragement, the long nights of proofing and the kindness and deep understanding she lavished on me in the face of her many medical problems.

To the eternal memory of
Madiba
South Africa's first saint

Violent storms often precede rainbows.
I was born and bred in South Africa long before
Nelson Mandela's rainbow.

Author Information

Born, bred and semi-educated in Johannesburg, Edward (Eddie) Joffe experienced a vibrant childhood as a privileged white South African. After dropping out of Witwatersrand University, he fumbled through tedious jobs while searching for some challenging creative occupation. In 1955 an opportunity arose to write and direct his first film *Tent of Stars* during a 7,000 mile African safari incorporating the only known motorised attempt to scale Kilimanjaro, Africa's highest mountain.

Unable to come to terms with apartheid or the Victorian mores of most white South Africans he escaped to Britain expecting movie moguls to be clamouring for his services. But alas, to his chagrin he again had to settle for odd jobs, including stints as a pop star roadie and a television critic for *The Stage* newspaper. He enrolled at the London School of Film Technique where his 35 mm graduation film featured Soho's iconic coffee bars before he went on to become the first South African-born director, producer, writer in ITV, the UK's commercial television channel.

His international award winning career encompassed approximately 4,000 films and television productions of every genre as well as consultancy work and lecturing on production techniques in the UK and abroad.

One of the founders of Britain's Directors Guild, he remains a member of BAFTA, the British Academy of Film and Television Arts.

He relished working with top British entertainers and thespians as well as paupers, prisoners, prime ministers, and lashings of famous nonentities.

In 1968 he was Tony Hancock's producer / director in Australia. The comedian's tragic death in Eddie's home inspired his first book *Hancock's Last Stand* which was highly acclaimed for its style and candour. The screenplay for World Productions' movie *Hancock & Joan* was partially based on Joffe's book.

Joffe claims that his book *Before Mandela's Rainbow,* based on his reminiscences of life in apartheid South Africa, took him longer to write than it did to live.

He unashamedly committed opsigamy in 2011 and is currently serving a life sentence.

Acknowledgements

Almost every person I encountered during more than eight decades on this planet has contributed to my story. Although I cannot possibly remember everyone, you were there and I tender heartfelt appreciation for most of the memories, good, bad and indifferent.

Huge debts of gratitude are due to umpteen especially wonderful people not individually named within the book itself, such as:-

Evelyn Hood, my dear friend and editor, whose painstaking checking of my first draft was ruined by my massive rewrite. Unfazed by an excess of split infinitives, hyperbole and highly dubious punctuation, Evelyn embarked on a second corrective odyssey with admirable courage and bravura to enhance this edition. A truly great *fidus Achates*.

Layne Cain, my daughter, for her invaluable editorial and proof-reading assistance.

Anne Joffe, a much missed cousin. Her voluminous knowledge of my father's family was inordinately helpful.

Brian Lapping whose exceptional insight into apartheid reminded me of horrors I had sublimated, forgotten or never knew. I am deeply grateful to him for his generosity in presenting me with DVD's of his entire television documentary series about apartheid.

Vivien McAlpine for access to the Sacred Heart library.

Dr. Bhaskar Ram for his time and advice.

Maria and Kenny Robinson for restoring a vital manuscript.

Pat Rogers for his constructive observations.

Plus other outstandingly talented and helpful folk listed in my bibliography.

And last, but by no means least, to my kid brother Justin, who was subjected to so much psychological stress by his older brother that he became a professor in that field. He waded patiently and unerringly through numerous drafts, providing invaluable, intelligent comments and vivid reminders of our childhood.

Chapters

A Sort Of Prologue

As the traveler neared the double gates misty clouds gently evaporated in wisps in the warmth of the sun, disappearing as if on cue. There was a lot wrong with the gates. They should have been wrought from pure gleaming gold or maybe platinum or, at the very least, shimmering silver. On either side of the gates the walls should have been supported by towering mother of pearl columns ascending upwards forever, blending, Cecil B de Mille style, into the azure blue of the heavens they pierced. They ought to have been wide enough to admit cavalcades of carriaged queens and kings, their dashing nobles, banners proudly aflutter, glitteringly astride identical, pure white, thoroughbred chargers, leading vast panoplies of soldiers in splendiferous, peacocked uniforms.

Instead, the gates, fabricated of plain black painted iron, were barely wide enough to allow two motor cars to pass through alongside one another.

Despite his disenchantment at their mediocrity the traveler instinctively knew he had arrived at his preordained destination because these gates were distinctly familiar evoking memories of passing through them hundreds, perhaps thousands, of times in the past. Was it *déjà vu* or had his brain cells shared the same fate as the swirls of melting moisture? He looked back.

There, behind him, somber clouds had banked up to form a barrier which would be impenetrable and in any case he had no notion which of the myriad paths terminating at the gates had led him here on a journey that had taken him more than three quarters of a century, traversing rugged mountains with perilous precipices and predators all along the way. Hence he dared not contemplate retracing his steps. Not through cloud that thick anyway, even though he might possibly pass along golden paradisiacal beaches on his way to a different place. He was puzzled that there was no one else outside those gates, waiting, as he was, for attention.

Considering the death, devilment, disease and destruction rampant in the world he had left behind, he expected to find enormous crowds patiently awaiting entry. He did not immediately realize that's not the way it is. He had long been mindful that everyone in creation is an individual and that so far as humankind was concerned there are no clones. Not yet that is. We are all special, he thought, all one-offs. We love, we lust, we fornicate, we live, we eat, we defecate, we survive, we perish, often sharing mass graves with brothers, sisters, children, parents, neighbours, strangers even. We are the masses. Yet we are all, every single one of us, on the small planet we have named Earth and in common with the trillions of intelligent life forms inhabiting the known and undiscovered galaxies, individuals, totally unique.

That oft repeated cliché 'I know how you feel old boy' is bullshit he told himself. You *don't* know how *I* feel - and I don't know how you feel. I may *think* I do, as you think you know my feelings but you don't. We may use the same terminology, the same language, the same software, come from the same country, the same town, the same village, the same house, perhaps even the same womb. We may share the same experiences, but they are shared differently. We may even have been to the same school where we were semi-educated by the same teachers who tried to inculcate the same values - perhaps not even *their* personal values, rather those dictated by custom, by politics or by religion.

'Only *I* can know how I feel,' he pondered. 'I may even try to explain it in words, in the same language as yours, choosing my vocabulary as precisely as possible. Regrettably *you* do not, indeed cannot, know how *I* feel. You're not me. You may well have tasted the elation of love or the deep, final sorrow of death's presence. But was your joy greater or your grief deeper than mine? Was the pit of your emptiness as dark as mine? Or more so? Or less? Of course I will listen to your version of how you feel and will nod in sympathy and proffer condolences and try to stop myself from uttering that lie - *I know how you feel.* Or worse - *been there, done that and sport two t-shirts to prove it...*

So, he thought, his discomfort about there being no one else at the gates was garbage, inexplicable garbage. Common sense told him there must have been hundreds, thousands, perhaps millions, present waiting to be processed. Only he was not aware of them, nor they of him. Where were all those who had formed the endless procession of refugees that were so ghastly a feature of the 'ethnic cleansings' of our planet's misnamed 20th Century? Where are they he wondered, the pathetic lines of sick people, of aged people of desperate parents weeping impotently while witnessing their innocent young die at the hands of genocidal, racist maniacs and megalomaniacs?

He waited a few minutes - or was it an eternity? - contemplating those gates and the low walls on either side of them. Too small, he concluded, to keep people in. Or out.

When, at last, the Keeper of the Gates appeared, the traveler was intrigued to find he knew him well. He was his mirror image, his doppelganger. Or was he? The traveler scrutinized the elderly, silvery haired, balding, bespectacled, overweight man with several days' growth of stubble, wearing a scruffy black track suit which had never been troubled by an electric iron. The old man looked him straight in the eye, not in the least curious about him. Nor did he say anything, he simply stared unblinkingly. Then, astoundingly, the doppelganger's tired eyes grew younger, brighter, clearer. The stubble dissolved as had those clouds. His lined face became steadily smoother, his hair thicker, darker, akin to an expensive effect in the movies. The Keeper's stature as well as his clothing altered until there stood before the traveler a schoolboy, scrubbed clean, replete with a blazer of navy blue with double golden-yellow pairs of vertical stripes on it. The boy revelled in the hedonistic aroma of his crisp, freshly laundered white shirt, tucked neatly into his long grey trousers supported by a blue and gold striped elastic belt whose buckle was a flattened snake frozen in a permanent metallic 'S' shape. Around his neck hung a crooked, gawkily knotted tie matching the colour and pattern of his blazer. On his head, perched at a jaunty angle, was a straw boater, its flat topped crown surrounded by a hat band in blue and gold.

The traveler smiled, recollecting how, at first, he'd hated that hat until he'd matured sufficiently to appreciate that it not only added a touch of distinction to his mien but also instilled in him an arrogant, fustian opinion of self-importance while wearing it on school outings. This and the combination of his colour coordinated uniform provided irrefutable evidence that he was not an impostor but one who belonged behind the gates.

It dawned on the traveler that the gates were in fact those of his school. Not much had changed in all those bygone years except that while he had been busy living his life the gates had shrunk. They were the same gates, oh yes, only far smaller than they had been seen from a child's perspective. His sixth sense assured him that the Keeper was himself; and that his life was not quite over; and that he was destined to relive parts of it; and that his newly completed journey was only the beginning; and that trying to alter it in any way would be both dishonest and impossible; and that even if he considered it from any other frame of reference, he would still have to relive it time and time again and again and again until it accurately reflected his life's blueprint. This reconfirmed his thoughts that all he had perceived in life *was* unique and that his narrative had to be truthful, to him at least, or he would be barred from passing through *his* personal gates.

He now knew for certain that he was but one of the uncountable sentient beings who had stood at their personal gates reflecting on their journey through life until being allowed through the gates into the unexplored galaxy of galaxies on the other side.

Then the traveler awoke and started writing his memoirs.

These memoirs are really all about quite a beastly little bugger born in Johannesburg, a sort of misfit super brat who truly deserved to spend much of his childhood incarcerated as a boarder at a private fee-paying Catholic school where he excelled at hardly anything apart from two uncommon achievements, one of which was having had prayers intoned for him at assembly by the entire school when he contracted meningitis. The other was the size of my gonads. Yes, the size of my gonads.

You see I had this friend whose given name, Achille (no 's' as with the hero) was of Greek origin, which was hardly surprising since his family was Greek. His name was pronounced Ack-kill-lay but non-Greek South Africans seemed incapable of manoeuvring their tongues round that, so his non-Greek friends all called him Ash-shill - or simply Ash as he preferred to be known.

Ash lived in Empire Road not far from my home at 55 Loch Avenue, Parktown West. He inhabited a grand mansion very unlike my parents' home or those of my other friends or any of my family who lived in bungalow style houses, there being no need in a country with an overabundance of space to erect tall houses or other land efficient edifices. Ash's house was completely white with a nifty green pantiled roof and a gorgeous garden with a highly enviable additional feature - a tennis court.

His was the first double storeyed house I ever entered. Ash's father was a shipper, whatever that was. He was seldom at home and on his rare personal appearances, he blurred past us kids without a greeting or even a glance, scurrying by in March Hare mode, to return to his shipping. Or maybe he was shy or just didn't relate to kids. Either way he was an unprepossessing man.

Ash's mother on the other hand, was a sultry, sexy lady for whom I developed an onerous teenage crush. Her presence always reduced me to silent idolization. I think she liked me, possibly mistaking my lovelorn silence as a sign of good manners and respect for my elders. I was indubitably quieter than any of her son's other pals and younger relatives who chattered away nonstop in Greek and hardly ever in English. I'm sure I would have received a healthy clip around the earhole if she'd ever suspected what I was really thinking.

To be honest, I wasn't that friendly with Ash, who was a year or two older than me, yet treated me almost as an equal, totally ignorant of the fact that I only visited him to admire his mama.

Ash was a keep fit freak whose mania manifested itself mainly in jogging in the days before that word had been coined and was still called running. He also rode a bike for hours on end, frequented a gym where he climbed ropes, leapt over wooden horses, utilised the parallel bars and that kind of thing. I kept forgetting to ask him why he bothered doing this only my thoughts were preoccupied with the hope that his mother would drop by to say hello, an event which hardly ever materialized. It was difficult to get a word in edgewise with Ash who was occasionally high on the rush of adrenalin brought about by his regular excess of exercise. This, in turn, made him far more voluble than your average South African of his age.

Although I played tennis at school, my game was significantly improved on the clay court in Ash's garden. What he lacked in subtlety he compensated for with aggressive strength. His serves were staggering, as were his forehand smashes

1

but he hadn't a clue about delicate lobs or tactical placement. Experience had taught me not to argue with him if he deemed his shot in when blatantly it was not. I managed to beat him now and then which wasn't a good idea as losing made him sulk for the rest of the day even refusing to cavort in and out of the spray gadget that endlessly sustained the Technicolor green of the manicured lawn neat as a new pin surrounding his house.

I told Ash of the ads I'd seen in a Superman comic about a guy called Charles Atlas who had once been a 97 pound weakling into whose face big, bulging, bicepped blokes kept kicking sand at him lolling on the beach ogling women. Atlas's intense dislike of mouthfuls of beach sand inspired him to invent a course called 'Dynamic Tension' which augmented both his physique and his bank balance. I had imagined that Atlas, 'the world's most perfectly developed man' had changed his name from Aronofsky, or something, to Atlas on the grounds that no one could possibly take anyone called 'Aronofsky the body builder' seriously, and, as Aronofsky, Atlas must have been aware that a substantial number of 97 pound weaklings proliferated in the USA so he proselytized among its younger citizens via comic books.

I don't think Atlas picked a particularly propitious period to capture the South African youth market since we're talking of the era in which Frank Sinatra began sashaying into the swing, as it were, of his chosen profession and all the girls I knew idolized and swooned as Young Blue Eyes, as he was then, crooned at them from the innards of every radio and every gramophone in every house harboring mutant teenagers. My circle of friends (except Ash) actually aspired to emulate Frank who looked like - yes, you're right - Aronofsky, the 97 pounder who kept getting sand kicked in his face.

Indeed, Ash proclaimed, the course wasn't worth the dosh because, in his opinion he had a better body than Charles Atlas to start with and, anyway, if anyone kicked sand at him, they wouldn't see any more of that day or the next for that matter. Know-what-I-mean?

Undeterred I applied my mind to finding means of assisting Ash achieve the muscular perfection on which he had set his sights only to have my suggestion to try weightlifting pooh-poohed by his declaration that he didn't think much of my idea since weights made you muscle bound hey man.

For a reason I can't quite put my finger on, I didn't visit Ash for a while. No, no, that's not strictly accurate. Ash had his eye on Nora, a scrawny but rather pretty platinum blonde who lived nearby and whom I thought was my girlfriend. Holding hands in those days was the equivalent of betrothal and, well, we were almost there until Ash appeared centre stage and as my physique had more in common with Sinatra than Atlas, her fickle heart performed a hop, skip and a jump, or, it may even have been a pole vault at the sight of all that burgeoning masculine musculature. That took care of me. Not that Ash was a back stabber or anything like that; he just wasn't aware that Nora and I had been on the brink of culminating our engagement, aka 'going steady', until I took her round to his house for a game of tennis. Ash's romance with my girlfriend didn't last very long given that he spent excessive time exercising and talking about himself, a trait Nora considered to be the feminine prerogative in any relationship. In due course, having found another girlfriend, I forgave Ash sufficiently to want to see his mother again, so I dropped in for a visit, to find him working out on the shady side of his house, near the tennis court, with a brand new, gleaming, very expensive set of burnished barbells.

I was amazed at how much his legs had developed in the few short months I'd neglected him. Yirra man they were humungous - awesomely so. His thighs, which resembled chunks of gnarled oak, were roughly the girth of my midriff.

He told me he only had another couple of minutes to finish his 'set' and I gawked, fascinated by his rippling muscles. Just watching him expend such prodigious energy wore me out. It was a hot afternoon and buckets of sweat were pouring off him so I abandoned hope of a game of tennis.

When he'd finished toweling himself down after a refreshing shower under the omnipresent lawn sprinkler, I reminded him that weight training would cause muscle-binding. His rejoinder was unequivocal. 'You're talking kak man' he said. Then he asked where on earth I'd got such a stupid idea from. I let it pass and helped him sort the glistening circles of chrome plated steel poundage into neat, matching piles, the biggest one on the ground with the smaller ones fitting snugly into the perimeter of the one below, all stacking up into a likeness of those phallic pagoda things you see in Far Eastern travel brochures. Naturally he finished his pile long before mine.

'You're a lazy beggar', he admonished, 'you should get some exercise.'

'I do', I replied, 'I swim, play tennis and cricket in summer and in winter it's rugby and ice skating.'

'That', he assured me emphatically, 'is no bladdy good.' (In South Africa, bladdy is the only recognized pronunciation of 'bloody' among English speakers. If you say 'blerry' it immediately reveals that you either had not received a decent upbringing, or that you came from the Orange Free State.)

'You should,' continued Ash, 'take up weights.'

I told him it was far too strenuous for my liking. Nevertheless he launched into an encomium on the merits of weights and generously offered me a crash course in their use with a view to our training together. Much as I savored the possibility of seeing Ash's mom more frequently, I preferred that pleasure to occur before, during, or after a game of tennis in preference to the back breaking effort of weight training, so I politely declined his magnanimous proposal which had, I suppose, been a gratifying compliment really, considering that Ash later became 'Best Legs, Mr. South Africa', or was it 'Mr. South Africa, Best Legs'? Either way it was difficult to get much more famous than that.

What, you may well ask, has all this to do with my balls? Kindly be patient - I'm getting there...

Ash continued to elucidate on the methodology of barbell exercises, ho-humming on about fiber diets, carbohydrate diets, symmetry, posing and muscularity, emphasizing which exercises related to what body parts and which muscles were best moulded by sit-ups, press-ups, squats or whatever.

Personally I was far more interested in female anatomy and since Ash's exposition was confined to the male physique I didn't pay much attention to his verbosity which included deltoids, obliques, the intriguingly named erectors and abbreviations like lats, traps, abs, pecs and assorted others I had never previously heard of. Ash's dedication to bodybuilding introduced me to a subject that served only to equip me with answers to that exasperating game Trivial Pursuit, a name which aptly summarizes what I believed Ash was up to with all that scrap metal in his garden. Since his exhortations failed to stir me into participating he selfishly began to demonstrate a 'clean and jerk' - a technique esteemed by those burly guys on television who heft hundreds of pounds of dead weight into the air above their heads and hold it there for a given number of seconds. No written description can do full justice to the clean and jerk so if you've not watched Olympic or any other weight lifting contests on television please do not feel excluded as my brief explanation may make as little sense to you as it did to me at the time.

Ash repeated his assertions that I was an indolent good-for-nothing which was, in truth, absolutely accurate as he prepared for the clean and jerk with its necessary preliminary ritual.

'Watch this,' said he, 'It's so simple I bet even you could do it!'

There he stood, legs slightly apart, concentrating, inhaling deeply before grabbing the bar, heaving it to chest height and sort of half kneeling, then straightening up simultaneously pushing the barbell skywards as nonchalantly as he would lift a spoonful of cornflakes to his lips. If you're not old enough to know better, dear reader, this is a feat you should certainly not even think of emulating at home, especially if you're on your own or have any doubts about the tensile strength of your bedroom floor.

'Gotit?' he demanded.

'Of course', I lied.

'OK', said Ash, 'let's see'.

My hesitation prompted Ash to resort to the dirtiest trick in the teenage repertoire. He dared me to have a go at the weights. Reluctantly I approached the barbell, contemplated it briefly, as he had, sucked in a deep lungful of air, regretted my folly, gulped a few more lungsful and began my first attempt at it accompanied by noises which would have qualified for inclusion in Spike Jones' mad immortal hit 'Cocktails for Two'. It didn't work, so I tried again. The blood rushed to my head as I hauled the barbell an inch or so above the ground.

Ash stood regarding me with a sardonic smile wordlessly confirming that I was incontrovertibly a prototype of the 97 pound weakling irredeemably condemned to a lifetime of sandy faces. That did it! I determined to prove him wrong so I persevered; managing to chin the bar to the accompaniment of further porcine sound effects, until, with a final, strangled grunt I raised all that metal slightly above my head. By now I was decidedly dizzy and let go of the bar which missed my skull by a coat of chrome as it squelched into the soft, over watered lawn. I remember being highly disgruntled at not hearing the clank of the barbell before I passed out.

Next thing I knew was - bliss of all blisses - Ash's mom was fussing over me pouring cool, fizzy lemonade down my throat all the while murmuring tender solicitations in a gentle, mesmerizing voice. There I lay, a cynic no longer, filled with admiration for the pleasures I now deduced could be achieved with weight lifting, and, taking full advantage of my position I luxuriated in the cooing and gentle clucking sounds being made for my sole benefit.

This took place during a winter school vacation prior to which I had remained unaware of any unusual testicular endowment which we will return to later.

As a very small boy my mother doted on me to the extent that I was in grave danger of transmogrifying into Little Lord Fauntleroy. She dressed me modishly and I have photographs to prove it. There I am aged 5 or thereabouts attired like a junior poof in black velvet short trousers, a pure silk, whiter-than-white shirt with genuine mother-of-pearl buttons, ruched sleeves and a black bow tie with white polka dots. On my feet are white socks and patent leather black shoes. And, to top it all off, my dark, naturally curly, frizzy hair was hidden by a French beret.

My finest childhood sartorial landmark was at a cousin's wedding where I shone as a page boy dressed in a replica of an adult dress suit, perfect down to the last detail - shiny lapelled double breasted black tailcoat, satin striped trousers, white ruffle-fronted dickey shirt, black bow tie, miniature cufflinks, patent leather shoes, white gloves and a tiny top hat - the full junior Monty. Vindictive relatives kept reminding me that my ensemble and my innocent, butter-wouldn't-melt-in-my-mouth, babyface look had attracted more attention than the bride herself and outshone her along with my captivating flower girl cousin dressed entirely in pink whose hand I clutched tightly as we strolled together down the aisle. Yessir - as well as stealing the show that day, I proposed for the very first time and was accepted. Aaahhhhhhhhhh!

I was absolutely, rottenly spoiled by my parents and inevitably got my own way. I guess it may have been the sissy clothing that activated my rebellious nature in that if I didn't get what I wanted precisely when I wanted it, I stored up my revenge until my parents had guests. I would sneak into either the lounge, or dining room, to perform a party piece I had perfected. Down came the trousers in synchronization with the removal of my underpants, baring my pink buttocks to all and sundry. The impact was further intensified as I bent forward, anus audience-wards while positioning one hand over the crack, patting it to give the impression I'd farted and was wafting the gas towards them. It was supremely satisfying to occasionally succeed in releasing a real burst of air. Their shocked reaction was enormously gratifying to me and their faces were, I'm told, wondrous to behold.

Lamentably my endeavors to follow in the footsteps of the 'Flatulist' or 'Fartiste' Joseph Pujol, (Le Petomane, of whom I hadn't yet heard) palled because those who could bring themselves to pay a second visit to our home ignored me completely thereby obliging me to devise other ploys to gain attention.

Predestination ordained that my life should begin in a road called End Street and in the same year that Boris Karloff's *Frankenstein* film was released. This ridiculous juxtaposition presaged a life of infinite variety and plenty of laughter punctuated with relatively infrequent bleak periods of sadness. The venue for my debut was the Colwyn Nursing home, converted from what had once been the Imperial Light Horse Headquarters, standing on a narrow island site running the length of End Street.

All babies, of my acquaintance anyway, made their first incursions into speech with simple words of one or two syllables at best - da, dada, ma, mama, or perhaps the mispronounced name of a sibling. Not me. I was a four syllabler with *afelifie* as my first word. *Afelifie* is Afrikaans for the Cape gooseberry... How I picked that up is unclear as no one in my family circle except my Uncle Ike was fluent enough in Afrikaans to know that word unless my father, who depended on fruit for a living, perhaps used it as a pet name for me spoken only in private one-to-ones between father and baby son.

It wouldn't have surprised anyone if my first words had been Hokey Pokey absorbed from the daily cry of a black ice cream vendor proclaiming he was in our street selling 'Hokey Pokey ice cream' from his tricycle cart with its commodious, white, cube-shaped airtight ice cream container at the front, filled with a selection of suckers (ice lollies as opposed to lollipops) of varied hues and flavors together with assorted ice cream all kept well chilled by dry ice - solid carbon dioxide. The regular ice cream man was always smartly turned out in a white jacket, well pressed black trousers and a black military officer's cap. He reinforced his presence with his bicycle bell while pedaling along, before emphasizing his arrival by tolling a heavy brass hand bell to entice the neighbourhood kids who flocked, in Hamelin mode, to his cart, besieging it even before it stopped. My preference was Eskimo Pie, an oblong ice cream covered in milk chocolate at the cost of a *tickey* (a tiny coin worth three pence.) Top sellers, at tuppence apiece, were ice creams the same shape and size as the Eskimo Pies except that they came between crisp wafer biscuits on both the larger surfaces. Suckers, today classified as drinks on a stick, were a penny each.

On rare occasions, if his wares were sold out he presented us with his residual dry ice and we'd quiver to the frisson aroused by the burbling white smoke-like clouds it precipitates when water is added.. We even drank this fizzy by-product, taking care to avoid swallowing the slivers of almost spent dry ice which rose to the surface. If he gave us any larger lumps of steaming ice we'd put them into screw-top ink bottles, hoarded for such occasions, and then fill them with water and quickly tighten the lids before shaking and hurling the bottles as far as possible, preferably onto the road or other hard surface where our home-made hand grenades would shatter loudly, thrillingly, propelling glass shards every which way. Amazingly no one ever got hurt indulging in so risky a pastime.

One spring cleaning day Mom laid my father's medals on the bed. My four year old brother noticed them and asked what they were.

'They're daddy's medals', my mother told him.

'What are they for?' asked my brother.

'For serving in the army' Mom answered.

'Oh', said he, 'did he serve dinner or lunch?

And that was the sum total of our knowledge of Pop's war because he never spoke of his military years to us. Not once. Not ever. And the slate remained blank. Until I went researching...

Private Harry Joffe, 1671, swore allegiance to His Majesty, King George V at Potchefstroom on 23 March 1916 on which date he was barely 18 but claimed to be twenty one, working as a 'conductor, municipal cars', and that his mother, Fannie, was partially dependent on him. He attested that he *'engaged and agreed to serve as an Imperial soldier under the Army Act in the Union's East Africa Expeditionary Force and to be attached to any arm or branch of the service therein for the duration of hostilities in Central and East Africa and for three months thereafter, provided that His Majesty should so long require his services or until legally discharged, such discharge to be carried out in South Africa should he so desire.'*

Pop found himself assigned to the 4th Field Ambulance Unit of the South African Medical Corps. He was posted to Dodoma in Tanganyika, today the capital of Tanzania, a town described by travel writer Phillip Biggs as 'eminently missable.' By chance I once visited Dodoma while filming in the early 1950's, 60 years before I found out that Pop had been stationed there. It was, and still is, an arid, dusty desert town over 3,000 ft. above sea level on the edge of the Great Rift Valley where extreme temperatures range from 35°C during the day to minus 10°C at night. Aside from the weather it was hardly the sort of place one would choose to spend a war in, chiefly since East Africa obtained notoriety for tropical scourges such as rampant malaria. So much so that Lieutenant-General Smuts, Commander-in-Chief, East African Force noted in a dispatch:-

'... the very rapid rise of the sick rate among all the troops... It was clear that white troops who had had repeated attacks of malaria or dysentery would be more of an encumbrance than a help... ''

Smuts lost no time evacuating all white troops declared to be medically unfit, resulting in close on 12,000 soldiers being returned home from East Africa. This possibly led to Pop being aboard the Kinfauns Castle, a passenger vessel with a proud record as an armed merchant cruiser until 1916 when she was pressed into service as a troopship capable of carrying 1,500 troops on each journey so it was hardly surprising that Pop contracted that disease diagnosed as 'type unknown' at Dodoma. These details only came to light thanks to the records held by the South African Army archives. On his return to Johannesburg he was hospitalized, granted a month's 'recuperative leave' and then discharged from the army.

Photographs confirm that Pop was a handsome young man cast in the Jack-the-lad mould at the time he met and married a woman called Annie Romain. Their marriage didn't last very long and ended in divorce.

Neither my siblings nor I knew anything about Pop's first marriage until I was about fifteen and chanced upon a key to an iron strongbox stored high up in a slatted, shelved, linen storage cupboard where it lay, concealed under piles of laundered sheets. It had, until then, been considered safe from marauding burglars but not from a nosey Parker like me. That box had hitherto secreted family records and other important papers. The pile included my parents' marriage certificate plainly stating in indelible ink that my father's marital status was 'divorcee.' Thus was the family 'skeleton' disinterred. I was foolish enough to tell my siblings of the discovery inordinately upsetting my sister Amelia, named after my grandmother. I would have preferred someone else to have broken the news to her, and although she would undoubtedly have found out in the course of time, I deeply regretted having been the bearer of the most dramatic tidings of her young life

Pop began dating my Aunt Clara until the grapevine notified my Gran that he was a divorcee (a heinous social crime in the Roaring Twenties) and she forbade my aunt to have anything to do with him. Aunt Clara heeded her mother's advice about not having a liaison with a divorcee and chose to forego the relationship. Undaunted Pop switched his attention to her attractive younger sister Rita, my mother, to whom he promptly proposed.

Mom was a well-read, well educated, adventurous young woman - a good swimmer, a keen tennis player a whiz at calisthenics, and could twirl those wooden Indian club things with noteworthy panache. The clubs reminded me of skinny, elongated tenpin bowling pins with rounded bottoms. These were ever so popular in white South African girls' schools, since, it was claimed; they 'stimulated the brain and invigorated the body.' Perhaps they also instilled in Mom the energy for all those activities over and above helping Granny bring up my two cousins Millie and Johnny Naar, my Uncle Alf's children, whose mother Myra had walked out on her family and both the very young kids were had to be taken in by my grandparents.

Mom plumped for an unprecedented job for a woman - driving a lorry for a soft drinks company in preference to becoming a shop girl or a secretary. Unheard of in those days - what, what? She ignored Gran's dire warnings about divorced men and my parents were wed in 1930 when Pop was 32 and had doubtless obtained Gran's forgiveness for his 'marital misdeed'.

Following their wedding my parents went to work for Mom's half-sister Aunt Stella, a formidable old gal of uberous proportions, who owned a hotel in Aliwal North, a dozy dump in the Eastern Cape and doubtless the place where I was conceived. This last factor resulted in my parents' decision to return to Johannesburg to live with my Gran at her home at 16 Webb Street, opposite the Nazareth House Convent in Yeoville.

The world had, by then, entered the Great Depression seemingly an inopportune time to open a business but Mom maintained that no matter how hard up people happened to be, they had to eat. The result was that my arrival on the planet helped her persuade my father to return to Johannesburg to open a business specializing in fresh fruit, vegetables, groceries and confectionery in Plein Street in Johannesburg's main shopping centre where all the major stores were located, naming his shop in honour of his firstborn son. It didn't take long for the word 'Eddies' to become synonymous with produce of the finest quality attracting both the city's gentry and the hoi polloi. The business prospered and my parents soon accumulated enough capital to make a down payment on their own house at 67 Joel Road, Berea.

Granny moved in with us and all in all I spent much of my first five or six years in her charge while my mother went to help Pop at the shop.

Granny was a Cockney of Spanish origin, born Amelia Espinoza. Her sister Arche married David Naar, a Dutchman from Haarlem living in London. Arche produced four children before she died an early death and David married my Gran. Soon afterwards he contracted a pulmonary problem. Doctors strongly advised him to migrate from the mists and chills of Northern Europe to sunnier climes if he wanted to survive. He did and migrated to South Africa where he lived to sire another eight children, bringing his tally to a round dozen, ten of whom survived childbirth. His chosen country had much to offer a man who not only spoke both white languages but also possessed a brace of highly apposite professions in a rough and ready mining town - those of diamond cutting and cigar making.

The Naar family reached South Africa at the height of the first Boer War. Their rail journey from the coast to the Witwatersrand, a thousand miles away, was interrupted from time to time by Boer or British combatants demanding to search their belongings, specifically an outsized wooden packing case that the soldiers suspected held munitions. They were exceedingly disappointed to find that the weapon inside was Gran's piano. My grandfather's fluent bilingualism was immeasurably advantageous on that hazardous odyssey since both sides thought them to be 'their' people.

Granny frequently regaled me with stories of her early days in South Africa during the Boer War. Being an ignorant young sod I switched off mentally whenever she reminisced about her adventures, the voyage out, the pound of butter costing a gold sovereign, the early pioneers... My idiotic attitude was 'Oh no, Gran, not again! You told me that story last week...' I heard her, but did not *listen* so that my information about their pioneering journey is partly speculative, partly half-remembered family yarns and receding echoes of snippets of conversations between relatives.

In the back yard of Gran's house there stood a wall like no other I have ever seen. Ten paces long it was fabricated entirely from empty Bols Genever Gin salt glazed earthenware bottles piled up neatly lengthwise, lying flat, row upon row, each row atop the other, bottoms to the front until it was twice my height. There must have been thousands of 'em. I failed to notice whether or not the wall grew bigger or who drank the contents. I never saw my Gran inebriated, so I have attributed the content consumption, design and erection of that wall to my grandfather who died before I was born.

Father time has erased any memories of my ever going to kindergarten or its equivalent. Perhaps I didn't go to one or mayhap they didn't exist in Johannesburg in the early 30's.

Anamnesis of my first school, Yeoville Boys, a pitifully dull institution just off Rockey Street, also remains vague except for two things - a snapping turtle of a teacher who forbade pencil sharpening during lessons, an instruction I flaunted because the tip of my lead broke, forcing me to employ a one sided razor blade on my pencil concealing it from the teachers' view as best I could under the desk. The blade slipped, blood gushed and I was rushed away for medical attention, retaining a lifelong scar on my inner thigh as a souvenir of disobedience.

The other razor sharp memory related to my daily transport to school and back ensconced in the metal goods carrier at the front of a bicycle powered and piloted by our black 'houseboy'. I relished those intoxicating journeys primarily because the speed at which we travelled with the wind in my face and hair and my urging my 'chauffeur' to pedal ever faster. Eventually the inevitable happened and the bicycle wheels caught in the sunken rails of the electric tram track toppling us off in a most undignified manner. We connected with the tarmac without the slightest damage - other than our hurt pride caused by the scoffing laughter of witnesses to so freakish a crash landing. Unfortunately the incident persuaded my mother to discontinue this dodgy means of transport for her cossetted sonny boy and from then on it was Shanks' pony there and back. How I ached for my inimitable daily woohoo on my bikemobile!

Not long afterwards we moved from Gran's house to Joel Road. The impendent arrival of my brother was the conclusive factor in my parents' decision to change my school so I was enrolled at a private, fee-paying college at 30 Koch Street run by the Catholic Marist Brothers. Yeoville Boys' inspired the title for this chapter - 'Carrots and Iodine' which was the original working title for this book. Admittedly Carrots and Iodine is an odd title, a very odd title, so what the hell does it mean?

Let me explain OK? You see as a schoolboy, a very young schoolboy, I didn't much care for Yeoville Boys where few kids were able to do things I could do, such as read and write, thanks to my mother who regularly read aloud to me. She introduced me to the works of Charles Dickens, Mark Twain, Jules Verne, Rudyard Kipling, H G Wells and Oscar Wilde, not forgetting the marvels of Captain William Earl Johns' Biggles books and my first role model, Richmal Crompton's William. It was from Mom that I learned to love literature and the English language so that my early teachers didn't bother with me, being content to let me read real books to myself while my fellow pupils were grappling with The Cat Sat On The Mat segment of the three R's – readin', riten and 'rithmetic. Bluntly, I was bored stiff. I felt that school was a waste of time. My pleas to stay home were ignored and each day I became a right royal whining schoolboy with his satchel and shining morning face, creeping like snail unwillingly to school. Well, all right, it *was* decidedly speedier in that bicycle carrier.

The time had obviously arrived to modify tactics, so one morning I told Mom I'd been puking, didn't feel at all well and could I stay home? Please! Much to my surprise and delight, she agreed but advised me that next time I vomited I was not to flush it away until she had checked the evidence. So production of counterfeit vomit became a preoccupation since my first test - sticking fingers down my throat - was as unpleasant as it sounds and made me retch for real. Even school was preferable to that. The concept of actually obtaining parental agreement to stay home and with a *bona fide,* parental sick note for being absent grew into a mini obsession to which I devoted much thought.

Nothing came to mind until I sat watching Granny grating carrots. I liked raw carrots and started to chew the grated ones until Gran presented me with my own peeled carrot and off I went contentedly gnawing it. Fortuitously a smidgen went down the wrong hole and coughing it up sparked off a Eureka Moment which flashed inside my brain like a neon sign undergoing a nervous breakdown. The chewed, regurgitated carrot reminded me of the sick my baby brother spewed and I immediately began experimenting with a scientific verve befitting a novice Doctor Frankenstein. My research showed that well-masticated carrots, preferably pre-grated for a convincing semi-digested look, provided the perfect base for my prefabricated, patent, pretend, puke added to other assorted well mixed ingredients which, floating in the lavatory pan, could be mistaken for the real deal. Drops of iodine from the bathroom medicine cabinet radically altered the overall colour providing the perfect finishing touch. I was in business!

My first legitimate, illegitimate day off was achieved with splodges of mashed banana, a soupçon of cooking oil and traces of lettuce added to the carrots and iodine formula which evolved appreciably once I fathomed that my pseudo emetic efforts needed to partially reflect a recent meal so I began foraging in the fridge for leftover meat, poultry or fish. When minced, or munched and mixed with porridge oats, mealie meal or even brown porridge (the latter sponged off the black people who worked for us) were added to bits of mashed peas, potato, scraps of apple peel, fragments of scrambled egg, recycled radishes and occasionally grains of Condy's crystals contributed to the verisimilitude of my invention.

Soggy cigarette tobacco harvested from ash trays provided further variety and texture as did brown bread crumbs, but in the long run it was carrots and iodine that proved the best basic constituents. My main worry was that it was odourless. Mom only gave a cursory glance at my creativity prior to the flush. However being a fledgling perfectionist I devoted pleasurable hours to perfecting pongs spawned by stink bombs obtained at the joke section of a toy shop. A dash of Jeyes Fluid lavatory cleaning chemical dropped into my concoction inadvertently induced a tribute from my mother about my thoughtfulness in trying to eliminate the unpleasant odour of raw sewage.

As life and boyhood advanced, the melange became ever more realistic and, used with discretion, did not let me down.

The profound aura of gold could be perceived everywhere in Johannesburg whose evocative, vivid yellow, chemically refined, flat topped geometrical mine dumps glistened in the sun wherever you looked, and on windy days the aureate dust spread and was inhaled throughout the satellite towns of Witwatersrand - Ridge of White Water - the richest gold reef in the world.

Excluding the mine dumps, Johannesburg is a city of a thousand undulating hills, or *koppies* as they're called in South Africa. Our house was itself near the crest of a moderately high *koppie* which sloped gently downhill until it dipped into a short, dangerously steep dogleg section running directly into Harrow Road one of the city's busiest arterial roads carrying heavy traffic from the northern suburbs towards central Johannesburg.

Joel Road, later renamed Joel *Street* for some unfathomably addle-headed bureaucratic reason, was an idyllic place to grow up in. Lots of kids to play with and lots to do. There were numerous nearby *koppies*, a few as yet unblemished by human habitations and surviving in as natural a state as they had been aeons before gold was discovered on the 'Rand'. Oft repeated familial instructions to their offspring not to play on the *koppies* ensured these became a regular hangout.

There we vigorously re-enacted the Wild West switching like lightning between Indians attacking the Wagon train to brave pioneers defending it. We cowboys, or crooks, or injuns built small rock walls here and there - well they were at least three inches high - to demarcate forts, saloon bars, sheriffs' offices, or anything else we needed for that day's fantasy. If anyone chanced upon an old sheet it easily converted into a snazzy wigwam, an army tent or an Arthurian knight's pavilion.

Our favourite *koppie* - today the site of Ponte, whose 54 storeys made it the tallest residential building in Africa and later the largest crack house on the planet - was once a place for running wild, whooping and emitting bloodcurdling war cries at the top of our shrill, unbroken voices. It was a place where there were no adults to chastise us or try to shut us up or stop us from making real camp fires on which to roast our imaginary steers or whatever it was we assumed cowpokes got up to. We were exceptionally careful with our matches having once started a veld fire which luckily did no damage as the rains came, heavily, just in time to rescue us from the verge of panic.

Expeditions to the *koppies* provided occasional booty such as the odd abandoned, rusted bicycle which could be stripped of its wheels if it still had any. Once the spokes were removed the rims made marvelous hoops which could be propelled at breakneck speed down the street, controlling them, more or predominantly less, with dowel sticks or selected tree branches.

Lots of black guys, mainly 'house boys' on their afternoons off, with nowhere else to go would use our *koppie* as an open air *shebeen* where they'd sit for hours, smoking *dagga,* a powerful local marijuana, and drinking *skokiaan*. We didn't go too near them and they ignored us until one day I spied our gardener among them. He waved to me and I waved back. Back home I asked about the strange stink of the drink with so evocative a name.

He chuckled a lot while downloading details about its manufacture in the townships by the numerous Shebeen Queens, local women who had no other source of income. The brewing of hard liquor by 'natives' was prohibited by law to prevent the government controlled beer halls from losing revenue. The SAPs - the acronym for the hated South African Police - devoted almost as much time hunting for *shebeens* and illicit *skokiaan* as they did to harassing black people to ensure that all black men carried the accursed obligatory pass books. Nevertheless the manufacture of so-called *kaffir* beer and *skokiaan* continued unabated in defiance of the unceasing police raids on the townships.

The home brewed beer was damned strong but not nearly as lethal as *skokiaan* whose potency had been known to kill debauched drinkers, particularly if heavily laced with methylated spirits. No one except the Shebeen Queens themselves knew precisely what went into it since each Queen zealously guarded the secrets of her recipe for fear of losing regular customers to a rival's new thirst treat with the result that they continually experimented with increasingly more repulsive ingredients such as overripe fruit, stale bread, rye and even selected animal parts, preferably sex organs, for the connoisseurs. It is not known if any of them thought to add carrots or iodine...

The Queens were wont to secrete their moonshine in sealed 44 gallon oil drums buried underground to ferment and to avoid detection by the police who employed long, pointed iron bars to prod the ground to try to locate the drums. One gung-ho greenhorn fresh out of cop college determined to make a name for himself by tracing more hidden *skokiaan* than his relatively laid back colleagues who were either *shebeen* clients or extortionists who received 'protection' payment from prosperous proprietors for ensuring a blind police eye was cast on bootleg booze businesses. The neophyte cop expended excessive energy stabbing the earth as if he were plunging a stake into Dracula's heart until he made contact with one exceptionally volatile drum which instantaneously exploded, hospitalizing him.

The *koppies* in each area had differing characteristics. A sprinkling of them accommodated the skeletal framework of unfinished blocks of flats abandoned by developers who ran out of finance on completion of the concrete and steel superstructure. One such had become a regular rendezvous for homeless black and coloured (mixed race) people including alcoholics, *dagga* smokers, *dagga* dealers and who knows who else. Even if we hadn't seen the profligates, the fetid odour of sweat, faeces, urine, vomit, beer and *skokiaan* would have kept us away from there after our initial visit.

Another frightening, forbidden - hence fascinatingly irresistible edifice to us was a derelict two storey house, a sort of local Gormenghast we called 'the haunted house' which stood at the corner of Joel Road and Harrow Road and had reputedly been built by an eccentric randlord who doubtless believed size to be more important than either quality or good taste. Within, the remnants of heavy, clumsy, old furniture stood decaying away unobtrusively alongside filthy, shredded curtains still clinging to rods on the boarded-up, glassless windows. It was exactly the sort of place Alfred Hitchcock would have selected to film one of his chillers. The creepy basement itself housed a goodly selection of live props such as rats, spiders, centipedes and other anonymous arthropods.

Apart from the reek of cheap tobacco, stale liquor and human waste, its nooks and crannies made it a perfect place in which to play hide and seek. The cobwebbed loft running the entire length of the house was spacious enough to engage in *bok-bok*, a nationally proscribed game at all schools, principally the rugby playing secondary schools. This was a game we engaged in whenever we could coax sufficient kids to join us in the creaky room with holes in the roof and rotting timber. We had to be careful where we trod but the risk of possibly falling through the wood made the planet's crudest, most senseless game even riskier than it was out of doors in parks, on the *koppies* or the rough kikuyu grass rugby fields. Rules? What rules? There were no rules other than by prior agreement between two teams. The game as we played it went more or less like this:-

There were two teams of four or more. Number one player - let's call him the prop - stood, back against a wall, a tree, or a rugby goal post while boy number two crouched down, his head against the prop's midriff, his hands clutched tightly together behind the prop. Another player crouched behind number two, hanging on with both hands, and then another and another until all those on the crouching team became a human centipede scrumming chain. One at a time opposing players took a running vault on to the backs of the crouching boys, sitting on them jockey style, legs gripping the boy below with crossed feet. Then another leaping team-mate landed behind him on top of the crouchers, then another and yet another, the object being to collapse or break the crouchers' chain while the crouchers tried unseat the leapers without breaking or collapsing their own chain. If one or more leapers fell off or touched the ground after landing, the crouchers became vaulters. If the crouching team withstood the weight of the jumpers the last leaper held both hands aloft to display his fingers (from zero to ten) while intoning the chant:

'Bok staan styf, hoeveel vingers op jou lyf!'

Which means:

'Buck, buck stand steady, how many fingers on your body?'

If the crouching team guessed correctly, it became the jumpers' turn to crouch, otherwise the crouchers re-crouched, I think! Punching, gouging, kicking and hair pulling were the order of the day in the process of a game supposedly invented by the Romans. If this is true those Italians have a host of damaged vertebrae, necks, arms, legs, assorted bones and squashed testicles to answer for. Not a game for the timid or squeamish. Unlike rugby it can be played anywhere at any time without a ball or any kit. Or brains.

One dank, rainy day ten of us chose to play bok-bok in the haunted house. Entering through our usual smashed back window we rowdily headed up to the attic picking sides as we ascended. While forming the first crouching line we saw a figure shambling towards us in the half light. For all we knew it could have been the Grim Reaper as depicted in old illustrations, you know the one - the faceless hooded guy carrying a scythe over his shoulder.

As it approached through the gloom and the curtain of water gushing through the leaking roof, it slowly lifted its arms and began to speak in a deep, husky voice at the very moment that a bolt of lightning momentarily illuminated the loft, precipitating a cosmic crash of echoing thunder above us a nanosecond later. We all wet or shat ourselves and were out of there in far less time than it takes to write 'thunderbolt.' Rain deluged down as we fled for shelter in the friend's home nearest the haunted house. Our clothes were soaking wet, our trousers soiled, yet we sat around trembling and speechless for a while summoning up the strength to go to the bathroom to clean up and dry off. We debated the matter in hushed tones and couldn't agree about what we'd seen. Common sense suggested it was merely a vagrant sheltering from the weather. Or was it an apparition or perhaps an escaped convict? None of us ever plucked up the courage to set foot inside that house again and we made damn sure we passed it on the other side of the road.

During the long summer school holidays which lasted much of December and all of January and February, Mom usually took me to Durban with its diversity of entertainment like whites-only 'midget' golf, fishing - not that I ever caught anything - sand castling on the whites-only beach, swimming in the whites-only sea or the fresh water whites-only hotel pool, visiting the whites-only amusement park, the whites-only bird sanctuary or the whites-only snake park where I was terrified by the way the black keeper antagonized an angry hissing cobra with a hook at the end of a long stick. Although there was thick glass between us and the snake, the mesmerized onlookers gasped and cringed when the snake spat at him almost ceaselessly which made us understand why he wore protective goggles.

Unquestionably my Durban favourite was riding on the rickshaws pulled by mountainously muscular Zulus wearing ornate, intricately hand-crafted beaded shirts and kilts. Their heads were crowned with enormous, multi-coloured, feathered, phantasmagorical, carnival-style headdresses with super-sized cattle horns presumably intended to assure passengers that the puller was strong as an ox. To enhance their warlike appearance pullers often carried miniature Zulu shields and life-size knobkerries. They plied their trade barefoot but looked as if they were wearing long white socks with their legs whitewashed up to their knees. A lot of them had tied shells to their ankles. Inside these shells hard seeds rattled as you rode. All these doodads seemed to me to double the wearer's apparent height and girth.

Oddly enough in the early 20th Century rickshaws had been the city's main transport system with thousands of them on the streets.

Even when simply lined up awaiting customers the carts vied with each other for the most dazzling wheel decorations which harmonized with the owners' outfits. The appearance of a camera was greeted by demands for a *tickey* to take a piccie. Their intimidating size and bearing warned you to refrain from thoughts of haggling.

I found the rides electrifying and yelled exultantly each time the puller, ululating lustily, leapt joyously into the air tilting our vehicle backwards at an alarming angle until a small 3rd wheel, a balance wheel beneath the seat, touched the ground to prevent any chance of the rickshaw overturning backwards. I wasn't taking any chances and clung to my mother like a baby monkey while we watched the horizon appear then disappear. It scared me to the degree that I kept begging for another ride... and another... and... until Mom got fed up and took me back to our hotel.

Guy Fox

Guy Fox, better known outside South Africa as Guy Fawkes, was responsible for Bonfire Night which was always celebrated *con brio* by white South Africa each year on the 5th of November. The date was keenly anticipated by children of all ages from 5 to 95 for that was the night of a *braaivleis* (barbecue) bash combining the burning of an effigy of Guy Fawkes, one of the conspirators who plotted to blow up the British Houses of Parliament in 1605. King James I of England decreed that bonfires be lit annually to commemorate the discovery and thwarting of the plot which, had it succeeded, would have been the gravest act of mass terrorism perpetrated on humanity prior to the horror of the destruction of the twin towers in New York.

This anniversary has survived for over four centuries, but we kids hadn't the foggiest notion of why we fashioned a man from old clothes stuffed with newspapers and straw then pushed it about in a purloined pram or a homemade cart outside local shops demanding 'a penny for the guy' from total strangers. On 'Guy Fox' night our dummy was deposited upon a large bonfire around which we danced chanting:

> *'Remember, remember*
> *The fifth of November*
> *Gunpowder, treason and plot.'*

Over the years the parents of Joel Road had concluded that the most sensible, not to mention cost-effective, way to whoop it up would be to pool all neighbourhood food, drink and fireworks thereby providing a top-notch display. This was always held at number 74, in the Solomon family's front garden, the biggest in the street. The house lay in a dip allowing the junketing to be viewed from street level by the local black people who weren't working on the barbecue, or serving 'cool drinks' like crème soda or fizzy lemonade to the kids and iced beer to the adults. Loads of black people gathered agog to watch the whites incinerate their money.

As soon as the bonfire was lit our mantra took on greater fervour. At a safe distance away the supervising adult began lighting the fireworks, always starting with the smaller ones, the simple hand-held Sparklers, Golden Rain, Golden Fountains, Fairy Glitters and Catherine Wheels nailed to a tree. Concertina-bellows shaped Jumping Jacks zigzagged dementedly as they exploded eliciting squeals of delight and fright from kids trying to dodge their haphazard progress. Jacks-in-their-boxes followed as the display gradually built up to more grandiose fireworks with exotic names like Mine of Serpents, Mount Vesuvius and Roman Candles. Rockets erupted skywards from their empty milk bottle launching pads in cornucopias of colour, concertos of clamorous crackles, bangs, whistles, whizzes, and of course, choruses of oohs and aahs from the entranced audience of kids and adults.

November 5, 1938 embedded itself in my mind because, for the first time ever, my mother was away from me, recuperating in a maternity hospital after giving birth to my brother.

Pop knew specifically how to alleviate my distress in her absence - he took me to the zoo, a treat reserved for notable occasions. Johannesburg's excellent, whites-only zoo (except for the black guys who fed, cleaned and tended the animals) included one of the most exhilarating adventures in the entire world for me as a small boy. An elephant ride no less. The elephant was parked between two tall, steep, crude but solidly built wooden stairways shaped like a wide capital 'A' with the triangle at the top cut away. This enabled passengers to board the elephant's custom-built, double-sided howdah with padded seats facing sideways across the animal's back. Each seat held four kids or three adults facing outwards. The white mahout, impressive and commanding in his khaki military Jodhpur uniform with peaked cap and brown leather riding boots, supervised the boarding before positioning himself on the elephant's neck guiding the whopping beast as it ambled along, its trunk held nonchalantly at the precise angle required to accept monkey nuts (unshelled peanuts) from spectators.

Johannesburg's elephant had been imported from the Far East where working elephants were commonplace. No one had quite managed to tame the larger African elephants and few people knew, or cared, that the zoo's elephant was a foreign immigrant. The comparatively inexpensive rides were only available on weekends for about three pence each for kids and a bit more for adults but the ride lasted less than five minutes so there were always queues of people waiting for their turn.

Those wanting a second go had to dismount and re-join the queue. Black passengers were not allowed.

Other attractions at the zoo were the camel back and pony cart rides but the elephant headed everyone's list. It's a pity they didn't have a stand-in for him because in time the elephant concluded he'd endured more than his fair share of dissonant yipping, yelping youngsters and bolted, heading for his elephant house at a rate that terrified the handler almost as much as the hysterical joy riders on its back. No amount of sweet talk or tempting titbits of its favourite foods could induce it to return to duty thereby forever ending elephant rides at Johannesburg zoo.

On Guy Fawkes Night Pop cheered me up once more, this time with a jumbo box of fireworks which I examined while he freshened up before taking me out. In that cardboard treasure chest reposed all the fireworks a kid could wish for including Chinese crackers wrapped in glossy red paper bearing labels illustrated with dragons and monsters with lions' heads. These were in great demand since they too jumped about crazily crackling like staccato Tommy Gun fire scaring the crap out of parents and kids alike.

We guzzled delicious hot dogs in buttered rolls oozing with mouthwatering yellow French mustard supplemented by burpy drinks and topped off with trifle, jelly and ice cream. But the evening, as always, ended far too soon with its climactic salvo of shrieking sky rockets. We dispersed slowly, reluctantly, wishing it could have lasted forever, or for another two or three hours at least. But this superbrat had indulged in forward planning about that, don't you worry.

My pockets bulged with small fireworks from Pop's box. I was bent on staging my own personal display on my return home. Instead of going straight to bed, I sneaked outside with my private fireworks which included a miniature top hat which didn't do much except exude curly black cylindrical ash as long as my arm. Waste of time. I lit a hand held tube thing delighting in its harmless spray of bright sparks. I lit another hand held firework and within seconds I was writhing on the ground screaming my head off in terror. Unfortunately I'd misread the instructions on the side as 'to be held in hand.' Or maybe the word 'not' had been rubbed off by other fireworks jostling in my pocket. It blew up in my face with a vengeance blinding me for days on end most of which I spent crying my heart out as I didn't think I would ever see again...

The news that my Mom would be home soon seemed to hasten my recovery. Ever since then I have retained a healthy respect for the dangers of fireworks.

I first met Justin, my baby brother, in the Frangwen Hospital high on Hillbrow Hill shortly before I was blinded. He wasn't much to look at then. Until he was born, I had never seen a baby at such close proximity and his resemblance to an overripe squashed tomato was a shock to me. I couldn't have guessed he'd be so small and so wrinkled and I doubted if he would ever grow big enough to play with and I didn't want to be the butt of redskin jests. Accordingly I was concerned about what my friends might think of his complexion. I was not convinced by my mother's assurance that lots of babies had red faces and that he would look just fine once he grew a bit.

It wasn't so much his appearance that disconcerted me most; it was my loss of family limelight. The prestige I had hitherto savoured was clearly diminishing. All activities in the house now seemed to revolve around him. It was, for me, what is today referred to as a 'sea change.' I had been demoted from my kingship. I was no longer *numero uno*. I had become an ordinary member of the family. I was hardly noticed any more. Not that I was neglected mind, far from it, but my equanimity was discombobulated until the day I overheard a joyous exchange between my parents one Sunday while we were preparing to go on our usual outing and I heard my mother call out, 'Harry! Harry! Have you or Mom changed the baby yet?'

'No!' Pop replied from another room, 'I thought you were going to change him.'

'Yessssss!' I thought, 'Yessssss! They've seen the light.' That afternoon was the happiest I'd had since my brother's arrival. Obviously they couldn't do anything about it that day since no one except black people worked on Sunday. I spent my time wondering what they were going to change him for. A bigger one perhaps? A girl? A puppy, eh? My mind was in overdrive.

Next day on my return home from school, Justin was still there, angelically asleep in his pram so I guessed they hadn't yet got round to changing him.

'Maybe tomorrow,' I assumed.

Gran was impressed by the devotion I displayed towards my brother and I overheard her tell my Mom, 'He's so sweet. First thing he does as soon as he gets home from school he looks in to see if the baby's all right.'

And Mom expressed her happiness at this manifestation of brotherly love. A week or so later I asked Gran when they were going to change the baby.

'Why,' she wanted to know, 'Is he smelly?'

It was only then that the penny dropped in my seven year old brain. It was the nappies my parents had been discussing.

My first holiday with baby brother was to a seaside village called Port Alfred which is; at least it was then, in the late 1930's, a sleepy village on the southern coast of South Africa. Who cares about Port Alfred? After all, hardly anyone in the world had ever heard of it - except my parents and me. I didn't bother to question my mother's reasons for choosing Port Alfred as she was a reasonably logical person whose decisions I seldom queried. Out loud that is.

I have no recollection whatever of Port Alfred itself as I was recovering from a major, self-inflicted trauma so that the only tangible evidence of being there is a photograph of my mother, brother and me. Nevertheless that place remains forever indelibly branded on my psyche thanks to the railway journey that took us there that summer over 70 years ago. It was a hot, hot summer so all the passengers on the whites-only S A R & H (South African Railways and Harbours) train wore as little as modesty and the Victorian mores of 1930s South Africa permitted. I was all of seven years old which entitled me to wear nothing other than a pair of thin knickerless shorts.

Our engine sighed to a stop at a nameless junction for reasons known only to those who ran the railways. During the wait the mercury soared higher than it had been while travelling and having the relatively cooler air sucked in through the open windows. I wandered up and down the corridor breathing in the sweltering heat wondering if it might be cooler on the platform than inside the coach itself. I alighted and my assumption proved correct. It didn't concern me in the least that the sheltered platform was derelict and totally deserted.

My self-congratulation ended abruptly as the train pulled away without so much as a warning whistle. I hadn't bothered to tell my mother of my intention to disembark. I later discovered that the junction was not a 'designated' stop and no one noticed this semi-naked child standing open-mouthed and speechless, gawping at the departing train. There was nothing for it but to give chase. I was barefoot and therefore able to run a little faster than if I'd worn shoes. I raced along the side of the track not noticing that my feet were cut and bleeding. I collapsed, exhausted, on the sleepers wailing my heart out, convinced that I wouldn't ever see my mother again. I was so preoccupied with my misery that I didn't notice the man standing next to me until he spoke to me in Afrikaans. '*Wat maak jy hier kerel?*' It was only when he used English that I understood him.

'Wotchew doing yere, hey *jong*?' he asked.

Between tears I explained that I had missed the train - pause for a fit of sobbing - and that my mother was on it and I wanted to be on it with her. The man asked where I thought the train was going and between renewed blubbing he caught the word 'Alfred' and whispered, 'Ach shame, but *moenie* worry *nie*, yaw trayne is still there.' His emollient words soothed my anxiety.

He pointed to the station where a number of engine-less carriages shimmered in the heat haze. I think I made a highly intelligent observation like 'But, but, but, there's no engine.'

'Yar man' said the stranger, 'another engine's on its way to haul them coaches to Port Elizabeth.'

He then nodded his head in the direction of the departing train which, by then, had almost blended into the khaki-brown of the distant *veld*. What had happened was that the front set of coaches had been disconnected from the rear coaches and had gone off to another destination whilst our coaches awaited the arrival of a second engine to take us to Port Alfred.

Pop only once accompanied us on holiday. This was due to two factors. He did his buying personally on a daily basis to ensure the freshness and high standard of his goods and no one else could do that for him. The other reason was that Eddies was a cash business with an excellent turnover making Pop apprehensive that staff might be unable to resist the temptation to help themselves to a few quid now and then. In fact cash was an issue between my parents and my mother often berated Pop for not emulating a precedent set by one of her brothers-in-law's proclivity to skim a tenner a day from his till without disclosing it in his books. Her stock, on-going argument was that if Pop did the same, the money would be better utilised in the family coffers than in the hands of the tax man. But Pop remained impervious to her pleas even when matters went pear-shaped due to the skullduggery of a nephew by marriage into whose care Pop had entrusted the management of the Plein Street shop while he launched his second shop in Eloff Street, the Regent Street of Johannesburg. The scale of his dishonesty almost bankrupted Eddies. Inevitably Pop found out what was going on and chivalrously wrote it off against experience rather than involving the police which is what the man really deserved. But Pop refused to bring disgrace on his sister and his niece and simply fired the guy. Mom took to working regular shop hours ostensibly to keep an eye on the staff and potential shoplifters but Pop was unhappy about it not simply because her presence inhibited his natural inclination to charm women customers but her compassionate nature prompted her to give elderly customers a little more here and there. The 'little more' might be twice the amount requested. When Mom was weighing goods if the scale indicator swung over the mark well, that was OK with her if she either liked or felt sorry for the customer. She ignored Pop's argument that he was running a business, not a charity. In fact it was not unknown for relatives to leave the shop without paying for anything at all. Aunt Minnie's driver Arthur collected her weekly order regularly and knew he could count on having my aunt's extras augmented by freebies for his own family. Hardly surprisingly this caused Pop a good deal of angst since Minnie's husband Harry Vorenberg, the family Croesus, was a business magnate who had once shown Mom his bank statement reflecting a balance of well over a million pounds credit.

Vorenberg was an unusual man who had arrived penniless in South Africa from Germany via the USA in the early nineteen hundreds. He managed to borrow enough capital to open a printing works which prospered prodigiously. He married Minnie, my mother's eldest full sister, whom he treated abominably, keeping her short of bank notes while conducting a long lasting affair with his secretary, as plain a Jane as ever there was. I don't know if that accounts for Aunt Minnie's compulsive hobby of turning seashells into figurines with crudely painted faces. Numerous display cabinets in her home overflowed with shell ladies holding shell umbrellas, shell decorated book covers, even shell coated match and cigar boxes all of which she bestowed on friends and family on birthdays and other occasions. She always ensured that her holiday destinations had beaches with abundant sea shells for her to harvest in order to create her *objets d'art*.

When the First World War loomed Vorenberg correctly forecast there would be a shortage of newsprint paper rolls in South Africa. He approached his mother-in-law for a loan to buy and import quantities of paper from Europe. Gran lent him as much as she could afford. The paper shipments landed at Cape Town shortly before the war began. The phenomenal profit from this enterprise was the foundation on which his financial empire was built.

He started buying up as many workers' cottages as he could lay his hands on in order to resell them. So far, so good. Nothing wrong with that except that as soon as a buyer defaulted on a repayment he was summarily evicted regardless of circumstances or how much of the bond (mortgage) had been repaid. No pay, no stay. Result - HWV to friends and foes alike - sold the house again and maybe again, and yet again.

The depression of the 1930's increased Vorenberg's property business exponentially while he sat rather like a voracious arachnid in the centre of a web awaiting fresh prey. OK, 'business is business' so they say.

In the course of time my grandparents decided to buy a new house. Unsurprisingly they turned to HWV for advice. This he willingly supplied and attended to all the paperwork relating to the transaction. No charge! What a good guy, eh, exuberantly reciprocating his appreciation for their loan. Fast forward to the mid 1930's by which time my grandfather had died and my parents had bought their own house in Joel Road and Gran came to live with us not only for company but to take care of me. Her house went on the market and HWV dropped by to say he would again take care of the documentation. 'Thank you son,' replied grateful Gran.

South African law, based on Roman-Dutch law imported by the Dutch colonists incorporated Latin which hardly any non-solicitors, other than Roman Catholics understood. Shortly prior to Gran having to sign the papers the buyer's solicitor told her that the Latin small print on the deeds specified that in return for the services undertaken by HWV on her behalf, the house belonged to him. The Latin stipulated that the house was Gran's for as long as she lived in it, but on her death or if she sold it, HWV was entitled to the proceeds. My five maternal uncles swiftly paid HWV a friendly visit and it took but minutes for a sweating HWV to assure them it had all been a 'misunderstanding' and that it would be sorted, in writing, the very next day. And it was.

The main theatre of marital conflict between my parents was pecuniary. Particularly the amounts Pop lost on the horses and the fact that he was an inveterate gambler. Fortunately the heated debates were confined to late nights behind the closed door of my parents' bedroom.

Pop relished his regular Friday night poker school which always took place at our house. Mom delighted in entertaining the players who included Pop's racing cronies and several uncles. The wives played rummy or gossiped in the living room, separated from the main event in the dining room. As I grew older Pop's pals had no objections to my watching the game provided I didn't disturb the play. At about 11 pm the men took a break to dig into a lavish buffet of cold meat, chopped herring and chopped liver washed down with Scotch and soda. I was allowed to join in the snacking and always went straight to bed as soon as Pop gave me the nod.

I'm reasonably sure that Mom's insight into Pop's gambling was nowhere near as clear as mine. I always knew when Pop had won. Not the amount, just the fact that he'd won which, now and again, occasioned an increase of my usual weekly half a crown allowance, a.k.a. pocket money, by as much as a shilling or more. And if he had a really lucky streak, he'd hand me an additional five bob. The law of averages dictated that he would lose more regularly than he won but the bad weeks which meant little or no dough were more than compensated for on jackpot weeks.

I think Pop may have had another school going on some Sunday mornings and my close friend Neville's father, whose men's clothing store was named after his eldest son, was a regular player. I soon got to know who was indebted to whom when Pop told me to nip along to Neville's for shirts, trousers or shoes. And each time Nev's dad won, he'd send his driver round to Eddies to collect crates of fruit, boxes of chocolates, whatever. The businesses were located a short walk away from each other in central Johannesburg and there was fairly brisk traffic between them,

Much as Pop loved his cards, his main weakness was the gee-gees to which he seemed addicted, only he seldom, if ever, had time to attend race meetings at Johannesburg's Turffontein race course, preferring to restrict his betting to the bar of Uncle Charlie's nearby hotel where Pop and his regular friends savored the *frissons* of hush-hush gambling over a drink or two.

Not that Pop was a big drinker, more a regular one, who limited his intake to one neat double Scotch at lunchtime and another on his way home from work. He'd gulp down his whisky habitually pulling a face as if it were an unpalatable medication. This was swiftly followed by a small tumbler of beer which he called a chaser.

His favourite tipple was Black & White whisky. He only got tipsy at family weddings where he'd always order that brand often refusing a glass if he decreed it was anything other than the real McCoy. We occasionally bribed the waitresses at functions to simply return the same drink whereupon he would knock it back with a sigh declaring, 'Aaaaah. That's better!' before ordering another. We once put his connoisseurship to a serious test after he rejected what he believed was not a Black & White. We persuaded the waitress to bring him a double brandy which he knocked back remarking, 'Aaaaah. That's better!'

Pop's reticence to speak about his gambling activities fueled my desire to penetrate his secret world to witness, with my own eyes, what took place in Uncle Charlie's bar on race days. But that never happened.

The time I became fully aware of Pop's passion for the ponies coincided with that first and last holiday together one July, the month devoted to the country's premier race meeting. This, the Durban July Handicap, was a race on which everyone in the land placed a bet. If I'd known how, I too would have risked a small flutter but only Pop was familiar with the arcane science of betting so most of our fecund family had him perform this annual chore on their behalf. Mom used to grumble to me about Pop's gambling, maintaining that although Eddies was very profitable it did not allow us the same degree of luxury living enjoyed by relations of both their families. Pop silently tolerated persistent nagging about his mild ludomania seldom retaliating or arguing about it or trying to justify it with me. Why should he?

The approach of the Jewish New Year heralded bonanza time for Eddies' presentation baskets of fresh and preserved fruit which proved incredibly popular as gifts to families, friends and important business associates. I think the baskets were my mother's brain child for she was always in charge of them and trained the staff in the esoteric aesthetic of artistically arranging fruit in wicker baskets. I even supplemented my pocket money helping meet the demand by becoming proficient enough to hear Pop admit that I was good at it then hastening to express the rider that I might, one day, be nearly as good at it as Mom.

On average the baskets were between fifteen and eighteen inches long. Bumper sized ones were available for wealthier clientele and businesses. A pineapple usually stood in the centre of the bottom row surrounded by fruit such as apples, oranges, pears, yellow peaches and guavas. The next row was built up with softer fruit such as *naartjies* (mandarins), nectarines, peaches, plums, apricots, mangoes and bananas topped with grapes, granadillas, litchis, kumquats and loquats. Fresh figs, soft berries and persimmons were out. Too squishy. Cherries, Cape gooseberries, dates, unshelled nuts and sweets filled any gaps. More expensive baskets would include red or green glacé cherries and preserved fruit such as watermelon *konfyt,* a famous, waist threatening South African delicacy. As an additional treat for the recipient, customers were known to ask for a box of chocolates or miniature bottles of alcohol to be added to the presentation.

When the basket was full you needed two pairs of hands to manoeuvre a sizeable square of cellophane paper carefully under the basket handle and tightly over the fruit to hold it in place while a second person positioned a very large elastic band under the basket's ridge. The cellophane was then trimmed with scissors and the rough edges neatly tucked under the rubber band in readiness for the finishing touch - a bounteous bow of bright ribbon tied to the basket handle. Eddies' staff constantly loaded the entire floor of the van with medleys of colourful baskets for speedy delivery to customers spread far and wide. Other stores copied the idea, but none were as successful as Eddies where demand always exceeded the supply.

Six houses away from ours in Joel Road was a block of four flats where the Paiken family lived. Seeing as how Mr. Paiken, a violin teacher, was so close by, Mom felt it would be a shame not to have me take music lessons with him, so I was duly enrolled for an introductory session. I didn't much care for the screechy, graunchy noises which were all I could coax from the instrument but I desperately wanted to please my mother and miraculously mastered the rudiments of Twinkle, Twinkle Little Star with the aid of mnemonics – simple sayings to remind learners of the order and letters of music notes such as Every Good Boy Deserves Fun and F A.C.E. But that's as far as it went...

Soon after I started my lessons Mr. Paiken, doubtless concerned about the assault my musical talent was inflicting upon his auricular senses, told my mother that I would have to practice at home which required her to buy me a violin for me. Sure enough, before the end of the week Mom came home with a brand new half size instrument in a swanky black leather case with bright red lining, a new block of resin and spare strings in a small compartment. I was pleased as punch with the case which was not dissimilar to those in which the American film gangsters toted their 'gats' for use against the G-men. In the familiarization weeks of my acquisition, I practiced myself silly almost deafening my dear old Gran who displayed her true Cockney resilience and London's East End stoicism with a strained smile but whenever I opened my case she swiftly retreated to whichever room was furthest away from my music stand.

White South Africans venerated cricket. My love for the game was nurtured at a very young age playing with other kids in the hood. Our quiet street's tarmac surface provided a better pitch than the uneven grass of Joel Road's gardens. Playing in the road itself diminished the possibility of breaking windows or being harangued by elderly neighbours. Our wickets were upended orange boxes or chalk marks on garage doors.

Not long after acquiring my weapon of mass distraction I was dawdling home and stopped outside the Solomons' garage match where the local boys were playing cricket. The fact that I didn't have a bat with me did not deter me from joining in. I assumed that the violin would make a satisfactory substitute. I mean we were only using a soft old tennis ball which I didn't think would harm the instrument if I used the back to hit the ball keeping the front and the strings safe. My batting worked out fine until an easy ball tempted me to hit it for six. My text book on-drive was worthy of any Springbok test match player if only it hadn't been accompanied by a fearful crunching noise as my 'bat' connected with that tennis ball. That classic stroke effectively terminated my first sally into the world of music.

My parents' reaction to my stupidity eclipsed my enthusiasm for both cricket and violins for a while until I was sent to boarding school. Oddly my Gran took to smiling a lot more once the violin lessons ended.

As well as street cricket we engaged in an offshoot called kennetjie (pronounced kennekie) a dinky name for a simple boys' game. All you needed was a thick stick - part of a wooden broom handle was preferable - about a forearm's length and a smaller piece of the same broom handle about as long as an open hand. Clutching the long bit in front of you with the smaller piece balanced across it, sword handle style, keeping it in place with your thumb until letting go to flick it up into the air then whacking it as far as you could. If your opponent catches it, you're out and your opponent takes strike. Or it can be a team game if there are other kids around.

The older we got the more inventive and ambitious our diversions became. For example, trial and error taught us to make crude go-carts from old wooden boxes of the type that are today exclusively reserved for fine wines. The boxes were sturdy enough to enable us to fix a long, rigid plank about twice the length of the box, to its underside.

Wheels were the other main D.I.Y. ingredient and if we couldn't scrounge a child's disused pram from neighbours we went scavenging on the *koppies* where, if you were very lucky, you might occasionally light upon an abandoned pram or even an old tricycle which would do if no other wheels were available.

In the Yeoville bike shop the guy who repaired punctures removed the pram wheels for us if he wasn't busy. His fee was a *tickey* and we'd pay him another *tickey* for cobbling together the axles. One set of wheels were fitted to the back of the box. At the front of a solid plank long enough to jut forward a few feet from the box, the bike guy drilled a hole through its centre. Then he added the front wheels to another piece of wood and drilled a hole matching the first one and a tuppeny bolt through both holes allowed the wheels to swivel. Once he'd attached the plank beneath the box itself, steering was achieved with strong twine or rope appropriated from somebody's washing line and tied `to each side of the front axle and Shazam! There stood a push-propelled chariot fit for a prince. Any spare rope was slung over a tree branch to make a swing.

We carved our initials on trees with sheath knives; we shot each other with rubber suction tipped pads that failed to live up to the pack promise to stick to smooth surfaces.

In wet weather we listened to the radio; built dens in coal cellars; fought pea shooter battles with the glass tube from refillable soda siphon bottles which carried a returnable deposit if the tube was still inside. Choosing between returning the siphon for cash or removing the Rolls Royce of pea shooters was always a major dilemma.

Joel Road was at the summit of the highest *koppie* in the vicinity. A main road sliced through it turning both halves into *cul-de-sacs* making it relatively traffic free, as were nearby streets down which we raced our carts. The main problem was stopping them in an emergency. We failed to crack the secret of making brakes that worked, obliging us to rely on the soles and heels of our shoes to slow us down, a distinctly essential skill on approaching hazardous crossroads while racing delivery boys on their bicycles. Parents were baffled as to how their offspring wore out so much leather so quickly. The astounding thing was that none of us had any accident more serious than skinned arms, legs and occasional nosebleeds.

You may recall my mentioning how spoiled a brat I was. In very cold or wet weather - or in the evenings - or if I was kept indoors with a chill or whatever, I had infinitely more playthings than all of my friends put together. My bedroom was chock-a-block with them. Toys that is, not always friends. If I'd had the foresight to accumulate a time capsule of valued toys they'd fetch a fortune at auction in the 21st Century. There were enough of them to stock a small shop. There were cars of top ranking marques; aeroplanes of tin, metal or wood; ships of Bakelite; cap guns; a chemistry set;, an assemble-it-yourself crystal set radio (known as a wireless in those days); board games, compendiums of them, containing pastimes such as tiddlywinks, snakes and ladders, table croquet, draughts, ludo and dominoes.

My collection included Escalado which was really more suited to adults than kids. I think it was the only game Pop bought me for his personal entertainment. It had wads of play money shared out by the player nominated as bookmaker to handle the betting. The green oilcloth track had a handle which you turned to vibrate it, causing five or six brightly painted metal horses and their jockeys to move along the course which had three rows of flat circular cork hazards across the track presumably to try to stop gee-gees from colliding. Or were they there to simulate steeplechase falls? Had we fully understood the rules of betting we may have enjoyed it even more if we'd had the skill to set it up unaided by an adult. You see it had to be clamped to a table to allow it to work efficiently otherwise the horses refused to race or if they did they consistently fell over and none of us had the knack of adjusting it correctly so that we considered Escalado to be a boring waste of time unless Pop set it up for us.

Another outstanding plaything and a must for the capsule was one that had no chance to gather dust. It was my Meccano set. Had they thought of applying the word to it in the 1930's this remarkable toy would, should, have been tagged 'educational' but it is probable that had it been so, it would not have attracted the unrivalled popularity it achieved over decades keeping boys of all ages between five and eighty five enthralled for hours, days, weeks, months, years even.

Meccano's main components were thin, strong, vivid red or green metal strips, three, six, nine and twelve inches long, each strip rounded off at both ends. The strips had perforated holes every half inch, designed to be assembled into a variety of structural engineering wonders with brass nuts, bolts and washers. There were oblong plates, flexible flat bits, rigid plates, double angle strips, half cylinders, axle bars, pulleys, hooks, wheels and dozens of other parts to allow you to construct anything you fancied from their illustrated booklet, or your mind's eye, using Meccano screwdrivers and spanners. Meccano's varied custom sets contained the entire kit and caboodle necessary to assemble a large selection of motor cars and aeroplanes. The genius of Meccano was that all components were compatible with what you already owned. Kits could be upgraded and lost pieces - even the smallest, cheapest parts - were readily available individually at hobby shops.

Siblings were known to run errands or perform chores for older brothers to earn a supervised turn or to inherit any Meccano bits which were passed on as if they were precious heirlooms by the older brother leaving school or taking an interest in other types of screw.

One of Pop's longest serving employees, Mrs. Mac, a charming, soft spoken Scot, was sufficiently fond of me to pass on her grown-up son's capacious Meccano coffer which contained the wherewithal to construct tottery towers, rickety roundabouts, forlorn Ferris wheels, crooked cranes - you name it... Another of her bumper presents included a wooden fort with a working drawbridge, peopled by Britain's brand lead soldiers in either busbys or combat uniforms; knights on horseback and assorted military vehicles including toy cannons which fired bits of matchsticks. In the wake of Mrs. Mac's son's death from diving into a natural pool and striking his head on a submerged rock, she gave me his expensive linseed oiled cricket bat and a beautiful, shiny brown leather oval rugby ball which I preferred to the round soccer balls used in football, a game we only played at primary school. To us, soccer was a sissy's game compared to rugby's physicality and non-stop action throughout the match whereas soccer frequently ended in deadly dull nil-nil draws.

Even without all that stuff my generation would not have found time to waste watching television or playing the computer games that separate modern kids (and adults for that matter) from human contact, sequestering them indoors like latter-day anchorites from the X-Box cult where the only body parts receiving any exercise are frenetic fingers abusing electronic keyboards. We were far too busy with self-invented pursuits.

Fast machines first seduced me thanks to a birthday gift of an especially treasured childhood possession - a clockwork motor tin replica of one of Sir Malcolm Campbell's beauteous Bluebird cars in which he broke the world land speed records no less than nine times in little over a decade.

I had no way of knowing or imagining that as an adult I would direct an award winning film, The Price of a Record, with Sir Malcolm's son Donald during his fatal attempt to regain his world water speed record on 4 January 1967 when his jet propelled Bluebird hydroplane somersaulted at over 320 miles per hour on Coniston Water.

I craved to find out what it felt like to control a petrol driven machine. But how?

One Sunday afternoon while impatiently waiting for Pop to finish his well-deserved nap ahead of our traditional family outing, I was killing time playing in the business van which was always parked facing downhill outside our Joel Road house. Having often attentively watched how Pop and Joseph, his black driver, worked things, I went through the same motions as they did, personally generating the essential sound effects. It didn't occur to me that the van was capable of moving with its engine off so I turned my imaginary ignition key - click, nothing happened. So I turned it again - yow-yow-yow - before I hit the accelerator and revved the engine vroom-vroom. Then I released the hand brake. For real. I could hardly see the road over the top of the dashboard.

Nothing happened at first since the van had been left in gear, a standard parking precaution on inclines, so I stre-e-e-e-tched my leg to reach the clutch and managed to depress it. Then I rammed the gear stick into neutral and to my surprise and delight the van began to move. We're talking like five em pee aitch max. But to me, aged about eight, I was Sir Malcolm Campbell driving Bluebird furiously along Daytona Beach USA one moment and Errol Flynn on dawn patrol proficiently piloting my Sopwith Camel into a dogfight with the Red Baron's scarlet triplane the next.

On reaching the level part of the road the van slowed down slightly by which time my father, not widely renowned for his athleticism, had equaled the world hundred yard sprint record to catch up with the van and to clamber onto the aptly named running board where he struggled to open the door to get inside which wasn't easy for him as I was in the driving seat. I've no idea how he managed to stop the van but stop it he did. He also stopped my allowance for a considerable period. Pop's temptation to beat the shit out of me must have been enormous and his reluctance to allow any future use of his vehicles was probably a result of my foolhardiness.

But it was encouraging to have proof that Pop had the heart of a lion compared to most other fathers who would probably have suffered a coronary by engaging on anything half as physically demanding. Another bonus was that the van hadn't hit anything on the way down the street except the kerb and, of course, my income.

I was never fully aware of how deeply this escapade had affected Pop until I was old enough to apply for my driver's license. But all will be revealed in a while.

Apart Hate

It's impossible to write about South Africa in the first half of the 20th Century without reference to that universally despised doctrine, 'apartheid'- a word coined by Afrikaners to describe the contemptible dual policy of Hitlerian discrimination and racial segregation which was, in fairness, not exclusively a 20th Century Afrikaner concept having been practised against non-whites from the day European ships commanded by a Dutchman, Jan van Riebeeck, first anchored in Table Bay in the 1650's.

The first recorded use of that abominable, xenophobic word is credited, if such a thing can be defined as a 'credit', to a speech made in 1917 by General Jan Christiaan Smuts who was destined to become Prime Minister of South Africa two years later. But it wasn't until May 1948 that the Afrikaner Reunified National Party - the 'Nats' - was elected by a slim majority of five seats ousting the predominantly English speaking United Party government, that apartheid entered the international lexicon to define the excesses of the most hateful word in the English language - after Nazism - and turned the land of my birth into an international pariah.

The clash between Holland and England regarding 'ownership' of South Africa appeared to have been finalised when the Brits annexed the Cape Colony in 1795. It wasn't until 1835 that the fiercely independent Dutch burgher settlers became totally pissed off with British legislation which abolished slave trading in 1833 and consequently put Boer noses further out of joint by proposing equality with the black population. Ten thousand Boers began to hit the dirt tracks, moving away from British jurisdiction by becoming *Voortrekkers* who undertook long, hazardous, heroic journeys by ox wagon and horseback into the wild, relatively unexplored Cape hinterland to escape England's burdensome effect on their lifestyle. They defeated the Xhosas and other gun free cohorts encountered on their quest for pastures new. The burghers established two Boer Republics, the *Oranje Vry Staat,* the Orange Free State and, in the Transvaal, Paul Kruger's *Zuid-Afrikaansche Republiek.*

The discovery of diamonds in 1867 and gold in 1886 precipitated a flood of English migrants suffering the twin curses of gold lust and diamond fever.

This influx forced the Republics into a second War of Independence, to try to evict the *kakis,* the British soldiers, and the *uitlanders* (foreigners) from the land the Boers had themselves wrested from black tribes.

It took nigh on half a million Brits the best part of three years and the deaths of 22,000 Tommies to defeat the guerrilla tactics of the Boer commandos who, justifiably, nurtured deep resentment and hatred towards the British. The Boers postulated that they had not been beaten on the battlefield but by the scorched earth policy and the repugnant invention of concentration camps by the British who interred entire Boer families. There were over 40 camps throughout the land for whites. Inside those, 27,000 Afrikaner women and 24,000 children died of hunger or disease.

Black people, held in over 60 segregated camps, bore the loss of 103,000 lives. 25,630 Boer prisoners of war were deported abroad to British possessions like Bermuda, Ceylon, India and St Helena. Many never returned to their homeland.

Three years of hostilities led to humiliating surrender terms being imposed on the Boers in 1902 by King Edward''s government did not exactly enhance the Brits' prospects of winning the hearts and minds of the Afrikaners.

The light in which the Afrikaners saw themselves was succinctly described by Patrick van Rensburg, himself an Afrikaner, whose apartheid epiphany forced him to abandon his diplomatic career and flee his birthplace to live in Britain where he published a ground breaking anti-apartheid book, Guilty Land.

'*The Afrikaners,*' he wrote in 1960, '*are a tiny people up against the world. Even in their own world they are hopelessly outnumbered. They are one and three-quarter million of the three million Whites in a total population of fourteen million. As a nation they were born in South Africa, and as a nation they grew up there: they belong nowhere else. They have developed their own way of life and it differs even from that of the English-speaking Whites. They have their own language and their own history. They jealously guard their way of life because they think it worth guarding: it means, for one thing, the religion they believe in. Their politics demand the maintenance of their identity. In the past they have felt the maintenance of that identity threatened by the British, and more recently by the African. In guarding themselves against the British in 1900 they gained the sympathy of the world: in guarding themselves against the African in 1950, they have lost it.*'

In 1910 South Africa became a self-governing Dominion of the British Empire so that at the outbreak of the First World War numerous white South Africans volunteered to fight for 'King and Country'.

Predictably, scarcely any Afrikaners served in the military since almost all of them identified with, and rooted for, German victories in that war and again in World War II. After all Germany had supplied both friendship and armaments to the Boers in their struggles against the British.

In 1939 the country was governed by a coalition between the Nationalist Party led by erstwhile Boer General James Hertzog and the South African Party also headed by a Boer General - Oom (Uncle) Jannie Smuts - a boyhood hero of mine until I learned that it was he who had laid the foundations of apartheid revealing himself as a hypocrite of the first order by proclaiming equality for all internationally while totally subjugating the blacks in his back yard. In fact it was Smuts who prefigured the brutal horror of Sharpeville when, in 1944, during a strike by black miners for an increase in their starvation wages, he sent in armed men to quell them. Five days later over 80 miners were wounded and nine lay dead.

Prime Minister Hertzog advocated neutrality in World War II but Smuts opted to fight for Britain as he had in World War I. Hertzog resigned and Smuts took South Africa's armed forces into the conflict where they served the Allies with distinction.

Between the two world conflagrations a number of paramilitary 'shirt movements' sprang into being. Italy spawned Black Shirts as did Britain. Germany chose Brown Shirts. In South Africa the Grey Shirts reared their repugnant heads, basing their philosophy on Schicklgruber's Mein Kampf. They were all male, all white pro-German, anti-British and anti-Semitics. Oddly enough, the latter led to their demise as we shall see. Flocks of them defected to newly formed secret societies, the *Broederbond* and the *Ossewabrandwag*, ostensibly to promote and pursue Afrikaner culture while synchronously vowing to retain the same discriminatory practices they had established in the era of Afrikaner Republics.

A hair's breadth whites-only, electoral win in 1948 presented the Nats, under the premiership of Doctor D F Malan, with carte blanche to promulgate ever more

31

pernicious laws, piling restriction upon restriction to further humiliate and demean non-whites who they referred to as 'the black peril'.

Two years later the Nationalists introduced the Population Registration Act to ensure that all South Africans were allocated to one of four racial categories - black, white, coloured or Indian. There were cases where the same parents had three offspring each adjudged to be of a different race to the other siblings making it possible to have four races wanting to share the same family home - a Catch 22 situation since that was illegal under apartheid law. The misery this caused cannot be assessed. Decisions as to who belonged to which race were entrusted to barely literate white officials whose reference terms were based on Gestapo style sophistry including pseudo-scientific tests such as whether or not a pencil would fall out if pushed into the hair as 'proof'' of ethnicity.

The Nationalists turned their attention to their 'Grand Plan' - the establishment of a series of 'Bantustans' designed to isolate various tribal and ethnic groups on islands of barren land often blighted by innumerable *dongas* and completely encircled by oceans of fertile farmlands belonging to whites.

After the so-called 'homelands' scheme passed into law, they were proclaimed Independent States thereby turning South Africa into the laughing stock of the world since the homelands were about as independent as Nazi labour camps. Any black person from any tribal group could be arbitrarily sent to any homeland selected by any white official for any or no reason at all. Nine million black South Africans were deprived of their citizenship and forced to obtain passports to enter the region in which they had been born.

Within three years of Nationalist government, the Immorality Act was amended to make sex between races a criminal offence. All 'skilled' work was reserved for whites-only. The Prevention of Illegal Squatting Act empowered the Government to raze black townships without the slightest pretence of finding alternative housing for the evicted inhabitants who had nowhere else to live.

By law, every black person had to carry a pass book at all times. These repulsive documents contained photographs, fingerprints and full information as to where the user could or could not go. The penalties for non-compliance included fines which could not possibly be paid by destitute people; detention without trial for up to six months; severe, unprovoked beatings; gruesome acts of torture and the serious possibility of fatal 'accidents' while in police custody.

The Suppression of Communism Act enabled the Government to ban from public life any person, or any party it considered endangered any aspect of its absolute dominance.

The suffering of black South Africans was horrifyingly analogous to those inflicted on the Jews of Europe, yet the Jews of Southern Africa mostly turned a blind eye to what was happening to the blacks under apartheid and the hateful, abusive persecution continued apace enforced by an implacable, predominantly Afrikaner police force which could rely on the country's well trained, well-armed military for ever-ready assistance in perpetrating tyrannical restrictions on all non-white people. Combined, these two despicable forces could indubitably have taught the Gestapo and Hitler's SS a thing or two. It is puzzling how the Nationalist government found time for any business other than that of oppression.

As a child I was surrounded by people who were deemed 'inferior' according to South Africa's custom and practice, bolstered by its invidious laws. I did not comprehend that millions did not share the way of life I inherited in the lottery of birth and it wasn't until I reached my teens that the imbroglio clarified itself for me and I came to realize that the Malan government ruled a country in which we, the minority whites, had exclusive use of over 90 per cent of South Africa's land. I was deeply ashamed that the supporters of the Nazi regime had managed to seize such demonic power. The indigenous blacks were regarded as cheap labourers whose sole purpose in life was to assist the European migrants on the road to untold wealth while the workers lived in abject poverty. The blacks were without any rights whatever and suffered draconian measures imposed on every facet of their lives.

Humankind continues to breed individuals who maintain a personal, inbuilt apartheid against other nationalities, races, creeds. This is their inalienable human right. But no government has the right to dictate to anyone that he or she shall, or shall not, associate with whomsoever they please publicly or privately.

Among middle class white families like mine, the norm was to employ at least two permanent live-in servants, usually a woman and a man, seldom, if ever, a married couple. The woman's duties included light cleaning tasks, washing and ironing clothes and linen, cooking, serving at table and caring for white children. 24/7.

The male servant's responsibilities included arduous physical toil such as scrubbing floors and tending the garden, in addition to sundry other duties embracing butlering in snow white linen uniforms. In winter they kept the fireplace clean and re-laid the coal brought in from the coal-cum-wood shed in the back yard. When our coal supply was low a team of hardy black guys would arrive on a horse-drawn cart to restock it. To keep the coal dust off their hair and backs they wore sinister Ku Klux Klan style pointed hoods made from jute bags slit down one side.

All these black folk, tradesmen and servants alike were unvaryingly referred to in disparaging terms such as 'kaffir' or 'nanny' or 'the girl' or 'the boy' even though they were mature adults. Not once did I hear any whites address them as Mr., Mrs., or Miss So-and-so. I doubt any employers even knew their surnames. The black form of addressing white men was 'boss,' or 'sir' or, the most subservient, demeaning 'master'. White women were 'madam' or 'missus.' White kids were 'baasie' (little boss), 'master' or 'missy'. Whites always referred to black kids, be they boys, girls, babies, teenagers or toddlers with the pejorative 'piccanin.'

Black servants were housed in what were called 'the boys' rooms' of which there were two at the back of most homes. These were invariably made of wood and capped with corrugated tin roofs, their stark ugliness concealed by a wall or high fence strategically positioned to avoid offending sensitive white eyeballs.

The meagre accommodation rarely included furniture other than a bed, a chair and maybe, if they were very lucky, an ersatz plywood wardrobe. Otherwise their clothes were hung on an indoor rope line or stored in a cheap suitcase or flimsy wooden fruit boxes kept beneath iron bedsteads raised at each corner with bricks not only to utilise the extra storage space but to prevent the possibility of *Tokoloshes,* mythical evil dwarfs, from skulking under the bed waiting to climb up to harm the sleeper.

Conditions were marginally better than those of the shanties in the infamous black labour reservoirs on the outskirts of Johannesburg, commonly known as 'locations'. The city is nigh on 6,000 ft. above sea level with icy winter nights. The servants' rooms were no warmer than the interior of an average refrigerator. In summer the searing Highveld sun beat mercilessly down on the metal roofs of the servants' quarters transforming them into tandoori ovens.

What ventilation there was came from a diminutive window high up the wall. Even a very small child would have been unable to squeeze through it thus disallowing sufficient light to read - if the occupant was able to read - during daylight hours. Leaving the door ajar at night for air was a definite no-no security wise. There was no electricity supply. Candlelight alone illuminated them. More often than not, servants were obliged to prepare their food in their rooms on small paraffin powered Primus brand cooking rings. These brass and copper appliances needed regular cleaning and valve maintenance failing which they were prone to flare up dangerously and were notorious for causing lethal fires in which cased employers simply shrugged it off while filing claims against their insurers for fire damage, mumbling, 'It's a tragedy man, 'cos now I got to train a replacement, dammitall.'

The arrival of the rainy season guaranteed ferocious pounding on Johannesburg's corrugated iron roofs but the ear-splitting racket was often, too often, merely a prologue to the destructive hail storms which propelled the noise into a whole new decibel dimension. Witwatersrand hailstones were often the size of golf balls capable of killing poultry and small animals. No one in their right mind set foot outside during those hail storms which frequently damaged windows, cars and all but the sturdiest garden plants. The hammering on the rooftops was frightening enough inside the whites' homes which at least had lofts and ceilings to reduce the ruckus but the servant quarters had neither and the din on the tin was as terrifying as a non-stop fusillade of heavy machine guns. The combination of ferocious sheet lightning and thunder simulated what it must have sounded like at the receiving end of a heavy artillery barrage.

The servants shared a primitive, often seatless, lavatory. Fresh water was only available from a standpipe installed for the benefit of parched plants rather than thirsty black throats. The communal zinc hip bath, barely big enough to sit in with knees bent up to the chin, had to be filled laboriously, bucket by bucket from the hot tap in the kitchen. Hot baths were not encouraged by employers due to the high cost of coal. Come to think of it, the bath was also used to wash the dogs which needed regular monthly dousing in dilute Jeyes Fluid to rid them of ticks and fleas. Our dogs unerringly sensed what was in store whenever a bath was being poured in the yard and they swiftly disappeared. We chased them for ages by which time the water had cooled and their opposition to being held captive by several pairs of hands while being thoroughly soaped and rinsed with cold water appealed to neither the dogs nor the servants but we kids regarded the mayhem of recapturing very slippery, muddied animals which soaked us to the skin by vigorously shaking themselves dry, as hilariously funny.

Married servants were not allowed to have their spouses or their children live with them except perhaps if there was some salient circumstance for which the employer's permission was essential and seldom granted. There would be hell to pay and the possibility of instant dismissal if an unauthorized friend spent the night in a servant's room which was, anyhow, too small for anything other than one single bed.

While many white madams treated their black women with respect, others preferred insulting disdain, referring to them as 'you kaffirs' prior to a diatribe about infringing a petty, or imagined or unwritten rule. Such humiliation following a fifteen hour day led to acute depression. They had nowhere to go other than their claustrophobic room with no one to talk to. They were often homesick, missing their children and family in a faraway township or village. Yet these black ladies were the self-same women to whom the whites entrusted their most precious possessions - their children - who the 'nannies' treated with loving-kindness at all times. I know. I was one of the kids who loved his black nanny whose name my brain does not retain.

Working hours were tailored to the requirements of the white household.

A typical day in their lives would pass along these lines - the male servant was always first up at around 4.30 am to light the fire to heat the water to ensure that it was hot enough for the 'master's' ablutions.

'Nanny' would be in before long to prepare the master's breakfast before delivering cups of wake-up tea to the 'missus' and children. The 'girl' then attended to the white baby while simultaneously ensuring that the older kids were clean behind the ears, well breakfasted and neatly dressed in time to be taken to school. The black woman would gulp her own breakfast of cold *mielie pap* - maize porridge - prior to bed making and preparing the mistresses' breakfast and bath. Next she would hand wash clothing and linen on a metal faced washboard and laboriously wring them out with a wooden mangle before hanging them on the washing line to dry. After the 'boy', her adult co-worker, had delivered the kids to school he got stuck in to polishing the red tiled front *stoep*, shining the parquet floors, washing the kitchen and bathroom linoleum and then tending the garden.

If the missus stayed home that day, she would expect the nanny to prepare a light lunch, to change the baby, to take the toddler for a walk to the park returning in good time to help madam prepare the family's evening repast by peeling potatoes, slicing onions, stringing beans, shelling peas and what have you. Broadly speaking, nannies were far better cooks than their employers and often carried out that task as well. Occasionally the missus would invite friends to afternoon tea, or perhaps a game of rummy or canasta, in which case the nanny would don a smart white uniform to make and serve dainty crustless white bread sarnies.

Unobtrusive they may have been in homes but the black folk were there all right. They were everywhere. Hundreds of thousands of them swarmed in and out of Johannesburg's central business area daily in fleets of mammoth, green, single-decker PUTCO buses often laden with at least twice the number of passengers prescribed by safety regulations, if indeed, there were any relating to Bantu (i.e. black) transport. These vehicles hurtled along the main highways between the shanty townships and the city, trailing black clouds of mephitic exhaust fumes and heaven help man or machine that got in their way on roads like Louis Botha Avenue between Alexandra Township and 'town' where non-whites eked out a pitiable livelihood as labourers, cleaners, delivery messengers and errand 'boys' for a meagre few shillings a week.

In the evening the buses returned their exhausted human cargo to their shanties converting central Joburg into a deserted ghost town of eerie, echoing, concrete canyons between tall darkened office complexes and shops invoking images of Hollywood's silent back lots of plywood streets standing by for the arrival of the film crew and actors.

Purged of its black and white workers, the 'city' became the purlieu of business cleaners, night watchmen and sundry other black folk who had to carry a 'passbook' permitting them to be there after hours. Failure to produce a pass if demanded to do so by a cop meant at least one or more nights' imprisonment, and/or a beating, and/or punitive fines and/or banishment to wherever the victim's tribal birthplace happened to be.

Next morning at about 3 am, the black work force again emerged from their hovels, the men all wearing wide brimmed American gangster movie style hats and every woman hiding her hair with a *doek*.

Those who had work, no matter how degrading, regardless of how badly paid, considered themselves the lucky ones compared to those without work or the 'correct' papers permitting them to seek work in preference to joining families scavenging for food on garbage dumps to try to stave off death from hunger, or condemnation to the scourge of diseases attributable to malnutrition.

The black people worked in my city and its suburbs only because we whites allowed them to be there, and then only if needed for menial tasks or to cater to our creature comforts - comforts they would never share under white subjugation. Without their labour the gold mines that provided countless whites with incalculable fortunes would have ceased to function. They were there, the natives, they were always there and they were taken for granted. They were no better off than bonded slaves struggling to survive and to raise families on weekly wages not much higher than the amount a white would spend on a Castle beer, 50 Springbok cigarettes and a packet of salted peanuts in the bar after work. They were black ghosts in front of whom white people spoke with impunity, often about them and their alleged shortcomings as domestic servants or delivery 'boys', the 'white' minds being incapable of imagining that the targets of their scorn were intelligent enough to grasp what was being discussed.

Although no one spelled it out, you just knew they were different. Their way of life, their homes, their food – were all different and unlike 'ours'. In particular they were inferior and seen to be so since they were not allowed in our buses, our trams, our trains, our parks, our schools, our universities, our libraries, our hospitals, our swimming pools, our sports facilities, our cinemas, our restaurants - unless they were waiting table or working backstage in the kitchens. And the only blacks who ever entered our houses were our servants or delivery men and for the latter, lots of homes even had separate 'servants only' or 'tradesmen only' side or back entrances for them. There were signs and notices everywhere in both 'official' languages, Afrikaans and English, stating *Blankes alleen - Whites only*. What if they couldn't read? And if they *could* read, did they understand either English or Afrikaans, spoken by, at most, fifteen per cent of the total population? The answer was simple. They were arrested and fined or jailed.

The lucky ones weren't beaten with truncheons or the egregious *sjambok,* a weapon of preference among the SAPs (South African Police) who were christened *Bar Mitzvah Boys* by my brother since their trousers were always too short for their gangly legs.

Just before the end of the summer holidays I was about to change schools so Mom took me on my first expedition to an ancient store pervaded by the strong, fusty pong of mothballs. At the emporium, McCulloch & Bothwell or maybe it was Ward & Salmons in Eloff Street, I was subjected to a thorough measurement session prior to being kitted out from top to toe. I tried on short navy trousers which I was allowed to keep on together with the colour-coordinated socks, belt and cap and, most essentially, my navy blue, gold striped blazer with its distinctive, curlicued M (for Marist Brothers College) machine embroidered on the left breast pocket - a far more impressive uniform than Yeoville's insipid grey gear. All in all, it was a very scientific outing in the course of which I stepped onto a machine which X-rayed feet to ensure that my new shoes were a perfect fit. I was allowed to look into the eyepiece to observe, with wonderment, the bones of my own toes wiggling beneath the leather down below.

The cash Mom paid the salesman was placed in a brass container about the size of a soup can which he inserted in a tube contraption pointing upwards from the shop counter into the ceiling. He pressed or maybe pulled something or other causing the container to be sucked into the tube with a superb schwoooosh sound from the compressed air operating this weird machine. Shortly afterwards the container returned in much the same way. The salesman twisted it open and presented its contents - change and a receipt - to Mom. Then I was hurried along, resplendent in my posh new outfit, to Pop's shop for him to see what Mom had spent a small fortune on. All Pop's lady assistants fluttered and flattered. And the black guys (who could have lived on the cost of that gear for a year or more) beamed and exclaimed 'Hau, hau!' and shook their heads in admiration.

The Marist College in Koch Street, on the edge of central Johannesburg, a short electric tram ride away from Joel Road, was a major private prep school located in a purpose built, prison-like multi-storey structure with a sizeable attached chapel.

The Marist Brothers are a Catholic teaching order. In 1889 a pair of them reached the shanty mining town that was the infant Johannesburg to establish a boys' school. Their first class numbered five pupils but their high standard of tuition speedily acquired so enviable a reputation that by the turn of the century they had some two hundred pupils. The original school in Koch Street boomed to such an extent that by 1924 the Brothers were able to establish a second school on an extensive site in Observatory with facilities for around 200 boarders and 400 day boys. The pupils were predominantly Catholic kids with a goodly percentage of other faiths. In fact there were so many Jewish pupils in those days that, for a while, the Brothers enlisted a rabbi to provide regular religious classes. Oy vey Maria with a vengeance.

Less publicized was their narrow minded teaching regime which relied, to a major degree, on the imposition of corporal punishment for relatively minor infractions of their strict, oppressive, medieval code of behaviour that held its boys in thralldom.

The College proved so startlingly different from Yeoville Boys' School that any thoughts I might have harboured of employing my carrots and iodine scam went straight out the window and I actually began to absorb knowledge, always achieving top marks in English and faring well in other subjects with the marked exception of arithmetic at which I proved quite hopeless. This was surprising really since my father was a virtuoso at sums. When working on his business accounts he would spread his fingers and move them down columns of figures taking under ten seconds to total up each ledger page. He would sometimes pass the ledger to me and ask me to check his figures. It took me ten minutes or more per page. I often had three stabs at it, coming up with three different figures none of which matched Pop's infallibly correct answer. In the 1930's we dealt in mediaeval pounds, shillings and pence, not forgetting fractions of pence so you'd have a page of forty eight lines of figures as bizarre as this - £165.17s.11¾d which is one hundred and sixty five pounds, seventeen shillings and eleven pence three farthings. Consider this - there were four farthings or two half-pennies (pronounced haypennies and spelled ha'penny) to each penny. There were twelve pence to a shilling and twenty shillings to the pound so that his arithmetical brilliance was astonishing. To me anyway. In those days calculators were but primitive mechanical adding machines which Pop reckoned were a waste of time thanks to his ability to add up columns of eight numbers across and about 48 lines down per page, in less time than it took a qualified adding machine operator to enter the figures. I hated sums which I found extremely boring and failed to figure out what use they could possibly be to anyone other than a businessman which I had no intention of becoming. Ever.

My first teacher at Koch Street, Brother Pius, a short, chubby, red faced, balding, genial, middle aged man, took a liking to me thanks to my vocabulary so that if he failed to get a response from the other kids, he would turn to me and I usually obliged him satisfactorily. One incident that clearly springs to mind was the time he asked how we would describe the coastline of Britain and I answered that it was rugged. Brother Pius was pleasantly heartened to hear such a word used by an eight-year-old. His favouritism did not endear me to classmates but it did protect me from strappings which might otherwise have come my way, so I resigned myself to the sarcasm of my peers which I comfortably countered, confusing them considerably with cynicism and complex conversation, concocting comments as I went along.

Another memory etched in my brain concerned the news, read out to us in class one morning, about a black guy in a native reserve whose only cow was killed by lightning. We had to copy a note from the blackboard to take home, asking parents to make a small donation to help replace the animal. I was given a sixpence and next morning while the other boys went to place their coins in a chalk box at the front of the class, I sat still, hesitating, fondly fingering my coin, turning it round and round in my pocket contemplating how much more I could do with it instead of giving it to an anonymous bloke whose livelihood depended on a replacement cow. I argued with myself that a sixpence would hardly buy even the tiniest portion of a cow, but then, I reasoned, if enough pupils contributed a single coin, no matter how small, there might even be enough in the collection for more than just one cow. Maybe there'd be sufficient to add a chicken or two. My conscience overcame my greed. As I stood up and stepped into the aisle to go hand in my 'sixy' I glimpsed something whish past my head before this frightful crash of the light fitting, situated plumb above where my head would have been had I been seated, smashed to smithereens on the seat of my desk. Had I hesitated but one second longer that light fitting might well have cracked my skull.

A big advantage of my new school was its proximity to Pop's Plein Street shop which enabled me to enjoy myself at the back of the shop, a unique locale for an adventurous boy to spend formative periods of his life.

Pop's small office separated the front of the shop from the warehouse sized storeroom behind it. The office doubled as a rest room for the white staff to brew and drink their *Mazawattee* tea, eat their lunch or smoke *C to C* (Cape to Cairo) cigarettes during breaks. I only spent hurried moments in there if I had homework to dash through, preferring to wait for my lift home in the Ali Baba cave at the rear where the black guys relaxed with their strong dark tea which was ninety per cent sugar or sweetened condensed milk and smoked their pungent, cheap *Springbok* cigarettes.

If there was no work to do they'd amuse themselves by playing either riotous card games or *umhlabalaba*, an African strategy game on a homemade 'board' marked with squares and diagonal lines and often seen in action on the streets with markings chalked on the pavement (sidewalk) or scratched on flat bare ground. The 'men' or counters are called cows. Players start with twelve cows apiece consisting of whatever was readily available. Smooth matching pebbles, buttons or draughts' checkers were utilised but Eddies' men preferred crown corks which were moved rapidly about a piece of suitably marked, thick brown cardboard. The non-stop kibitzing was a noisy hubbub invariably accompanied by ceaseless contagious cackling. My requests for an explanation of the rules never failed to trigger convulsive laughter.

I gloried in the company of those seemingly happy-go-lucky guys sitting on apple boxes upholstered with empty jute sacks, listening to their non-stop natter and developing a predilection to being addressed as 'Baas Eddie' or 'Little Baas' which I regarded as a sign of respect and comradeship.

Adventures in that warehouse were limitless. In a far corner there stood an enormous, but really enormous, mountain of empty jute potato sacks piled up to a height of perhaps 25 ft. and covering a good deal of floor space. I have no idea how many thousands of brown sacks it had taken to build it up that high but the mountain grew steadily higher by ten to fifteen bags per day, six days a week awaiting collection for reuse as recycling was then called. Luckily for me that never happened.

Two other mountains dominated that store room - Mount Orange Box and Mount Apple Crate later renamed Everest and Kilimanjaro. My mates and I used to rearrange the boxes to serve as pretend trains, planes, cars and even skyscrapers. Pop's black staff let me help them flatten the produce boxes using their chrome plated claw hammers before removing the nails and filling the business van with the wood in readiness for delivery to the coal shed of our home for use as kindling.

I made a secret den, invisible to any casual passer-by, under Jute Sack Mountain by tunnelling into it utilising extra-large crates to support the weight of the sacks above. Inside I stashed away a torch, comic books and a pen knife. Only my closest friends were allowed into this sanctum. It didn't occur to me until I started writing this, that if the top of the den had collapsed under the weight of the sacks I'd probably have suffocated. But it remained intact whatever I did to it.

Naturally I looked upon the store room as my personal domain and, as its ruler, it was my sole right to position those sacks any way I pleased enabling me to alter the shape of the mountain to form a jute sack toboggan run. The black guys helped me make a sledge from a box. A long wooden ladder afforded access to the summit. Up and down, up and down I went for as long as I liked, interrupted only occasionally by a message from my father enquiring if I'd finished my homework.

A significant, life-changing development arose around the time my brother was due to graduate from kindergarten. My mother was pregnant with my sister Amelia. Sadly Granny died before Amelia's birth. No doubt realising how difficult it would be to cope with two frisky boys and a new baby girl without Gran, the easiest solution seemed to be boarding school for me.

That was the cover story but my theory is that I was packed off because I was an impossible kid and although my habitual misbehaviour had improved marginally after leaving Yeoville Boys, I guess I deserved what destiny held in store.

Marist Bothers College in Eckstein Street sat on the crest of a *koppie* facing another *koppie* across the valley where the Johannesburg Observatory stood sentinelling the suburb bearing its name.

Formidably impressive, double wrought iron, Gothic style gates incorporating an ornate, gold painted 'M' for Marist, guarded the main entrance. The purpose of these gates was purely ornamental as they were never shut.

Many years later while attending a film festival in Krakow, the Polish hosts chose to organize a visit to Auschwitz where I saw for myself that infamous gate bearing the obnoxious wrought iron sentence *'Arbeit Macht Frei'* evoking memories of my school gates except that while I'd been busy living my life the gates had shrunk. They were the same gates, oh yes, only far smaller than they had been when viewed through a child's eyes.

The College's vast rectangular building encompassed numerous classrooms, a huge kitchen, the boarders' dining room and administrative offices at ground level. On the first floor were the Brothers' quarters, the chapel, the junior dormitory and the boarders' ablution area - the lavatories, showers and serried rows of white porcelain hand basins with mirrors for brushing hair and shaving once your facial bum fluff blossomed and started to darken, mimicking a strange mange related malaise. In a semi-basement music rooms and the school tuck shop could be found. A long first floor corridor lined with shower cubicles linked the main building to yet another double storey which housed the senior dormitory and the infirmary above ground level classrooms.

The main building had a tarred quadrangle with a fishpond and fountain at its centre. Here, in weather fair or foul, over 600 boys gathered for morning assembly where prayers were intoned and important announcements made before we filed off 'in an orderly fashion, no talking allowed' to our classrooms.

Completing a trio of buildings facing onto the wide driveway was another two storey classroom-only block. Next to that was the school cadets' rifle shooting range and adjacent to that was the toilet block comprising two rows of lockable cubicles and two separate sets of urinals - one for the seniors and another for the juniors. This area was very busy indeed especially after the evening meal - a time when most of the seniors flocked there to partake of forbidden fags. Despite there being abundant cubicles, it was always difficult to find one that was not occupied by several boys puffing away for all they were worth, their smoke billowing out of the open tops as if the place was a practice ground for squads of Red Indian smoke signallers.

There were, naturally, sporadic raids by the Brothers, spearheaded by one Brother Raymond, an ultra-strict martinet who matched his sadistic sobriquet - Cossack - to

41

a 'T'. He was wont to bang on the doors, loudly demanding, 'Open up you seely fellows!' He often apprehended four felons per booth. They were ordered to await him in his study for 'a couple plus one' before he moved on to check if there were any offenders who were not fast enough to vacate their booths.

From time to time practical pranksters would frighten the daylights out of their peers by imitating Brother Raymond's curious Spanish accent, a talent that was unappreciated by the smokers who wreaked disproportionate physical vengeance on the scoundrels, pitilessly *donnering* (beating) them up so that in time the only diehard impressionists left were among the school's fastest runners.

One night all the toilet block lights fused and a new junior unwittingly chose the wrong urinal. Unluckily for him a tall senior who was engrossed in chatting to his friends over his shoulder failed to notice the hapless kid who received the most disturbing emotional upset of his young life before he howled off banshee fashion, into the night drenched to the skin by the senior's golden shower.

In a cottage next to the toilet block stood the school armoury of Great War relics - .303 calibre rifles (none of which worked) rusting forsakenly away alongside the .22 calibre rifles and live ammunition used at the shooting range. The cadet corps' band instruments, drums and bugles were shelved near the rifles. The rest of the cottage was crammed with bedraggled sports gear such as tennis nets and rackets; cricket mats and bats, pads, wickets and assorted balls - tennis, cricket, medicine and rugby - an agglomeration presided over by the multiskilled, blotchy-faced Brother Ralph. This guy also taught Afrikaans (a compulsory subject) and history and applied the *Broederbond* concept of teaching *geskiedenis* (history) in Afrikaans. The result was that we all did well at Afrikaans but dismally failed *geskiedenis* which didn't much matter really since South African history text books were heavily biased in favour of Boer heroics due to the overwhelming influence of the racist *Broederbond* whose adherents were mainly schoolteachers and academics so that there was hardly any reference to European history other than its direct effect on South Africa's Afrikaners.

Backing on to the cottage was a walled-in outdoor swimming pool with dressing rooms, showers, diving boards and a well kempt garden with shrubs and a lawn on which to relax.

Facing the college's main buildings stood an orchard the size of a soccer field, entry to which was absolutely prohibited. Few foolhardy lads ever courted disaster by entering that sanctuary where the Brothers meditated, enjoyed a quiet cigarette or simply escaped to take respite from their charges.

Disciplinary infractions at Marist Brothers College Observatory were dealt with far more strictly than those at the Koch Street primary school. Punishment at Observatory was so stringent that none but the boldest or dimmest pupils infringed rules for fear of instant retribution of up to six 'cuts' by strap or by cane.

Worse still, and reserved exclusively for boarders, the physical assault was often an overture to the ultimate chastening - black marks - which, if exceeded, led to the loss of the monthly weekend home visit privilege.

At boarding school, privacy wasn't part of the package. Privacy, with over a hundred blokes in each of two dormitories, one senior and one junior, was in short supply, particularly since the shower cubicles had no doors. The lavatories themselves did. Sort of. The door bottoms were a foot above the floor and barely high enough to conceal your seated body ensconced on the built-in blocks of wood screwed to the top of both sides of the rim of the bowl. These blocks were all that separated our delicate young arses from the chill of raw porcelain. It also meant that there were no seats to lift while peeing so that the wood was perpetually damp requiring a thorough papering over prior to being seated. This involved the careful positioning of squares of shiny primordial toilet paper called Izal which came in individual six inch square sheets dispensed from tiled, refillable receptacles slotted into the wall. This stuff had more in common with sandpaper than toilet tissue. If the boy in the next cubicle opened or closed his door before you'd finished papering, the draught blew it off and you had to start over again.

Such discomfort must have been sedulously planned to ensure that no one squandered too much time skiving in the bogs. In addition, the seniors were able to chin up to peer over the top of the door 'to ensure you were all right!' But their real motive was to catch you playing with yourself. It was not only the toilets but the entire school which seemed to have been designed for the specific purpose of making it impossible for boys to find anywhere to commit self-abuse in peace. Dire warnings from prefects and seniors that such deviant behaviour by juniors would result in hairy palms proved a singularly effective deterrent and I am able to report that no one in my dormitory ever suffered from that particular ailment. I pored over the Catholic catechism for ages without acquiring either enlightenment or ancillary information relating to hirsute hand syndrome.

If there were no Crows in sight (a Crow being the boys' apt name for the Brothers who wore long black *soutanes* with white, starched, split oblong collars at the throat, comparable to those worn by barristers in British courts of law), the less inhibited seniors pranced to the showers, clutching bars of red Lifebuoy soap, pre-pasted tooth brushes, jauntily clenched between their teeth, stark naked except for towels proudly draped over their early morning erections. The best endowed blokes, chiefly final year youths and the 1st rugby XV, even managed to transport a slipper in this manner by hanging it on the helmet end of their phallus. We younger inmates tried to preserve a vestige of dignity by progressing to the showers wearing pajama pants or a dressing gown or, at the very least, a towel round our waists. Even so everyone knew what everyone else's genitals looked like.

I accepted the situation without giving it much thought other than to try to imitate my seniors by rehearsing the slipper trick at home where I could practice in the comforting solitude of a warm, lockable bathroom with its faint, reassuring fragrance of my mother's green Palmolive soap.

As I grew older, taller and more virile at the onset of budding pubic hair, I succeeded! I was far too repressed to share details of that particular achievement with anyone until now.

The outbreak of war in Europe and its subsequent escalation added yet another dimension to my childhood. The radio, newspapers, magazines and newsreels overflowed with details of battles won and battles lost; of air raids on faraway cities; of attacks on British colonies in the East; of American landings on islands all over the Pacific Ocean; of convoys of ships being sunk by U-boats in the Atlantic.

All Johannesburg cinemas screened reports of major world news bringing home the global magnitude of the war to our far off Dominion at the bottom tip of Africa.

A wall of my bedroom at home hosted a large scale world map with drawing pins connecting bits of string delineating battle lines and other data which I updated sporadically.

Senior classrooms at school had similar maps to keep us informed about Allied developments. Our 'Boys up North' as our soldiers were styled, fought in far-off places which South Africans would never have heard of but for the war.

We were transfixed daily by radio news bulletins, newspaper and magazine stories and photographs of the astounding array of the machinery of war, the tanks, the guns, the ships and above all, the aircraft.

I marvelled at the dynamic beauty of flying machines, collecting all the pictures I chanced upon to supplement my ever expanding scrap book. I failed to take into consideration that they were all killing machines whether they were British, American, German, Italian or Japanese – Fiats, Zeros, Messerschmitts, Stukas, Mosquitos, Spitfires, Typhoons; bombers, fighters, transport planes - they all featured in my book. To me their sounds - as heard on the wireless, newsreels and war movies - were music to my ears and reinforced their grip on my imagination by stimulating the adrenalin to flow supersonically around my body. I avidly sought out one cracking magazine which illustrated aircraft from three angles, top, sides and front superimposed on graph paper squares, each representing a square foot to convey their size. These drawings were designed to assist servicemen to identify both Allied and Axis aircraft. I conscientiously measured them out step by step on a sports field and could recognize all the aircraft that flew in World War II.

The war taught us that there was far, far more to history than what was to be found in the skewed South African school text books which concentrated on the way brave Boers outgunned hordes of 'uncivilised black tribes.' It was indeed humbling to us to us to be aware that we were experiencing the unique opportunity to more or less witness history, albeit from afar, while it was actually in the making without waiting for lumpen historians to slant the truth to satisfy political ends.

Although Marist boarders were deprived of the most desirable of life's blessings like adequate sleep, tasty food and access to freedom, we didn't feel claustrophobic thanks to the well-managed grounds boasting sufficient space to accommodate a variety of outdoor sports. There was the pool, eight tennis courts, three rugby fields, and a full size athletic track doubling as the main cricket ground where the 1st and 2nd X1 cricket matches were usually played. Two of the three rugby fields were transformed into cricket pitches in summer by laying coir matting on top of the rough, tough kikuyu grass.

On the other side of the public road at the rear of the school were three or four red clay soccer pitches which were hardly ever used, even unofficially, since almost all Johannesburg boys' schools played rugby which was, after all, *the* national winter sport.

It was widely recognized that the Marist Order had a nose for property. Wherever a Marist College opened up, surrounding land values soared as did the rush to buy nearby homes. Those soccer fields were subsequently sold for an undisclosed profit and were used to erect high-class luxury houses. Lack of expansion space caused Koch Street's closure. On that site arose Mariston - a pricey multi-storey apartment block. The Mariston mazuma was added to the income from the soccer fields and invested on another Johannesburg Marist College in Inanda, a place considered to be in the *bundu* of the city outskirts where, previously, only an isolated brace of tacky riding schools had existed. Inanda swiftly evolved into a highly desirable, outrageously extravagant suburb in which to build mansions. But I digress...

Running down the side of the Observatory College a 500 yard dirt service road led from the rear street entrance before taking a left past the school buildings into Eckstein Street. Mature pine trees lined the top of this quiet, seldom used thoroughfare where we younger boarders exercised our architectural potential, enthusiastically constructing villages from pine twigs with roofs of cardboard covered with glued-on pine needles.

All the villages had roads connecting each village to its neighbour's. Hardly anyone bothered the builders creating this miniature world on which to 'drive' Dinky toy cars from one end to the other of the area which was moderately protected from the hailstorms which often beat down upon the pines only the depredations of sudden downpours of monsoon magnitude gave rise to floods which entailed rebuilding again from scratch.

This area was the natural habitat for strange black beetles called *tok-tokkies* so named for the sound generated by them rapidly moving their rear ends up and down on hard surfaces to produce a frenzied drumming noise to attract female company. We harvested them for amusement but they proved unhappy at being corralled in crude pine twig pens, so we built what we believed to be the first purpose built *tok-tokkie* race track in history.

Its design incorporated a relatively straight trench about six inches deep in order, we thought, to thwart any notions the *tok-tokkies* might nurse to abandon the course during race meetings.

On race days the *tok-tokkie* wrangler doubled as the starter. He stabled the runners in a flat, lidded biscuit tin with air holes at the top in readiness for the off. We would drum our fingers on pieces of wood positioned at the winning post end which the beetles would head for in a straight line, more or less, fully expecting a sexual encounter on reaching the finish line at the end of the hollow racecourse. But instead they were subjected to ignominious re-capture and re-stored unfulfilled, in a container to race again another day.

Because our beetles, male and female looked identical we were unable to differentiate between the sexes so we deduced that it was the males who did the drumming but to be sure we hadn't got it wrong we sorted them into known drummers and non-drummers if we saw them drum.

Each *tok-tokkie* was branded with a microscopic dab of model enamel paint to ensure which *tokkie* belonged to whom. Each winning beetle was honoured with a gold dab on its glossy, patent leather black back. Such accolades were infrequent since it proved almost impossible to keep a *tok-tokkie* longer than two or three races before it escaped.

Goggas, a guttural word (with the three g's pronounced as if clearing your itchy throat) is the generic collective noun for insects, creepy-crawlies or winged beasties which abound in South Africa where tourists and townies alike regard them as annoyances which constantly target humans as prime snack-mobiles. But in rural areas *goggas* are often a valuable and sustainable food source for humans as well as an amazing variety of reptiles and the exotic birds which grace South African skies.

I was first introduced to the nutritional value of one edible species by Enos, our house servant, who rushed inside to call me to witness the phenomenon of swarming 'flying ants' - an awe-inspiring sight of hundreds of thousands, maybe millions, of them whirring through the air at low level, pursued by black people feverishly garnering them with hats, pillowcases, shopping bags and even battered suitcases.

Once the swarm had passed, the harvesters squatted down to feast upon their prey by pulling the fat white abdomens away from the moving parts of wings and legs at the front and gorging on them greedily as if it was their last supper. This fascinated me and I gingerly tasted them. I could find but one descriptive word for them. Scrumptious! To my palate they smacked of rich creamy custard similar to the famed Afrikaner *melkterts*, only more trendy. Enos assured me they were hyper delicious cooked so he fried a handful in a dry pan. I preferred them raw but either way was fine and from then on, I was out there with the locals whenever there was a swarm, catching the termites, for that is what they were, and avidly enjoying so novel a taste of Africa. At school none of the other guys would try them. They'll never know what they missed.

Another *gogga* which enjoyed enduring popularity at my school was the silkworm, tolerated by the Brothers because the shoeboxes we kept them in didn't take up much space inside our lockers; and they were odourless and anyway, the Crows reckoned, quite rightly, that starvation would take its toll as there was a paucity of mulberry trees around that part of Johannesburg and, as any schoolboy could have told you in those days, that's the only stuff the little blighters will eat.

We boarders didn't allow a small matter like that to discourage us and nightly incursions were undertaken into more far-flung gardens. As insurance we persuaded daydog friends to bring us regular supplies of mulberry leaves from the outside world in exchange for future silkworm eggs or flat fees of a marble or two per brown paper bagful.

Aside from providing them with food, the worms didn't require any attention and happily munched away night and day, moulting from time to time until they began creating their cocoons heralding intense activity for the owners to make crude spinning wheels or winding bobbins out of cotton reels and, once having found the end - or maybe it was the beginning - of the silk the worm had spun, we began to unwind the silk.

It seems silk farmers chucked the cocoons into boiling water to simplify the unwinding procedure. Regrettably this practice cooks the pupa inside and even if we had been aware of this, we wouldn't have wanted to harm our 'pets' so we loosened the strand of silk using the spittle in our mouths.

Pupae that survived such oral indignity transformed into flightless moths which spent the rest of their brief lives bonking back to back until the males popped their little clogs, doubtless exhausted from their prolonged sexual antics. The fertilized females then laid hundreds of tiny yellow eggs before they too passed away. The eggs hatched fairly soon and the new generation began to engross us again. All very exciting for impressionable kids, but a polite word of warning will not go amiss if you want to evaluate our method of silk harvesting - ensure that you don't try it at a place where you may be liable to be startled as the pupae are nowhere near as tasty as the termites should you accidentally bite into one.

Food at Marist Brothers was startlingly unimaginative. Not that there was any shortage of it, only it was perpetually repetitious and flavourless. The cooks' ambit was restricted to two menus - one for summer, the other for winter. If any of us had gone into cryonic hibernation for future defrosting we'd have known for sure which day of the week it was when we were thawed out and saw what was being served for either lunch or dinner.

During the war fresh meat was in short supply and except for Fridays which was ineluctably fish day for Catholics, we were served bully beef (corned beef) in guises galore - plain and cold with salad for lunch, as hash with potatoes for dinner. Next day it reached the table in the shape of a powdered egg omelette with bully beef filling and in the evening it might be curried corned beef. The following day would bring forth minced bully beef on rice or with cabbage or fried with potato chips and so on ad nauseam.

All this bland mush caused the condiment table to creak under the weight of the boarders' personal supplies of ketchup, mustard, piccalilli, vinegar, brown sauce and Worcestershire sauce on which I became totally hooked and still cannot eat fried or poached eggs without it. But my addiction paled into insignificance compared to a lad called Richardson who even sloshed it on his porridge. Whether or not the Crows shared the same menu in their dining room was not in the public domain but the Crow in charge of mealtimes consumed the same food as we pupils.

Each table seated eight boys. Two seniors, the table captain and vice-captain were allegedly in charge of conduct and the democratic sharing of food. Democratic? Hell no! They controlled our intake more severely than any of today's faddy, foodie dieticians. The table captain was first in the pecking order. He helped himself to a king-size portion of any dish he fancied before passing it to his gluttonous vice-captain who served himself similarly leaving hardly anything for the others to share. It was not unknown for the captains to allow drops of surreptitious saliva to dribble onto food from time to time thereby ensuring that none of us would eat any of it. Complaints to the Brothers were pointless as the captains unfailingly denied them and the complainants risked further deprivation for as long as the captain's whim demanded. Weeks often passed by without the juniors receiving butter or portions of desert.

Neville Marks, a dayboy whose lovely mother, bless her, was the kindliest of all my friends' mothers, helped rescue a number of boarders from nutritional deprivation by concocting the most delicious sandwiches in the history of the world. Come to think of it, I reckon she may have invented the first known designer sandwiches *a lá* Dagwood. Rye bread with *schmaltz* (chicken fat) and garlicky polony, my favourite, still has me drooling at the thought of them. Nev didn't go much on sandwiches and I'm sure his mother knew he was sustaining boarder pals so she always loaded his neat greaseproof paper sandwich parcels with supplemental sarnies in case Nev actually ate one or two himself. Monty Legator, a close friend from Koch Street days, also had a generous mother who ensured that his lunch included spares for his ever hungry boarder classmates. Other daydogs occasionally contributed, but the majority abstained from sharing since the notoriety of 'boarders bites' was such that a new daydog once lost three quarters of an outsize apple in one monumental mouthful.

The College's two dormitories - one for juniors, one for seniors each slept over 100 boys in rows of metal beds backed up against the walls on each side of the long rooms with two rows in the middle. Adjacent to the junior dorm was a large narrow enclosed balcony with yet another row of beds.

At the pillow end of each bed stood five foot high cupboards called lockers - a contradiction which mystified us since none of them had locks. The tops each had a hinged, lidded compartment for toiletries and small personal belongings. Inside were shelves to store shirts, trousers, underwear, socks, handkerchiefs, pullovers, pajamas and clean towels. A bit of string, drawing-pinned to the inside of the door held a 'best' school tie and belt. The bottom was reserved for dirty clothing, rugby boots and sandshoes aka *takkies* or plimsolls - prototypes of today's Nikes - consisting of white canvas uppers and gummy, tan rubber soles, the compulsory footwear for tennis, athletics, gym and other sporting activities. Each and every item, even socks, bore our name and the letters 'MCOJ' (Marist College, Observatory, Johannesburg) to identify ownership if mislaid, lost or mixed up at the laundry.

The predominant odour of the lockers was a combination of reeking *takkies*, ancient soap, old orange peel, sweat, jockstraps and toe jam matured over generations of lads plagued by athlete's foot. No matter how often the locker was cleaned, the smell had permeated the wood to such an extent that even the strongest disinfectant merely served to intensify the pungency.

School blazers and overcoats hung on wall-to-wall rails erected at the far end of the dormitory. This clothing was hidden from view by thick, turd-brown drapes. Many a lad escaped detection by hiding behind them to avoid being caught in the dorm at a prohibited time.

Considering the fact that the two dormitories housed over a hundred of us few shenanigans worth recording took place there since dorm discipline was such that the Crows, who all possessed radar hearing, had no compunction about caning pajama wearers. You really knew you'd been caned if you were in pajamas and were unlucky enough to have been punished once this way, you made damned sure not to repeat the offence, or at the very least, you became ultra-cautious to avoid being caught a second time. In parentheses, anyone who tells you that the pain of corporal punishment can be pleasurable assuredly did not attend a Marist Brothers' College.

Schoolboy honour was another matter. Squealers seldom survived boarding school life unscathed and by far the worst crime any kid could perpetrate was to breach the unwritten Number One rule - never, *ever*, be a stoolie, not even against your worst enemy. This meant biting the bullet when older bullies tried to exact a tithe as part of a protection racket imposed on those junior to them. Pay up in coin or with a valued possession to escape physical harm. The non-payment alternative was to await inevitable revenge - a threat far greater than the Crows' Damoclean canes. Rule Two - share your tuck with friends from time to time. Failure met the same Machiavellian consequences as Rule One which introduces us to the Case of the Pawpaw Guts...

Richardson, the Worcestershire sauce fiend's father was a fruit farmer. On family visits to the College on one designated Sunday each month, Richardson's father customarily brought him a wooden box full of pawpaws, the South African name for papaya, a luscious tropical fruit. They weren't those tiny gourmet jobs one sees in up-market supermarkets these days, they were the real South African, man-sized McCoy, each one resembling an overinflated rugby ball.

Richardson was wont to secrete his fruit under his bed. As soon as the lights were turned off by the dorm Crow he would nip out of bed armed with a bowl, a knife and a spoon to guzzle away at his pawpaws under the bed.

In the dark, the dorm Brother progressed along the aisles between the beds in slow motion telling his rosary until everyone was sound asleep or seemed so to be. After circumnavigating the two main dormitory aisles he would enter the balcony sleeping area making a U at the end of it, returning to the dorm and retracing his route in the opposite direction. The juniors' dorm Crow Brother Marcellan - Marcie - never deviated from his habitual circuit. Richardson therefore knew exactly how long it took Marcie to pass his bed but as a precaution Richardson had devised a crafty ruse. As soon as Marcie went out to the balcony area Richardson sprinkled granular sugar at the start of his aisle. Since the concrete floor was covered with tough, shiny, hardwearing linoleum, any sole treading on Richardson's sugar produced a barely audible crunching noise which alerted him to the fact that the Crow was within range allowing him time to scramble quietly back into his bed with the Crow oblivious that any tomfoolery was in progress. Richardson became so cocksure that he took to stuffing pillows in his bed on moonlit nights to avoid the effort of getting in and out of bed to finish his selfish gorging.

It didn't take too long for a clutch of conspirators to conclude that Richardson's arrogance and greed rendered him ripe for revenge. In order to ensure his come-uppance we scrounged a few overripe pawpaws for their slimy, gelatinous seeds which looked for all the world like black frog spawn. No sooner had Marcie entered the balcony than Richardson's opposite neighbour hastily spread excessive quantities of pawpaw pips across the aisle at the foot of Richardson's bed while the guy at the start of the aisle quickly wiped away Richardson's alarm granules.

As Crows went Marcie was a moderately nice old guy in his late fifties, a very tolerant, enlightened man compared to his brethren. Marcie's vows had obviously excluded gluttony to which his corpulent belly silently attested. Marcie was the *onlie begetter* and the butt of all the fattist wisecracks schoolboys could concoct. The size of his impressive *boep* convinced us that he hadn't seen his penis from above for many years and we figured that the only way he could verify it was still there and in good nick was to employ a mirror.

The dorm seemed quieter than usual that Sunday night and all that could be heard over the chirruping cricket concert from the orchard was an occasional snore and the odd fart as Marcie trod slowly by, conscientiously, devoutly, silently, reciting his Hail Mary's. We all listened intently for the outcome self-righteously certain that Richardson's reprisal was merely moments away...

Suddenly there was this sloshy, slurry sort of sound accompanied by a high pitched yelp as Marcie upended on the slithery pawpaw pips and landed heavily on his butt with a crump, akin to that of an artillery shell in those movies about the Somme, as he hit the deck with a gasp of wounded pain.

We were astonished by the alacrity with which this portly person sprang into action. He sprinted for the light switch, flicked it on and returned to the scene of the crime to discover an ashen faced Richardson emerging from under his bed, shell shocked and disorientated at being caught so blatantly red-handed. Marcie took one glance at the incriminating mound of fresh pips in the aisle which condemned the wretched Richardson without further ado. Marcie was deaf to his pleas of innocence as the boy was ignominiously dragged by his ear to the door of Marcie's room where he was left standing, trembling until Marcie emerged, nanoseconds later, armed with a three foot long cane with which he swiftly administered six cuts on the culprit's pajama'ed rear.

From then on his contemporaries enjoyed a decent share of Richardson's father's superbly succulent pawpaws.

Family Frolics

The bigger and older my kid brother grew, the more I liked him. In fact I enjoyed reading him stories and showing him how to play the games in my boxed compendium. He was the only kid I knew who couldn't see through my clumsy card tricks but then Justin was a bright boy and I suspect he was humoring me.

One day he was in our back yard, no more or less than a bare dirt patch where forlorn weeds struggled for survival here and there, playing with Sorrel, one of the two Solomon brothers, engrossed in digging holes with a small, blunt, rusted axe and a trowel. While they were busily burying broken bricks in the holes Sorrel had an idea.

'You put your finger here,' he suggested, pointing at a brick, 'and I'll chop it off.'

Justin obliged and true to his word, Sorrel chopped. Fortunately he wasn't strong enough, nor the axe sharp enough to sever Justin's finger but I had never before seen so much blood. Luckily my Mom's youngest brother, Uncle Willie, happened to be visiting at the time and he whisked us off to hospital in his car with Mom holding Justin while I clutched an enamel bowl to catch the blood flowing through his hastily bandaged finger.

This wasn't the first time I'd accompanied my *boetie* to hospital. Uncle Willie was a first rate fellow with a whimsical wit and inclined to prestidigitation. He practiced his sleight of hand whenever he came to visit and always willingly demonstrated a selection of his wizardry for us. Justin adored Uncle Willie's speciality - the disappearing marble or coin - that he would pretend to thrust up his nostril, retrieving it from either his ear or one of ours. We were ecstatic if he used a coin 'cos he always let us keep it. Now this, surmised my brother, was easy as pie and any kid could manage it. He resolved to put it to the test immediately but he didn't have a coin and his smallest marble didn't fit so he tried it with a bead and, hey presto, hospital.

Justin was born on the same day as Uncle Willie's only child Yvonne who was gravely mentally handicapped and spent her entire life in the care of an order of nursing nuns. Even though Uncle Willie always referred to the Mother Superior as 'Mrs. Shapiro' it was faith in spiritualism that helped him and my Aunt Freda retain their sanity. Long after Uncle Willie died, I used to ask my aunt to give him my regards and she always responded graciously and civilly saying he appreciated my enquiries...

Justin often accompanied me to the cinema which he hugely enjoyed as did I especially since I always received a cash bonus to take him with me to the swimming pool and the movies. One Saturday we went to a kids' screening of *Abbott and Costello meet Frankenstein* (as well as the *Wolf Man* and *Dracula*). The age limit 'Not for Children 4-12' was prominently displayed at the box office. At the time Justin was about nine, a very small nine. The box office lady looked quizzically at my pint-sized pal whose face she could hardly see above her counter despite his standing on tiptoes. 'He doesn't look twelve,' she observed. My reply was 'That's because he doesn't eat his Wheaties.' She grinned broadly as she handed me two tickets.

The spoof horror movie was very much my cup of tea, but Justin was really too young for it and in later life he confessed to me that he'd had nightmares about it for years.

The Solomon boys seemed to attract more problems than other kids in the street such as setting fire to their house while investigating the arrival of a litter of kittens born in their cellar. They chose to use a lit newspaper which ignited the wood stored there... Oh well, maybe that paper torch had been my idea but no animals were harmed.

One afternoon while playing draughts with Rael, the elder Solomon boy, in his parents' bedroom he asked if I wanted to see his dad's gun. Naturally the answer was 'Yes!' So he clambered onto a chair to feel around the top shelf of his father's wardrobe, producing a really impressive chrome plated revolver just like those we'd seen in gangster movies. We oohed and aahed at it for a while before we went to my house to see if perhaps my father kept a gun in his wardrobe. He didn't.

No problem - I owned a six shooter cap gun and we played cops and robbers rampaging up and down the passageway. Mom stuck her head out of the door to tell me that Aunt Ray was visiting and that I should come say hello which I did. Rael trailed behind me into the lounge, bang banging vocally while ducking behind an armchair.

'What's your name son?' asked my aunt.

'Rael', he answered, 'I'm a detective.'

'Well,' said Aunt Ray quietly, 'that's a mighty fine gun you have detective Rael. May I look at it please?'

Rael drew a bead on her but before he could say 'Bang, bang.' my aunt again ducked.

'Pow! Pow!' exclaimed Rael.

Encouraged by her spontaneous participation in our game Rael again aimed the gun at her and repeated his "Bang-bang, pow-pow" powwow before handing her the gun, barrel first. She gingerly took it from him.

'This,' she sighed to my mother, 'is no toy. It's a real gun. It's fully loaded and the safety catch is off.'

I thought my mother was about to faint.

Aunt Ray had recognized it as being identical to a weapon owned by her husband.

Had Rael been slightly stronger and able to exert a fraction more pressure on the trigger there might well have been a corpse in our house that day...

Soon afterwards a very real tragedy occurred in our home. Sadly my dear Gran died shortly after I became a boarder at Marist 'Obs'. My parents felt I was too young to attend the funeral and it wasn't until I came home for the holidays that I was told that Gran had gone away for a while. They kept the truth from me until they thought I became used to not having her around.

My mother again went to the maternity hospital, this time to give birth to my sister whose arrival coincided with one of my home visit weekends and rather than have me forfeit that, Mom arranged for me to stay with Aunt Clara and my cousins Melville and Ivan at their home in Becker Street where I slept in the spare bed in my younger cousin Ivan's room.

Seeing him naked for the first time shocked me. Unlike any of the other guys at the swimming pool whose suntan stopped between the waist and thighs, Ivan was brown all over. I'd wondered why he had a slightly darker complexion than any other members of his family. It wasn't until I shared a bath with him that I discovered his bath water was always a purple coloured solution matching one of my rejected carrot and iodine ingredients called Condy's Crystals, the common name for permanganate of potash, widely used as a disinfectant which tended to stain pink skin light brown. And there I had been thinking that Cousin Ivan was a changeling or from a different race and that the suspicious tidemarks in their white bathtub were from plain old fashioned dirt.

We two youngsters had been given strict instructions never to disturb Melville in his room where he conscientiously beavered away at his dentistry studies.

At that time I was obsessively into philately and assembling model aeroplanes from balsa wood kits bought at Yardley's, a hobby shop opposite another frequently patronized haunt, the stamp shop in a small shopping arcade just off Market Street over the road from the Johannesburg Town Hall. My best pal Monty and I often frequented both shops during school holiday Saturdays once we had received our pocket money. We invested in our mushrooming collections of Hitler Head and Nazi swastika stamps. Beneficial philatelic by-products were the magnifying glasses we both used to minutely examine our purchases hoping to spot a printing flaw which, had we miraculously found one, would have hugely increased the stamp's value. Magnifying glasses also proved useful for starting fires on sunny days and surprising friends dozing off while sunbathing at the swimming baths by focusing the sun's rays on their bums which always provoked yelps of angry protest from the quarry.

Yardley's was next. Their aircraft kits included full instructions and blueprints of models from all angles. Every box contained thin, flexible strips of balsa wood and flat pieces on which the complicated curved bits were printed. The latter were carefully cut out with a sharp scalpel tool then sandpapered. The plan itself was laid onto a cork or softwood base and the strips were fixed to it by pushing straight pins through the paper plan into the base to form a ladder like skeleton glued together by rapid drying balsa cement gingerly squeezed from lead tubes. The adhesive often stuck to your fingers and you spent satisfying time biting it off and spitting out the dry residue.

Once the fuselage was ready the wings and tail sections were similarly formed. Tissue paper was glued on to all sections, then lightly sprayed by mouth with tap water which tautened the paper as it dried, leaving a smooth surface which could be painted with stuff called aeroplane dope. Then the bits were all glued to the fuselage and there stood your magnum opus awaiting its final coat of paint and respectful admiration from parents and pals.

Although it was a slow, painstaking pastime requiring great concentration, its therapeutic effects partially dispelled junior boarders' homesick blues and the longing for wholesome home-cooked meals.

In retrospect I'm convinced it was not merely a creative urge that kept us building model aircraft. This divertissement was certainly enhanced by the euphoric 'high' induced by inhaling the balsa cement fumes and those from the dope. At my young age of nine or ten glue sniffing was unheard of, but that's what we were doing while working on those aeroplane models. In the fullness of time I discovered that the word 'dope' derived from the fact that men who used it to waterproof real canvas-covered aircraft were all affected by the daily inhalation of the fumes from commercial quantities of the same liquid I used. This overdose acted much like alcohol, making the operators drowsy, befuddled and unsteady on their feet. Ergo 'Dopey.'

Where was I? Ah yes, spending a school weekend break at Aunt Clara's nearby house while my mother was having her baby. At the time I was wholly committed to my most ambitious aircraft. It had a wing span as wide as my outstretched arms and all that was needed to finish it was to paper the wings, spray them, allow them to dry and attach them to the fuselage. I spent the whole of Saturday working on it at Aunt Clara's.

Cousin Melville was at dental school that day and I felt the safest place to leave my plane to dry out was in his room which always had drawn curtains to keep it cool. Sadly Melville returned earlier than usual and went straight to his room where he sat on his bed without turning on the light having no idea that my masterpiece was there until his rump flattened it. I had never lost the plot as badly as I did on seeing the destruction he'd wrought on weeks and weeks of my spare time labour of love.

I virtually took off and chased this guy, who was at least a head taller than me, round and round the house into the garden, down the street and back again for fifteen minutes until I caught him determined to inflict bodily harm upon him - except that I wasn't big enough or strong enough to do so even after he collapsed in fits of helpless laughter.

Of course it hadn't been his fault and he had the decency to apologise and later he bought me a new kit which helped me forgive him. To this very day he always reminds me of the first seat he'd had on an aeroplane. My aeroplane.

It always struck me as odd that Marist Brothers College accepted quite so many Jewish kids. What was equally odd, or odder even, was that most Jewish parents wished their male heirs to be educated at a private school on the assumption I guess, that paid tuition provided a higher standard than the free Government schooling available to white kids and if it happened to be a Catholic school, vell, so be it already.

Although we Jewboys were a minority at Marist's there were sufficient of us among the boarders to warrant a part time Hebrew teacher to provide religious instruction which, I was advised 60 years later, was classified by the Crows as Jewish Studies under the tutelage of Mr. Lazar - Lizzie to his victims. His mission was to teach us sufficient Hebrew to read a portion of the *Torah,* the first five books of the Old Testament - the Books of Moses - to mark the day on which boys become 'sons of the commandments' at the age of thirteen. This is known as a *Bar Mitzvah* which is not so much a religious requirement as a modern practice among Jews throughout the world, not to mention as good an excuse as a wedding to throw a pizzazzy party.

No one abhorred those lessons as much as me and I frequently bunked them. Lizzie was not exactly a Top Ten Teacher contender and the only positive element to emerge from his classes was that he kept us fully informed of the definitive calendar of Jewish Holidays which we 'observed' with a day off 'to attend synagogue'. Only we detoured to the movies or one of the 'caffies' in Yeoville or Hillbrow to play the pinball machines or to simply laze about.

Combined with Catholic Saints Days which meant that everyone at Marist Brothers' Colleges had a holiday, we Jews were the envy of our schoolmates who contemplated converting to Judaism to qualify for our privileged days off but as soon as they discovered that circumcision went with the territory they all flinched and executed a swift volt-face.

In Johannesburg *Bar Mitzvah* festivities were almost as lavish as those of Jewish wedding receptions. Mine was no exception. The Ginsberg Hall in Bertrams had been booked a long time ahead as had musicians and *Beth Din* validated *kosher* caterers in deference to those among us who observed the ancient custom of *kashrut.* Gilt edged invitations duly went out to all and sundry.

While I was away at school during the run-up period, arrangements moved along smoothly until about a week prior to my *Bar Mitzvah* Lizzie suddenly perceived he'd been teaching me the wrong portion of the law and panicked accordingly. He telephoned my parents to ask them to postpone events until my segment caught up with the correct date four weeks later. Until then I'd no idea of how elaborate the planning had been and my parents were absolutely adamant that there could be no postponement of the reception which had monopolized months of their time and would be impossible to reorganize even if they wanted to. The one thing Lizzie did get right was recognizing the certainty that there was no chance that I could possibly master the obligatory portion in the ten days left prior to the ceremony. So... the compromise reached was that my portion of the law, the correct portion, be written out phonetically for me to learn off by heart as I was unable to read most Hebrew words. I had to spend several painful hours a day for four days having Lizzie coach me in the correct pronunciation. The relative ease of this simple idea made life a lot less stressful and I wondered why the phonetic route had not been trodden originally thereby sparing us the agony of Lizzie's deadly dull droning on Friday afternoons.

It was necessary for me to turn up at the Berea Synagogue on the eve of my *Bar Mitzvah* for a rabbinical briefing on the fine detail of the forthcoming service.

The rehearsal, held immediately afterwards, went smoothly enough and I left for home cock-a-hoop at passing that test with flying colours. About half way home the heavens opened up as if the Almighty was wagging a finger of displeasure at my disrespectful behaviour. It was a typical Johannesburg flash downpour which lasted less than five minutes but left me wringing wet within seconds and even though it was high summer, by the time I reached home my teeth were chattering and I was shivering from the ice cold shower. This necessitated an immediate hot bath, dinner and straight to bed with two aspirin swallowed with hot milk laced with honey.

Next morning the symptoms of an oncoming cold were emerging. Nevertheless the ceremony went very well and my proud parents were overjoyed. I was hustled home for a quick lunch and another helping of aspirin, hot milk and honey and obliged to spend the afternoon in bed before the evening reception, another daunting challenge.

Two hundred guests filled the hall to the gunnels consuming enough food to nourish an African village for a week. Gifts included quantities of prosaic stuff like wallets (no less than a round half dozen), a lifetime supply of fountain pens, two watches, numerous leather-bound books and zipper bags containing writing pads and envelopes. My preference 'though, was the pile of cheques all made out in guineas (one sterling pound and one shilling).

My duties that night included being pleasant to the guests and making a speech in the English language both of which justifiably impressed my parents. I had hoped that my demonstrable maturity displayed by this, my first public engagement, might influence them to release me from incarceration at boarding school. No such luck. But I was mollycoddled for the next ten days at home in bed with pneumonia.

I had to wait another three years for my next close encounter with Judaism. Aunt Minnie's son, cousin Cyril, and his wife Edie invited me to become their firstborn's godfather which was quite a surprise in view of my overt lack of interest in the religion into which I was born. This invitation was, apparently, a singular honour and I duly turned up in my suit at the maternity hospital where the *Brit* - the covenant of circumcision - ceremony was to take place on the eighth day of the child's life in accordance with the seven biblical days of creation. The full name of the ritual is *Brit Milah* aka *Bris*.

Representatives of both parents' families were in attendance. I was led to a chair and as soon as I sat down a whopping great cushion was placed on my lap. Moments after being asked if I was comfy my 'God-wife', the baby's godmother, brought the infant to me and placed him on the cushion, whereupon this bearded man wearing a prayer shawl and a *yarmulke* removed the kid's nappy. It was only after he'd finished instructing me as to how to keep the little creature still that I realised with horror that he was actually going to snip the diminutive dong while the mite was on my lap. I then knew for sure what the phrase 'left holding the baby' really meant. The *mohel* - he who snips - shoved a soggy cotton wool ball into the infant's mouth, apparently dunked in wine or maybe a top secret rabbinical pacifier which made the baby lick his lips and relax. I think he was probably *shikker* and therefore blissfully unaware that part of the tip of his miniscule manhood was about to be sliced off. Whatever the liquid was, I was the one who needed it more urgently than the babe. Now that I was fully aware of what was about to happen I felt chronically queasy so maybe my memory isn't too clear but what I think I saw was the *mohel* producing a small shiny ring thing from a kidney shaped enamel bowl and intoning a Hebrew benediction while attaching it to the baby's petite prick. I was giddy and breathing hard before I passed out so that I missed the snip itself but I recovered to the buzzing of a room ringing with *mazeltovs* all-round while the poor little bloke yelled his head off at the undignified loss of his foreskin. He was given another lick of the alcoholic cotton wool. It was difficult to desist from puking until I was able to get out of the room to visit the men's toilet - not an easy place to find in a maternity hospital...

Among the mass of madcaps at Marist Brothers College was Dimitri Papadopolous, a recent immigrant from Cyprus whose home language was Greek. Problems with his English, a handicap which initially generated a superabundance of teasing, were swiftly terminated by him firmly clouting the bully no matter how much bigger the blighter happened to be. Dimitri was possibly the strongest boy in the school but being a stocky lad he was unable to run very fast so he always played rugby as a forward whose strength enabled him to ward off other heftier opponents who tried to tackle him.

Dimitri had developed an imbecilic party piece which handsomely boosted his pocket money. His trick was hair-raising. Using a ruler or a stick in his left hand he'd place his right arm under his left arm and grab his left ear lobe. Then he bent down to allow the stick to touch the ground using it as a pivot to rotate himself round and round and round in circles umpteen times until he collapsed from giddiness. He'd bet all comers that no one could match or beat his total. No challenger ever did.

The *dramatis personae* of Marist Brothers' teaching cast included a troupe of zanies recruited from a downmarket theatrical farce. The starring buffoon was played by Jack O'Malley whose apposite epithet was Pegleg. Rumour had it that he'd mislaid a leg one inebriated evening by falling under a moving train in Ireland where he had been a champion boxer.

For us boys Jack's disability proved to be a blessing. You see the Crows tended to sneak up on us silently on rubber soled shoes whereas Jack's clanking metal leg was audible from a long way off, ensuring that we could immediately stop doing whatever it was that might remotely be construed as an infraction.

O'Malley's nose was not dissimilar to the ski jump, typically Irish hooter, famously sported by Bob Hope except that Jack's was bigger, its size enlarged by his skanky habit of constantly playing pick and flick with its contents during class or whenever he was in charge of study (prep) periods. Pretending to be reading, but keeping an eagle eye on us his excavations were industriously, almost lovingly, rolled into perfectly round pellets which he propelled in our direction caring not a jot where they landed.

Unsurprisingly Pegleg was also the college boxing coach. It was a given that those who failed to take an interest in his sport could expect a very bumpy ride. I don't think he took to me at all, instinctively realizing I was inherently a coward who found no pleasure in being beaten to a pulp for no apparent reason, so he ordered me into the ring with the school champion who delivered one or two resounding thumps and it was all over for me. My nose bled profusely and I had problems with the resulting deviated nasal septum for years afterwards.

Jack O'Malley was notorious for his largesse with his strap. Being a former boxer the strength of his right arm placed him on a par with Brother Raymond as the most fearsome of all those who inflicted corporal punishment upon us. The straps employed by Crows and lay teachers alike must have been obtained from the same dishonourable manufacturers in that they all looked the same - about an inch and a half wide, eighteen inches long, crafted from heavy, double-sided stitched brown leather which may possibly have concealed lead or something equally heavy inside to provide added weight not to mention pain. The handle part was curved to ensure that the torturer had a good, solid grip.

A newcomer to our class, the son of recent German immigrants was actually called Fritz. O'Malley took a dislike to the luckless lad and made life unnecessarily difficult for him. We reckoned the friction between them was due to the fact that O'Malley did not have the patience to decipher Fritz's Pidgin English and, in turn, Fritz was unable to make neither head nor tail of Pegleg's Irish brogue, a speech impediment even thicker than his strap. One day Fritz was summoned to the front of the class for an unspecified indiscretion. Pegleg tetchily indicated that he should hold out his hand at arm's length, palm upwards, a procedure that most of us had sampled. Fritz held out a trembling hand. O'Malley took a vicious swipe at it but Fritz yanked his hand away a nanosecond before the strap was due to connect resulting in a resounding thwack on the thigh of O'Malley's good leg. The class tittered as Pegleg winced. His expression was thunderous. In the throes of a fit of pique he warned us that anyone displaying the merest hint of hilarity would be next in line after he'd finished with Fritz. Pegleg readjusted his stance for a second go at Fritz's hand. Again Fritz pulled it away. This time the leather clanged melodiously against Jack's metal leg. So outraged was Jack by then that he grabbed Fritz's fingers grasping them tightly to ensure the boy's hand was where he wanted it for the third swipe.

Pegleg underestimated Fritz's adrenalin augmented strength and Fritz again wrenched his hand away, but this time the strap met something and that something happened to be the tip of Fritz's middle fingernail. O'Malley's brutal force had snapped off a chunk of nail, precipitating a fountain of claret coupled with a horrified scream from Fritz who hurtled away, fast as a greyhound from a trap, as he headed, hysterically hollering, out of the classroom as if a hundred demons were hot on his heels. A pallid-faced O'Malley immediately ordered a class prefect to undertake a search-and-find quest with instructions to escort Fritz to Matron for treatment. The messenger was thrilled to oblige and out he went following Fritz's blood trail - for a short distance that is - until he decided to exploit his luck to the full by retiring to the lavatory block for a smoke and not bothering to return to class until home time, claiming to have left no stone unturned in a meticulous search for Fritz.

Twenty minutes after Fritz's dramatic exit the door of the classroom was flung open with a bang loud enough to awaken the dead and in burst a very angry woman whose resemblance to the guppy-eyed Fritz left not the remotest doubt that she was his maternal parent. Thanks to her accent and her conniption fit her words were, by and large, incomprehensible yet her tone and her body language ensured that Pegleg clearly understood her animus towards him.

We all sat there open mouthed, wide-eyed, flabbergasted by so fabulous a diversion from lessons. Words like 'swine,' 'monster,' 'bully,' 'brute,' and 'Hitler' tumbled from her lips. Seemingly without drawing breath she told him what she thought of him and his illegitimate parents and threatened to have the police arrest him for inflicting grievous bodily harm upon her son.

O'Malley was thoroughly shocked to be thus berated in front of his class. He vainly sought to persuade her that the broken nail had been an accident; that her son had deserved the punishment but had pulled his hand away at the last second, and... She was having none of it and her tirade did not diminish in either volume or venom.

The teacher next door came to investigate the cause of the commotion which had interrupted his class. His equally futile bid to calm Fritz's mother merely resulted in further lurid language.

Eventually she ran out of steam leaving O'Malley and his colleague mopping their brows with palpable relief. Normally the recess bell precipitated a pell-mell rush to leave the classroom. Except that morning. Not one of the 29 boys in the class moved a muscle. We were enjoined not to mention the brouhaha to anyone. Fat chance! Moments after we left class for our break, the entire student body was rocking with glee.

It was the last time O'Malley used his strap on hands and many a young rear bore welts attributable to Fritz and his momma. But it was a small price to pay for ringside seats at the most far-fetched phenomenon ever to take place in a Marist Brothers' classroom.

And, by the way, unsurprisingly, none of us ever saw Fritz or his mother again.

Another participant in the pantomime parade of educators at Marist was 'Congo Bill,' a lay teacher whose real name is lost in the mists of time. The college's uniformed Cadet Corps was considered by all us 'privates' to be an unmitigated waste of time and energy. It was operated one afternoon a week by a murder of Crows who dressed in dog-collared army uniforms to supervise the posturing senior pupil sergeants and NCO's in charge of drilling us. The only practical occasion relating to Marist's military malarkey was the day in mid-1947 that the entire Marist cadet corps together with all other Johannesburg school cadets lined Louis Botha Avenue, the main road out of Johannesburg, where we all stood to rigid attention in honour of the King and Queen of England and both Princesses as their open Rolls Royce drove slowly past us en route to Pretoria.

Cadet days invariably saw Congo Bill wearing a different uniform from the one he'd worn the previous week. In fact he sported a different uniform every cadet day leading to our assumption that he'd served in the armies of numerous unspecified nations. Or maybe he had learned the art of 'mix 'n match' long before that phrase passed into common usage. Or perhaps he had an arrangement with a fancy dress supplier. His most ridiculous uniform included riding boots and jodhpurs which still make me smile if I re-run that image in my mind's eye.

Not so amusing was Bill's arsenal of straps and canes which he had maliciously christened 'Salt', 'Pepper', 'Mustard' and 'Ginger' - among others - and he, too, was excessively liberal when deploying his weapons. He further exhibited his macabre mentality by allowing miscreants to choose from his selection. No one remembers what subject he taught only that he was in charge of the .22 rifle shooting range where, as cadets, we were instructed in the art of shooting with live ammunition. We assiduously collected the copper plated *doppies* which we conspired to utilise to persecute Congo Bill. We shaved the sulphur ends off matchsticks with razor blades and inserted the bits into the *doppies*, sealing them by closing the open ends with pliers. The doctored *doppies* were placed on tramlines where they exploded triumphantly when a tram ran over them.

Our devious schoolboy cunning worked out that the same would happen if we dropped weighty rocks onto the *doppies*. Tireless experimentation and tweaking went into working out how best to support said rocks above the *doppies* using sticks attached to string, and yes, tug the string and BANG!

Outside our classroom a rock garden provided camouflage for a battery of doctored *doppies*. One afternoon while Bill babbled on interminably the planned barrage began. The classroom was a long way from the shooting range and lots of our rocks failed but it sounded as if we were actually at the range. Congo Bill panicked and rushed to the window to see where the enemy fire was coming from.

We were hard put to curb our mirth but Bill did not find it in the least amusing and raved indignantly about it, threatening to summon the police to deal with the criminal hooligans perpetrating the reprehensible offence of firing live ammunition at *his* classroom, endangering life and limb.

One intrepid guy - Joel Joffe, no relation - expressed the class's thoughts by stage whispering 'Oh do shut up!' Whereupon Bill lost the place. In the blink of an eyelid he was at the cane cupboard. Again ignoring his personal protocol of permitting a choice, he seized the first one that came to hand simultaneously ordering Joel to bend over so that he could administer four bloody hard whacks on Joel's rump, calling out a letter with each blow, 'S' pause, 'H' pause, 'U' pause, 'T' long pause. By then Joel thought it was all over, but Bill delivered two more savage swipes in swift succession - 'U. P.' Joel returned to his desk mumbling words to the effect that he preferred to endure Congo Bill's thrashing to the bullshit he bloviated every time he conducted a lesson. This earned Joel another two landmark wallops by rocketing him to immortal fame as the first kid ever to have been punished so severely with a total of eight cuts in one 'hit', as it were, at Marist Brothers College.

Joel's courage stood him in good stead in later years. As a young lawyer, he became one of Nelson Mandela's defence team during the so-called Treason Trial. At the conclusion of the three year trial Joel wanted to leave South Africa but the Nats revoked his passport yet later offered him an 'exit permit' allowing him to migrate to Britain on condition that he would never return.

In England he became an influential insurance tycoon who was later ennobled by the Queen to serve as a Lord of Her Realm. This was, without question, the most illustrious accolade ever bestowed on any old Maristonian.

Motion pictures had an inordinate influence on my life. So much so that at a very early age I had made up my mind that what I wanted to be more than anything else as an adult was Errol Flynn, the pre-eminent swasher of buckle in cinematic history. For me anyway. Not even the strict school regime succeeded in deterring me from catching his latest film the very week it opened. Flynn was the only actor who could possibly tempt me to risk eternal damnation and 'six of the best' by bunking school which I did by relying on the latest incarnation of carrots and iodine in order to see one of his *fillums* - a forged dispensation to a fictitious dental appointment signed by Brother Justin, Brother Raymond's predecessor, whose signature I had practiced for months on end for just such a purpose. My forgeries were so convincing that I signed notes for friends who needed them. I wrote his name so often that it became second nature to me and to this day my signature remains based on that of Brother Justin.

In South Africa movie houses were always referred to as 'bioscopes'. The Plaza bio in Rissik Street was *the* rendezvous and forum for junior white Joburgers on Saturday mornings in the 1940's. Its audiences were preponderantly pre-teens. Adults knew better than to attend screenings, except in emergencies, because the decibel quotient was high on the Richter scale, especially during serials and the entire audience knew full well that the next line the Lone Ranger was going to utter was 'Hi Ho Silver!' It was essential to beat him to it by hollering the words before he did. And again, in synchronization the instant he did. The same applied to other catchphrases in vogue at the time.

If the *fillum* broke, which it did periodically, the place would erupt into a cacophonic Krakatoa of derisory boos and incessant raspberries until the unfortunate projectionist fixed it.

Each time our screen heroes performed a feat of derring-do or outwitted the villains they were acclaimed with fervour while the baddies were booed with even greater gusto. It was so simple then to differentiate between the goodies and the baddies in cowboy movies in which the bad guys always, but always, wore black Stetsons while the good guys owned white ones which remained pristine if the wearer fell off his horse and he and his hat rolled a hundred yards down a dusty canyon.

The language of American movies was a strange one indeed, filled with weird words and sounds voiced nowhere else in the country except by me and my contemporaries. Although we could only guess what most of them meant, it did not discourage us from articulating them at every possible opportunity, unaware *that* the USA was subliminally brainwashing us (and the rest of the world) to absorb and speak their language through the medium of their motion pictures.

Americanese, both written and spoken, was fervently frowned upon by teachers. I was proud of my word skills and could count on an A plus or an A at the very least for my essays until I wrote one cramming in all the US words as I could think of into a work entitled The Bone Orchard (American for cemetery.) My C minus came on top of a severe admonishment together with an instruction that in future I was to stick to English words both written and spoken. 'And...' continued Mr. Devine the English master vehemently, 'that applies to all of you.'

He picked up my exercise book between his forefinger and thumb as if it was contaminated by life-threatening germs and condescendingly read out excerpts starting with the opening sentence... 'Down at the bone orchard not a creature was stirring, not even a mouse...' 'And that, class,' he commented, 'is as gross an example of plagiarism as you will ever exhume.' He paused for effect, eyeing me as if I were a recently arrived green blob from Mars before resuming a litany of embarrassment by selecting and sarcastically emphasizing random words from my masterpiece in what he considered to be an American accent, each word or phrase prompting chuckles from all present except me: 'Hep cat... bebop... doodah... stick 'em up... skedaddle... kiddo... humdinger ... zowie... okeydokey... wisenheimer... palooka... skidoo... vamoose... sourpuss... moniker... kibosh... glass jaw... holy smoke... floppo... sockerino... southpaw... oomph... toots... you're darn tootin'... zombie... wise guy... torch singer... lingo... beat the rap... bunkum... wampum... vamoose... loopy... lollapalooza... jalopy... schnozzle... wisecrack... spondoolicks ... aw shucks... go tell it to the marines... how's about it?...'

The recess bell sounded. It had seldom been so welcome. In the playground classmates wanted to know what my essay was about. I told them it was a parody about a man suffering from lead poisoning - US-speak meaning he'd been shot – which led to their swift departure in the belief that I was trying to bamboozle them. Attaboy!

The main feature at the Plaza kids' morning matinee (sic) was preceded by comedy shorts with the Three Stooges; cliff-hanger western serials like The Lone Ranger with his sidekick Tonto and an early science fiction 'epic' called *Flash Gordon* or was it *Buck Rogers in the 25th Century*? It didn't matter to us in the least that we spotted the wires suspending the crude model rocket ships as they journeyed through the galaxies propelled by exhaust effects closely resembling common or garden sparklers which was exactly what they made 'em with. We were probably too young or too naïve to care about the repetitive gags and embarrassingly awful dialogue between Bud Abbott and Lou Costello or the happy slapping performed by the Three Stooges Moe and Curly (both Horwitz) and Larry (Fienberg).

Come hell or high water we continued to visit the cinema weekly to check up on how the heroes always escaped 'in one bound' from the inevitable death threat they'd faced at the end of the previous week's episode.

But cartoons were the firmest favourites with Bugs Bunny and Elmer Fudd never failing to tickle us. No barracking or booing once Bugs was on screen. We waited in eager anticipation for the immortal words, 'Eh, what's up, doc?' and 'Of course you know dis means war!' enunciated in Mel Blanc's unforgettably mellifluous voice.

The ill-tempered, hot-headed Donald Duck was more popular than Mickey Mouse, Goofy, or Pluto. Donald's original, inimitable voice, Clarence 'Ducky' Nash, inspired me to teach myself to talk duck with expressions like 'Aw, phooey!' and 'Oh boy, oh boy, oh boy!' a phrase which earned me my first professional showbiz fee for recording it for a radio commercial for the princely sum of £2 and 10 shillings in cash for less than five minutes work. Taking inflation into account, it was the highest fee I was ever paid for so little effort. This money for old rope convinced me that a show business career would be a perfect profession.

The Plaza's jumbo stage and the Wurlitzer organ played by Dean Herrick provided an ideal setting for talent contests and competitions such as paddle ball which became an even bigger craze than yo-yos. The paddle, a flat wooden bat about the size and shape of a ping-pong bat had a red rubber ball attached to its centre by a length of strong elastic. The idea was to whack the ball forward as hard as possible, then hit it again... and again... If you happened to possess good hand-eye coordination you could keep hitting that ball indefinitely in any direction that took your fancy. Loads of us could do this in excess of 200 times while competing for prizes such as free entry to the flicks for weeks, the on-stage contest winner being the kid who continued to hit the ball after all the other competitors defaulted.

Another lodestone attracting us to the Plaza was the American comic book market conducted on the pavement outside the cinema before Saturday morning screenings. Kids brought piles of comics, Batman, Superman, Captain Marvel, The Phantom, Archie, Dagwood and others to sell or swap. To ensure you didn't miss an instant inside the bioscope, the dealings were fast, furious and to the point - 'gotit, gotit, gotit', 'readit, readit, readit,' 'seenit, seenit, seenit.' None of us ever dreamed that these comics would one day spawn myriads of major movies...

Bioscopes would not have been the same without popcorn to munch or jube-jubes to suck, or pink, powdery, rubbery marshmallow fish with which to dislodge your teeth while tugging to break off, well, try to break off, a mouth sized piece to chew. If you could resist eating them for a week or two they lost both moisture and elasticity and you could snap bits off 'em.

Lots of kids came along wearing those ruby red wax lips which were in fact bubble gum. And yes, there were onstage bubble gum blowing contests until parents complained they couldn't remove the stuff from their kids' hair. Mind you I may have had summat to do with that.

The example of gum chewing G.I's in US war movies had promoted chewing gum from digression to obsession in South Africa, especially Chiclets in their distinctive yellow boxes with ten or twelve tablets inside. Then there were flat strips of Black Jack gum in blue packets and Dentyne in red wrapping. Come to think of it, World War II was the most efficacious free sales tool for selling products in the history of marketing. Almost every war film made in the USA featured chewing gum, the staple diet, it seemed, of all the macho G.I's portrayed in them. Sales soared internationally and acceptance of the gum habit spread even unto South Africa where it was banned from schools, a dictat about as futile as trying to ban breathing.

My Plaza choice was Topps Chewing Gum which came in ten inch double drawer cardboard boxes. Since they were free from my father's shop I usually took a full box containing about 30 pieces to the Plaza and shared them with friends. If things got dull, the Topps gum came into its own. As soon as the flavor was chewed out we rolled the gum between the thumb and index finger into small pellets even deadlier than O'Malley's nasal harvest. We discharged these from the balcony seats in the circle on to the unfortunates seated in the stalls below by employing drinking straws as peashooters with gum pellets as ammunition... It was hardly surprising that chewing gum in any form was outlawed at the Plaza. The bulk of my cinema visits took place on religious holidays, home visit weekends or during school vacations which lasted three months in the summer and a month in winter.

Thankfully the Crows also enjoyed movies and every Saturday night *fillums* were screened in the college hall for them and the boarders. Black cinemas as such were unheard of and since there was ample room in the hall to accommodate all the school's black workers, to their credit the Brothers allowed them in provided they sat at the rear of the hall.

More often than not the ancient movies were rigorously censored by the government and the Crows who knew they could rely on British 'B' movies, mostly low comedies starring people like Will Hay whose brand of humour seemed to be exclusively aimed at morons. Not a single movie screened at Marist Brothers contained the vaguest intimation of sexuality, or even holding hands, or swearwords stronger than 'dang' or 'doggone.' The result was, yep pardner, you guessed it, a heavy diet of sex free Westerns overburdened by singing cowboys.

The projection booth had only one machine which meant reloading intervals of about ten minutes between reels during which time the tuck shop was open for business. And an excellent night it was for trade. Subject to the proper disposal of wrapping paper and empty 'cool drink' bottles we were allowed to take refreshments into the hall where we sat in cliques and drew up schedules as to which pair would go fetch the next round of goodies for the others.

Marist myth maintained that lacing a Coca Cola with aspirin induced drunkenness. During a reel change break one Saturday night we tested this out on my friend Mike whose tuck shop order included a coke. On the way back we added not one, but three crushed aspirin to Mike's drink causing it to effervesce so alarmingly that we had to buy another bottle to top it up to ensure that Mike didn't suspect anything. We timed the return to our seats to coincide with the start of the reversing numbers 5...4...3... as they appeared on the screen for the last reel. As the movie ended the lights went up we saw Mike's coke bottle was empty and he looked perfectly all right. We filed back to the dorm believing we had put paid to an old wives' tale. Until... en route to his bed Mike started discarding his clothes while trampolining all the way along a row of beds, gibbering like a supercharged baboon on heat, creating quite a stir with everyone either egging him on or yelling at him to stop - the main objections emanating from those who were already between the sheets. I was aghast at this performance as I'd been the one who'd initiated the experiment.

Suddenly a voice cried out, 'Chups! Chups!' ('Chips! Chips!' pronounced the local way). This was the time honoured warning signal that a Crow was nearby. I would like to think that this was based on James Hilton's book *Goodbye Mr. Chips* but I have doubts about any of my contemporaries or predecessors at Marist Brothers being capable of so perceptive a literary analogy. Mike lay on his bed burbling incoherently before falling off onto the floor apparently unconscious. By now I was convinced that, as the ringleader, reckoning was nigh so I hastily put trousers on under my pajama pants and crawled under the beds searching for Mike.

'Mike,' I whispered with real concern, 'Mike are you OK?' There was no reply other than a slight groan. I tried again. By then the dorm was silent except for the dorm Crow's approaching footsteps. I was now certain I was doomed. Until Mike burst out laughing, as did the rest of those in the know who'd told Mike about the aspirin and he'd come up with a counterplot to teach me a lesson with an Oscar award winning performance... Biter bitten. Never again did I put anything in anyone's drink without knowing for certain what the outcome would be.

Movies governed white Johannesburgers' Saturday Big Night Out.

Cinema-going was always a most congenial outing except for one factor - car parking. The only way to get to the cinema was by car and to find parking as close to the cinema as possible, preferably at the Albany or Embassy Parking Garages. Street parking was free but space was at a premium and the further you were away from the bio the greater the possibility of having your car nicked. One night, on an *en famille* outing to a movie, Pop was overjoyed to alight upon an empty space near the cinema. Afterwards we couldn't find the car and held a debate as to which street Pop had left the car. It was only when the streets emptied that we realised that Pop's faithful old Chevrolet had been stolen. It was found months later on the outskirts of a nearby township, wheel-less and burnt out.

Attending bioscope was no mere casual affair in those days. Oh no. The ladies from the northern suburbs did not necessarily visit cinemas to view motion pictures, they went to see and be seen by friends or acquaintances they wanted to impress so that everybody dressed, or rather overdressed, to undertake the Saturday night pilgrimage to the cinemas which were usually packed to capacity for both evening screenings, the first at six pm catering to families with kids and the other at nine o'clock which was usually an adult only performance.

Johannesburg women wouldn't dream of visiting the cinema without having their hair done for the occasion. Why anyone wanted to visit a hair salon simply to take in a movie, which was far shorter than the time it took to have the hairdo, was beyond my comprehension. One of the limitless facetious jokes about those dim-witted dames went like this:-

'Do you have the time Mrs. Cohen?' asks Mrs. Shmaltzgroof seated next to her in the front row of the dress circle, to which Mrs. Cohen replies in a whisper loud enough to be clearly heard by everyone within a range of 20, no make that 30, feet, 'It's seventeen jewels to eight.' Apocryphal perhaps, but not that far off the mark since bejeweled *nouveau riche* matrons were always dressed to kill wearing the latest fashions and expensive furs. Yes, even in the hottest summer months.

Advance booking was essential. Every seat in the house was numbered and browbeaten hubbies had to ensure that their pampered wives sat in the very best seats. Whites were averse to standing in line personally, not just because they were lazy but to avoid squabbles and occasional fisticuffs with potential queue jumpers who laboured under the misapprehension that the presence of a friend or acquaintance nearer to the ticket booth conferred precedence to join that person in the line thereby possibly preventing those at the back of the line from obtaining tickets if seats to a box office blockbuster were sold out. Hence the queues for advance bookings were mainly black employees sent to stand in line to buy tickets for their white employers.

The Metro, MGM's flagship showcase in Bree Street was the acknowledged favourite Johannesburg cinema. It seated 2,800 people, making it the largest bioscope in the country. Whites-only of course. The Metro was the most modern, most opulent Joburg venue, designed as it was, in Hollywood Ocean Liner Art Deco style echoing the elaborate sets in MGM's trademark musical movie extravaganzas.

A huge staircase swept extravagantly down from the first floor into a spacious lobby with deep, plush carpeting. Dignity was ensured by the management's insistence that jackets and ties be worn to their late show. Signs to that effect were displayed at the box office. No jacket, no tie, no movie, no argument. Patrons were escorted in by impeccably liveried ushers and usherettes whose torch beams aimed unerringly at your seats.

Supporting features such as The March of Time, Pathé Pictorial newsreels, cartoons, trailers for forthcoming attractions not forgetting the 'filmlets' (ads) lasted half an hour or so. The African Mirror, a local newsreel was often included. Then there was a ten minute intermission to allow you time to buy ice cream tubs with flat wooden spoons from lasses wearing trays round their necks. If you needed to leave the auditorium to answer a call of nature or whatever, an usher would hand you a pass-out. If you lost it, too bad, you stayed out no matter what excuse you cooked up. And, would you believe, at the conclusion of the movie, the entire audience stood to attention while pictures of the Royal Family and the Union Jack appeared on the screen accompanied by a gramophone recording of 'God Save the King.'

The Colosseum in Commissioner Street was noted for its romantic ambiance thanks to its splendid Gothic décor which was for me, and my contemporaries I might add, an idyllic place to take one's 'special' or 'steady' girlfriend. The auditorium created the illusion of being in an open air amphitheatre, surrounded by turreted fairy tale castles with lambent light shining through its windows. Above us astral numbers of pea lights representing stars twinkled down through lazily moving clouds projected onto the ceiling.

Another auspicious Colosseum attribute was Charles Manning's orchestra whose repertoire of selections from hit movies, stage musicals and light classics was conducted by Manning whose leonine mane of long white hair bobbed up, down and sideways in time to the beat. On Saturday nights this orchestra replaced the usual overture of newsreels and whatnot.

What was showing was of no consequence provided you were armed with at least two packets of Sen-Sen breath fresheners, a box of chocolates and, the ultimate in wishful thinking, a tin of prophylactics in your wallet pocket for later.

Ah yes, those really were halcyon days!

The Colosseum and its sister theatre, the Empire, across the road could, and often did, accommodate full-fledged stage productions. The one I remember most nostalgically was The Danny Kaye Show. I queued at the stage door for half an hour to ask him to autograph a photograph I'd bought in the foyer. I was so enraptured by meeting a real live movie star that I was utterly unable to say a word to him. I still have the signed picture.

At the other end of the cinematic spectrum in the heart of Johannesburg just off Eloff Street, the 'Tearoom' or 'Café Bioscopes' were to be found. Here diluted soft drinks or weak tea were included in the entrance charge of a *zac* (sixpence). For another *tickey* you could buy an unsavoury, inedible pie or a tired cheese and tomato sandwich to nibble while you watched scratched B, nay C or maybe even D, movies so well past their shelf life that no other cinemas would dream of screening them. The backs of the seats in front of you had shelves on them for you to set down your 'refreshments' between bites and sips. The box office presented you with a saucer to place on the shelf to indicate you hadn't been served and when you were, the saucer was removed. The management disallowed brought-in food but that didn't matter as long as you had the balls to risk eviction if you were caught consuming contraband chow.

One such establishment, the President, in the street of the same name, seated about 40 people. In common with all tearoom bios, it was on the first floor of a building above a shop: its seedy staircase walls plastered with ancient, peeling Western movie posters bore no relation to those currently screening. Such bios were solemnly denounced by most parents who (accurately) regarded them as 'bughouses' or worse still, dens of iniquity where unemployed and/or drunk 'poor whites' went for warmth in winter or for a peaceful snooze in summer. Other habitués included truants and teenagers coming in for a *fray* which translates into 'heavy petting'. There was much rivalry for back row seats between off duty bus and tram drivers and conductors from nearby termini who also frequented these bios before, after, or between shifts to have a quickie with a girlfriend or a tart. These cinemas were all white of course.

If patrons wished to stay on for protracted petting or even to watch the programme again - the screenings were continuous - there were no intervals - it didn't much matter. Even those who got their timing wrong or came in out of the rain in the middle of a picture could remain there as long as they pleased, which satisfied the needs of all its clients.

If your appetite remained unassuaged on leaving the tearoom bio, Easy Eats was just round the corner. This was probably the first instant, well, almost instant, food takeaway establishment in South Africa – or in Johannesburg at least, and it seems that no one has since tried to emulate it. Easy Eats had no visible staff. They were hidden from view preparing the food behind curved Plexiglas windows containing samples of the day's menu. You strolled up and down past twenty or so windows inspecting the delicacies on display such as hamburgers, hot dogs, pies, Cornish pasties, *boerewors* (farm sausage), pastries and a variety of sandwiches. You inserted coins into a slot beside your chosen item and a turntable delivered your nosh and any change. The idea was okay except that hot food didn't arrive as quickly as readymade sandwiches. If the service was adjudged too slow or if the mechanism developed an attitude or jammed, loud altercations would take place between the customer on the pavement and the invisible drone bellowing back from behind the Plexiglas.

Another dish - Elizabeth Taylor - entered my life at a very early age. We were both fourteen and it was love at first sight for me. Nonetheless it was a very one-sided romance what with me living in the Transvaal and she in California failing to respond to my letters. That and a fixation on my idol Errol Flynn meant a total rethink about my future. Before Elizabeth I had this yen to be a pilot but on giving it deeper thought I concluded that flying would require expensive lessons and besides I was too young for it. So it seemed the acting profession was the way to go. Imagine that! Meeting Elizabeth and Errol in person while becoming rich and famous in double quick time.

Bearing in mind my mother's interest in literature, I don't remember her taking me to anything theatrical and it was only during a school outing to the Technical College opposite Johannesburg station to see a semi-pro performance of *Romeo and Juliet* (one of my set works in the English curriculum) that the theatrical bug bit me and I thought 'That's for me! Yes sir!'

My scholarly thespianism did not exactly prove earth shattering. My stumbling block was an inability to memorise my lines, so the Crows took not the slightest interest in me during casting sessions for the annual production. I had therefore to content myself with Mercutio in Romeo and Juliet in the classroom where I was a whiz at emulating Errol's swordplaying expertise by ostentatiously flaunting my wooden ruler with aplomb. OK, that role was a doddle for words as we all had our books in the non-sword hand.

At around this time Mom divulged that I had a cousin in Hollywood called Reska Law, only daughter of my eldest Aunt, Bea, who lived in England. Reska's father was the South African agent for De Reszke cigarettes, endorsed by Jean de Reszke a world famous baritone from Warsaw - hence Reska. Presumably the cigarettes were profitable enough for the Laws to migrate to England in style and to ensure that their children accomplished a high standard of education. Reska moved to Hollywood where she worked as a technical adviser on three time Olympic gold medal skater Sonja Henie's films. What that technical advice was remains unrecorded.

In 1945 Reska had a bit part in Gregory Ratoff's film *'Paris Underground'* starring Constance Bennett and Gracie Fields, then the world's highest paid actress. The male lead George Rigaud, was an Argentinian who featured in 200 movies!

To a youngster fanatical about films, having a cousin in Hollywood was amazing and I wrote to Reska. Long months of impatient waiting for the postman were rewarded on receipt of a small parcel containing a friendly, cousinly note and no less than a dozen autographed photographs of film stars. This manna gained me a great deal of kudos among my friends except for a cabal of churlish blighters who refused to acknowledge the veracity of my story and tried, unsuccessfully I hasten to add, to diminish my pleasure by suggesting I'd forged the signatures.

My earliest sortie into real theatre took place thanks to my girlfriend Claudette, a talented soprano, landing a leading role as one of the Three Little Maids in *The Mikado* staged in the University Great Hall for one week. The production required male extras to play the Mikado's bodyguard and she felt I would be eminently suitable, assuring me it didn't matter that I couldn't sing for toffee.

I went to meet the director who immediately gave me the nod. The wardrobe mistress took me backstage to try on my 'armour' which fitted well and even without Japanese make-up I looked the part. It was only necessary to be around for the last few rehearsals but it wasn't until dress rehearsal that members of the Emperor's Bodyguard discovered the drawback. The armour, ingeniously fabricated from dozens of freshly minted golden crown corks skillfully sewn together to form splendid, kilt length tabards were hellish difficult to get on and off. Being merely set dressing, we six guards were onstage only when the Mikado was, which wasn't a lot, but since there was no time to remove and then replace our costumes, we had no choice other than to stand for the entire performance as we were unable to sit down backstage in our armour without acquiring painful crown cork shaped serrations on our posteriors.

South Africa is a country where sport is King. Sport transcended politics and creed, but drew a firm line when it came to skin colour. About the only belief common to all South Africans was, and still is, sport. Male offspring were, and still are, forgiven almost any transgression except failure at sport. People often ask why Serthafrikins are so damn good at it. The answer is that everyone transmogrifies into a fanatic in respect of sport and if the national team or an international competitor fails to win, the country enters a state of National Mourning. Being second doesn't count and it would be difficult to run into a South African who does not concur one hundred and one percent with that famous dictum coined by Mohammed Ali's iconic manager Angelo Dundee, 'I only talk winning.'

Schools were judged by their prowess on the playing field rather than in the classroom. The mere idea of allowing kids to play or not to play games is a concept South Africans cannot comprehend. They play to win - losing ain't an option. Whichever sportsman claimed 'Winning isn't everything, it's the *only* thing' must have had South African genes.

My own sporting life did not harbour so demanding a criterion for the simple reason that I was far more interested in chasing girls than running after balls. Luckily my parents didn't seem to mind what I wished to do. In addition I was a very laid back kid. Lazy is probably a more accurate definition and I was relatively happy to belong to the 97 pound weakling category.

However, sport was impossible to avoid at my school or any other 'white' school in a country where sport was compulsory for white kids.

Other than chatting up girls, swimming was my preferred recreational pursuit but I can't remember how or at what age I learned to swim thanks to my mother's deep affection for swimming inculcated in me by her often taking me to the Yeoville Baths, a nearby whites-only public pool in Raleigh Street where I spent untold hours practicing the crawl. If I thought any girls on the raised patch of lawn were watching I managed over 40 lengths at a time. I could hold my breath long enough to swim an Olympic size pool under water. Occasionally I would dive from the high board but only if I was certain I had an audience. As I got older I grew a little wiser and mindful of Mrs. Mac's son's fate while high diving, I usually stuck to the low level springboard.

On quiet days there was sufficient room on the grass to laze about on spread towels, or to play 'leggy', a game in which you stand legs apart and try to lob a tennis ball underhand i.e. no hurling, through your opponent's open legs. He / she had to prevent that without moving his / her feet at the cost of a lost point. This harmless game could also be played by teams facing one another at an agreed distance between them depending on how many sunbathers there were on the lawn or, for that matter, anyone else likely to complain which could result in expulsion from the Baths.

Below the lawn was a kids' paddling pool, the second of two pools qualifying the place for its plural.

Bikinis were still decades away and although Yeoville Baths didn't harbor any Betty Grable or Esther Williams lookalikes, my friends and I savoured the sight of the alluring, well-basted feminine flesh decorously roasting in the glorious sunshine.

At a very young age I twigged that onlookers often admired the style and athleticism of good swimmers and I soon realised this so that even without an audience I delighted in practicing the sport. Another self-evident benefit was that if swimmers sweat, they do not smell sweaty - a decided advantage in the arcane art of chatting up girls.

Those of my pals who hadn't been taken to the coast for the summer holidays passed most daylight hours at the Yeoville Baths during the three month break, a period we dedicated women watchers lay bronzing while admiring the scantily clad lasses. Occasionally we summoned up enough courage to talk to them. The poolside lawn was also the summer rendezvous where the foremost topic revolved around which parties to gate-crash at the weekend. As soon as it got too hot for comfort we dived into the pool and swam underwater to admire girlish curves from inconceivably perverse angles the minute they too deigned to enter the water to refresh themselves and daintily emerged to dry instantaneously in the scorching Highveld heat.

Swimming at the Yeoville Baths entailed one vexatious disadvantage for me, brought about by a bloke called Percy Buntman, an excellent swimmer, who played a mean game of water polo for the local A Team. I knew Percy from various parties where we traded nods. An unkind quirk of coincidence had determined that he and I looked vaguely alike so that I was often mistaken for him and took to returning friendly hellos to those who greeted me as 'Percy.' The problem was that Percy, an incorrigible borrower, either forgot to repay his debts or didn't have the wherewithal with him to do so or so he told his creditors, resulting in my repeatedly being accosted in the changing room by someone threatening to bugger me up if I didn't pay soon and, to emphasize their intent, often delivered a warning punch on my upper arm by way of a farewell. I was similarly buttonholed in the tea-room-cum-milk-bar, another meeting place for the local kids twenty seconds walk from the baths, by *okes* demanding payment frequently with menaces. They simply did not believe I was not Percy, particularly if they'd seen me swimming loads of show-off lengths. It was a relief if Percy was in the vicinity allowing me to point him out to his creditors. In middle age the poor guy topped himself on account of debts far more pressing than the paltry petty cash he'd purloined in his youth.

Despite the pool at Marist Brothers College being kept locked and out of bounds unless supervised by a Crow or a lay master, we often scaled the high wall on hot summer nights and dropped noiselessly, commando-style, into the pool where we swam breaststroke or under water lest any passing Crow heard us. Most of my contemporaries couldn't swim without the accompaniment of their own loud splashes and snorts but I perfected a silent crawl and preferred swimming solo at those wonderfully refreshing illicit nocturnal dips.

For competitive purposes, Marist pupils were divided into four 'houses' each having its own distinctive colour. Mine was O'Leary, yellow. Geddes was blue, Patrick's green (naturally) and red belonged to Valerian's. No one ever knew how or why which boys were allocated to which house. Even your close mates were foes apropos house loyalty. On rare occasions house allegiance didn't matter – for example during weekend matches between teams of boarders.

My innate laziness bred certain talents such as a knack for choosing sporting positions requiring the least expenditure of energy, an asset which stood me in good stead with cricket. I had diligently practiced catching in order to become a reasonably competent wicket keeper, he being the person who spends the entire fielding session behind the batsman. After bowler 'A' has delivered six balls the umpire calls 'Over' and bowler 'B' takes over from the opposite end of the pitch requiring the fielders to reverse all their positions but instead of traipsing round the large field at the end of each 'over' the 'wickie' only needs to stroll along to the other end of the pitch itself, a mere 22 yards away. More importantly, he did not have to frantically chase the ball speeding to the boundary to try stop it crossing the boundary to score four runs. Unequivocally fielding was far from my idea of enjoyment on sizzlingly hot days.

The other secret of my summer survival relied on my being a meticulously neat scorer who is one of two guys, one from each team, who record the number of runs amassed and balls bowled by both teams to ensure that the numbers match precisely. The main attraction of scoring was being able to choose the shadiest area of the field from which to conduct our business. I refused to brook any argument or colloquy with the other scorer by dint of browbeating him into believing that his tally was incorrect and that mine was the definitive version. Consequently I was much in demand as scorer for senior teams which occasionally lost tight matches if I wasn't there to help them. Had I been a player, my efforts would have merited my achieving the College's highest batting and bowling average for the season. Indeed, if 'colours' had been awarded for scoring, I'd have got 'em. 'Colours', by the way, meant that the recipient was eligible to wear a highly prized blazer of pastel blue with navy, yellow and white vertical stripes, embellished with an embroidered scroll sewn on below the college badge on the breast pocket proclaiming the wearer's achievement(s) - such as 'Rugby', 'Athletics', 'Prefect' and so on.

Like it or not, on weekends all boarders were obliged to participate in a sport, preferably a team sport, failing which we forfeited our daily swim. I was hopeless at a lot of sport, principally athletics. Except once, during a Saturday cricket match between boarders' teams.

A distinguished member of those weekend cricket matches was an albino called Johnson whose poor sight forced him to undertake weird eye exercises every night in the dormitory hoping to strengthen his eye muscles to try to overcome his attendant squint. Happens he was the fastest bowler in the school and but for his visual handicap he would have been a permanent member of the First Cricket XI. He spent ages at the cricket nets practicing his bowling trying to perfect his natural aptitude.

One afternoon I played wicket keeper to Johnson's blistering bowling. His lightning fast deliveries made this a hazardous task and I always positioned myself half a pitch length behind the wicket, since I was not only terrified of being hit but because Johnson's hostile balls often went wide or over the top of the batsman's head and the extra distance ameliorated my chances of stopping the ball since the farther it travelled the more its momentum diminished. But if perchance Johnson bowled a straight one, the batsman was out. O. U. T. No question. The ball simply blurred by, seemingly passing straight through the batsman's willow.

One of the opposing batsmen was a bloke called Oakes, not one of the best liked boarders. You see Oakes came from Australia or somewhere in the antipodes and, predictably, he was very good at sport except that his braggadocio together with his bullying of younger boys did not appeal to his juniors, his peers, his seniors or anyone else for that matter. He owned two pairs of kangaroo skin boots, one for boxing and another for cricket. These boots, he alleged, had been sanctified by a genuine Aborigine medicine man rendering him (Oakes) unbeatable in the boxing ring or outside it whenever he wore the boots. We believed him. He was a very good boxer and few boys, including older, bigger seniors and even prefects baulked at standing up to him in or out of the ring.

Oakes' consummate claim to fame was that nature had favoured him with the biggest appendage in the school. It reminded us of a very healthy, newly hatched, python pup or whatever a young python is called.

To the casual, non-participating observer the noble and ancient game of cricket may well appear to be a refined, gentlemanly game played by two teams of eleven chaps clad and shod in white. The batting team wield willow bats, towards which a member of the fielding team hurls a bright, shiny, extremely hard red leather ball down the pitch time and time again until the batting side are all 'out' and then it's the fielding side's turn to bat.

This ritual regularly takes place on summer afternoons on rural England's village greens o'ershadowed by 15th Century church steeples, while, in the clubhouses lavender-scented, pert bosomed, blue eyed, blonde English roses in crisp, freshly laundered, impeccably ironed white frocks, produce liberal quantities of crustless sandwiches from wafer thin bread and semi-transparent slivers of cucumber. A mere tennis lob away from them, contentedly snoring, a blazered, retired colonel recumbent on his tree-shaded brightly striped canvas deckchair near the hand-operated scoreboard tended by enthusiastic urchins in return for a handful of coppers, his recurring dream of hitting the one and only six of his lifetime disturbed occasionally by the sound of prolonged applause for a player given 'out' on the greensward. Awakening merely to applaud the bowler or the outgoing batsman, who may even have recorded a duck - a zero - next to his name in the score book, before again succumbing to the effects of his post prandial brandy and soda.

Tosh!

In reality cricket is a very dangerous game. Being struck by a sphere with the constituency of reinforced concrete, travelling at over 90 mph in top class cricket and 'tests' - international matches - can cause serious damage. Even at half that speed, concussion, broken fingers, ankles and teeth are common. So are black eyes and bent noses. Bruises abound and hamstrings are frequently unstrung.

A degree of protection is provided by leg pads and thick gloves for the batsmen. Other devices such as helmets, now considered *de rigueur* by serious cricketers, had yet to be introduced in my youth but the main safeguard - a 'ball box' later known as a groin guard - had long defended the most vulnerable portions of the male anatomy. This box, a triangular codpiece conforming to the shape of the average male genital accoutrements was constructed from lightweight metal such as aluminium with rubber rimmed edges covered with soft white suede leather was designed to withstand a force equivalent to a powerful kick in the crutch which is what an exceptionally fast delivery of the ball hitting one's groin area feels like.

I, as 'wickey' - wicket keeper - always wore one, as do all wicket keepers and batsmen. As did Oakes. The problem was that his organ, the envy of every last one of his contemporaries, was too long to be properly contained in even the largest of the school's assortment of well-worn boxes available to our scratch weekend teams. The result was that a portion of Oakes' anatomy refused to remain within its constraint and, emulating the curious young python it resembled; it succumbed to the urge to explore the world about it.

Johnson was on top form that Saturday, having already clean bowled three early order batsmen. Oakes, wearing his enchanted kangaroo footwear naturally, swaggered confidently to the crease to take his guard, looking around 360 degrees to judge where best to hit the ball past, or over, the fieldsmen's positions. Johnson waited tetchily tapping his feet while Oakes pretentiously went through the full rigmarole of taking guard, finally banging his whitewashed crease with his bat before patronizingly nodding his preparedness.

There was an expectant hush as Johnson began his 30 yard run-up. His first ball was adjudged a 'no ball' by one of the two umpires, the reason being that his foot had overstepped the whitewashed 'popping' (delineating) crease so that it would not have counted had his delivery resulted in the batsman being bowled, caught or stumped off that ball. Johnson's second ball was wide which meant that it was beyond the batsman's reach. As with a 'no ball', a 'wide' also counted as one run credited to the batting side, thereby spoiling Johnson's 'average', his runs-per-wicket ratio, of which he was justifiably proud. This riled Johnson no end and his third ball was jaw-droppingly awesome. It was a ball which any top international test match bowler would have been proud to deliver. From my vantage point directly behind Oakes, I knew beyond doubt that the stitched lump of rock-hard red leather hurtling Oakes' way was going to earn Johnson his fourth wicket of the match.

Oakes, who had not previously faced Johnson's demon deliveries, would have scoffed had he guessed my thoughts as he squared up intending to knock Johnson's next missile over the boundary for six. Or four at least.

However, Oakes' consecrated boots let him down. He misjudged both his stroke and the velocity of the ball which struck WHA-HAM! - not the wicket, but Oakes' box almost decapitating his adventurous python pup. Oakes screamed loudly enough to awaken his Aborigine medicine man's deceased ancestors in the faraway Australian outback as he dropped like a lead weight, writhing about in agony on the ground while several fieldsmen ran to his aid realizing he would have to be carried off the field of battle. Since both Oakes and his bat were well outside the crease markings I removed the bails from the wicket with the ball.

A stump, that is a wicket, is a cylindrical oak stick with a conical metal spike at the bottom to allow it to be hammered into really hard cricket pitches. A set of three stumps is topped by two bails of lathe-turned wood resting in grooves across the top. The batsman has to defend these stumps from being hit by a bowled ball. Should the ball strike the stumps removing at least one of the bails the batsman is out. If, on the other hand, the ball strikes the batsman's legs and the fieldsmen think the ball might otherwise have struck the wicket, they yell 'Howzat?!' (How is that? Meaning Is That Out Or Not?) at the umpire who decides whether or not the batsman remains at the crease or has to make way for the next man from his team. If the batsman fails to hit the ball and either he or his bat is not behind his crease - a chalk or whitewashed line on the ground in front of the wickets - the batsman can be dismissed if the wicket keeper is fast enough to remove a bail with the ball in his hand in which case the batter is out, stumped, by the wicketkeeper which is what

I did - I stumped Oakes. Technically he was 'run out' but I hope you will agree that 'stumped' sounds so much more interesting.

Not that it would have made any difference to the match or its outcome as Oakes was totally out of action for the game and, as it transpired, for the remainder of the season. There were heaps of risible theories as to how Matron had reacted to so bizarre a case which effectively sabotaged Oakes' self-esteem. Thereafter he was ruthlessly ragged about his magic boots and, worse still, he became the butt of derogatory schoolboy jokes such as his willy being encased in splints or plaster of Paris for evermore.

My swift 'stumping' was definitely not appreciated by Dave, my very best boarder friend, who had been fielding nearby in the 'slips' position merely feet away from me. He was so incensed at my blatant display of despicably bad sportsmanship that he ran up to the wickets and ripped a stump from the ground.

Instinct warned me that Dave's objective was to use that stump on me. Calling to mind that discretion was by far the better part of valour I took off as fast as I could. Dave pursued me across the field on which we were playing, over the athletics track, past the swimming pool, across the rock garden, into the tarred play area at the lower end of the school all the while brandishing that steel pointed wicket in an aggressive warlike manner.

I was wearing cumbersome pads on each leg while Dave was in shorts and *takkies* yet I smashed the school records for all the sprint races by significant margins. On the verge of expiring from exhaustion I reached the sanctuary of the toilet block where I locked myself in an unoccupied cubicle.

It took a lot of smooth persuasion from inside that bog to convince Dave that my stumping had been intended as a joke. He didn't believe me, but conceded that I was an unsporting arsehole who should have known better. Perhaps he figured that calming down and refraining from assaulting me would avoid a lot of awkward problems for him, not least of which might have meant a merciless caning. Eventually he grudgingly admitted that he too disliked Oakes and he congratulated me on my sprinting. It was the only time I'd ever seen Dave lose his temper and over ensuing decades we often shared chucklesome hours reminiscing about that chase and Oakes' magic boots.

Although school sports and games were often interesting and intermittently challenging, our most enthralling extracurricular sport involved girls. Regrettably the only physical game we were aware of that could legitimately be enjoyed with them - in public that is - was tennis. Accordingly I devoted far more time to tennis than I did to rugby or cricket, spending long hours hitting a ball against a suitable wall until I became moderately proficient at it which proved a good thing because Nev's family moved into a grand home close to the school by virtue of his dad winning shedloads of lolly in the Rhodesian sweepstake. The house's finest asset was its tennis court. Neville's parents were very generous sociable folk who adored entertaining and tennis and scarcely any summer weekends passed without friends gathering there for heartily enjoyable tennis afternoons.

Nev always had scads of mates round to play, with the result that I became acquainted with a flock of birds I would not otherwise have encountered.

Neville's dad had a wry sense of humour about our behaviour towards our girlfriends, especially during mixed doubles. You see we were apt to hug our partners if they gained a point, more often in relief that they had actually managed to hit a ball over the net, because our girlfriends were selected for their pulchritude rather than an aptitude for tennis. After observing our antics through a window Nev's dad was heard to comment that love-all in tennis meant the score was nil-nil rather than a prelude to physical congress.

Neville's regular 'crowd' consisted of Monty, Dave, myself and our respective girlfriends. Irregular players included Pete, Mike and Arnie. The latter wasn't terribly welcome since he was widely considered to be 'a pair of pants' - i.e. always on the bum. This was attributable to his seldom buying his own cigarettes, much preferring to cadge off others. He was also well-known for being bonkers about Biggles books. Even during our university years every time I saw him he would unfailingly enquire if I had any Biggleth bookths to thwap.

His prime qualification for inclusion in this narrative arose from an unforgettable incident he experienced as a houseman during his medical training. A male patient had been fooling around in bed with a girlfriend who slipped a brass curtain ring over his limp penis. His arousal caused the ring to transmogrify into an exceptionally tight tourniquet endowing him with a permanent erection. Nothing they did to try to remove the ring was of the slightest use leaving them no option but to hurry along to the emergency ward where Arnie worked. By then the penis had developed an effulgent purple hue. A gaggle of student medics had reached an impasse as to how to help the luckless lover who was obviously suffering a great deal of pain. A black cleaner happened to observe their dilemma and told them his wife had faced a similar problem with a ring on her finger and that she'd gone to a jeweller for help. 'Amazing!' they chorused and found a nearby jeweller to co-operate and *voila*! It worked.

Forgetting financial fracas detonated by Pop's gambling, family life moved along placidly. There was something reassuring about being able to forecast what we would be doing on Sundays a year hence. Or ten years hence for that matter.

On Sunday mornings Pop routinely went to one of his two shops, ostensibly to catch up on the bookkeeping but we knew he'd be visiting his bosom buddies Barney Kotzen the butcher and Solly Salit the gambler at Barney's house where, in modern parlance, they used to 'hang out' discussing momentous matters relating to the past week's horse racing - who'd won or lost and why, and, more importantly, which trainers' gee-gees were in form in the coming week. Occasionally Pop would silently reinforce his cover story by bringing home a parcel of 'boys meat' (the very cheapest cuts) for our black workers.) And I think he and Solly played poker one Sunday morning a month at a school hosted by Neville's dad.

Sunday afternoons were reserved for family outings. A big drawback was to have to kill an hour or so for pop to enjoy his regular chill-out snooze before we all crammed into the car to drive to Rosedale, a tea garden north of Johannesburg where we'd meet up with friends and assorted uncles, aunts and cousins.

Rosedale's recreations included pony rides and miniature golf. While the adults sat around chin wagging in the shade of outsize colourful sunbrellas, sipping tea and downing copious quantities of buttered scones piled high with thick dollops of strawberry jam and clotted cream, we kids had an uproarious time in a swimming pool which would horrify modern parents with its algae green water covered by hundreds, nay thousands, of deceased insects - bees, wasps, flies and other nameless creepy-crawlies which had drowned in a Sargasso Sea of dead leaves, mown grass cuttings, bird feathers and multitudinous other unmentionable flotsam and jetsam which was only removed on a monthly basis by a one-eyed black bloke with a long-poled fishnet the blunt end of which, we speculated, had been responsible for his resemblance to Lord Nelson. We tried to catch frogs whose home we invaded with raucous rapture. No one ever thought what we'd do with one if we'd ever succeeded. The only care we needed to exercise, apart from not swallowing water, was avoiding collisions with divers when swimming and with swimmers when diving.

We would occasionally visit the Lido, south of Johannesburg where the water was considerably cleaner than Rosedale's. It was a pleasant enough place only not quite so popular with us as our allowable loudness level was a lot lower than Rosedale's. Another reason for looking forward to Lido visits was the nearby Tampico, a Mexican snackery, where we stopped on the way home to wolf down lip-smacking steak sandwiches served with hot onion and tomato sauce and the greasy, deep fried delectable potato 'chups'.

Christmas was always a big deal in our household because it fell on Pop's birthday. 'The whole world celebrates my birthday', he'd unfailingly, proudly, declare every 25th of December. On that day, Pop opened his cards to the accompaniment of his offspring jigging up and down impatiently while he slowly, ever so slowly, solemnly unwrapped his gifts announcing that each was an object he'd always wanted, adding that it was one of the nicest presents he'd ever received. Then we'd tuck into a whopping lunch banquet.

An ostrich size turkey always complemented a mouth-watering selection of delicacies such as chopped herring or chicken liver scooped out of capacious cut glass bowls using those sugary egg-yolk yellow, diamond shaped, biscuity things called *kichel* from Crystals a huge widely known delicatessen in Beit Street, Doornfontein. Crystals was a place filled with exotic eastern European food, served by Jewish immigrants whose native tongue was Yiddish so that if you didn't happen to speak it, your business was conducted with your forefinger and the only English you'd hear from staff would be the total you had to pay.

I occasionally accompanied Pop to help carry the innumerable goodies he bought there; thoughts of which still tempt my gustatory glands to run amok ... brisket, pickled herring, smoked salmon, snoek, potato *latkes, tzimmis, taiglach, hummus, blintzes, sauerkraut, gefilte* fish with eye-watering *chrain* (finely grated fresh horseradish dyed pink with beetroot) and other tracklements such as pickled gherkins, olives and sweet and sour cucumbers fished out of huge barrels with long handled trident forks.

Then there were bagels and *challah* bread and, most importantly, chicken *schmaltz* to spread on Crystals' freshly baked rye bread...

As if this weren't enough Mom would tax the strength of the dining room table by augmenting the meal with fresh fruit or ice cream or both.

The repast was conventionally washed down with beer shandy. Family tradition allowed us kids a thimbleful of beer in our lemonade. Apart from boiled chicken and chicken soup (Jewish penicillin), the only other Jewish dish I failed to come to terms with was *kugel* which loosely translates into a sort of bready, noodley, sickly sweet pudding overloaded with raisins and topped with cinnamon, jam and sour cream which may help non-Jews understand why Phillip Roth elected to name his overly materialistic embonpoint Jewish princesses after it.

Looking back at the ghosts of Christmases past, in all honesty they weren't that different from our usual Sunday lunches except for Pop's birthday cake.

Mom's unequalled culinary achievement, fresh fried sole, was always on our table. Eaten with *chrain* or piccalilli or a dash of Worcestershire sauce, it had to be the finest fish dish in the universe. Friday afternoons were literally Fry Days in our kitchen because Mom spent that whole afternoon frying fish while we kids hung around drooling in anticipation of the perks we were to receive for our patient impatience. These took the form of chunks of fresh challah bread generously topped with hot froth skimmed from Mom's secret recipe fish frying oil - served in strict rotation - eldest first of course.

My birthdays usually attracted an increase in my weekly allowance of perhaps an extra threepence or even sixpence a week. I was seldom short of cash because I entered my misbehavioural mode and nursed no qualms about raiding Pop's wardrobe where he kept empty Dimple Haig whisky bottles in which he deposited loose threepenny and sixpenny bits. He couldn't understand why those distinctive triangular bottles never filled up.

Bottled money apart, Pop also stored expensive Cuban cigars in there and once, when I was about fourteen, he caught me smoking one. He didn't chastise me. Instead he made me puff it until I turned a peculiar shade of green prior to running off to throw up. Since then I have been unable to smoke cigars and the faintest whiff of cigar smoke still makes me nauseous.

Eddies stocked Johannesburg's largest selection of loose sweets, tastefully displayed in the drawers of glass fronted showcases. Each drawer had a removable wooden backing inside, close to the glass. This space was always filled with sweets so that the drawers never appeared empty. I was allowed to help myself to anything I fancied any time I felt like it. Just as well I didn't suffer from the sweet cravings to which the majority of my schoolmates were prone else I'd have lost all my teeth at a very young age. And for free.

Flavours of my childhood return to my mental taste buds with uncanny clarity and fondness. I recall those wafer thin 'penny nessels' (Nestlés) chocolates in their red wrapping being so small that if folded in half they easily fitted into even the littlest child's mouth. And budget.

And those chalky white sugar sticks with dyed red tips supposedly resembling a lit ciggie spring to mind. You toyed with them, emulating your repertoire of smoking gestures, as copied, so you thought, from the elaborate poses of a debonair old movie matinee idol you'd seen acting his socks off. You'd tap one end of the cigarette against the packet imitating what you'd seen adults do without even guessing that the reason was to compress loose tobacco. Then you'd insert your sugar stick carefully into your make believe cigarette holder impatiently waiting for your imaginary manservant to light it for you. That done, you'd dismiss him with a perfunctory wave of your hand whilst exhaling a perfect imaginary smoke ring. You then turned to your astoundingly glamorous co-star for approval of your stellar performance. You sucked that 99% sugar ciggie until the one end was thin as a matchstick before turning it round to suck the 'lit' end until it too was matchstick thin so that if you crunched the matchstick against the roof of your mouth with your tongue the teacher wouldn't hear it.

Peppermint crisps! Honeycombed, crispy green bubbles covered with chocolate. You tried your hardest to suck out the peppermint before the chocolate melted. As always that failed so you resigned yourself to the old fashioned, traditional chewing method. Chocolate Logs! Soft, brown, mushy stuff atop a crunchy biscuit base encapsulated in sweet milk chocolate. Real melt-in-the-mouth bliss found nowhere else in the world. Sweeties wrapped in bright paper with illustrations of the fruit whose flavour you were about to sample came in translucent brick-shaped sugar cases containing syrup. It was hard to resist your self-imposed rule no chewing OK. It was essential to tickle it with your tongue until the juice inside was released to overwhelm your taste buds. And peppermint humbugs with swirly shaped flavouring. Not forgetting Walnut Whips with real walnuts on top - more delicious than any other Walnut Whips in our galaxy.

Then there were those whatchamacallits - sort of cylindrical tube things with sherbet in them which you sucked out through a liquorice straw after biting off its sealed top. We delighted in those translucent flying saucer shaped lemon acid drops which dissolved to detonate those taste buds with flavoured fizzy powder. Another lip smacking treat was a flat Catherine wheel of liquorice which you unrolled with your tongue to set free the small white aniseed ball at the centre if that's what you wanted to start with.

Without doubt the most esteemed member of the college staff was Matron O'Connor, a pleasant, no-nonsense woman in her late forties with twinkling blue-green Irish eyes. No one had ever seen her wearing anything other than her immaculate nurse's uniform complete with its long, white, head veil, the merest hint of her greying ginger hair peeping out from under it.

Her infirmary contained ten beds, a bathroom with a toilet and a separate consulting room-cum-surgery-cum-pharmacy. There was a ground floor entrance and she had her personal door to admit her to the dormitories if necessary. I think there was also a private suite in which Matron slept if anyone had anything drastic enough to warrant overnight observation or attention. The substantial number of boys in her care kept her extremely busy, and markedly more so during the rugby season - a season of Vick's camphor vapour rub, eucalyptus and wintergreen oils.

As a rule Matron maintained a benign smile and kind words of sympathy and encouragement to those who deserved them. She held strong views on what was best for 'her' boys. Standard remedies were castor oil and/or aspirin with which she cured most ailments. Once I visited her with a headache which she treated with a whole aspirin with water. The next guy claimed a stomach upset. He too received an aspirin, only crushed, with his water and the third guy with toothache was instructed to chew his. I still suspect that almost all Matron's aspirin were simply placebos.

Matron did not take kindly to skivers. Her uncanny knack of sniffing them out made me unenthusiastic about chancing my arm with the carrots and iodine ruse because instead of reporting would-be frauds to the Crows which would have guaranteed 'a couple plus one, seely fellow' she dispensed man-sized portions of castor oil and an order to return in four hours for another tablespoonful. Her ultimate weapon of mass medicinal deterrent with persistent fraudsters was to administer a dose of what we called her Lourdes Liquid since the mere mention of cascara was enough to affect instant miracle cures. I still suffer collywobbles thinking of that noxious black syrup.

She well knew how to treat those who tried to refuse castor oil or other revolting medication. She simply sat the boy down in a chair, went behind the chair to tilt his head back, placing one hand under his chin to close his mouth with her palm and his nose with her fingers so that the kid couldn't breathe. He soon opened his mouth for air and abracadabra, in went the medicine no problem. This was always a joy to behold as it happened so fast that if you flickered an eyelid you'd have missed the rapid subtlety of her well-practiced manoeuvre. Once the squeal of shock subsided, the kid would leave contentedly sucking a piece of barley sugar.

A panacea beloved by boarders was a preparation called Radio Malt, a dark toffee brown, treacly gloop contained in huge brown glass jars. Everyone clamoured to get on Matron's winter malt list, not only to boost our energy levels with a pleasant tasting substance, but the weekly malt visit to the infirmary could be relied on to shorten our early evening prep period by as much as fifteen minutes or, if one was lucky and she was particularly busy, we could spin out the visit even longer and the smokers among us skipped their malt in favour of a nip down to the lavatories for a quick drag.

Winter Saturday afternoons were Matron's busiest. Three rugby fields often catering to two consecutive matches per field provided her with queues of walking wounded awaiting treatment for injuries even more serious than those sustained during the cricket season.

Naturally, among all the other joys derived from the dynamic game of rugby, there were occasional stretcher cases who wound up in the infirmary or hospital with broken legs, arms, fingers, noses, teeth or ribs.

Probably Matron's most dramatic case concerned my classmate Derek Sammel. PT - Physical Training - was another compulsory Marist activity. None of us cared for the gym sessions which were too much like hard work without any observable benefits and many of us preferred occupations less tiring than climbing ropes dangling down from the ceiling twenty five feet above. Nor did we see any purpose whatever in leaping over wooden so-called horses and the like.

Derek was in strong contention with me for the laziest-bloke-in-the-school title vis-à-vis PT. He detested the climbing rope which is why the gym Crow consistently ordered him to climb as high up it as possible and hounded him to improve on the mark he had stuck at for months which was, a meagre one, at most, a quarter of the way up the rope. Finally Derek was told in no uncertain terms that unless he reached at least the halfway mark that day he would acquire six parallel marks on his buttocks. With a deep sigh of resignation he set about tackling his lose-lose task. He put his all into it and on reaching ten feet he reaped a round of applause from his peers. This encouraged him to climb another foot by which time he was suffering from both exhaustion and giddiness and began to slide down the rope, burning his hands badly. As he descended he made the life changing decision to let go.

Those of us present at the time were startled by his chilling scream a nanosecond before his plummeting body hit the floor with an ugly thud. By the time we gathered round him a pool of blood was oozing steadily across the floor. It wasn't until Matron hurried into the hall that the full horror was revealed. Derek's scrotum had been ripped open by the metal hook fixed to bottom of the rope which secured it to the wall at the end of climbing sessions. Derek was rushed to hospital where he spent months recovering from the loss of a testicle.

Another messy hospital accident occurred during the rush to get through a classroom door before it swung shut. The last running boy put out his arm to prevent it from closing only to connect it with the frosted glass instead of the wooden part of the door resulting in his arm smashing straight through the glass, severing both a tendon and his aspiration to become an architect.

Had these disasters arisen later in the 20th Century, the school would doubtless have been sued for substantial reparations.

We often speculated about Matron's relationship with the Brothers and whether or not she undertook hanky-panky with any of them. Having had dinner one evening Dave and I were relaxing in the dormitory, a mortal sin in its own right, since being in the dorm was prohibited until bedtime. There we were, in convulsions at the thought of Matron fucking the ugliest Crow of all, Head Crow Brother Raymond, who suddenly materialized as dramatically as a panto wizard, lacking only the crash of cymbals or smoke and mirror effects. We were gorgonized.

'Come with me you seeley fellows,' he ordered.

Brother Raymond who doubled as the science master, had recently been appointed to Head Brothership or whatever it was called, as a result of his predecessor Brother Justin being promoted to Brother Provincial or some other grandiose title relating to the Marist hierarchy. Strict though he had been, Brother Justin was a fair man, respected rather than liked by his charges. Cossack was a horse of a different colour. No one had ever seen him smile. Being a Spaniard he spoke with what, to us, sounded similar to a poor Hollywood B movie Russian accent to which he owed his positively perfect appellation. He was an intolerant man whose brutish ferocity was nefarious. His autocratic power over everything in the College had gone to his head. And we knew it.

Two very pasty faced boys fearfully followed him forlornly to his office where he sat us down and gave us each a pencil and a piece of paper while trying to terrify us with steely-eyed hostility. He succeeded.

'Write down that word you used,' he commanded.

Very reluctantly and very, very slowly we each wrote 'fuck' on our piece of paper.

'Now' snarled Cossack, 'fold the paper and give it to me.'

We duly obeyed. Cossack stared at the folded papers for what seemed like half a century. Then he opened them and stared at the words for another interminable period.

We nearly jumped out of our skins when he stood up, unintentionally knocking over his own chair, intensifying his liverish glower. Slowly, purposefully, he crumpled each sheet of paper into a tight ball, hurling them into his waste bin with as much disgust as he would have displayed had they been Satan's very own genitals. The psychological war was over. He strode to the cupboard in which he stored his personal implements of torture.

We knew before he opened that cupboard that we were not going to get off relatively lightly with the strap.

'Bend', he ordered.

We complied.

'You first,' he said to Dave.

Cossack was a small man, no taller than we were - about 5 foot 6 inches at most, and weedy with it, but he reputedly boxed above his weight and wielded the wickedest cane in the school. It was one of those really whippy ones with a diabolical swish akin, in our minds at least, to the scream of the Stuka dive bomber's siren designed to frighten the shit out of its victims before releasing its bombs. Both Dave and I were veterans of the weaponry deployed by Crows and lay teachers alike but neither of us had yet come face-to-face with Cossack's fury...

I'm not sure which was worse, the swoosh itself or the dreadful thwack of connection. Unable to bear witness to what was happening to Dave I tightly shut my eyes while listening for the swish-thwack-gasp three times. Cossack's shibboleth 'Seely fellow, I give you a couple plus one' did not apply that day, and the count rose to six. Was it possible, I wondered, that he might increase the number? Six had been the very maximum number of cuts dished out by any teacher at one time except for Joel's showdown with Congo Bill. But our crime, our double crime, was so repellant to Cossack that we could not rule out the possibility that he might break his own unspoken punition code that very evening. After the sixth stroke I opened my eyes to see Dave still bending, his eyes shut tight to deprive Cossack of the additional satisfaction of seeing his tears. One of our instinctive defence mechanisms was blinking back our tears so as not to allow the enemy to know he'd got the better of these encounters. Dave did a fine job of this. I hoped I would be able to match his fortitude.

'You!' Cossack snorted at me.

I bent down praying that the force he'd just expended on Dave had diminished his energy.

No such luck.

I think my senses shut down at around the third stroke.

When it was over Cossack scowled at us malignantly, reserving his most excruciating lethal salvo until last. 'No weekend for either of you. Go!'

We left silently. Cossack slammed the door behind us. Dave and I were in accord that we'd rather have had an extra cut or two in preference to the gating.

As slight compensation for our ordeal we gained celebrity status among our peers as well as seniors by displaying our not insignificant weals which took nearly a month to fade but entitled both of us to add six carved notches to the lids of our desks.

After Granny's death the family moved from Berea to a genteel, more salubrious suburb called Parktown West. Our Loch Avenue home occupied a sloping site at the lower end of Westcliff Drive. The front rooms faced the street while the rear backed on to a neglected no-man's-land fenced off from a Portuguese market garden and its neighbour, the Sans Souci Hotel. The fence, more a safety measure than one of security, had been erected to keep people away from a treacherously vagarious stream flowing from the vegetable garden's irrigation dam which was itself replenished by a voluminous concrete open storm water drain upstream. Behind our house, a few yards from our fence the stream became a natural stepped waterfall dropping about ten feet from top to bottom. In good weather the water trickled down in five or six lazy stages but rain transformed it into a rapid torrent.

No one knew nor cared where the excess water went from there but it was at this place that our twig rafts floated over the abyss while Tarzan looked down from a high tree, beating his chest in self-congratulation at foiling the baddies' plan to cheat the tribesmen out of their ivory by diverting their raft from the safe channel to the one that flowed over the waterfall. It was an unparalleled, world famous location, for it was here that Stanley met Livingstone. Here the top secret Allied strategies were hatched between Churchill, Roosevelt and Stalin. This was where the Germans built bridges along the Rhine only to have them annihilated by RAF bombs drowning hordes of Nazi troops before they could invade France a second time. Here it was that Monty destroyed Rommel's tanks the very day before Waterloo. Here stood Custer. Here Pearl Harbour was avenged. Here no mission was impossible. Here our clothes were always covered with spiky blackjack weeds armed with stubbornly sticky tips that could only be picked off one at a time - a tedious task that always took forever but had to be done to avoid motherly suspicions that we'd been where we shouldn't have.

In this waste land my friends and I honed the art of catapult shooting at glass jars until we were able to hit them from a range of maybe 30 feet. We then turned our attention to stalking the only available moving targets - birds. It took a month or more before one was killed. That seriously sickened us, forcing us to conclude how senseless it was to try to emulate big game hunters by taking life in the name of sport, so we abandoned hunting even though I received a birthday gift of a Daisy air rifle which fired small, round, copper pellets. Friends were allowed to use it if they provided their own ammo - which they did - and we all became reasonably proficient at it, aiming only at tin cans and water filled bottles. This experience stood me in good stead at the school rifle range.

The dam water irrigating the market garden doubtless contained mosquito larvae, frog spawn and well, better not to think too deeply about anything else. Today's kids would not be allowed to play in such waste areas for fear of attack by snakes, vagrants or an unspecified tropical ailment contracted from unclean water of dubious origin. Then there were miscellaneous creepy-crawlies to contend with including the dreaded stinkbugs, and their vile neighbours - ticks - whose repulsive, bloodsucking habits were anathema to us.

Our house, built of mellow, honey brown bricks, sported two majestic, mature palm trees twenty or more feet tall that endowed our front garden with a touch of class.

The driveway could accommodate five parked cars. A detached block at the back of the house contained two servants' rooms, their shower, their separate toilet and a lockup garage for one car as well as a disused, lockable, second toilet from which all the plumbing had been removed. The previous owners had stored garden tools in it. I was tickled pink because, wonder of wonders, my mother agreed I could have exclusive use of the room in which I built a work table with a secret shelf underneath it specifically for storing my Men Only magazines, 'girlie' publications and personal treasures too precious to leave unattended while I was away at boarding school.

The incline on which our house was built dictated that the garden had three flat terraces at different levels, each supported by well-crafted stone retaining walls. At the bottom there grew a quince tree, a pear tree and an apple tree whose fruit was too tart for the local avifauna but when rotting, the fruit attracted multitudes of bugs ensuring that our garden was often graced with hordes of birds gorging on them.

A path beside the house led into the back yard past a large circular, rusting, green painted metal rain water tank that was only ever used if Mom was tending seedlings too fragile to be hosed. A leaky mains garden tap contributed to the proliferation of a huge clump of mint from which I made sauce if leg of lamb was on the family menu. I always felt a glow of pleasure at Pop's unfailing compliment 'Hmm, nice mint sauce.'

The house had two cellars. One, under the fourth bedroom, an addition my parents had built for me, was deep enough to allow standing room for a small child.

There was another shallow, wedge-shaped cellar beneath the house. Unfortunately this cellar was unusable because wild bees had colonized it via an air vent and passers-by were always in danger of being stung. Several so-called experts had attempted to remove the bees but none of them had been successful. Even a fine metallic mesh fitted inside the vent did not stop the bees from finding their way back into the cellar, so we resigned ourselves to an uneasy truce with them and accepted the permanent, unmistakable odour of beeswax. Nevertheless that cellar was a happy hideaway for kids brave enough to venture near the humming hive. It was our loss that no one ever bothered to work out how to harvest the honey.

My good friend Enos, our dapper, slightly built black servant, handled the heavier garden chores such as mowing the lawn and weeding while Mom took care of planting, pruning and hosing which often coincided with returning home time for the foraging bees and Mom frequently came inside nursing a sting or two until the day the bees swarmed while she was gardening without her hose. Within seconds infuriated bees were all over her, getting angrier and angrier, especially those caught in her hair. Had Mom's screams not alerted a passing hospital nurse Mom might well have died. The nurse had the presence of mind to rush her indoors and into the bath, clothes and all, possibly saving her life.

Anyone meeting my Mom would have regarded her as far too sophisticated to be superstitious. No one could have had the slightest notion that she was that way inclined. No one, that is, except her kids - well me, at any rate.

Everybody, it seemed to me as a boy, was superstitious and I therefore assiduously observed most of the universally accepted no-no's such as walking under ladders, stepping on cracks on pathways and opening umbrellas inside the house. Leaving shoes on the bed was prohibited - which may have been the cover story to keep the covers clean. We were never, but *never* allowed to bring anything green into the house. Mom's aversion to green puzzled me because of her devotion to plants all of which were green. Opals were unlucky according to Mom. 'If you are ever given a knife you must pay the donor a penny in return to avoid cutting the friendship', she'd tell us. If there were crossed knives on the table, Mom immediately straightened them to 'avoid quarrels' in the house. *That* didn't always work. A dropped knife heralded a male visitor while a fallen fork foretold the impending arrival of a female. Spoons were ignored.

If you gave anyone a wallet, a purse or a handbag, Mom asserted it was imperative to include a coin to ensure the recipient would always have money inside it. Finger and toenail cuttings were always burnt in our combustion stove to avoid a possible miscarriage should a pregnant woman walk on them. Thirteen was the unluckiest number. (Maybe it had to do with my birthday falling on the thirteenth.) And... pulling out a grey hair caused ten more to grow in its place. Now that worked on me. I started going grey at about thirteen years old! Go figure.

We were instructed to always throw a pinch of salt over our shoulders if ever we spilt any in order to confuse the Devil who was constantly on standby awaiting salt spills and the opportunity to capture our souls if perchance we sneezed and no one was fast enough to bless us. Why salt was selected and not pepper was never explained to us.

If ever our clothing needed a button replaced or any other minor repair my mother made us take off whatever it was, since, she apprised us, 'The only time you sew clothing on a person wearing a garment is when that garment is a shroud.'

Neither of my parents displayed much leaning towards religion except that Mom always lit Sabbath candles on Friday nights which, I suspected, may have been out of superstition rather than a belief in the Jewish custom of welcoming the Sabbath. There were hardly any discussions about religion other than my *Bar Mitzvah* arrangements, yet years later Mom was unequivocally opposed to my marriage in a Reform Synagogue rather than an Orthodox one.

Mom's main religious superstition remains pellucid in remembrances of my early childhood. She would lick my forehead and spit, lick again and spit, repeating this frequently before tucking me in to sleep. I could not understand why until, as an adult, I asked her and was told that the purpose was to preserve me from the wicked, envious thoughts of other people pre-eminently those who stopped to admire her cute little boy. Me. As an adult my research revealed that this 'lickspittle' ceremony is an ancient Jewish custom to protect children from the evil eye.

Garlic was reputedly another sure-fire method of avoiding evil eyes. My brother reminded me that when he was aged nine around 1947 there was a grim infantile paralysis epidemic in Johannesburg. This dreaded disease, polio, or to give it its full name, poliomyelitis, was so critical that government schools shut down to avoid the possibility of contagion among pupils. Public swimming pools were closed as well, and my mother took to hanging garlic round his neck, and my sister's, to defend them against it.

'It worked for us,' my brother recollected, 'we didn't catch polio. In fact no one came near us because of the smell...'

I loved our Loch Avenue home even more than Joel Road and sorely missed it while I was away at boarding school. My monthly home visits were spent wallowing in the hedonism of lying abed for as long as I pleased instead of being rudely awakened by a Crow turning on the lights and loudly clapping his hands at six am seven days a week. It was also a joy not to have to make one's own bed, leaving it to the black maid who brought in morning tea or even a hot breakfast, in bed if you felt like it. And the home cooking! To die for!

The roof of our house extended over the front *stoep* which was always shaded and cool even in the hottest weather. At one end of this porch grew a passion fruit creeper providing attractive foliage and flowers but very sour granadillas.

Our *stoep* boasted a spacious aviary which had once been home to a noisy colony of Technicolor budgerigars, cute Australian parakeets much admired as a gourmet delicacy by the Aborigines who named them 'Good-to-eat'. I'm not sure whose brainwave it had been to breed budgerigars in the first place but the attempt proved unsuccessful and the cage remained there long after the inhabitants escaped or were given away. I housed my pet chameleon in it for a while but the creature didn't thrive in there and no one else was prepared to take responsibility for it while I was at boarding school, so it too, was given away. The aviary just stood there, empty and neglected until one day, while sharing a quiet chat about it with Dave between sips of lemonade, we considered what a waste it was having a cracking cage like that just standing there doing nothing. Vying to think of a use for it led to a jokey discussion about maybe housing my kid brother in it, a possibility scathingly dismissed by Dave who opined that, thin though he was, there was no way Justin, about six at the time, could get into the aviary through its door that measured, at most, a foot square. I argued that he could. Dave contended he could not. All this persiflage sparked off a bet of major proportions. A shilling no less.

To persuade Justin to help me win I took him aside and offered him a penny, in cash, if he'd try. Initially he refused, and then haggled the ante up to a *tickey*. That still represented nine pence profit, but to ensure he wouldn't renege I placed the coin beyond his reach in the corner furthest from the cage door and told him he could only have it if he collected it from the inside.

A couple of hearty pushes later my panting brother managed to squirm diagonally through the cage door. He and I were jubilant at his success. His newly acquired wealth influenced him to remain in the cage while I fetched my state-of-the-art Baby Brownie camera to record his achievement. Once the photograph was taken of my brother proudly grinning at us, clutching his shiny *tickey*, it was time for him to come out. Oh yes? Oh no! En route to put the camera away my mother asked if I knew where Justin had got to. I volunteered to find him.

Back on the veranda Justin was manfully struggling to get out but as he'd literally been pushed inside, that proved impossible as did trying to pull him out legs first. By now he was getting quite agitated. So was I. There was only one solution - to confess my misdeed to my mother. She was utterly unamused. Her concern was such that she recruited a neighbour with wire cutters to release Justin from a lifetime diet guaranteed more effective than that concocted by Dr. Atkins - of millet and cuttlefish bone.

To this day Justin insists he has been unable to overcome this sibling inflicted psychological setback, steadfastly maintaining he's never been the same since, but that is contradicted by his maturing into a reasonably well adjusted, respected Professor of Psychology. My brother has spent a lifetime reminding me of the incident and I continue to remind him that he was a *tickey* richer and that, regardless of my winning the bet with Dave, I was the real loser having had two weeks' pocket money docked for my misdemeanour.

By way of a postscript, the photograph of the cage containing Justin took pride of place at his retirement party nearly a lifetime later when he became an Emeritus Professor.

Schoolboys love farting and its associated vulgar limericks, especially classics such as:

There was a young man from Umtata
Who was a champion farta
He could fart anything
From God save the King
To Beethoven's Moonlight Sonata.

Just why the noisy release of human methane into the atmosphere has given, and undeniably continues to give, infinite pleasure and unlimited laughter to most kids and immature adults (bless 'em all) has not been adequately explicated to date. Maybe it's because everybody does it and the word itself is not as unacceptable as that other four lettered 'F' word. If kids are down in the dumps all you need do is say 'fart' or 'someone farted' and a resulting smile is guaranteed. No other single word I know can activate so much hilarity. In addition to exchanging inexhaustible fart gags, we schoolboy boarders even held farting contests for the loudest, longest, most melodic, and so on. Such practices were frowned upon by near neighbours and hooted at by those a safe olfactory distance away.

The boarders' obligatory supervised study sessions totaled over three hours *per diem*, all devoted to homework, revision, reading set work books and swotting for exams. Woe betides the boy who smuggled in a comic book and was caught reading it during 'study'.

Talking during study hours was also strictly taboo and we longed to have the odd gentle fart intrude upon the silence of bleak boredom to spark off brief levity before we resumed our work. Noisy farters were punished if the Crow or teacher knew, or thought he knew, who the perpetrator was. No one ever owned up to disturbing the peace so that miscarriages of justice were rife. Those stealthy ill winds often provoked fist fights between victims and culprits during breaks.

Most of us perfected the art of noiseless farting by flexing our gluteus muscles to facilitate the silent expulsion of loathsome emissions of greenhouse gas. The annual fartology medal, had there been one, would indubitably have been awarded *cum laude* to a boy called Rupert who was far and away the school champion. His farts, the strong silent variety, always placed his neighbours' nasal passages in jeopardy. Rupert's intestinal gases were nauseatingly hircine and although we all knew what caused them - those potato chips that came with a tiny blue bag of salt and were called crisps in South Africa. Rupert persisted in devouring packet after packet after packet after packet of them in quick succession as if they were his last meal. It would not be an exaggeration to state that he was addicted to them. The result was that on the annual seat allocation day for the study intense jostling took place to secure one furthest away from his potent exhaust fumes. Rupert's regular robust releases may well have kick-started global warming.

One night in the dormitory we persuaded him to let us test the veracity of a schoolboy fable about farts being flammable. We impatiently waited until all the conditions were right for the experiment to commence. It had to be dark at a time we could be reasonably sure there'd be no Crows about before Rupert shed his trousers and adopted a suitable position on all fours on a bed. The prudent ones among us had taken the precaution of protecting our lungs with handkerchief face masks covering our noses in the style of the villains we had seen in those cheapo *skop, skiet en donner* (kick, shoot 'n fight) Wild West movies when the outlaws were robbing banks, rustling cattle, sticking up stagecoaches or engaged in other heinous undertakings calling for disguises.

'Yes,' hissed he, 'I'm ready.'

A match was struck, a countdown from three commenced and at zero, Rupert farted bang on cue so to speak. We held our breath as the match was applied to the fetid gas emerging from his orifice. To our delectation this produced a small blue flame about six inches long. Of course Rupe warranted a hearty round of applause as he arose from the bed to bask in his undeniable success.

One of the Lebanese cadre was so impressed by this accomplishment that he insisted on having a go himself. Determined to observe the result he preferred not to attempt Rupert's exemplar. Instead he lay on his back and, with his parted legs pointing at the ceiling, he manoeuvred pillows to raise his arse as high as possible. Unlike Rupert, who'd kept his underpants on, the Lebanese guy completely bared his bum. The countdown began but he failed to perform and we only wasted six matches before a slow, satisfying phhhhrrrrrrrtttttttt commenced. We naturally accorded him an ovation in the wake of his fart igniting with an even larger flame than Rupert's. It was only the whiff of burning flesh that made us realize his shrieks were not of triumph but of agony caused by the blue flame singeing the hair surrounding his anus and testicles.

By chance one of the boys found a tube of ointment to soothe the Lebanese's barbecued balls because he flatly refused to consider a visit to Matron for running repairs on the grounds that he would have been at a total loss trying to explain the cause of his injuries. This led to a surfeit of intellectual speculation as to what he might have told her before receiving his aspirin. Our only regret was that it hadn't been Rupe's balls on the line...

Victims All

Not all the Brothers at Observatory were good teachers. For instance, Brother Patrick (Paddy) the Latin master was a dismal failure. I loathed Latin. All that *amo, amas, amat* garbage and translating Caesar's Gallic Wars into English seemed pointless to me. English was my favourite subject but the Crow singularly failed to inform us how much of the language I loved was derived from Latin. Had he done so I am sure I would have displayed a keener interest in it. Instead the only knowledge that Paddy the gerund-grinder imparted, not by teaching, but by example, was about homosexuality. In retrospect I think he probably became a teacher in order to obtain access to boys. I'm not sure when exactly I became aware of what homosexuals were and what they did. That it existed at Marist Brothers was certain since a small coterie of boarders who we called bum boys displayed all the signs today associated with being gay. Strange behaviour certainly took place between Paddy and selected classmates.

While we were hard at work laboriously decoding Virgil or Ovid, Brother Patrick strolled up and down between the rows of desks ostensibly keeping an eye on what we were doing. Frequently he would 'accidentally' drop a bunch of keys down a kid's collar as a prelude to spending a good deal of time playfully fishing around inside the boy's shirt pretending he couldn't find them. Paddy seemed to pursue this avocation with one boy in particular. No one ever questioned Lennie, the victim, about his thoughts on the matter. Nor was it discussed outside the classroom. Lennie was liked by everyone he came in contact with - the Brothers, his school mates and the opposite sex. His personal charm ensured his ability to get away with pranks which would normally have meant six cuts if enacted by any other Marist scholar.

Fully aware of Paddy's favouritism, Lennie took advantage of his privileged position by becoming increasingly adept at creating distractions which everyone looked forward to as they helped lessen the lethargy of Latin lessons. Lennie's party piece was his curtain caper. The classroom's tacky window curtains that scarcely shaded us from the blinding sunshine were suspended by brass curtain rods resting unreliably on the cheapest of cheap cup hooks. Lennie's desk was against the window wall and with judicious manoeuvring of the hem at the bottom of the curtains he could manipulate the rod fractions of an inch at a time until it slid off its hooks and clattered to the floor. Played judiciously, Lennie could spin out the interruption for at least five minutes, always claiming unexpected difficulties with repositioning it and the curtains.

One memorable morning when the rod 'fell', Paddy instructed Lennie to replace it and the curtains 'as quietly and as quickly as possible'. The rest of us were told to carry on with our work while Lennie clambered onto the lid of his desk to replace the rod. Before Paddy resumed his walkabout he had a gander at the work of the boy whose desk was in front of Lennie's. The temptation was too much for Lennie who coolly positioned the rod above Paddy's head shouting 'TIMBERRRR!' just before releasing it. An incredulous Paddy looked up to see the brass rod heading for the bridge of his nose. He staggered sideways to try to avoid it, succeeding only in tripping himself and collapsing onto the floor. Lennie leapt down to 'help' Paddy who looked a bit groggy, more from shock than pain, and for the first time ever at Paddy's hands Lennie sustained several cuts while protesting vociferously that the rod had slipped and the only word of warning he could think of was 'timber'.

Next day a handyman replaced all the fittings to permanently keep the curtains affixed to their rods. As a result Lennie and others were spared from having any more keys deposited down their collars.

Fausto Barbosa da Silva was one of a cluster of Portuguese Catholics at Marist Brothers hailing from what was then the city of Lourenço Marques, (now Maputo) the capital of Portuguese East Africa (today's Mozambique). He was born with a good brain, a quick wit, an ebullient smile and a flair for marbles or 'marlies' as Maristonians called them. In fact had there been a 'colours award' for that game Fausto would have won it hands-down.

The marbles site was the driveway between the buildings and the main rugby field. Contiguity to the classrooms enabled us to extract every last moment of playing time before the bell summoned us back to lessons. The area was sheltered by mature pine trees and riddled with small shallow craters used when playing holey-holey at which the Portuguese guys were unusually skilled. This game was vaguely reminiscent of billiards without the cue stick and demanded remarkable dexterity.

The more popular version was a less complex game in which players simply shied their marlies at small pyramids of three marbles topped by a fourth, which, if dislodged, won four marbles and the return of the shied marble. Enterprising pupils offered castles of sixteen or more marbles. The shying distance from the castle depended on the number of marbles in the pyramids, starting from a few paces away, the distance increased in relation to the quantity of marbles in the pyramid. In order to reduce their risk, castellans would strengthen the base by embedding the bottom row firmly into the earth by standing on them. The best time for shyers coincided with a famed South African weather paradox known as a 'monkey's wedding' - a short sharp rain shower in bright sunshine. Almost as soon as the rain stopped the sun baked the clay so that marbles could be rolled along a relatively smooth, hardened surface in preference to the full toss method. Since shying success necessitated dislodging marbles fist fights occasionally erupted if castles remained intact after being hit.

Variations of shying at castles involved inverted boxes with cut-out arches of differing sizes. The smaller the arch the larger the number of marbles you won. The targets ranged from cardboard shoe boxes to elaborately decorated wooden structures with the stakes clearly displayed above each hole.

Other shying games had targets such as 'goons' (large glass marbles) or 'ironies' our name for steel ball bearings of varying sizes...

Fausto was the college's most successful marble entrepreneur. After every break he'd return to the classroom with pockets brimful of winnings, often so plenteous that he had to keep a book recording who owed him how many marbles. Anyone failing to pay his marlie debts within a stipulated time was honour bound to produce an alternative payment of either cash or kind, making Fausto the only boy in the school to own ten penknives.

The hour-long lunch recess often netted Fausto brilliant results and one outstandingly lucrative session included a number of ironies which further strained the marble-worn lining of his trouser pockets to such a degree that one of his bulging pockets burst as he sat down at his desk. The marlies went scattering, clattering helter skelter on the floor against the metal desk frames. Chaos ensued as dozens of marlies, goons and ironies cascaded over the classroom floor. In his panic to salvage them, Fausto's other distended trouser pocket also gave way. The door opened and the teacher, Congo Bill, strutted into the class room, failed to see the marbles and performed a faultless 'Marcie' by falling flat on his arse, immediately releasing a loud, unexpectedly indecent expletive from him and squalls of delight from us. Bill picked himself up, did an absurd jig through the marble minefield to avoid a second accident on his dash to his cane cupboard where he selected the one he knew would inflict more pain than any other and delivered six unto Fausto - loudly spelling out the word M. A. R. B. L. E as each stroke landed. His blows were delivered with such force and manic fervour that they caused a breeze strong enough to produce small dust clouds on the blackboard chalk rack. The instant he was done he told Fausto 'You're lucky to get away without the plural. Now, you, you and you,' glared Bill, pointing at three of us, 'pick up every single marble and put them in here.' He handed us an empty wooden chalk box. Fausto watched his confiscated winnings disappear into the cane cupboard while he ruefully rubbed his raw red rump.

School rules dictated that *cleanliness was...* well you know. So clean clothes, clean fingernails, clean everything were the order of the day - every day. Decent haircuts and neatly combed hair - often flattened with pungent lavender scented brilliantine from oval tins or Brylcreem 'a little dab'll do ya' - of an approved length and style received close scrutiny from the Crows. Therefore the local Sweeney Todd visited the school fortnightly to tend to the boarders. Those of us whose turn it was dutifully reported to the classroom designated as the barber shop. Many Marist day boys prided themselves on what they considered to be their trendy crew cuts as worn by American GI's in all those war movies. I too wished to make a similar fashion statement and instructed the barber accordingly. Unfortunately the barber was new and probably more used to burnt hair and bay rum than the hasty back and sides of his predecessors. He held the mirror up to show me the end result. It seemed that one side was thicker and longer than the other. By the time he got them to match, all that was left was a partially bare skull bestowing upon me a striking resemblance to a semi-shorn sheep or, as one of my classmates tactfully remarked, 'a badly worn lavatory brush.' I told the barber it looked awful. The other guys awaiting their turn immediately formed a committee which collectively agreed, *nem con*, that it would look far better entirely shaven and, again collectively, dared me to do that. I thought it couldn't look any worse and moreover a peer dare was equivalent to a double dare which could not, under any circumstances, be ignored. Therefore I accepted it. Stuuuuupid. Verrrry stupid. I resembled a freakish mutant. I rushed around in search of a classmate who owned a moth-eaten beret. When I found him and after I'd swallowed his inevitable caustic comments about my being the first of the Marist skinheads, he agreed I could keep it for as long as necessary. I wore it all weekend, even in bed, in the forlorn hope of avoiding further disagreeable, barbed jibes from churlish schoolmates.

On Monday morning in class we all stood up as usual when our first master of the day, Brother Ralph, another hyper-strict disciplinarian, entered the room. His eagle eye immediately homed in on me.

'You should know better than to come into the classroom with a hat on. Take it off immediately!'

'Please brother,' I begged, 'please let me leave it on.'

'Take it off!' he insisted, deliberately enunciating his stentorian words as if I were a simpleton.

'Please...' I repeated...

Everyone in the class was having a hard time keeping straight faces since mostly they knew what I looked like without the beret.

'Take...'

Knowing that continued palaver would instantly precipitate physical pain I reluctantly, very reluctantly, very slowly began to slide the beret off... Of course by now the entire class was corpsing. As soon as Brother Ralph saw what the beret had concealed he barked 'Get out of here and do not return to my class until your hair grows back again' Me, I was staggered at what he had told me and all I could stammer was: 'But, but, I'll be out for the rest of the year Brother ...'

'Right,' said he, reluctantly relenting, 'sit down and do not take that thing off your head under any circumstances.'

The Crow ended the frivolity decreeing, 'Very well, the entertainment is over for today, turn to page...'

'And you,' he addressed a boy at the back who continued to snigger when everyone else had stopped, 'I said the entertainment was over. C'mere!'

The lad stepped forward to receive a hefty larruping.

To their credit the Marist Brothers partially ignored apartheid so that boys of assorted nationalities, creeds, shapes and sizes, heights and weights and colours - except black kids - were present - all learning a lot about other beliefs by mixing freely and imperturbably with one another.

One particular boy of Lebanese origin was the hairiest creature I'd ever seen except for the gorilla in the Ape House at the zoo. This guy, whose name was Khouri which, I was informed, meant priest, had hair almost everywhere on his body, from head to toe, the only exceptions being his forehead, his nose, the palms of his hands, the soles of his feet and his penis. So hairy was he that he sometimes needed to shave twice a day and he was only sixteen or seventeen. As my facial bum fluff began to sprout and darken the prospect of evolving into a Yeti lookalike having to shave twice a day did not fill me with a shred of anticipatory pleasure and I began to think of means of circumventing such a future

I spotted an advertisement for a product called Veet in one of my mother's magazines. I reasoned that if it could remove hair from women's legs it would certainly eliminate my face fuzz so I bought some during my next home leave. At home alone I considered the time was right to apply the Veet. I locked myself in the bathroom and smeared it liberally all over my face. If you, dear reader, have not used a depilatory, do yourself a favour and abstain from applying it to your visage. The sulphurous odour did not auger well as the stuff was so powerful that it ate into my skin which began to bubble like a painted surface copiously doused with paint stripper. The pain was intense and the scabs took months to clear. Its full impact only manifested itself in my teens when I started growing a beard which, thanks to the bald patches left by the Veet looked conspicuously moth-eaten. It hadn't occurred to me that female leg skin is far tougher and thicker than that of an average teenage boy's face.

Intermittently a nugatory accident would enliven the Marist monotony. For instance Yazbeck, one of the less hirsute Lebanese boarders managed to trap his head between the bars at the back of his iron bed. He screamed his lungs out until he was freed by a Crow with a hacksaw.

Another dormitory inmate, given to sleepwalking, took full advantage of his affliction by faking things. Once he'd fallen from a first floor balcony, merely breaking an arm. Marcie bought his somnambulistic story but we all knew he'd frequently been shinning up and down a drain pipe to call his girlfriend from the telephone kiosk in the street just outside the school's main gate.

Even though that booth was officially out of bounds, it was always in demand since it was our sole means of communication with the outside world and, most importantly, contact with girlfriends. After school and during evening meal breaks boarders risked Brotherly bile by joining the impatient queue waiting to use it. Sometimes we'd amuse ourselves by making anonymous calls to local shopkeepers. The prime quarry was the owner of a soda fountain-cum-tearoom-cum-snack bar called Teddy Bear's Tearoom located at the Yeoville tram terminus about a mile from our school.

As with all calls, these cost us nothing and the telephone company recouped scant income from that box since every Marist boarder knew how to operate it for free by sticking a pin through the live cable and once the call was answered, tapping the pin on the metal inside a small hole near the mouthpiece to replicate the sound of a coin dropping and we were connected. None of us ever knew why that worked but it did.

Removal of that kiosk by the phone company was by no means a great surprise to anyone.

Teddy Bear's Tearoom, named in honour of King Edward's School - KES for short - just across the road from that school, was a revered haunt for Maristonians, being the nearest place where we could supplement our school's detestable diet with remarkably delicious toasted cheese and tomato sandwiches or, if we were really flush, perhaps a gourmet meal of steak, eggs, and chips liberally splashed with vinegar and Worcestershire sauce. We spent a lot of dosh there feeding ourselves and the ancient, well-worn pinball machines. These were, I suppose, the obsessive forebears of computer games. Practice made perfect allowing us to squander entire afternoons playing the free games won by attaining high scores. Since this precluded younger, less accomplished kids from inserting *zacs galore* into the machines the owner didn't much care for us.

Teddy Bear's was a place where we could be reasonably sure of relieving ennui by trading insults and taunts about sporting incompetence with KES boys who, needless to say, also spent time there either waiting for a tram or enjoying a cool drink, a Perks meat pie or a snack. No matter how much we spent as customers, the Cypriot owner was curt, often to the point of rudeness to all Maristonians, whilst being obsequiously polite to the King Edward's boys. I suspect he probably knew that Marist pupils were responsible for plaguing him with nuisance telephone calls in voices disguised by holding a handkerchief over the mouthpiece, asking if that was

Teddy Bear's Tearoom on the tramline. The reply was invariably affirmative and our invariable retort was 'You'd better get it out of the way quickly, there's a tram coming'.

Predictably the owner refused to serve anyone wearing a Marist uniform and his frequent complaints to our headmaster resulted in the tearoom becoming another no-go area which was most regrettable since it was also a rendezvous for those of us who had girlfriends at Yeoville Girls' Convent, a block away from the tearoom. The convent, Marist's 'sister' school, reputedly had a secret tunnel joining our schools so that the nuns had access to the Brothers and vice versa.

Marist Brothers College was renowned as a rugby school. Well, OK, come to think of it 'notorious' would be more accurate. We had a lot of very beefy boys in our First XV all of whom revelled in the sheer delight of battering their adversaries into submission. These guys were glorified role models. All our rugby teams were very good, notably those with lots of boarders in them. This was partly due to the fact that the boarders could vent their pent-up frustration with the school's rigid discipline by expiating their melancholia when playing rugby where the rules of that game could be imperceptibly modified, resulting in a mess of wounded antagonists queuing up at Matron's after every game.

The only rivals Maristonians respected were Jeppe High which bred topnotch rugby players, and Helpmekaar, (Help Each Other) an Afrikaans school whose tactics were nearly as unsporting as ours and whose pupils, in the main, consisted of huge brutes with hands resembling bunches of bananas genetically modified to carry rugby balls. We all reckoned Helpmekaar's first teams were in their mid-twenties rather than the seventeen and eighteen year-olds who played for Marist's senior teams.

St John's College, Johannesburg's only other fee paying private boys' school, fielded first rate teams who refused to play us because, so the story went, we were unsportsmanlike and, as scions of predominantly expatriate Brits, they preferred to pit their skills against gentlemen in preference to us, the 'Marits Buggers' (sic).

But KES was the real enemy.

Johannesburg's venerable Ellis Park rugby stadium, the equivalent of England's Twickenham, was the birthplace of abundant South African rugby legends, and the venue where international test matches and all Southern Transvaal's inter-provincial games were relentlessly played, no quarter being asked or given by either side.

The match of the season between the country's two top teams Transvaal and Western Province always turned the principal stadium in the Union of South Africa into a sardine can of spectators. Johannesburg schools occasionally provided curtain raisers to important games. The Ellis Park management invited Marist Brothers and King Edward's schools to play against each other, secure in the knowledge that such an inter-school match would be played with the same chauvinistic fanaticism as that of the provincial teams.

Even though schools matches began well in advance of the main game they always attracted crowds of supporters from opposing schools. Every ticket available to each school was taken. To discourage bangarangs within the grounds, contesting supporters were assigned to opposite ends of the stadium. The Marist versus KES match day was no exception. Cloudlessly clear blue winter skies smiled seraphically down upon us. Minutes after kick-off KES scored a try for their wildly ecstatic supporters. By half-time they were in the lead by seven points.

This was too much for the Maristonians to bear and after the teams had sucked their half-time oranges KES was playing into the sun and the Marist supporters began to deploy their secret weapons - mirrors - to reflect the sun's rays into the eyes of their fullback while he was trying to field high balls from Marist's kicks.

The detonation of protest emanating from the opposite side of the field built into a crescendo after one such act thwarted their fullback trying to catch an up-and-under kick from our team, resulting in an interception and a levelling try for us. This impelled a KES contingent to make a foray in our direction. Their intentions were obviously hostile which was what a lot of our guys had hoped for. The face-off resulted in the eviction of most of the spectators from both schools. We won the match together with the doubtful distinction of being banned from Ellis Park and all future fixtures with KES, who also refused to play us again for years. Regrettably other schools espoused similar values so that our rugby standard deteriorated due to the lack of regular worthwhile opposition to keep our firsts on their toes.

Once in a while during school vacations I accompanied Pop to the Johannesburg produce market where, without exception, he was known as Eddie disregarding the fact that the business was named after me, his firstborn. Or was it the other way round? I was always addressed as 'little Eddie', a compliment echoing those received from Pop's black employees. They always filled me with a glow of pride reflecting as they did, the esteem Pop enjoyed among his peers. I didn't know of any other kid who accompanied his father to work.

Most of the traders at the market were of Indian descent which made it one of the rare places in South Africa where no apartheid existed, at least amongst the buyers and sellers.

My father's popularity led to wedding invitations from his Hindu business associates and, as a particular treat, he sometimes took me with him. The celebrations were usually held in a suburb called Melrose I think it was. The venue, a dilapidated corrugated tin roofed hall was dominated within by a huge portrait of Mahatma Gandhi in a gilt frame surrounded by a carload of Christmas tree lights.

The ceilingless hall which doubled as a temple was decorated with flowers and paper streamers creating a joyous, jubilant, festal atmosphere.

I felt very much at home there among the elaborate saris and ornate gold jewellery worn by Indian matriarchs, reminding me of the *yentas* at Jewish weddings except that the Hindu ladies' vivid outfits were far more evocative and exotic. Apart from the expensive finery of female apparel, the similarities between Hindu and Jewish weddings seemed remarkable, to me at least. I was intrigued with the wonder of this new world so far removed from mine yet so similar in various ways.

At Hindu weddings the ceremony was immediately followed by a banquet in the same hall, unlike other weddings I'd been to where the receptions were not held at the place of worship. The bridal retinue entered the hall making their sedate way past the guests en route to the stage at the far end of the temple. Here the barefoot bride wearing a saffron sari and red shawl stepped elegantly onto the stage to be met by a priest beneath a *mandap*, a canopy not dissimilar to the Jewish *chupah* except that the Hindu version is self-supporting whereas the Jewish equivalent has groomsmen (pole-holders) at each corner. The Hindu ceremony required two young men to hold a white sheet in front of the shoeless bride to hide her from the groom until she took up her position next to him. He too was shoeless.

Tradition had it, I was told, that the bride's sisters kept the shoes until the groom paid to redeem them so that he could walk home afterwards. The groom wore white trousers and a matching knee-length 'Nehru jacket' with a stand-up collar and buttons down to the waist. He joined his bride at a hallowed nuptial fire of twigs and ghee smoking away centre stage in a copper brazier, reminding me of the Eternal Light that burns in synagogues 24/7.

On seeing one another for the first time that day the couple exchanged garlands before seating themselves on a pair of low stools where they invoked sacred vows dating back millennia. Another feature of the ceremony called for them to step on a large stone together to remind them that they would need the marriage to be as firm and strong as a rock in order to withstand life's obstacles. For me this echoed the Jewish custom in which the groom crushes a drinking glass with his shoe as a reminder to co-religionists of the destruction of the Temple in Jerusalem by the Romans 2,000 years ago. Many a Jewish groom has had cause to remember the broken glass as the last opportunity he had to put his foot down!

The number seven plays a significant role for both Jews and Hindus. At Jewish weddings seven cups of wine are consumed. The Hindus circumnavigate their holy fire seven times pausing briefly to allow the bride to flatten seven small piles of rice with her feet to record the lap count.

My clearest recollection is of a Hindu ceremony that took place in the afternoon of a witheringly hot, parched Witwatersrand summer's day. The exhausted electric ceiling fan's brave struggle to reduce the inside temperature was matched by the couple's fortitude in surviving without passing out from the intense heat.

For the benefit of guests of other faiths, a scholarly elderly gentleman with a microphone provided a felicitous commentary in English about the significance of each stage of the proceedings. The rites were carried out in accordance with the Vedas, the holy scriptures of Hinduism, the oldest known religion in the world. He explained the significance of the necklace which the groom tied about the soigné bride's throat to the accompaniment of unconstrained ululation from the guests. The groom then marked the bride's forehead with a dab of orange powder to signify that she was now a married woman.

The conclusion of the ceremonies heralded the beginning of feasts fit for royalty, matching, if not surpassing those of Jewish receptions where the quantities of food could probably have fed thrice the number of guests present. I relished the spicy vegetarian food served up on giant banana leaves, inculcating my predilection for Indian cuisine that has lasted me a lifetime, except that I have been unable to find a restaurant anywhere whose food is quite as delicious as that served at my South African Hindu weddings. All the while a host of noisy little girls in enchanting saris frolicked around boisterously.

An Indian matron smiled at me and crooned indulgently, 'It is not a wedding without the children...' You can't get much more Jewish than that.

I'd always believed that my father was Lithuanian from Panevyzys (pronounced Ponevezh) until I began researching my family background. The South African Defence Force records unearthed a document which Pop had signed stating that he was born in Petrograd, the northernmost city in Russia. Until 1914 it was known as St Petersburg but was subjected to a name change because the Russians felt it sounded too Germanic. Ten years later, under communism, it became Leningrad until, late in the 20ᵗʰ Century, it reverted to St Petersburg. The reasons for these changes are less of a mystery to me than the information on Pop's army enlistment form. Numerous possibilities spring to mind but the likelihood is that my grandparents were there to buy ship cards (boat tickets) for two of my teenage uncles Sam and Robert to reconnoitre South Africa to provide feedback before the rest of the family joined them. My father's innate sense of fun may have nudged him to upstage his brothers by arriving prematurely. Or maybe Pop deliberately misinformed the South African recruiting officer thinking that if he mentioned Panevyzys it would take all day to get it spelled correctly. Or was it simply a mistake?

Apartheid was but one of only two topics of mutual interest shared between Afrikaners and English settlers. The other was anti-Semitism.

It is an historic given that wherever in the world Jews settle, the spectre of anti-Semitism follows to haunt them. South Africa was not to be the exception to prove the rule.

Vasco da Gama retained a smattering of Jewish navigators, cartographers and mariners aboard his famed exploratory journeys round the Cape of Good Hope in the mid-15ᵗʰ Century. A hundred years later a handful of Jews from England and Holland settled in Cape Town. Jews were of so inconsequential a minority that they were, at first, totally ignored until their numbers increased substantially with the arrival of the 1820 Settlers from Britain.

In Europe, especially e0astern Europe, things hadn't gone too well for the Jews. In 1791 the Russian ruler Catherine the Great, under pressure to *'rid Moscow of Jewish business competition and evil influence on the Russian masses'*, designated a portion of her vast Empire as a Pale of Jewish Settlement. This stretched about 800 miles from the Baltic to the Black Sea. The region included fifteen of Russia's western provinces and ten of her Polish provinces. These were the only places where Russia's Jews were permitted to live. Life in Russian Lithuania was not exactly easy for poor Jews and not much better for those who had any rubles to spare.

All we knew of my family's life in Panevyzys was gleaned from a school project by Uncle Robert's grandson Charles who recorded that:

'Robert and his brothers had to walk a distance of one kilometer to school... There was a river not far from the town and all the brothers and sisters learnt to swim there... On Saturday nights the gentiles used to walk along the streets and hit the Jews like some gangs in South Africa hit the blacks. This was the favourite so called sport of the Gentiles before the Russian revolution. The Cossacks used to cause a lot of anti-Jewish feeling and life became very hard for the Jews in Russia... A lot of Jews in Eastern Europe wanted to emigrate because of anti-Semitism and the poverty that surrounded them... The Jews from Russia spoke mainly Russian and Yiddish. They were an educated minority group in that area whereas the Russians who used

to persecute the Jews were illiterate... My grandfather was on the intellectual side and to earn extra money he used to teach Russian to little Russian children. It is unbelievable to think he was only twelve years old when he did this... Although there were some wealthy Jews most of the people lived in one area. This was known as a shtetl... My grandfather's family decided to leave Russian life and find a better life. They heard of all the wealth in South Africa... but they found nothing was as they had expected... They came by boat from the Baltic Sea to Cape Town. Most of their passports were Russian. Others were German. They couldn't speak English and added any Christian name to their correct surnames.'

Conditions in the Pale were terrifyingly similar to numerous South African apartheid rules. Within the Pale, Jews were restricted to poverty stricken urban areas, which meant severely limited economic opportunities. They paid double taxes; were barred from leasing land, running taverns or receiving higher education. Their teenage sons were conscripted into the Russian military and seldom seen or heard from again. Discrimination ruled and these depredations led to the creation of Zionism, the aim of which was to create a Jewish state in Palestine.

Matters continued to worsen for the Russian Jews. When Czar Alexander III was assassinated in 1881, the blame was laid at the doors of, yes; the Jews. The cataclysmic, increasingly violent pogroms, boycotts and other horrific anti-Semitic activities became so intolerable that millions of Russia's Jews sought ways and means of migrating. North America was their first preference until gold was discovered in the Transvaal. The mass exodus which began in 1880 totaled six million departures from Eastern Europe. Four million of them, including my paternal grandparents and their children, were Jews.

During this period of turmoil a Scotsman, Donald Currie from Greenock, entered the frame. As a very young man his dynamism had so impressed Charles MacIver, a partner in the Cunard shipping line, that he had no hesitation in hiring him. Currie rapidly rose through the company ranks to become a senior executive until he felt it was time to start his own business, the Castle Mail Packet Company, plying between Liverpool and Calcutta. He then initiated regular sailings between South Africa and England. Currie was quick to realize that the migrants of Eastern Europe presented a challenging business opportunity. He was an astute man, well aware of the obstacles facing refugees - long, gruelling voyages, language problems and rules they could not comprehend.

The refugees needed transport to get the hell out of there and Currie's ships needed passengers. His Castle Line vessels were primarily mail carriers with plenty of spare passenger capacity. Currie became, in that awful modern word, a facilitator. He appointed agents throughout the Pale and arranged accommodation for his Jewish transit passengers to South Africa through a charity he sponsored called the Shelter for Poor Jews in London's East End. This provided free accommodation and sustenance for passengers awaiting their ships. Lithuanian Jews took up Currie's affordable fares to South Africa in preference to going to the United States where the numbers of immigrants were being restricted. Currie's business boomed benevolently, allowing him to increase his fleet and to amalgamate with the Union Line which was rebranded as the Union Castle Line. It wasn't until 1892 that the

Baltic exodus gathered real momentum. The majority of Currie's migrants started their voyage at Libau, a Latvian port with a thriving Jewish population.

Donald Currie could not have guessed he was instrumental in saving Jewish families from future Nazi gas ovens on a scale which made Schindler's World War II effort almost fade into insignificance.

In addition to his humanitarianism, Donald Currie had profound effects on South African history. His intimate, incisive knowledge of the country led to his becoming an advisor on South African affairs to the British Government. But probably the main reason for his name being forever enshrined in South African history was his interest in sport. On his first visit to South Africa in 1888 he handed a trophy to Major Warton, team manager of the first English cricket tourists under the captaincy of Aubrey Smith (an actor who became a Hollywood movie star) to award to the team delivering the best performance against the tourists. This was the first Currie Cup.

In 1936 Donald Currie sailed to South Africa on the maiden voyage of his newest vessel, the Dunottar Castle. On board he entertained the first British Rugby Union team to tour South Africa. In Currie's luggage was a gold cup which he planned to present to a South African team on the same basis as the cricket trophy. The Brits were too strong for the locals and the cup went to Griqualand West who suffered the smallest defeat with a score of 0-3. Today that cup, the famed Currie Cup, remains South Africa's most prestigious trophy in the fiercely contested annual inter-provincial rugby championship.

The flood of Currie's Jews into Johannesburg between 1880 and 1910 enlarged the city's Jewish population tenfold - from four thousand to forty thousand predominantly Yiddish speaking Lithuanians - causing consternation among the Boer Republics who took steps to limit the 'Jewish threat.' One such move was to classify them in the same category as Asians since, the Boers asserted; Yiddish was not a European language.

Jews settled in Johannesburg in such quantities that it was scathingly referred to as Jewburg or Lithuania on the Veld. But it didn't take long before thousands jettisoned their traditional garb along with the conventions of the Pale to acculturate exceedingly well to their new environment. A goodly number started out as peddlers, or *smouses* - often contemptuously ridiculed as 'Peruvians', who eked out a living hawking eggs, matches and other goods door to door, catering to the mainly illiterate poor whites - all Afrikaners whose only skill was their stamina to handle farm labour.

The barbaric British scorched earth policy carried out during two Boer Wars left innumerable concentration camp survivors homeless, farmless, jobless. The Boers resented the success of the Jews who settled, acquired an exiguous amount of English and blossomed into prosperous citizens. The scarcity of work opportunities in a city bursting at its seams led to a Jewish overspill which travelled north to less inhabited places where they started farms and shops. But they did not engage Afrikaners since black labour was far cheaper.

Hardier, more ambitious hawkers scraped together enough money to acquire a horse and cart to travel to shop-free rural areas selling all manner of goods.

The really resourceful Jewish go-getters often became wholesalers or entrepreneurs rapidly acquiring the purchasing power to pay for their progeny to qualify for professions such as law, medicine, education and the arts. Top of the pecking order were the property and mining potentates and stockbrokers, all of whom enjoyed a life style akin to feudal barons in mansions rivalling those of European aristocracy.

All this success irritated the non-Jewish population no end, particularly the most virulent Jew hater of the era, a certain Charles Penstone, an Englishman whose scurrilous weekly rag *The Owl* flopped on the Witwatersrand at the turn of the 19th Century yet found 16,000 receptive readers after he moved to Cape Town. The Owl's obscene cartoons doubtless inspired those that Hitler employed to denigrate German Jews. In the 1930's Germany reciprocated by exporting foul propaganda to South Africa. Afrikaner newspapers needed no coercion to replicate *The Owl's* racist cartoons which, in turn, goaded the government to introduce a quota act in 1930 expediting a dramatic decline in Jewish immigration which fell below a thousand a month.

The early 1930's saw the birth of several paramilitary 'Shirt Movements'. In Italy and England they wore black. In Germany they were brown. South Africa chose grey. These Greyshirts were a virulently anti-Semitic, neo-Nazi group closely allied to the South African Gentile National Socialist Movement and the South African Fascists led by one Johannes von Moltke. These factions made not the slightest pretense to disguise their compulsion to inflame hatred against the Jews. The Greyshirts hatched a plot intended to besmirch the Jews and were taken to court by a rabbi. They were prosecuted for libel and heavily fined, signalling the end of the Greyshirts who snuck off to form their secret societies, the *Broederbond* and the *Ossewabrandwag* whose more prominent members included Dr. D F Malan and Hendrik Verwoerd, who shared and nourished the same fervid Nazi-incited views behind closed doors.

Before WW2, according to a report by the Jewish Board of Deputies, *'The Jewish community was anxious to avoid a confrontation with the government without compromising its own rights and principles.'*

As I grew older I felt progressively more ashamed that they did not, as a community, identify with the unremitting suffering of their black countrymen especially since the majority of South Africa's Jews had families wiped out during the Holocaust.

One would have thought that the Holocaust which imbued the Jews with a dynamic sense of international solidarity would have motivated them to oppose the apartheid regime whose policies were not dissimilar to that of the Nazis.

Of course there were liberal minded Jews, prominent Jews, in the forefront of the anti-apartheid movement but they were a minority among their co-religionists who perpetuated the doctrine of remaining *shtum* rather than risk the slightest possibility of disturbing the Kraken. They continued to thrive and prosper. And I felt impotent at my inability to think of a system to at least reduce the incessant battering ram of apartheid on the black people of Utopian white South Africa.

My brother and I often speculate about our Lithuanian family roots and wish we had more details about their lives in that small Baltic town. I regret never having quizzed my uncles about their childhood there, losing forever priceless details about the ordinary, everyday experiences of their growing up over a century ago in so isolated a corner of the world.

In the school project mentioned earlier, my cousin Charles Joffe relates that Uncle Robert's first job in South Africa was in a store wrapping food in newspaper for black customers. He taught himself English from those papers. His hours were 6 am to 6 pm. He slept in the back of the shop for a rental of sixpence a month including food. He sent whatever was left back home to his parents. He later taught himself accountancy which led to a job offer at an outlying Northern Transvaal *dorp* called Louis Trichardt. At that time a cruel 'flu' epidemic struck South Africa in which thousands died. In appreciation for his nursing his boss back to health he was rewarded with a diamond which enabled him to marry my Aunt Sophie from England in style.

They moved to Bloemfontein where they produced three children. Uncle Robert's eldest son Jack was killed in action at El Alamein in 1942. He was 21. His younger son Henry (pronounced Hendry by all and sundry, including Henry himself) was an accomplished rugby fly half whom I idolized. He was very kind to me and whenever I needed advice he always made time to listen carefully to what I had to say. I in turn, listened raptly to his views. I had to, as I needed to concentrate on his heavy Free State accent to work out what the heck he was saying.

Henry played for both the universities he attended - UCOFS - University College of the Orange Free State and Wits, the University of the Witwatersrand. Most importantly Henry played at provincial level for the Orange Free State. On 30 July 1947, the Port Elizabeth *'Daily Advertiser'* rugby reporter wrote of his performance in an interprovincial match: *'I liked his speed off the mark as he came up to take Dantjie Strydom's excellent passes, while his engineering of the winning try was a brilliantly executed piece of work.'* In the 1949 Springbok trials in Pretoria Henry was one of 30 players on the short list selected from 114 trialists to play New Zealand. Both the press and public were in accord that he was unlucky not to have made the final team.

He was my most famous relative - a lovely man who I was proud to have as a cousin.

Pop's sister Janie married a man named Epstein who fathered her four daughters Minnie, Ettie, Annie and Betty. Poor Ettie suffered a complete mental breakdown in her teens when a callously ignorant policeman knocked on the front door to ask if hers was the Epstein household to which she replied in the affirmative. The man spoke but one brutal sentence 'Your father's just died,' he said and left. So severe was her shock that she went berserk and had to be confined in Sterkfontein, a Dickensian mental home whose nightmarish methods included regular ECT (electroshock) treatment. These had no positive effect on her so the doctors recommended a lobotomy. Providentially my aunt read of a medication unobtainable in South Africa but she hunted out a source abroad which proved so efficacious that Ettie was allowed to leave the institute where she had resided for much of her adult life.

Charlie, my jovial paternal uncle was in the hotel business and his hail-fellow-well-met outlook admirably suited his life style. How he retained his constant smile was an enigma since his chunky wife Fanny henpecked him unremittingly. Maybe it was their three daughters who kept him smiling. Mavis and Ruby were older than I and the youngest, Phyllis, a talented, delightfully charismatic kid with a million dollar personality, was an outstandingly gifted dancer and a steadfast friend. As a young mother of two small children she was tragically killed in a car smash while still in her twenties.

As I sit tapping away at my pc, my attention wanders because reminiscing about my family reminds me of those biblical begats for which I sort of apologize and beg your forbearance as I'm nearly finished with the family tree as such by mentioning that while the children of Israel were being instructed to go forth and multiply, my ancestors must have been issued with calculators because my father was the youngest of six - three brothers and two sisters. My mother, the youngest of the Naar children was one of ten.

Now, where was I? Ah, right - the begats... It would fill the rest of this book to detail all of them so I'll stick to those whose influence on my life was greatest. You may already have gathered my mother Rita's family was far more cosmopolitan than Pop's. Grandfather David Naar, the Dutchman, begot my eldest uncle Isaac - Ike to all of us - who left home in his teens to join the South African Post Office. With his fluent Dutch and a surname like Naar, he was readily accepted by the predominantly Afrikaner civil service of the era, none of whom, I suspect, would have taken to him so willingly had they been aware of the faith he was born into. Karma led him to marry an Afrikaans woman. They lived in the Afrikaner-dominated southern suburbs of Johannesburg and we hardly ever saw him. Nevertheless, he knew I was a keen philatelist and every Christmas he would send me a biscuit tin brimful of stamps from every corner of the earth still stuck to bits of envelope. I spent a lot of time soaking the backs off the stamps, drying them carefully, sorting them into countries and sticking them into albums with transparent gummed paper 'hinges'. My love of philately was responsible for my becoming the school's smartest kid at geography.

My maternal uncle Jack Naar was a munificent man who often slipped me a threepenny bit or more if my parents weren't looking. Uncle Jack was not only Pop's brother-in-law but also one of his closest friends, and a co-founder of the poker school held at our house every Friday night. Uncle Jack married a lovely Irish lady, Kate O'Malley (fortunately unrelated to 'Pegleg' O'Malley of Marist's.) Jack and Kate lived in a luxurious, spotlessly clean penthouse maintained in showroom condition. We kids were not invited there for fear we might sully the place or damage anything.

Uncle Jack more than made up for that by encouraging me to pop in to his printing works in Albert Street, a short walk from central Johannesburg, any time I felt like it. Here I spent idyllically happy hours being pampered by Mom's youngest brother Willie, and cousin Johnny who both worked for Uncle Jack. They allowed me to delve into ink- stained wooden boxes in which were stored sufficient mysterious treasures for a kid to amuse himself for weeks on end. All the staff, black and white, knew me and usually presented me with a squidgy jam doughnut and a convivial enamel mug of tea on my visits to the 'works' which I made at every opportunity. At lunch times after the machines had all shushed to a standstill, the white employees adjourned to their staff room where they dined on packed lunches or fish and vinegary chips while seated at a grimy, oilcloth covered table on which the men played rummy while eating, and the women pored over their ladies' magazines or blathered away breathlessly in Afrikaans.

Then the machines started up again with their rhythmic rackety clack, clack, clacketty-clacking until the decibels built into a crescendo too loud to allow any gabbling on the machine shop floor leaving me alone to explore dozens of magic boxes on the long wooden shelves where hundreds of lead typeface and fonts were stored. I was overjoyed to discover a paltry cache of live dumdum bullets which I was allowed to keep after my cousin double checked they were safe by removing the lead tips to ensure there was no gunpowder inside them.

In my pre boarding school days, I'd done my homework or read comic books in Uncle Jack's jumbled, untidy office while he was out hustling up business. The enormous contrast between his meticulous home and the shambles of his office made me wonder if Aunt Kate had ever visited him there and, if so, what she thought of it.

The printing works occupied a building with a small open-air space at the rear for light and ventilation. As there was no access door, window cleaning necessitated having to climb in and out through the window. This area had been a weed infested wilderness until a black guy called Jim started to work for my uncle. Jim volunteered to clean it up in his own time if my uncle would allow him to grow vegetables there, since, he asserted, he had nowhere near his Johannesburg home to grow anything, and coming from a farming family he wanted to again savour the feel of the soil. My uncle did not vacillate about granting Jim the green light to tidy up the eyesore and for years the garden was lovingly tended and treated as if it was Jim's personal property. He even cleaned the windows, inside and out in his own time. Now and then he'd supply the staff with fresh tomatoes and beans that proliferated alongside his beautiful bushes.

Uncle Jack displayed great pride in the oasis at the back end of his premises.

During his annual leave Jim returned to his tribal village to take unto himself a wife. In his absence my uncle had a tap installed in the garden for him in recognition of his unselfish, devoted gardening services. He figured this would save Jim a lot of time and energy climbing in and out, back and forth through the window with a watering can to nurture his beloved plants. The black handyman my uncle hired to fit the tap showed a keen interest in the garden and asked my uncle if he could have some seedlings or cuttings, but his request was refused.

On his return to work Jim was startled to learn about the enquiry and when the handyman arrived to talk to Jim a tremendous argument ensued, culminating in a bloody fist fight which resulted in a visit by the police who inspected the cause of the disturbance – Jim's horticultural haven. My uncle was questioned as to why he had allowed the cultivation of 'certain plants' on his property.

It took an awful lot of persuasion from him to convince the cops that he was unaware that Jim's crop was mainly *dagga*, a type of South African cannabis, the proceeds of its sale having financed the purchase of sufficient cattle for Jim to pay *lobola* (bride price) for the most attractive virgin in his village.

107

As a teenager I had several close friends with whom I spent school vacations and sublime holiday images still inhabit corners of my brain except for those involving horses - well, one horse in particular. My first skirmish with these animals concerns my friend Monty whose father owned a farm. Monty, an excellent rider, persuaded me to go riding with him. He chose a horse for me which, he averred, was a very tame old nag, far and away the most placid, easiest-to-handle animal in the entire stable. The only danger Monty envisaged was that the horse might fall asleep under me.

I mounted up no bother and soon, there we were, two happy horsemen meandering along at a quiet walk with Monty furnishing tips about my seat, holding my reins at the right height, slouching and what not until he adjudged the time had come to go a bit faster. 'Right' he declared, 'You're not up to Cocky Feldman's standard yet but you're doing well. Time for a trot.' And off he went. Monty soon noticed that we - my bag of bones and I - had halted where he'd left us, so he made a U-turn, stopping only to break a dry branch from a tree. He handed it to me with instructions to hit the horse with it. I took the stick and gave the horse a gentle tap which it totally ignored. Monty told me to hit it harder. That didn't work either.

'Come on Ed,' urged Monty, 'hit the bugger. Hard.'

I did. Again nothing happened. Monty grabbed my stick and whacked the poor beast with such force that the stick snapped with a crack like a rifle shot. To my horror the darned thing took off as if it was a thoroughbred intent on defeating the entire field in the Durban July Handicap. I couldn't help but notice it was heading straight towards a barbed wire fence. I assumed that would stop it, but the gee-gee seemed to have emulating the Light Brigade in mind and summoned up extra acceleration. I was now gripping the animal's mane as tight as tight can be, convinced that my steed was about to leap the fence. It didn't. It stopped. I didn't. I flew over that fence as gracelessly as a dodo and if it hadn't been for a small, strategically positioned cluster of bushes I would probably have broken something but, scratches ignored, the worst consequence was Monty's ribbing all the way back to the stables.

My next equine experience was on holiday at Witbank, a somnolent wee town where my closest boarder friend Dave's dad lived on a sizeable property close to the general store he owned. Witbank was not exactly at the cutting edge of leisure activities for young guys like us other than swimming and riding. Dave's father kept a small stable and Dave was easily as good a rider as Monty, only a better instructor so I gained a tad more confidence around the beasts.

Regrettably Dave's cousin Sid, a dull, pompous fart of the first degree, came to join us. One morning while Dave was saddling our horses Sid appeared and announced that he would be riding with us. Dave offered him the horse he had just saddled which I thought was very kind of him, but Sid ungraciously refused; stating, without so much as a thank you, that he knew all about saddling horses and would do his own. I'd watched Dave saddling our horses and knew he was no slouch at it. After Sid had fitted the girth strap round his animal Dave suggested that the cinches weren't tight enough.

'I've done this before, you know', bragged conceited Sid.

Dave shrugged and we watched Sid mount up and settle into his saddle. Slowly, very slowly, Sid began to tilt sideways until he was almost upside down before falling on his head into a steaming pile of newly minted organic fertilizer rendering Dave and I unwilling and unable to attempt to assist him or to control our horse laughs for hours on end.

Shortly before Sid appeared on the scene to taint our holiday a young newlywed immigrant couple arrived to work for Dave's father in his store. They were temporarily billeted in Dave's dad's home. One night we sneaked quietly outside to investigate the accuracy of our speculations of what went on when the lights went off. We positioned ourselves below the open burglar proofed window of their bedroom. All that could be heard was a snoring duet and we returned to our beds seriously disappointed. Undeterred, we tried again the following night with much better results. There was a load of grunting and groaning in addition to the passionate pillow talk that took place on the vibrating bedsprings. They may have been speaking Lithuanian or Yiddish or Greek or Japanese, as we couldn't work out what they were saying, but we knew for certain that they were 'at it'. For teenage imaginations as fertile as ours, it was highly erotic stuff and we soon nipped off to indulge in a quiet masturbate.

The most truly memorable holiday of my life thus far was spent with my friend Mike at his uncle's home in Bethlehem in the Orange Free State. This uncle owned both a butcher's shop and a bicycle shop, and he and his cuddly, roly-poly wife pandered to our every whim.

Bethlehem itself was a town that time had ignored. Naturally it had been named by the religious Voortrekkers. However the only thing it had in common with its Middle East namesake was the oppressive heat. It was a typical example of other South African dorps, only slightly larger than average. When left to our own devices the acme of excitement was to fish for barbel, a very ugly antediluvian looking catfish, in a very ugly, muddied dam in a biblical rowing boat which might well have served as a lifeboat aboard Noah's Ark. We spent half our time bailing out water, sharing the chore in five minute shifts. We'd probably have capsized if we'd actually hooked a fish.

So - fishless fishing remained our primary leisure highlight until a cousin of Mike's arrived to spend part of her school vacation with us and life took on a new meaning for me. Late in the evenings after our host and his wife had gone to bed, Mike's cousin and I spent our time *fraying* on the double swing seat on the *stoep* well into the early hours of the morning until one night we both became somewhat over-stimulated.

When she stood up I guessed she was going to tell me we'd gone far enough. Instead she gently but firmly took my hand in hers and led me to her bedroom where she quietly closed and locked the door. Being another stiflingly hot summer we were both dressed accordingly. Within seconds she had shed her flimsy dress, her knickers and her brassiere and started on my fly buttons before I even had time to take my shirt off. All in all it was a sweaty, sticky, messy but torridly gratifying introduction to a congenial hobby which has lasted me a lifetime. Thank you Bethlehem for my first opportunity to reaffirm the *Bar Mitzvah* declaration: 'Today I am a man.'

My next holiday was a visit to the youngest of my mother's half-sisters, Aunt Ray, an aristocratic looking woman of gentle manner and dignified bearing who married a Portuguese man, Chico Vasconcellos. Their home was in Lourenço Marques (always referred to as L M) in Portuguese East Africa. She and my mother, the youngest

109

sibling, were very close and we occasionally went to L M to see her. My mother repeatedly expressed my Gran's oft quoted sentiment 'Where you're liked a lot you go a little and where you're not liked you don't go at all.' As a result of this truism Mom always booked in at the reputable Polana Hotel rather than intrude on my aunt's hospitality in her magnificent home with its chic, mirrored art nouveau furniture and ornate ornaments. However, we spent much of our time with Aunt Ray at the beach or lunching al fresco at her home.

In my sixteenth year my mother agreed that Dave could come with us to L M in reciprocation for the holiday I'd spent at his father's home. We had not been on holiday together at the seaside and could hardly wait to get to L M, which promised to be incontrovertibly preferable to Witbank.

Lourenço Marques was a classy, cosmopolitan city with wide boulevards and elegant European style buildings, one of which, the railway station, was designed by Gustave Eiffel, the engineer whose work includes the Parisian tower bearing his name. The jewel in the architectural crown was the striking modern Roman Catholic Cathedral pointing its impressive, streamlined, white steeple towards the sky as if awaiting the countdown to launch itself into orbit.

L M was the nearest harbour to Pretoria, justifying the expense of constructing a railway between the two cities in the late 19th Century thereby enhancing Mozambique's swift growth and importance. L M's lovely Indian Ocean beaches and exotic Portuguese food made it a tourist mecca for European Portuguese and South Africans.

It was very plucky of Mom to have undertaken this journey since she had to keep an eye on two wayward teenagers, my lively young brother and my baby sister. In the second of the three weeks of our holiday Justin contracted mumps. The situation demanded that my mother got my siblings home pretty damn quick. But, joy of joys; she felt that Dave and I were mature and trustworthy enough to spend the last week in L M on our own. We were optimistic that this would be the ultimate holiday of our lives. No adult supervision at all in a quality hotel where we could do more or less whatever we wanted to do. It was our first taste of unfettered freedom. We could sleep as late as we liked. We could stay on the beach or at the swimming pool as long as we pleased and our only obligation to the clock was to check what time meals were served. Had we been slightly more sophisticated we'd probably have used room service continually.

We returned to Johannesburg in high spirits sporting superb suntans. Our train pulled into Johannesburg station on the Friday afternoon preceding the Sunday return to boarding school. On Saturday a jubilant Dave telephoned to make the triumphant announcement that he too had contracted mumps and that he wasn't going back to school on Sunday...

'You lucky blighter,' I told him, 'I wish it was me!' I got my wish and wished I hadn't.

College rules stipulated that boarders had to check in prior to the 6 pm Sunday evening meal. Pleas that I was unwell fell on deaf ears and Mom pooh-poohed the idea, even suggesting that I was shamming, trying to avoid returning to school. This was true. I felt glum as a gillygaloo in the laying season. All the dramatic training I'd undertaken in my carrots and iodine era had been wasted since I hadn't had time to mock up any counterfeit puke. I was therefore duly delivered by Pop to Observatory; bag and baggage, well in advance of the deadline.

On Monday morning I awoke with a genuine fever, unable to get out of bed to visit the infirmary and Matron had to come to the dormitory to examine me. She swiftly diagnosed mumps and immediately telephoned my parents to collect me as a matter of urgency as she didn't much care to have a mumps epidemic around the school, thank you very much. On reaching home Dr. Freed, our family doctor, was waiting for me. He wasn't convinced that all I had was mumps and felt my condition warranted an immediate lumbar puncture. He telephoned a junior colleague to bring the necessary apparatus and to assist him with the procedure. During this lull I summoned up enough energy to stagger to the telephone to report to Dave that I too had mumps and we both rejoiced at our reprieve from school for another week or more. Hallelujah!

Dr. Freed soon put paid to my jubilation by inserting what might have been a blunt knitting needle into my spine to extract fluid. This had to be the nadir of unpleasant experiences of my life. The junior doctor was forced to pinion me to the bed face down, holding me immovable whilst I vainly struggled to prevent the needle being shoved into me. I panicked from the pain and screamed loudly enough and long enough to attract the attention of neighbours. I cannot understand why I wasn't given an anesthetic. The fluid was immediately rushed by the junior doctor to a laboratory where it was analysed so swiftly that within an hour I was in an ambulance wailing its way to the Johannesburg Isolation Hospital. I don't know whether I passed out from the pain or if I'd been sedated. Either way I was in a coma for a few days and awoke in agony unable to notice anything other than being surrounded by glass. I was unaware that there was a nurse wearing a face mask beside me until she stood up to ask how I was feeling. My lips refused to comply with my thoughts and I couldn't answer. I could hardly move my head which ached like hell. I felt giddy and drowsy and all I wanted to do was die. I believe the nurse had anticipated this reaction which was apparently common in cases of meningitis. She told me where I was and that she'd been briefed by my friend Dave to tell me he was in the same hospital, in the same ward. I think I may have managed a small smile before I passed out again.

It was a week before I was well enough to sit up and wave back at Dave's Cheshire cat grin through his glass box across the aisle. Visitors other than my parents were not allowed to enter my glass enclosure so Dave and I could only communicate with a sort of sign language and I didn't realize what his praying hands meant until my nurse went to ask him for me. It transpired that my meningitis, an inflammation of the tissue surrounding the brain, could have killed me and that the entire school had prayed for me at morning assembly.

In the late 1940's penicillin was relatively unheard of outside the armed forces and had only just come into use in the treatment of critical civilian ailments. My doctor later told me that my case had been cited in the *South African Medical Journal*, the local equivalent of *The Lancet*, as being the first case of meningitis in the country to be cured by that wonder drug to which I owe my life.

It so happens that my local hospital, St Mary's, Paddington, in London where Alexander Fleming discovered the drug, was less than a fifteen minute walk away from my London home. Whenever I'm nearby I always nod my thanks to the great man's commemorative plaque on the Praed Street wall.

On my return to school after a lengthy home convalescence I was treated with a hundred per cent more compassion than I ever thought possible from the Crows. My illness proved to be the dawn of a new era, finally ending the heady days of carrots and iodine. If I didn't feel like attending classes, simply claiming a headache unreservedly excused me from lessons, enabling me to spend the day sitting around the college fields reading books or comic books, training *tok-tokkies* or snoozing on my dormitory bed. My condition disallowed rugby or participation in vigorous activities such as gym or athletics or the senseless parade ground drilling with the school cadet corps. I was considered very brave when I played tennis or went swimming.

The only after-effect I was aware of at the time was a swift deterioration of my eyesight and ever since then I have always had to wear tinted spectacles.

Dave hadn't been as lucky - or was it unlucky perhaps? - as me, for his mumps had evolved into encephalitis whose symptoms are close to meningitis but less virulent or life threatening, so Dave had been neither prayed for nor later granted as many privileges as I was accorded.

All in all I missed about three months of the academic year and the forecast was that I would fail dismally so that passing my penultimate school year junior matric exams astounded everyone including me.

The final week of the academic year was traditionally marked by the Matriculation Year Class Dinner, hosted by the entire teaching staff for the 60 boys who were concluding their schooling. This was held in a good hotel where, for the first time at an official school function, the boys were allowed a few beers. For a negligible number of them it marked the first time they had swallowed alcohol with the result that the boarders among them who were capable of walking at all returned to the dormitory singing lecherous rugby songs.

It was traditional for the less senior boys in the dormitory to apple-pie their beds and so it was in my Junior Matric year. We'd been instructed by the prefects, matriculants all, not to follow that custom or else!

Naturally we ignored their threats by making a professional apple pie-ing job by removing the mattresses, hiding the blankets under them and replacing the covers to look as if there'd been no tampering.

Had we been aware as to which Crow would leave the dinner to check on us that night we may not have added the final touch - the positioning of water filled balloons on top of the dormitory door rigged to burst and inundate the first person to open the door. At about midnight we heard stealthy approaching footsteps. We suspected it was the vanguard of the returning matriculants but we were too canny to take any chances and the stage whispered warning words 'Chups! Chups!' sent us scudding back to our beds. By now everyone was wide awake anticipating the discomfort of a well drenched colleague.

The door opened and the cry of anguish would have done credit to any cinematic virgin confronted by Count Dracula. The lights went on seconds later to reveal a sodden Cossack almost foaming at the mouth. But not even he had the energy to cane everybody so he announced that every man jack of us would forfeit the next scheduled home weekend. Since that was only due the following academic year, three months away, we weren't all that fazed by it and fell asleep secure in the knowledge that our victim was better by far than one of our peers.

Regrettably Cossack did not suffer memory lapses and duly enforced his threat.

My Matric year passed pleasantly enough as I was neither caned nor strapped that year. I believe Matron spread the word of my meningitis among lay teachers and Brothers alike. My main regret was not playing rugby so that the opportunity to display my crown jewels was confined to the dormitory shower area.

There was however, one occasion where I thought I'd run out of non-punishment luck just as the Senior Dance loomed on the College's social calendar.

It seemed to me to be a total contradiction that, excluding this upcoming function, the Brothers totally ignored the fact that a ruck of adolescent boys whose hormones were on the rampage should have girlfriends. We pupils had very little to hope for socially in terms of the opposite sex - to whom we were obliged to refer as 'the opposite gender' - other than at that dance.

My girlfriend at the time happened to be Catholic - Irish Catholic to boot - and on telling her parents that her new boyfriend was a Maristonian they accepted it with equanimity. Until they discovered that their worst nightmare had come true and that she was dating one of the Chosen People. The ordure collided with the fan with an almighty splash. Claudette's parents had no compunction about contacting Cossack who summoned me to his office a week prior to the dance. I had no indication of why the sadistic Spanish goblin who had undoubtedly been an *eminence grise* in his country's Inquisition in a previous incarnation wanted to see me this time.

As soon as Cossack returned my obsequious 'Good afternoon Brother' with the dreaded words 'You seely fellow,' I was convinced that I was in for the high jump. I wilted and shuddered, racking my hard drive for a clue as to what felony I had committed this time to end my cut-free truce. period. The answer was evident as soon as he asked me if I knew Claudette Reilly.

'Of course I do, you cretinous old fart,' I thought, while working out that my *auto de fe* was due any moment for the cardinal sin of having a Catholic girlfriend. Was it to be a set of four, or maybe only two - or - whoa, hold it a minute! Since when was having a girlfriend punishable? There was no alternative but to answer in the affirmative whereupon Cossack cautioned me that henceforth I must have nothing whatever to do with her. This was as barefaced an instance of racism I'd experienced at Marist Brothers College and I knew that meningitis or not, any contact with Claudette would immediately lead to my becoming an endangered species.

No girlfriend. No reserves. And the dance was approaching fast. The chances of finding a partner in time were virtually nil but I knew that any plea to Cossack for a reprieve - at least until after the dance - would fall on tin ears and would probably incur his most rabid wrath. So I left his office feeling sorry for myself but relieved that, for the first time in the course of previous personal visits to Cossack's office, I had, at last, departed with a welt-free backside.

My other regret was wasting all those evenings in the school hall wrestling with the rudiments of rumba, foxtrot and the waltz with clod-footed schoolmates as partners. However there was no time for brooding as my immediate problem was to try to find a stand-in partner to take to the dance. Dave's girlfriend Minnie happened to be Claudette's soul sister but since Claudette was barred from the ball, Minnie wouldn't go without her. We later discovered that both girls had also been subjected to peremptory warnings from Mother Superior at their Convent School (Yeoville Convent, regarded as Marist's 'sister school') that neither girl was to associate with Jewish boys even though Minnie herself was Jewish.

Dave and I spent a lot of time in the phone box outside the school fruitlessly ringing round all the Rand's Rosies to try to find replacements for Minnie and Claudette. But where? We neither of us had female cousins of the right age and ex-girlfriends were adhering to Sod's law by going steady with other guys or saying so even if they weren't.

With only days to go before the dance, my Pop, unaware of my quandary, must have had a favourable win because he sent me to Neville's in President Street to obtain a new shirt and tie for the dance.

The junior sales guy there wasn't a whole lot older than me and on hearing of our date dilemma he gallantly suggested that his seventeen year old sister might be interested, adding that she had a lot of lovely friends one of whom, he considered, might agree to have Dave escort her to the dance. He produced a photograph of his sibling who didn't look at all bad. I telephoned Dave at his mother's flat in Rissik Street in the heart of Johannesburg a mere five minute walk away. He hurried round to Neville's, by which time the sales guy had spoken to his sister who assured us that she and one of her friends would definitely accompany us to the dance. Bingo!

Dave's father provided us with his car as well as his driver to chauffeur us on the night. Bang on the appointed time the car drew up outside the shop guy's parents' house in Kensington and Dave and I sauntered down the garden path to collect our dates. Through the stained glass door we discerned the outline of a very shapely girlish figure gliding forward to open it. I whispered, 'Mine' to Dave. 'No way!' he hissed, 'Mine!' 'No!' 'Yes'... until the door opened... 'Yours!' I retorted. 'No, yours' muttered Dave.

There, in the entrance lobby, stood this apparition clad in a sort of fluorescent emerald green ball gown, closely followed by another girl in a startling, clinging scarlet dress which left very little to the imagination. Later Dave confided that he had an urge to flee to the car to order the driver to make a fast getaway. I'd felt much the same but had been rooted to the spot in horror. Neither girl would see twenty again and, although their figures, specifically their cleavages, beguiled us, they were hardly suitably dressed to take to a Catholic School Dance. There we were, lumbered with dates one short of a coven.

The event took place at the Selby Hall, an adjunct to the Johannesburg Town Hall. Here we tried to distance ourselves from our dates by pretending that we weren't with them. But it happened that a lust of Lebanese lads, mainly the hairiest of them hadn't found dates and to them any girl was better than none so both our dates were danced off their feet while Dave and I drowned our sorrows in Coca Cola on the rocks.

My mother had long been convinced that dentistry would be the perfect profession for her elder son because, she reasoned, I was good with my hands thanks to my model making skills. And, in addition, there was the added bonus of my becoming known as 'doctor', a title enjoyed by South African dentists (and more so by their Jewish mothers) without having to adhere to the antisocial 24 hour availability that was the norm for medical practitioners in those distant good old days when they still made house calls which my mother approved of but not for her son.

I wondered if she had discussed the implications of dentistry with cousin Melville the plane crusher, whose first surgery was in Mayfair, a ramshackle Johannesburg suburb a million light years away from its renowned London namesake. To call the equipment primordial would be a compliment. As one of his first patients I distinctly remember the room where one sat in a sort of tilting barber's chair with a treadle attached which the patient had to pedal in the same way as those mechanical foot controlled sewing machines. This treadle worked the drill. Mind, it focused one's concentration on the feet instead of the mouth. The thought occurs that maybe such drills should be re-introduced to reduce the dental energy footprint er, toothprint er...

Plans for my future did not embrace the prospect of being assailed regularly by the reek of rotting roots and rancid respiration but for my mother's sake I chose to give first year a shot and take it from there.

The surprising success of my junior matric results led me to believe that I would sail through my final school year by continuing to take advantage of my meningitis. Wrong! Although I attained a distinction in English and reasonable passes in Afrikaans, History, Geography and Science, I barely scraped through Latin and comprehensively plugged Mathematics. This meant I had to sit supplementary exams. With the benefit of extra lessons from a tutor, a defrocked Catholic priest whose crime it was that he'd fallen in love with a woman, I squeezed through my exams. The pass wasn't good enough for admission to first year dentistry so I settled for the B A course since it was by far the easiest at the university in a faculty renowned for the quantity, quality and availability of its women students. I was convinced that I would have ample time to catch up on social activities and on my writing should the spirit move me.

Wits - pronounced 'Vits' - the University of the Witwatersrand, the largest learning institute in the land, was conveniently located less than a 30 minute walk from where we lived in Parktown West. I preferred not to walk, relying instead on the whites-only, red and cream double decker municipal bus service which was very reliable on the Parktown route.

Being a fresher at Wits was no hardship since a number of Marist schoolmates including Dave, Nev and Monty were also there, enabling us to organize spending our summer holidays together in Durban, the closest seaside resort to Johannesburg. This was an ideal choice, marking the beginning of a lethargic, dissolute time for me. During vacation periods Wits students were eligible to rent rooms from the University of Natal's residences at concessionary rates far below those of even the cheapest hotels so we were really well off compared to others of our generation who had to work for their living, had far less vacation time; and could not afford the cost of high season hotels.

The university summer break lasted from early December until the end of February and we stayed in Durban until our funds were exhausted, but even before that, long lie-ins were the order of the day, every day. Then we went to the beach to meet other friends. There'd be between eight and twelve Old Maristonians and their girlfriends basking on bright towels on that whites-only beach, tanning ourselves on the golden sand, either leaping into the sea or frolicking under the fresh water whites-only public outdoor showers to cool off before repeating the cycle.

If there were no parties we went for a meal or visited the bioscope or, best of all, indulged in protracted snogging sessions. It would be difficult to conceive a more sybaritic way of life for lazy teenagers recovering from the academic year at Varsity.

After the war ended in 1945, Wits expanded enormously because, in addition to the normal annual intake, extra room had to be found for returning servicemen who had exchanged their university blazers for battledress. To cope with the increased demand for space at Wits, prefabricated huts sprang up on campus. Overlooking the university's open air swimming pool, the huts were marked with a bold 'T' signifying 'temporary.' T5A was the only noteworthy hut, housing as it did, the student canteen and the Rag office, both much frequented adjuncts to university life. T5A was in fact the hub of the university's social life for me anyway, since I spent more time in there than at lectures or tutorials. Rag office became a second home to me because I joined the Rag Committee as assistant editor of 'Wits Wits' the Rag magazine which, overflowing with exceedingly silly undergraduate gags, was a useful money-spinner amongst the public as well as the student body.

The Wits canteen was never nominated for any Michelin stars but it was an ideal place to enjoy an inexpensive cuppa with friends between lectures; to shelter from inclement weather; or to devote time to the study of an important course absent from the official curriculum but fundamental to the further education of male students no matter which faculty they belonged to. This was the Ancient Art of Poker Playing, where tyros such as myself paid our tuition fees in hard cash. My personal tutors remained lifetime friends but failed to present me with a hard earned graduation diploma.

I often ran out of poker cash in which case I'd drift along to the nearest student Mecca, a local café called Phineas', to play their pinball machines. Here proficient players could *jol* all afternoon by gaining high scores to win free plays. I managed to hold my own against most of my fellow students except for Ian Heideman, a student architect from Port Elizabeth who was the number one pinball player for miles around. He lived with his uncle and aunt at nearby Woodview Road a few minutes walk away from my home in Loch Avenue.

Dave was also a student architect and he, Ian and I became inseparable and took to spending much of our free time between lectures playing pinball.

If we could afford it, we took our dates to Saturday night dinner-dance places like the Balalaika, a romantic candle-lit venue a short drive from the main suburbs. A pleasant night out could be had at a club located at the summit of Northcliff - a high, craggy *koppie* called Aasvoëlkop (Vulture's Head) which had a splendid panoramic view of the lights of Johannesburg. The club, once a film studio, kept burning down regularly, ignited by local vigilantes pissed off by the din of revving car engines and their *poegaai* passengers singing loud, lewd rugby songs every night without respite except for Sundays since the club was closed. But that didn't deter those who drove up for the view from the car park and for risqué wrestling in their motors.

The Coconut Grove in the Orange Grove Hotel on Louis Botha Avenue was another famed Joburg rendezvous where Dan Hill's band's popularity made advance booking essential. The hotel clung precariously to the side of a steep *koppie* overlooking the affluent suburb of Lower Houghton where Nelson Mandela settled on becoming president. Coconut Grove also developed a habit of burning down probably for the same reason as Northcliff and in time the owners capitulated and abandoned the properties to the vagaries of vandals and the weather.

On party free evenings we'd do the movies or maybe the ten-pin bowling alley at the Casablanca Bowling Club at the top of End Street.

The drive-in cinema, an American innovation, eventually reached Johannesburg where it proved a compulsive attraction to me and my friends combining as it did two of our favourite things - a good movie and a *fray*! Now and then we'd visit the ice rink, an ideal place to pick up girls - but more of that presently.

The Dev, real name 'Devonshire Hotel', once owned by Ian Heideman's uncle, had become a thriving den of iniquity akin to a training ground for student alcoholics thanks to the availability of the cheapest booze in the area and the only place within walking distance from the campus to take a girl for a shag in one of its cheap rooms which could be rented by the hour. Happens that long years later one of my second cousins went there on an 'assignment' to find himself accosted by the woman's so-called husband who tried to blackmail him. Being a feisty young man didn't prevent my cousin from being murdered in the fight that ensued.

All these activities distracted me almost totally from thoughts of apartheid's ugliness which was now approaching juggernaut proportions.

Former Marist schoolmates at university included a small contingent of Lourenço Marques boys, most of whom had been unable to obtain places in the official men's residences. They were housed in redundant army barracks at Cottesloe, a relic from the war. The prefabricated buildings, affectionately abbreviated to 'Cot' had originally accommodated discharged servicemen students. As their numbers dwindled by graduating or dropping out, their places were swiftly filled by out-of-towners such as Fausto the redoubtable Marist marbles mogul.

The ex-soldiers were all mature men which meant the authorities saw fit to employ a handful of administrative staff at Cot making it an ideal place for students to live relatively free from supervision. It was here that Fausto again exercised his precocious entrepreneurial panache by converting his room into a mini shebeen providing him with a nice little earner. Almost every student at Cot was a qualified drinker and the old barracks proved a pre-eminent place to carouse with Fausto supplying the booze at less than bar or bottle store prices and, as a result of his stumbling across a wholesale liquor source, his endeavour took off like greased lightning and prospered. At first.

However Fausto was prone to swallow most of his profits so that his only option was to increase his prices. Accordingly the prices spiralled upwards, a fact resented by his impecunious neighbours who set out to teach him a lesson.

It was common knowledge that Fausto had a habit of leaping out of bed the moment his alarm clock went off. One night he passed out, a victim of over imbibing his own liquor. His disgruntled clients pushed his wardrobe into the centre of his room and placed his mattress on top of it before adding the comatose Fausto to it. The finishing touch was to set his alarm to go off five minutes later. True to form Fausto leapt out of bed and in so doing fell to the floor, tilting the wardrobe which collapsed on top of him.

They say that angels protect drunks and Fausto may well have had a flight of them hovering around on standby that night because apart from insignificant bruises, he escaped unscathed except for his damaged ego and his depleted commercial enterprise. As with Richards the pawpaw guy, way back in the Marist dorm days, Fausto ceased trading immediately.

Outré Okes

It was at Wits that I renewed contact with one Jack Sholomir, a nodding acquaintance from the Yeoville Baths. This *oke* was as eccentric as a March hare and, as I was to discover, a man who would crisscross my life from time to time. He and his closest friend Arne Gordon were denizens of the Yeoville Baths who happened to crash parties on the same northern suburb circuit as my circle of friends, only I didn't get to know them well until I left school.

Sholomir was the first of the South African 'flower people'. It was to be at least ten years or more until that subculture was born. Standing no more than five feet eight inches tall, Jack's broad shoulders, stocky muscular build and bellicose stance made him appear even smaller. His thyroid-induced protruding eyes and long hair, relatively untouched by brush or comb years before bushy, unkempt hair became modish, conjured up images of the mythic Wild Man of Borneo, a character he once portrayed while working at a circus side show. Jack displayed all the finesse of a rampant Godzilla on speed. In brief, he was a person who stood out like a sore thumb wherever he went.

Jack regarded himself as an intellectual, believing he was artistic but his inability to live up to his imagined image of himself led to his hanging out with literati in the hope that perhaps he might absorb some of their qualities by osmosis. A clique of unconventional burghers who chose to call themselves 'Bohemians' chilled out at the East African Pavilion, a well-established coffee house in central Johannesburg. How Jack managed to inveigle his way into this group of poets, painters, journalists, actors and musicians is a matter of conjecture. In order to give them the impression that he too was qualified to partake of their pabulum, Jack maintained he was striving to make sufficient money to study law. Verisimilitude took the form of a briefcase which always accompanied him on his visits to the Pavilion until, one day he left it behind and when they opened it to see if his address might be inside, out tumbled its entire contents - an American comic book and a loaf of bread.

Jack was born in 1930 at a who's-ever-heard-of-it place called Thabazimbi near Rustenburg in the Northern Transvaal. His father, a farmer, whose wife's nagging had matured into physical assault, left him no option other than to literally head for the hills where he lived as a hermit for an unspecified number of years. In the fullness of time he returned to civilization to open a small trading store which took off to such a degree that he became very rich. Jack must have fallen out with his father since, he said, he did not benefit from the family fortune in either cash or kind.

Jack's early life in Thabazimbi accounted for his appalling Suid Afrikaner accent which, combined with his slow, heavy asthmatic type breathing made him sound as if his nasal passages were permanently blocked. He blamed it on boxing but no one really believed that. Articulacy was not his strongest suit perhaps due to his brain working too fast for his mouth or maybe it was the other way round. His inability to finish sentences often rendered him totally incomprehensible.

From an early age both he and Arne determined to follow their friend and schoolmate Larushka (Larry) Skikne into show business. You see five year old Larry from Lithuania's parents migrated to Johannesburg and as a young adult he went to London where he changed his first name to Laurence and his surname to Harvey. In his new persona Harvey never looked back. Arne maintained that Larry had

120

wooed and won Margaret Leighton yet all Arne had to show for his (alleged) superior thespianism was a half share in a clapped out lorry he jointly owned with another unconventional character, Hymie Blechman, to pursue their jointly owned scrap metal business in Johannesburg, a business that kept them both out of mischief and off the streets while they sought their niche in life.

Harry Houdini, the splendent Jewish American escapologist, was Arne's idol. Arne unearthed a replica of Houdini's fantastic milk churn illusion which helped him survive financially during 'rest periods' in England while looking for acting work. He and Hymie took it in turns to go abroad while one remained in Johannesburg partly funding the other's quest for fame and fortune.

Arne struck the mother lode by landing the leading role of Fagin in Lionel Bart's Oliver! during its stage run in the Union. This success finally convinced him to follow his star to England where he settled permanently.

Meanwhile back to Jack. Although he passed his matric qualifying him for university entrance it is unclear as to whether or not he was a registered student at Wits. He attended whatever lectures took his fancy and since security at Wits was lax to the point of invisibility Jack's *chutzpah* enabled him to participate in unlimited University activities, including the annual student Rag Week.

No one has yet provided a definitive definition as to why it's called RAG, but the commonly accepted version is that it's an acronym for 'Raising and Giving.' In Wits terms it was the *raison d'être* for students to plunge into the most uninhibited time of their lives by getting plastered out of their minds for a week or more.

Wits Rag Week climaxed on a Saturday morning when the Rag Procession, a colourful carnival of student-built floats, wound its way along a traffic free, police controlled route through Johannesburg's main shopping area.

Traditionally the procession was preceded by a marching band behind which a bevy of nubile, scantily clad 'drum majorettes' led a beribboned open top Cadillac conveying the curvaceous Rag Queen contest winner perched on top of its rear seat to ensure that spectators received a good view of her. Following the Queen's car, a second open convertible carried the two Rag Princesses, runners-up to the Queen. And, as if that weren't enough eye candy, the next vehicle, a gaily decorated open lorry, overflowed with more pulchritudinous Rag Queen also-rans waving as if their lives depended on it.

The parade drew throngs of cheering Joburgers into the city centre. People hung out of the windows of tall offices and apartment buildings showering donations down upon the phalanx of floats.

Every faculty built floats. Some ingenious examples designed by the Architectural and the Engineering Faculties rivalled those of Rio's renowned carnival. These faculties strove to outdo one another with imaginative creations ranging from working scale models of mine headgear to scenes and mechanical characters from Alice in Wonderland, The Wizard of Oz and American comic books. All these were constructed on lorries borrowed from various businesses.

The entire parade foregathered at the Union Grounds, the army parade ground corner of Plein and Twist Street, where they were judged by a panel of celebrities prior to their progress through central Johannesburg. This was the closest Johannesburg ever came to a carnival to rival the phenomenal Cape Town 'Coon Carnival' whose post-apartheid name was, wisely, amended to The Minstrel Capers.

The sheer size of the Wits student body did not enable everyone to be attached to a float and in my fresher year Jack and I joined forces as solo collectors.

My ability to do a reasonable imitation of Donald Duck's voice prompted me to make a crude duck head mask from thin wire mesh and *papier- mâché*. One of Pop's old shirts stuffed with a pillow and a pair of outsize hobnail boots sloshed with bright yellow paint gave a slight clue as to what I was trying to represent. Small kids loved the voice and giggled madly at my rag party piece, which was saying their name in 'duck' a stratagem rewarded by charmed mums depositing a large coin in my tin collecting box instead of the usual average of a penny or *tickey*. Of course the anonymity provided by my mask proved invaluable in befriending young women by talking 'aphrodisiacal duck' to them. Pity I hadn't had the foresight to carry a pencil and paper to record telephone numbers...

In the year of the duck, Jack Sholomir wore a ragged hodgepodge outfit of tatty clothes and a disconcertingly ugly rubber monster mask. His *pièce de résistance* proved to be the hit of the day. He had acquired a mangy, ill-tempered, elderly donkey upon which he proposed to allow children to ride in exchange for coins in his collecting tin. The problem was that the donkey strongly opposed the idea and unseated every child who tried to mount it. Jack tried another tack. He sat on the donkey, hoping to hold on to his small passengers. This didn't work either as both he and the kids were bucked off PDQ. Jack then tried riding the donkey solo evoking applause from the crowds lining the route who thought Jack's continuous falling off the donkey all over the place was an integral part of his repertoire.

As the morning drew on Jack's adrenalin level reached his eyebrows and he rapidly became ever more manic, ever more daring with his acrobatic tumbles off the donkey's back. His collection box was bursting with money including a surprising number of ten bob notes until, spurred on by the most appreciative audience he was to encounter in his subsequent 45 years as an entertainer, he became reckless and the donkey, by now totally nettled by his antics, threw him so violently that he broke his arm and was taken, collection box, donkey and all, by ambulance to hospital.

The next year brought an even more memorable Rag. My parents allowed us to build a float in the garden. The theme we chose was 'Heaven on Earth'. What a great idea we thought - a cloudful of seraphim. All we needed was a cloud on which angels could frolic. A simple wooden framework of chicken wire would be covered with a substantial quantity of waste cotton wool donated by a sanitary towel manufacturer and glued to the wire. No complex plans needed. After all, the cotton wool would disguise all the flaws from our collective lack of basic woodworking and constructional skills. No fuss. No bother. Simple eh?

Because the lorry arrived three hours late on Rag eve, work only began around sunset. No one had had the nous to measure the lorry beforehand and it proved much larger than we'd assumed so we all scuttled about around like headless chickens knocking on neighbours' doors and checking nearby wasteland to find additional wood to extend the frame. Therefore the gluing only began around midnight, the only disadvantage being the stench from the gelatinous liquid adhesive smelling suspiciously similar to Jack's donkey.

More than a few lagers had been downed by the 40 or so students working on the float with their energy levels reinforced by my mother producing a non-stop flow of sandwiches, sausages, meat pies, potato chips and cold drinks.

We packed it in at well past two in the morning and since a lot of the students hadn't arranged transport home and the bus service had shut for the night, most of them slept at 55 Loch Avenue. About twelve of them crashed on the living room floor and another half dozen did the same on my bedroom floor. The hardiest *okes* took their shut-eye in the cellar under my bedroom.

Came the dawn I was first up. I stepped circumspectly over the bodies on the floor to go outside to see what the float looked like in daylight. To my horror it seemed there'd been an overnight blizzard. Every scrap of the thousands of blobs of cotton wool we had so painstakingly stuck to the wire had blown off, transforming the front and side lawns of the house into a reasonable facsimile of a set on which to film Scott of the Antarctic. The float itself was reduced to its woebegone wood and wire skeleton.

It was hard to decide which was more daunting - my parents' reaction to their white lawn or the possibility that we might not be able to take part in the rag parade. I hastily woke everyone and by about 8 am the float began to look vaguely like a cloud, albeit a singularly shambolic cloud. We reckoned we had adequate reserve cotton waste to carry out running repairs en route to the Union Grounds and again, if necessary, the moment we parked there.

The lorry driver, a thickset Afrikaner, arrived on time and shook his head at the sight of our manky float and its weary angels clad in shoddy white sheets. The more enterprising angels wore wings and one or two had carefully twisted wire coat hangers into halos painted gold or covered in silver paper from cigarette packs. We were a highly disheveled, disorganized lot, but off we drove singing ridiculous, meaningless University songs of the sort that stick in your mind for no reason other than their ridiculousness. One went like this:-

> Aye zicker zimba, zimba, zimba
> Aye zicker zimba, zimba, zay
> Aye zicker zimba, zimba, zimba
> Aye zicker zimba, zimba, zay
> Hold him down you Zulu warrior
> Hold him down you Zulu chief,
> Chief, chief, chief...

At which point you stomp your feet vigorously in time to the chant of 'chief, chief, chief,' until you feel like stopping or restarting. Unforgettable eh?

This song and even worse folderols were practiced at sing-songs held regularly at lunchtimes on the terraced stone seating surrounding the university swimming pool in preparation for the other major university epic, the annual intervarsity rugby match between Pretoria's Tukkies (Transvaal Universiteit se Kollege) and Wits. The rivalry between Marist and KES was child's play compared to that between the English-speaking Wits team and the Afrikaners from Tukkies.

123

Back on our Unheavenly Cloud, the lorry had barely reached top gear before the freshly applied cotton wool began to disappear. Banging on the roof of the driver's cab to try to stop it took a while and by the time he'd found a safe place to do so much of the cotton wool had vanished. The monologue that ensued was quite Kafkaesque.

'It stands to reason man,' the driver told us, 'that the faster we blerry well go, the faster the blerry cotton wool blows orf.' He was, he said, approaching a main thoroughfare and would therefore be obliged to travel at least 25 mph. 'Besides,' he added, 'if I drive any slower we'll be late at the Union Grounds.' By now our morale was at rock bottom. But he wasn't finished. He was bent on rubbing it in.

'That glue you used was either too diluted or too old. It needed to dry out for a long tarm to make it stick properly, hey man.'

It was only then that we became aware that the glue had been affected by the heavy early morning dew.

He told us we'd have been better off covering the wire with *papier-mâché* and then painting it white. Dammit his summation was one hundred per cent accurate and we reached the Union Grounds with a very hollow cloud of wire mesh covering the worst example of a wooden frame ever assembled by humans.

The driver exited his cab to stretch his legs. He slowly sneered his way round the lorry shaking his head while the more obstinate members of our team doggedly continued their struggle to add more cotton waste to the mesh but only succeeded in further soiling their white angel outfits.

'Crawst,' observed the driver, 'a gang of bobbejaans (baboons) could of done a better job.'

Regrettably he was again perfectly accurate and had there'd been a trophy for the worst float on parade, correction - ever - we'd have been runaway victors.

We were well aware that most onlookers lining the route couldn't figure out what our farcical float was supposed to be. But it only took a few lagers (more or less) for us to forget our frigging flawed flop of a float and focus our feeble faculties on filling our tins with finance.

Soon after the Korean War began in 1950, South Africa sent a squadron of aircraft to fight for the United Nations. A bunch of students resolved that we too wished to be included in the action so we volunteered for service at the recruiting office at the Drill Hall opposite the Union Grounds.

Two weeks later we were bussed to Voortrekkerhoogte (Voortrekker Heights) near the huge, ugly monument built as a tribute to a huge, ugly philosophy. At the nearby military base recruits underwent medical tests. Once we had completed some forms, we were ordered to strip naked except for the towels presented to us to cover our privates. There we sat in a shivering row in a draughty room awaiting our turn with the Medical Officer.

'Next!' he called. My turn had come. I stood to attention in front of the officer's desk. Having observed what happened with others we all knew the procedure was to remove our towels and wait until the M O was done with his notes about the previous recruit. He carefully blotted the ink with a curved thingamajig before being confronted by his first view of my genitalia dangling at him.

'*Yirra* man!' he exclaimed, 'Wot have we got yere?'

I preened with pleasure at his appreciation of my widely admired bollocks, trying hard not to overplay it.

'C'mere,' said he, beckoning me to move closer and to his side. As soon as I was in range he grabbed my balls with his ice cold rubber gloved fingers, squeezed them, and then stuck two of his fingers up into my scrotum.

'How long,' he asked, 'have you had this, hey?'

Unsure as to where things were leading I stammered, 'I've always had them sir.'

He was too busy writing to say anything other than, 'OK. Go get dressed then come back and see me again.'

I returned from the changing room curious about my treatment compared to all the others who'd each been poked and prodded for several minutes. None of the other ten guys he'd examined had been sent away to dress.

'Ah.' he said, 'take this.' He handed me a letter. 'Give it to your family doctor OK.'

I queried this and was told I had a rupture probably caused by lifting heavy weights...

'Hmph,' I thought, 'thank you Achille.'

After Dr. Freed examined me, he sent me to hospital where my left inguinal hernia was repaired and my genitals returned to their original format. The surgeon disclosed that it wasn't my testicles that were abnormal. The size was due to a puncture in the lower body cavity where an intestine had ruptured a weak point in the gut wall, pushing itself down into my scrotum. So, at long last the secret of my bollocks was solved and all the pretentions I'd cherished about my super masculinity disappeared. As had my flying career which had ended before it began.

However, one of my school friends, Brian Singleton, who'd been with us on the bus to Vootrekkerhoogte, made it and flew with South Africa's Squadron in Korea winning medals and accolades in air battles that killed 34 of his fellow pilots.

I had always nursed twin yearnings - to fly aircraft and to drive motor cars. Joseph, a good natured but lazy black bloke who'd worked for Pop forever, turned out to be my mentor. It was maybe because I'd passed him toys I'd tired of for his kids that he liked me sufficiently to risk his job by teaching me to drive in Pop's delivery van.

Tuition took place in quiet back streets after Joseph had finished his deliveries or had dropped my mother home early from the shop, he'd leave the van at the house and take the family's Chevrolet into town for Pop. Now and then Joseph let me drive it as well so that by the time I was sixteen I was competent enough for Joseph to allow me into traffic.

Had Pop had but an inkling of this furtive tutoring he would probably have taken an apoplectic fit and/or fired Joseph because the last thing Pop needed was his son abusing his vehicles. Not that *he* looked after them and apart from filling up with petrol at weekends he seldom, if ever, checked the oil, water, battery, tyre pressure or servicing. Joseph mostly saw to all that.

Pop was an easy-going father who never upbraided me over below par school reports. Nor did he punish me physically even after I'd committed unforgivable acts of impropriety like mooning and nicking his cigars. His way of registering serious displeasure was to stop my pocket money for as long as he felt necessary - a far more painful, longer lasting retribution than a sound wallop on the backside.

All things considered, Pop respected me as an individual and I admired him unstintingly for his restraint but the main bone of contention between us was my use of either his car or the van. He had not forgotten my escapade with his van all those years ago and had doubtless experienced continuing nightmares about my solo down Joel Road. Not even passing my driving test first go during the week of my eighteenth birthday influenced Pop's mind about my borrowing either of his vehicles except in dire emergencies or on celebratory family occasions. Johannesburg public transport was woefully inadequate making it abnormally awkward to get anywhere minus wheels. But although Pop was very possessive about the vehicles he occasionally let me fill up and check the necessary for him, a task I volunteered for hoping to make amends for my childhood misdeeds, but these overtures were in vain and not once did he reciprocate by offering me the occasional use of the car in the evenings. I felt this was dog-in-the-manger behaviour since his working day always started at 5 am and accordingly he was too tired for evening outings during the week.

Mom frequently championed my cause by lobbying Pop on my behalf, but her successes were few and far between and only granted under protest in order to stop her nagging.

Uncle Jack, the printer, usually changed his car biennially and after Pop's ancient Chevrolet was stolen it luckily coincided with my uncle taking delivery of a new car and he sold Pop his low mileage two-tone fawn and brown, right hand drive Oldsmobile from the USA. I regarded this magnificent vehicle as a status symbol of sexual potency among the girls I dated. The only problem was the rationed use thereof, a situation which did not remain a long-term problem since his firstborn had a personal key cut without his father's knowledge and often used his car but only if circumstances guaranteed it was safe to do so. Friday nights were perfect since they were time-honoured poker nights at our home.

The house itself stood at the curved end of a U-shaped driveway with wide wooden double gates at the top ends of the U. To one side of the house was the garage where the Oldsmobile languished, uselessly gathering dust. Since Pop's

Friday poker schools were sacrosanct I could always rely on 'borrowing' the car without his knowledge. Before I took it out I disconnected the odometer to make one hundred per cent certain that the gauge showed the identical mileage level it was at prior to my removing the car.

On Pop's return from work he invariably parked the van close to the garage doors making it essential to shift the van to get the car out. My praxis was to take the Olds from the garage on Friday evening well ahead of Pop's homecoming. I'd leave it round the corner at the house where Ian lived with his aunt and uncle. I then walked back home for dinner. Thus the car was available for the night and was returned to the garage on Saturday morning after Pop left for work in the van.

This worked smoothly enough until one fateful Friday night. I was in the bathroom preparing for my evening out. I heard a gentle knock on the door. It was my faithful confidant Enos who whispered that he'd heard Pop on the phone to one Uncle Jack (I had two uncles of that name) who was unwell and therefore the poker school was cancelled and Pop was going to visit him.

This was shocking news. The unthinkable had happened. My dilemma was how to return the car to the garage with the van blocking its way. I had no key for the van and although I had occasionally reversed the van out of the way to help Pop access the Oldsmobile, that night he refused my repeated offers to lend a hand by insisting there was no problem as he wasn't in any hurry. Being too much of a coward to confess in person, I asked Enos to tell Pop that the Olds would be outside the house next door.

Neville's father was far more obliging with his car so I telephoned Nev to scrounge a lift for me and Ian in his dad's black Chrysler and we went to the Johannesburg Girls High Schools inter-school swimming gala at Ellis Park, not so much to witness the sport but to check out which of the schools had the most fetching females but I paid scant attention to the plenitude of pulchritude being preoccupied about the vituperation I knew awaited me when I got back.

How right I was. On my return around midnight the house was lit up like a Christmas tree.

Normally, if anyone was out late, the only lights left on were those on the stoep and the inside passageway. Not tonight Josephine! We had two bedrooms and two living rooms facing the street and all the lights in all the rooms blazed angrily at this wayward son.

There were five of us in Nev's Chrysler. Naturally my companions knew what deep excrement I was in and while they were sympathetic and consoled me with pledges that they would be mourners at my imminent funeral carrying bunches of whatever flowers I cared to nominate, it was all tinged with a degree of sarcasm. They even quibbled as to who should inherit my address book by playing rock-paper-scissors. The seconds flew by and soon passed the midnight mark at which juncture Nev felt it wise to be on his way in order to adhere to his father's imposed time limit. Reluctantly I opened the car door and off they drove, sardonically waving goodbye.

Despite the hot summer's night I shivered as I made my tardy way to the stoep. I fumbled for my house keys as I went up the four steps but I didn't need them as the front door opened, seemingly of its own volition, and my father stepped out wearing his pajamas and dressing gown and the fiercest look I had ever seen. He stood there breathing heavily, glaring at me. There was no rehearsal script for a scene such as this. I had this mental image of sparks flying from his eyes. I had no idea of what to do or to say.

Nor could I guess what he was going to do or say until he shouted, 'My son's a thief!' His nostrils flared and his lips curled. Suddenly he swung back his right arm as if to hit me. To my eternal regret I instinctively lifted my arm to protect my head. His slap, aimed at my ear I think, appeared to be a clenched fist. My reaction timing was excellent and I jinked swiftly, intending to deflect his blow away from where he'd aimed it... Instead his hand bounced off my arm and connected his head.

But he didn't see it that way. He was incandescent.

'Strike your father', he roared, 'you bastard!'

My brainless, ill-considered riposte was regretted almost before I uttered it. 'You should know,' I blurted. At which he turned away silently, speechless, and went into the house without even slamming the front door. In all my young life my father had never, never ever, struck me or threatened to strike me for behaviour unbecoming. He was too gentle a human being to engage in physical violence and this was the first time he had ever raised his hand against me in anger. Even as I type this, over 65 years later, in my mind it is, and was, analogous to viewing a television replay over and over and over again.

What had incensed my father was that Enos - who was saving up to buy a zoot suit to go with his massively expensive Fedora hat - had, sensibly, been disinclined to jeopardize his job by giving Pop my message about the car with the result that when Pop moved the van and found the garage empty he'd rushed inside to summon the police.

On arrival they started taking details of the missing vehicle and Pop described the make and the two-tone colours. One of the cops said he'd observed a car matching that description in the street outside the next door house ... and yes, there it was, exactly where I'd left it. It was not merely my dishonesty that made Pop lose the place; it was the embarrassment that he had suffered.

There were other ways that I could have handled the situation if only I'd had the balls. Pop didn't speak to me for about a month and I had, of course, destroyed any chance of borrowing the family car in the foreseeable future. I only wish I'd had the courage to confess my misdeed before leaving for that gala.

My crass fatuity left me no alternative but to acquire my own motor vehicle. Finances did not permit anything other than a banger and the one I bought lived up to that description in more ways than one. I took possession of a British 'Flying Standard' which cost all of twenty borrowed pounds. The eponymous 'standard' itself was a tiny enamel Union Jack emblem on the front of the bonnet. The attributes of my little black two door 1021 cc rattletrap were its sliding sun roof and the way it could be forced to backfire by turning the engine off then rapidly on again. The resulting explosions were preferential to, and far more satisfying aurally, than the pathetic sound of its own hooter, which was something like a cross between a constipated castrato and a seasick soprano, but. Additionally it was completely ineffective trying to summon friends when calling for them without having to leave the car. The bang method was perfect for that and highly effective at warning tardy pedestrians to dodge away pronto. Little did I realize that my ignorance was buggering the tappets which were obsoletely irreplaceable. To have new ones made would have cost as much as the car itself, making it essential to find a replacement.

This time my only affordable choice came in the shape of a virtually indestructible, improbably speedy second hand Ford Anglia which was to convey me from Johannesburg to Port Elizabeth in under nine hours' driving time which elicited a letter of commendation from Ford of South Africa.

With the aid of a generous loan from Mom, I was, at long last, able to purchase my first brand new car, a Citroën Light Fifteen. This motor was a delight to behold. I'd only previously seen them in France where Citroëns were undisputed queens of the road. They had only recently started gracing South Africa's tarmac. Mine had wide tapering mudguards, even smoother and more streamlined - so it seemed to me - than its predecessors. The colour was an imposing metallic silver, shot with a sparkling rich red tint if sunlight hit it at certain angles. The inside was quintessentially French - stylish red leather seats, a gear shift lever built into the lustrous polished wood fascia housing laudably clear instruments... I still nostalgically retain the memory of that Citroën which was for me Chambertin, Chanel, Champagne and Brigitte Bardot all rolled into one. I was so proud of it that I had bespoke silver initials fixed to the front doors. One day after completing its regular chamois rubdown I stepped back to admire it glistening at me in the early morning sun. Happens a discarded tin can lay in the road detracting the perfection I was enjoying so, in order to remedy that I kicked the can away. Only it didn't go where I'd expected but bounced off the street brushing the duco, leaving a mark smaller than an average comma. But to me it seemed as large as Nelson's Column and was enough to send me into mourning for the rest of the week.

The most unforgettable journey the Citroën ever made was from Johannesburg to Durban where Nev and I were to be pole holders at Monty's wedding. Our girlfriends had also been invited. On fetching Nev he produced this giant box containing his wedding gift - a complete dinner service. One thing Citroën designers hadn't taken into account with the Light Fifteen was boot space, and what little it had was filled by two smallish suitcases. The result was that Nev and his lady endured the eight hour drive sharing lap space with the dinner service. Nothing daunted they snogged away blissfully for over seven hours. The return journey was more felicific for them without the dinner service to impede their enjollyment.

Nev, Monty and I had previously made that self-same journey to Durban in my Anglia. Whilst traversing the Drakensberg Mountains at night there had been a mist so heavy that we had to take it in turns to walk in front of the car with a torch to allow the driver to negotiate the twists and turns of the tortuous bends.

Dave Bean, another friend from Wits, a car fanatic if ever there was one, took to rebuilding an old MGB with the aim of racing it. He persuaded me to join the Sports Car Club of South Africa to participate in their hill climbs. From there to racing the Citroën was a logical progression and although my car wasn't fast enough on the straight, its superb front wheel drive roadholding on corners usually meant finishing in the first five or so. But I wanted go one better than that and Bean's motoring contacts helped me acquire a brand new Triumph TR2, one of the first two in South Africa. As it was capable of over 100 mph on the straights it wasn't long before I won a few heats and even managed to finish in the top three in handicap races held by the SCC at the disused Palmietfontein airport. Motor racing was an expensive avocation costing at least a set of tyres per race day but the problem soon ended thanks to the steep slopes of adjacent Johannesburg *koppies* between the southern suburbs and Kensington in the north.

Visibility was good and my familiarity with a road I had often travelled enabled me to judge the time it would take for the traffic light (known as a 'robot' in Southern Africa) at the crossroad at the top of the hill to change in my favour. Certain I'd be through it with time to spare I gunned the accelerator to catch the light. I was not to know that all four traffic lights were stuck on green and another driver equally unaware of the faulty light was also accelerating and our timing could not have been better if we'd been stunt drivers on a movie. My car was t-boned by his. The impact cracked my chassis and both cars were write-offs. We were very fortunate to have survived a pretty serious accident and although the insurance companies paid out, that smash nullified my motor racing ambitions.

Pop was a remarkable man of great integrity and indubitably the most honest person I ever knew. When I collected my allowance at the shop he'd take change from the till (cash register) and carefully record the amount. He was equally thorough with his accounts.

But for his honesty and his gambling Pop may well have become super rich because Eddies bloomed into a small gold mine thanks to his enterprise and astute bargaining skills. At no time did he ever cheat anyone out of anything. I did not realize how honest he was until long after he died my mother disclosed the story about him and a bent hospital administrator. Shortly after South Africa entered World War II, Pop was approached by the man who appointed buyers for edibles for all hospitals on the Witwatersrand. He'd heard of Pop's business acumen and wanted him to handle the acquisition of all fresh produce for the hospitals under his jurisdiction.

The offer would have made Pop the biggest buyer, by far, at the Johannesburg market and his business turnover would have increased substantially. Pop went to discuss details with the official whose brief to him was for him to keep his eyes open for good value for money. Payment would be twelve and a half per cent of the price of invoiced goods.

'That sounds fine to me,' said Pop.

'Ja,' replied the man, 'that's ten per cent commission for you and two and a half to me. In cash.'

'I don't quite understand...' Pop paused. 'Let me get this straight. You want two and a half per cent returned to you in cash? You're paid a salary aren't you?'

'Ja, but *luister* (listen) man, I have to ...'

Pop was not a violent man but he stood up, knocking over his chair, leaned across the desk, grabbed the guy by his lapels, hauled him out of his chair and shook him as a dog would shake a rag doll.

'You lousy bastard,' Pop shouted, 'there's a bloody war on. Our boys are getting killed in the desert, and you want me to help you get rich at their expense!'

'But, but...'

'Don't say another word,' said my father, 'and if I hear that you make one single farthing this way, I'll report this conversation to the hospital authorities and the police.'

And out he stormed.

Only once did my faith in Pop falter. Over the years he was amicable towards all my girlfriends with whom he often had long friendly chats. Except for one who perhaps he thought I was becoming too fond of. Or perhaps he just didn't relate to her.

At the time I was in my second year at Wits having transferred from BA to first year BSc where I was kept busy dissecting dogfish and frogs pickled in formaldehyde, with fresh rodents thrown in for variety. A pass would have resulted in my being accepted into second year dentistry or medicine. One of Pop's wealthier acquaintances happened to be on the lookout for a suitable match for his daughter and, believing I was destined to become either a dentist or a doctor, he promoted me straight to the top of his potential sons-in-law list. I was totally unaware that he had discussed a fulsome dowry with Pop.

I suppose I should have sussed that something was afoot when Pop took the exceptional step of offering me the use of the car on Saturday nights before broaching the possibility of my meeting his friend's daughter who wanted advice on university life or some such and, it would be appreciated if I would have a chat with her about it. I could hardly turn him down since he even agreed to foot the bill for an evening out with her.

Sensing that my date was bound to be a spoilt Jewish princess, the imp in me opted for Pop's business van in preference to the car since I wanted to witness her reaction to being transported in a malodorous van prominently proclaiming in bold logo emblazoned at the sides and back that it belonged to Eddies The Fruiterers.

She turned out to be a pleasant enough, slightly plump young woman clearly destined to evolve into a buxom Yiddisher Mama. She was well worthy of the mental note I made to encourage her to become one of my patients after I graduated if only to treat her halitosis and straighten the teeth of a brood of children which I confidently predicted she would produce well in advance of my graduating as a dentist. Her breath wasn't quite as overpowering as the perfume in which she must have bathed.

I collected her from an upper crust Lower Houghton home and I must hand it to her - she didn't bat an eyelid at my choice of conveyance. 'Oh what fun,' she said gamely as she heaved herself up into the van. We went to the movies and then on to the northern suburbs' post-bioscope rendezvous where I knew I'd probably meet friends with updates of parties to crash.

The Doll House on Louis Botha Avenue which was - and still survives as such over 60 years later - a drive-in restaurant serving toasted steak sandwiches and excellent banana malted milkshakes so thick they could not be consumed with the outsize drinking straws supplied until the ingredients thawed sufficiently to suck it through them making gratifying slurping sounds. Some mates who spotted the Eddies van came over to say hello and passed on details of a party to visit after I'd dropped off my date.

I couldn't figure out why Pop enquired how I'd got on with her, a question that was another first for him. Decades later Mom revealed that the date had been arranged in the hope that I might marry her because her father had promised Pop a dowry consisting of payment of my university fees, a new car and an expensive block of twenty deluxe Flats Facing North.

The girl Pop didn't like? My first wife.

Both my parents believed that property investment was the yellow brick route to prosperity but lacking Vorenberg's entrepreneurial ability they had no success in that arena. I remember being taken with them to view a splendacious house in Yeoville called 'Chip Chase' which occupied an entire block and even had its own tennis court. As Mom loved tennis maybe Pop felt that investing in such a home might keep her away from the shop, so he too was keen on it only they procrastinated a tad too long, losing out to a developer who easily outbid them for a house that trebled its value within five years.

Pop acquired a small, single storey, disused hospital in Auckland Park. He had it converted into ten flatlets which were rented out at reasonable rates. His tenants were all on low incomes and not averse to midnight flits to avoid having to pay overdue rent. Pop tolerated this for as long as he could but his bond (mortgage) repayments soon exceeded his income forcing him to chuck in the towel and sell the property. This proved to be a misfortune for the family because years later the South African Broadcasting Corporation erected their 30 floor television and radio headquarters less than half a mile away triggering the transformation of the area from a sleazy, rundown neighbourhood into a gentrified media enclave where property prices rocketed.

But who am I to criticize my parents about property deals? Having noticed the way Johannesburg was expanding in the early fifties I chose to invest my modest savings on a small parcel of undeveloped land, about a quarter of an acre in a new suburb rejoicing in the name of Berario. I had a choice between two 'stands' as the plots were known locally. I viewed them both, chose the cheaper one and paid a deposit of half the asking price of £100, with the balance due in affordable installments of £2 per month. It was not until I wanted to sell it prior to leaving South Africa that I discovered why my stand had been so cheap. I'd bought a frigging swamp.

Prophylactics

Prophylactics, today's condoms, were always a botheration for me and my mates. In truth they were the ultimate embarrassment for young men in South Africa's narrow minded, prudish society. Condoms were commonly known as 'effells' (F L's short for French letters) or frenchies, or skins, or johnnies, or rubbers. Condoms were only available in packets of three, exclusively from chemists so that if you entered one with a female behind the counter, you'd feign shopping for a comb, or hair tonic or, well anything, rather than suffer the ignominy of actually asking a woman for contraceptives. Those brave enough, or desperate enough to do so always elicited a witheringly raised eyebrow plainly reading, 'You're the second arrant sex maniac I've served this week.'

But the cavalry was on its way thanks to my friend Mike - he of the aspirin and coke experiment - opting to become an apprentice pharmacist, thereby eliminating our embarrassments and the purchase of unwanted merchandise. His pals undertook lengthy detours to beat a path to Bregy's Pharmacy in Beit Street where Mike was serving his apprenticeship. Come to think of it that job turned Mike into the most popular guy in our circle.

My parents were very generous to me. To a fault. Their 21st birthday gift was a student tour of Europe due to depart just days before my birthday in December. Several friends who were coming on tour entreated me to buy frenchies for them from Mike in case they got lucky enough to lose their virginity abroad.

I'm assured that my premature 21st birthday bash was memorable. Had I not imbibed in an excess of brandies and coke I would be pleased to précis the evening but alas, all I readily remember, apart from a wretched hangover, is that we had a full house brimming with friends, family and members of the gate-crashing circuit which was fair enough since I knew 'em all from parties our crowd had crashed. Those who arrived sober and suitably attired in collar and tie were admitted to the speech-free celebrations. Apart from a brief pause to sing Happy Birthday after I'd clumsily extinguished my candles, we got on with the drinkin' and dancin' 'til dawn, at which time I remembered to open my numerous gifts among which were two neat parcels from Mike. The one in bright birthday wrapping revealed a quality zip-up leather writing case and t'other, in plain brown paper, contained 24 tins of Sheik.

The night before the boat train left for Durban where I and a number of other Wits students were to board ship, I went to a party with friends. On my return home in the wee small hours I immediately knew that an event of significance had again happened because, yes - all the lights on the porch, in my bedroom and the two interconnecting front living rooms were still on. This time there was no angry personal greeting awaiting me so I turned off the lights and went to my room wondering what it was that I had done to be accorded the blazing light treatment. I soon found out.

There, strewn across my bed were 24 orange condom tins with their distinctive black edging and the illustration of a haughty desert Arab astride a horse - far too small for him - toting a huge, suggestive, ornately engraved Jezail musket. Appropriately named 'Sheik' after the world famous silent film starring Hollywood's most illustrious lover, Rudolph Valentino, in his immortal portrayal of a randy desert lothario, the packaging unmistakably promised its purchasers erotic pleasure. Apart from the Sheik brand, in those days condoms were anonymous and did not feature the portraits of individual members of a British boy band called JLS. Had he known, dear old Rudolph would doubtless have somersaulted in his grave.

My mother, bless her once more, had wanted to surprise me with an extra ten pounds planning to secrete two fivers in Mike's writing case in which I'd placed not only my currency, my tickets, and my passport but also the entire contents of Mike's second parcel. Mom unzipped it to insert the two fivers, whereupon the condom tins cascaded all over the quilt. In the middle of the scattered tins lay a missive scrawled in an angry hand which simply read 'I am disgusted. Rita.'

It was the first and last time my mother ever signed herself to me with her first name.

The matter was never again raised by her - not even once - for the rest of her life. Sorry Mom, they weren't all mine. Lady Luck wasn't that benevolent.

The Grand Tour of Europe, South African style, is, or was, in the nineteen fifties, the NUSAS tour, NUSAS being the acronym for the National Union of South African Students. Shortly before the off Jack Sholomir (the donkey dingdong) dialled my number to thank me for my birthday booze-up which, he claimed, he had attended.

'Could you,' he asked, 'possibly let me have any spare NUSAS labels?'

These were very large, very bright red, gum backed stickers with NUSAS printed in heavy black letters for quick identification of students' luggage. His answer to my query as to why he wanted them was that he was 'starting a label collection.' The next day he picked up two spares from me.

My NUSAS journey began at Johannesburg station. We had a choice of embarking on our ship, the Union Castle liner Winchester Castle from any of South Africa's four main ports. Durban was closest so most Transvaal students embarked there to avail themselves of the opportunity to view the southern coastline of Africa from the sea.

The station platform was jam-packed with friends and families of the students whose parents could afford to fund so rare a pilgrimage. Just as the guard's whistle blew shrilly Jack bustled through the throng to say goodbye. The train had its first spasm and pulled out with Jack waving and calling, 'See you in Cape Town!' I did not give this another thought.

The voyage between ports was enhanced by a superabundance of marriageable maidens, enrolled on the tour by parents who regarded their investment more as a husband hunting expedition than a voyage of cultural discovery. The gallant male students were instinctively aware of this danger so that instead of snaring a husband a lot of the girls only succeeded in losing their cherries almost as soon as they boarded ship at the start of the four day cruise from Durban to Cape Town.

True to his promise, there, on the Cape Town quayside waiting to meet our ship, was Jack, who'd been lucky enough with his thumb to have made a thousand mile hitchhike from Johannesburg in a mere two days. He asked if he could leave his knapsack in my cabin - tourist class cabin number 537 - as he had nowhere else to put it. I had no problem with that. Or so I thought. Jack revealed his plan to hitchhike around the world, starting from Cape Town. He proposed to obtain the signature or mayoral seal of the mayor of all the important cities he visited. The Mayor of Cape Town was to be the first on his list. Would I, he asked, care to go with him to the Town Hall that morning? My curiosity got the better of me and off we went. En route we picked up a couple of chirpy Capetonian chicks who accepted our invitation to join us.

At the Town Hall Jack engaged the urbane uniformed doorman in an earnest parley and, surprise, surprise, we were soon ushered into the Mayor's Parlour where the secretary had Jack follow her into the Mayor's private office. She took in a tray of tea and biscuits while the girls and I sat there awaiting the outcome. Ten minutes later Jack emerged, triumphantly waving his autograph book replete with His Worship's signature. He also flourished a separate, handwritten message on headed mayoral notepaper wishing him success with his venture and duly rubber stamped with the Cape Town coat of arms.

Next day, just before departure time, Jack materialised on the main deck to wish the few he knew and many he didn't, bon voyage. Days later someone told me he had expressed the hope that he would see each of them very soon.

The ship's loudspeakers instructed visitors to disembark and shortly afterwards the gangplanks were removed and, blowing evocative farewell blasts of its foghorn, the Winchester Castle was tugged away from the quayside precipitating the release of hundreds of paper streamers thrown down by passengers on deck to well-wishers on Duncan Dock.

The Technicolored, spaghetti link between ship and shore soon stretched past breaking point and the strands cascaded gently down to the surface of the ocean where they fleetingly rode the wash before drowning.

As our liner eased her way languorously out to sea, passengers remained on deck until the unforgettable vista of the unparalleled Table Mountain, elegantly exhibiting its wondrous 'tablecloth' of snowy white clouds, disappeared below the horizon. We were well and truly underway. Next stop Madeira! Or so we thought.

I went to my cabin where, to my dismay, I found Jack lounging on my bunk studying a Superman comic. At first I was lost for words. In response to my question as to what he thought he was doing I received a broad grin, 'I'm stowing away,' he told me.

The penny dropped. Now I understood why Jack had wanted those NUSAS labels.

I shivered slightly. 'Not in my cabin you aren't.' He gave me a breathless argument that he might be locked up and why, he asked, couldn't he stay in my cabin as no one would know about him and I could bring him food from the dining room now and then.

'That,' I emphasized, 'is not on. In any case I don't think my cabin mate will take kindly to your sleeping here.'

'What am I going to do then?' he whined.

I made it plain to him in no uncertain terms that he was to go straight to the captain to inform him that he'd come to collect his ruck sack and had fallen asleep from exhaustion and was, of course, prepared to face the consequences. Jack expressed doubts about the captain accepting such a yarn so I told him to concoct his own excuse. A lengthy debate led to his agreement to give himself up. I was enormously relieved by his departure but seconds later he returned.

'Will you look after something for me?' he asked, groping round inside his rucksack. To my horror he produced a small handgun.

'Rightho,' I replied, taking it from him while opening the porthole.

He was shocked and upset when I tossed the pistol out of the porthole while assuring him that was the safest place for it. He skulked off with his rucksack and I didn't hear from or about him until the next morning, bright and early, he materialized on the sundeck with an expansive smirk to disclose that the captain had refused to allow him to work his passage to England but had allocated him a bed in the ship's hospital and a seat in the crew's mess area. He was cock-a-hoop at being granted the freedom of the tourist class section of the ship.

From then on Jack busied himself scuttling here, there and everywhere organizing things. Whether or not they wanted his clumsy attention no passenger was too old or too young, too unattractive or too good looking, too slow, too fast or not fast enough to escape Jack's bumptious, self-appointed agenda. He took charge of everything, from deck quoits and bridge tournaments to collecting entries in the daily lottery for the closest guesstimate of the number of sea miles sailed in the past 24 hours. Since he took his meals with the crew, passengers assumed he was working his way to England until he began winning prizes for activities judged by ships' officers.

During the time-honoured crossing of the Equator ceremony the role of King Neptune's assistant was played by - right, you guessed it - Jack Sholomir.

Next day there was an announcement advising passengers that anyone wishing to send mail to South Africa should place it in the ship's mailbox by midnight.

Jack disappeared.

Rumours abounded. The ship was abuzz with excited speculation. They were going to make him walk the plank. Naah that was wishful thinking. They're going to cast him away in a small boat. Naah, too expensive. Keelhaul him. Naah too complicated. They'll lock him away. This is exactly what they did.

Neither Sherlock Holmes nor Dr. Watson were required to deduce that the captain had arranged for him to return to South Africa and that the call for mail was directly related to the strong possibility of Jack's impending departure. There was no future in quizzing the crew who had doubtless been sworn to secrecy but word quickly flashed around that a lifeboat was being readied.

The equatorial sun had only just begun to blink good morning as the ship's engines slowed down and our vessel stopped in mid-Atlantic. Normally there was no one about at so unsocial an hour but on that morning every passenger on board was up, crowding the decks to the extent that our ship seemed to be listing to starboard. About half a mile away another Union Castle liner, the Pretoria Castle steaming towards us from the north was slowing down to the acclamation of all our passengers. Its decks were as crammed as ours and as the vessels hove to the volume of approbation from the passengers of both vessels at such skillful navigation could doubtless be heard in Timbuktu which we guessed was the nearest city to where we were in mid Atlantic, about half way to Southampton.

A shout that sailors were boarding a lifeboat led to a passenger stampede towards Number One Lifeboat in which Jack sat wearing his distinctive blue and yellow-striped Witwatersrand University blazer and a straw hat with matching hatband. It being the festive season, he was clutching one of those Christmas novelties with bright paper streamers stuck to one end of a short piece of dowel which he waved vigorously at us. And his audience vigorously waved back. Hundreds of cameras clicked merrily away as the lifeboat began its slow descent from its davits into the relatively calm Atlantic Ocean on our vessel's starboard side

Jack had been positioned alongside the master-at-arms to whom he was handcuffed. Eight strong men rowed Jack and a stack of mailbags towards the Pretoria Castle. The lifeboat bobbed along and soon reached its destination. There Jack was jerkily winched upwards in a canvas harness. As soon as the mailbags had followed suit the lifeboat turned away and came steadily back to its mother ship sans mail, sans Jack and his knapsack with my red NUSAS labels stuck on it.

Our paths were destined to cross again on my return to South Africa, but Jack always refused to discuss the subject with me and it was only by talking to his erstwhile friends that I was able to piece together what had subsequently happened.

His treatment on the journey to Cape Town was far harsher than he'd experienced on the outward voyage. He was not allowed to mix with the passengers and had a six pm to six am curfew imposed on him. Police escorted him from the docks and shoved him in a cell until the following day's court appearance before a magistrate. He refused a *pro bono* solicitor, opting to defend himself. We can only speculate on the magistrate's reaction to this wild looking, long-haired hippie weirdo appearing in front of him wearing a university blazer. The outcome was a ticking off and a suspended sentence. My guess is that the magistrate harboured a degree of admiration for Jack's exploit which undoubtedly made a welcome change from the usual petty misdemeanours swamping apartheid courts of law. The judge could not previously have dealt with cases as noteworthy as this and Sholomir the Stowaway unquestionably provided him with an ideal conversation piece in the magistrates' common room. After all not many people could stop two ocean liners synchronously. Not even Superman.

Our ship anchored at Funchal, Madeira's port, where passengers were allowed ashore for a while. We'd heard of a famous brothel called Madame Jesus located near the dock. None of us had ever been inside a knocking shop and most of the men looked forward to the visit.

A friend called Ivan - *not* my cousin of the same name but one who cannot be afforded a pseudonym, for a reason to be revealed later, was due to celebrate his 21st next day. Since he was still a self-confessed virgin I determined to splash out on a gift he would remember all his life.

The ladies all sat about Madame Jesus's ornate reception room redolent of a Toulouse Lautrec painting. Her damsels were a mixed bag, some old, some medium and some who looked as if they might have to hurry back to school as soon as the nocturnal high jinks ended. I identified one I thought might suit my shipmate and following my causerie with Madam Jesus in person I paid the five pound fee, took the girl's hand and led her to Ivan.

'Happy birthday mate.' I said, 'Here's your pressie.'

His eyes opened wide as he stammered breathless, unfathomable words of pretended protest as the tartlet escorted him coyly up the staircase to her bedroom. I bought a drink for Madam Jesus and tried to have another talk with her without much success seeing as how almost the entire NUSAS male contingent had, by then, found their way to the brothel so that Madam J was rushed off her feet choreographing the comings and goings of her girls' perambulations in and out of the boudoirs with their clients. The waiting patrons from our ship systematically emptied the liquor supply at the bar where the price of drinks had doubled since I arrived. Then I heard Ivan's voice. 'Ed! Ed!' he called, leaning over the top of the banister grinning like a Cheshire cat, 'have you got another fiver on you?'

To the strains of a gramophone loudly playing 'Sarie Marais' assorted launches conveyed us back to the Winchester Castle. We'd all had a fantabulous evening. Especially Ivan.

The turbulent final leg of our voyage had passengers and crew donating their dinners to Davy Jones during gales of hurricane force sweeping across the Bay of Biscay. We didn't know at the time that we had encountered the fringes of the worst storm there for 75 years. It sank seven ships, heavily damaging others including the Queen Mary, a far larger liner than ours. The protracted storm entered the maritime hall of fame because the skipper of a stricken ship refused to abandon his severely listing vessel until the very last moment before the vessel, Flying Enterprise, its hull cracked by a 30 foot wave, sank into the depths of the angry Atlantic. The captain, Henrik Carlsen, had remained aboard the doomed vessel until its ten passengers and forty crew members were rescued by an American navy ship. Miraculously only one person died and that was from exposure. Captain Carlsen's bravery captured front page headlines, newsreels and radio coverage throughout the world.

The NUSAS itinerary organized by the UK's National Union of Students travel department was unparalleled. On arrival at Southampton, we were met by NUS representatives who supervised our coach transfer to London's Cranston's Kenilworth Hotel near the British Museum. We were each presented with a kit containing stamps, air mail stickers, tickets for a ballet, a concert and a performance of *The Winter's Tale* starring John Gielgud, Flora Robson and Diana Wynyard at the Phoenix Theatre. Afterwards we were taken backstage to meet the leads who were all most affable and not in the least patronising. Flora Robson was particularly gracious and I had no way of knowing that one day I would work with her and be invited by Dame Flora, as she was to become, to her Brighton home for tea.

Also included in the NUS kit were bus and underground (tube) maps of London, a copy of *Vogue's Gastronomic Guide* to the city and an envelope containing English currency totalling two pounds nine shillings and sixpence broken down as follows: Seven lunches at three shillings & sixpence (3/6) each = one pound four shillings and sixpence. Four dinners at 4/6 each (four shillings & six pence) = 18 shillings. Fares during sightseeing, seven shillings (7/-).

Cigarettes were expensive, nearly four times more than the duty frees at sea. In the shops they were a shilling more for twenty than they were in South Africa.

The *Times* newspaper was threepence with the Daily Mirror half that. Savile Row tailor-made suits were under £18. The best seats in theatres were sixteen shillings or you could queue outside the theatres, on folding rented stools if you preferred not to stand, to buy unreserved gallery seats for one and six. Tap dancing or violin playing buskers provided entertainment for the waiting theatregoers.

Unlike South Africa where our movies always started at specific times, London cinemas ran continuous screenings of back-to-back feature films without the supporting programmes we were used to in Johannesburg. London's mini cinemas charged a shilling to view around an hour and a half of cartoons, comedy shorts and newsreels.

Until I visited Britain I had but a sketchy idea of the immeasurable scale of adversity endured by its civilians during the blitz. Much of the appalling evidence remained and boarded up bombsites could still be seen here and there. Cosmopolitan though London was with its plethora of theatres, dance halls, coffee bars, museums, art galleries and wondrous shops, it suffered from a discernible lack of colour not solely attributable to the lousy weather but to the dearth and outrageously high cost of good quality clothing.

The people too were grey, the shade of grey you see in hospital patients who hadn't breathed fresh air for a while. Doubtless the overall British pallor could be attributed to the years of privation and inadequate nourishment.

The more I spoke to people about the ruthless, remorseless bombing inflicted by the Luftwaffe, the more I admired the indestructible Cockney wartime grit and wit that still prevailed. Bus conductors all sounded as if they were radio comedians as did the market stallholders, particularly those at Petticoat Lane where we were treated to the badinage of Pearly Kings and Queens as the costermonger traders were known. They wore outfits with hundreds of mother-of-pearl buttons sewn all over them in imaginative patterns. Their scripts were even better than those of the infamous 'spivs' with outsize kipper ties, trying to palm off cheap Japanese replicas of famous brands. One of our group bought what he thought was a bargain price Parker pen only to discover - too late - that there was an almost invisible dot between the P and the A making the pens P.Arkers.

All paper sellers, shop keepers and publicans were cheery experts on every subject known to man. Miserable exceptions were to be found underground where grey zombies rode up and down, down and up all day on endless conveyor belts like dun-coloured bottles en route to having crown corks plonked on the heads of those devoid of bowler hats.

The tube system was nothing short of incredible to us South Africans. For a penny ha'penny we could travel about five miles beneath the bustling city in five minutes.

A group of us spent New Year's Eve at the Hammersmith Palais where two bands provided nonstop music for 5,000 dancers. No drunks, no fights. Happy 1952!

Our British schedule included three free days which allowed me time to travel to Bulwell near Nottingham in a remarkably shabby British Rail train reeking of tobacco, sweat and tears. My journey was to meet distant cousins Pat and Bill Townsend, a homely working class couple who fitted the description 'salt of the earth' to a 'T.'

Throughout the war years my mother had regularly mailed food parcels to them. There was no such thing then as airmail between South Africa and Britain resulting in lengthy delays to private parcels and correspondence which had to wait until spare space became available in ships transporting vital war supplies to Britain. It could take six months or more before we heard if our parcels had escaped the Atlantic U-boats.

Mom sent them canned butter, jam, corned beef, chocolate, sweets, biscuits, sugar, and dried and crystallised fruit. To ring the changes she once included biltong hoping to augment our cousins' sparse meat ration. Except that the cousins had never heard of biltong. Nor, for that matter, had anyone else in Nottingham. The outcome was that a year and a half later, Mom received a letter thanking her for the latest parcel adding 'P.S. over a year ago we planted the roots you sent us. Maybe England is too cold because nothing came up.'

I explained to them that biltong is as quintessentially South African as roast beef is British and that it is made from raw, lean venison, preferably springbok thighs, cut into strips, heavily spiced, salted and sun-dried by the Voortrekkers to sustain them on their long wagon train journeys lasting months into unknown territories, tiding them over until fresh meat became available by bartering or hunting. This dark, dried-blood coloured delicacy could easily be mistaken for black drift wood. It was ages since any of us had as good a giggle as we did about the 'biltong roots.'

Seven years had passed since the war ended yet the Brits were still subjected to severe rationing and meat, bacon, dairy products, tea, sugar and sugar products still required ration certificates. I didn't fully realize how seriously deprived they were until breakfast when I was served a hardboiled egg with my tea and toast. My cousins' five year old son Tony stared goggle-eyed at me while I ate it. I gave him half and his face lit up. I later found out that I'd breakfasted on a quarter of the family's total egg ration for the week. I made up for it by using all my tourist ration coupons to buy them a supply of sweets and chocolate that was in excess of their entire annual allocation.

The lad followed me into the bathroom where he stared intently while I cleaned my teeth. I asked him why he was staring and he told me he had never before seen a toothbrush! Later we went shopping and I bought him his own 'teefbroosh' and a tube of toothpaste which I suspect he actually ate. Or maybe his tummy upset that day was due to a surfeit of sugar from all that confectionery. 'Addie', he smiled, 'you're loovelley.' I unashamedly confess to a large lump in my throat. My letter home resulted in further parcels of nourishing goodies from Mom to Nottingham. Sans biltong!

Back in London I traced another long-lost family member Harold Law, one of Reska's two brothers. He invited me to meet him at the Automobile Club in the West End where I swam with him in a borrowed cossie in their heated indoor pool. This too was unfamiliar to me as it was the first time I'd ever seen an indoor pool let alone swum in one. Then he wined and dined me and invited me to attend one of his court cases the following day. That sounded very promising. It took place in the hushed, echoey caverns of the awesome Royal Courts of Justice. Truth to tell I'd envisaged a juicy criminal trial along the lines of those marvellous courtroom movies. Disappointingly, criminal cases don't happen there but at the nearby Old Bailey instead so I was obliged to listen to bewigged barristers conducting a polite conversation about tree roots and overhanging branches between two suburban gardens.

Years later after I'd settled in England, my cousin Pam visited London and took me to meet Aunt Bea Law, my mother's eldest half-sister, for the first and only time. She was about 90 then but looked twenty years younger. Time had not been as kind to her memory as it had to her physical wellbeing and she kept calling me Harry, thinking I was my father!

The NUS had laid on whistle-stop tours of the paramount unmissables - Hampton Court and Windsor Castle one day with Buckingham Palace, Westminster Abbey, Downing Street, and the Houses of Parliament augmented by a real, live Member of Parliament as our guide, the next, not forgetting a NUS New Year's Eve shindig in between. Then, soon afterwards, a coach trip to Cambridge and Ely overwhelmed my mind and left even the blasé, toffee-nosed members of the tour with a sense of veneration and appreciation of Britain's heritage.

Europe was substantially bigger than anyone had thought and furnished us with an abundance of wonderment. So much so that we wished we'd had four months instead of four weeks to try to absorb it all but the fleeting glimpses reinforced my determination to see much more of Europe in the future.

Paris was another dream come true. It is a difficult place not to fall in love with. It was bright, colourful and positively effervescing with champagne bubbles of *joie de vivre*. The women were bodacious and plentiful. How I wished Marist Brothers College had taught French instead of Latin.

We'd all led stultifyingly insular lives in South Africa and Paris, being our first contact with genuine continental sophistication, proved light years more stimulating than I could ever have surmised. It was here that we began to shed the shackles of the intolerant attitudes of South African whites and the oppressive government that controlled us. It was here I first saw black people sharing the same lifestyle as whites. OK, London had a smattering of black folk around but in France they mingled freely with white people which was most pleasurable to observe. Oh, in case you hadn't guessed, there was not one solitary black South African on that tour.

Taxi fares in Paris were cheap, but that was about all. It took a while to come to terms with service charges demanded by the busty, belligerent women attendants in men's lavatories whose frowns and Gauloise tobacco coloured teeth made you queasy enough to go back into the WC to be sick. We were told five francs was the average gratuity but when one of our colleagues mistakenly handed over a 500 franc note and asked for change, the madam swore he had only given her five francs. Obviously he was greatly miffed that no one sympathised with his expensive lesson.

Our Parisian sojourn started on a high note for four of us who drew the lucky straw in the bedroom lottery at the Hotel Palais D'Orsay where we were allocated a sizeable, well-appointed room affording a splendid view of the river Seine from its balcony. It had its own en-suite bathroom. In London none of the hotel rooms had private bathrooms and we revelled in our Parisian plumbing, inviting less blest close friends in for hot baths. It was so unusual that I drew a plan of the accommodation to mail to my parents. I wrote each guy's name on the bed in which he slept. One of them was Ivan - he of the Madeira bordello. At first I was puzzled by my mother's terse question in her reply to my letter. "Who's Nan?' she asked. I realised I'd printed the name IVAN in block letters. The 'I' was too close to the 'V' making it look, to Mom's suspicious mind, exactly like a capital N. In view of the condoms on my bed I very much doubt she believed my story that it was an innocent typographical error.

An organized NUSAS outing included a coach tour of Paris night clubs, each providing free liqueurs - green crème de menthe for the men and purple parfait d'amour for the ladies, who were conjointly TT. The men, loath to waste all that free alcohol, ensured that it wasn't. If you have not binged on either of those two liqueurs, be advised and do not risk it unless you are prepared to undergo the most abysmal crapulence on earth.

The *Folies Bergères* proved underwhelming. Mediocre performers failed to match the sumptuous costumes and fabulous stage effects. What with heavy, acrid Gitanes smoke choking us, the milieu was neither as exotic nor as oolala as we had anticipated from a theatre with so charismatic a reputation.

The official tour ended early and a clutch of us set out to explore Montmartre's darker side by wandering about seeking we knew not what. We frequently bumped into other NUSAS groups with whom we exchanged meagre information none of which amounted to anything interesting until a Frenchman called Pierre - what else? - harpooned us. 'Wanna see live exhibition?' he enquired. Silly question. Of course we did. I mean live sex shows were unheard of in South Africa. Problem was, we told Pierre, we students couldn't afford his quote. Pierre resolutely tagged along with us reducing his figure ever so slightly as we wandered aimlessly around Place Pigalle haggling with him until it dawned on us that if we could round up extra NUSAS students to share Pierre's price we'd be able to see his show. We told him what we wanted to do. It was a chilly night and business must have been very slow because, surprisingly, he agreed to our proposal if we kept the number under twenty, hokay?

Off we went in search of stragglers and by the time we returned to the rendezvous with Pierre there were fifteen of us following him into a sordid tenement block. We climbed rickety stairs to the third floor landing where we waited while he went into an apartment saying he had to ensure that his stars were ready for us. All we could hear was the muffled sound of rapid fire French. Minutes later he came out asking for the money. In his absence we'd all agreed that we would only pay at the end of the show. Pierre recognized we were serious and resentfully herded us into a downright seedy, musty bedroom barely large enough to contain everyone.

Apart from an iron bedstead in the centre, the room was empty. Pierre knew his attempts to express himself in French was a waste of breath, so, drawing himself up to his full height and taking a deep breath, he proclaimed, circus ringmaster style, to his men-only audience, 'Laddy an gen'man, Colette et Claude!'

He then tapped on the door whereupon a middle aged duo in dressing gowns almost as ancient as they were, pushed past us to reach the bed. They removed the bath robes to reveal bodies well past their sell-by date and as sexually provocative as a plunge into the Arctic Ocean. She was as stout as he was skinny and whoever whispered 'Jack Sprat' accurately summed up all our thoughts. They began to caress one another in a desultory fashion and would not have shed their knickers had Pierre not instructed them to get on with it but it was all too apparent that neither of them was aroused by the other and we'd paid to see 'em at it. The woman understood full well what we wanted and started to caress her co-star's testicles. But all that stood up were his goose pimples and it wasn't until she embarked on giving him a gamaroosh that he managed a semblance of an erection so we resumed our earlier chant 'Get 'em off, get 'em off, 'get 'em off...' so she removed her bra and out tumbled a blubber of unsightly flab. This seemed to further dampen lover boy's ardour and we decided en masse to leave and let them work things out without us. Our spokesman told Pierre that we'd been brought here under false pretenses and we were leaving and would only pay a quarter of the agreed price. Pierre wasn't too keen about this unforeseen turn of events and mumbled something to the effect that his regulars had been detained and the stand-ins (stand-ins!) on the bed were the apartment owners who always did the warm-up but his star had now arrived and would proceed to entertain us 'Immédiatement hokay?' OK, we agreed, but if it was as half-hearted as the first act, we were off.

Pierre again banged on the door. In shimmied our top of the bill in a very sexy transparent negligee. This was more like it we felt, wonder what she does? Happened she was a talented contortionist who writhed sinuously around that bed provocatively removing fishnet stockings, her bra and tantalisingly slowly, her briefs, all to the accompaniment of scratchy gramophone music coming from the room next door. She showed off her body from angles we had not, in all our young, relatively innocent lives, have believed possible. We considered that probably only anatomists or gynaecologists could have seen as much of a woman's anatomy as we did that evening. After a while she stopped writhing and indicated that she wanted a cigarette break. Immediately all the smokers proffered their packets. She took her time in choosing a brand she fancied, settling for a cork tip. Immediately a dozen Zippos sparked into life. The lady took a long, leisurely drag and exhaled even more slowly. Before her next puff she opened her legs wide and asked, 'Wanna see pussy smoke?' With one voice, as if rehearsed, all fifteen of us chorused 'Yesssss!'

She took a huge drag at her fag then inserted it in her vagina. She flexed some secret internal muscles somewhere, causing the tip of her cigarette to glow bright red. She serenely savoured our expressions of awe which increased tenfold a few seconds later as she slowly discharged the smoke from her cunt. We applauded this with the enthusiasm such talent deserved. She leant back on the pillow took a long double draw i.e. oral and vaginal, then exhaled synchronously from both orifices, a feat which prompted even louder approbation, whereupon she opened her legs and began to pat her pussy in a blatant invitation to jump on in. No one moved a muscle. We were all mongooses hypnotized by a cigarette smoking cobra. One of the older members of our gathering, a post graduate student, indicated that he would sample the goods on offer whereupon Pierre advised us in his fractured Franglais that the show was over. We paid him in full and left satisfied that we had witnessed everything there was to see in this life.

I doubt anyone forgot that night in Montmartre, particularly our colleague who'd stayed on for 'afters' that included a nasty case of crabs which, to coin a pun, bugged him for the rest of the tour. On the return sea voyage weeks later, the only way he got any relief was by having sympathetic friends drag him by rope round and round the ship's small saltwater swimming pool.

From the gorblimey to the sublime Louvre for inordinate platonic pleasure. None of us had ever seen original classic oil paintings, yet here we were, in an immense museum housing thousands of the finest masterpieces in the world among its three million works of art as dizzying as the immortal names - Leonardo, Uccello, Vermeer, Rembrandt, Watteau, Michelangelo, Raphael... There seemed no end to them and the half day we were allocated was months too short.

We beelined to the *Mona Lisa*, taking it in turn to check on the story we'd heard about her eyes being able to follow those of the onlooker. For some they did. Others scoffed. The painting stirred much debate as we wandered off happy to have seen it but very disappointed by its size of 30 by 20 inches which was far smaller than I, for one, had expected. About five minutes later one *oke* suddenly squawked '*Mona Lisa? Mona Lisa!* Where is she?' He'd been standing in front of the painting for over ten minutes without realizing what we had all been looking at and discussing. This same oaf was deeply underwhelmed at Versailles in the staggeringly spectacular Hall of Mirrors - probably the most famous room in history - complaining that he'd expected an accumulation of those funfair distorting mirrors. Definitely a few sandwiches short of a picnic, but then he was from an inferior university.

For sheer opulence and extravagance of scale Versailles provided another mind blowing experience making us acutely sorry to have to leave for Florence where we were dazzled by the Ponte Vecchio, the Campanile, the Opera House, the Pitti Palazzo and the Uffizi, housing works of art any one of which would have made the visit worthwhile.

The highlight of the Roman leg was the colossal Coliseum second only to the grandeur of the Vatican City, the smallest sovereign state in the world. Here the Pope lives in the splendour of one of the largest, most immoderate palaces ever built at a cost beyond imagination, funded and maintained, in part, a large part mind, by the contributions of millions of Catholics living half a loaf of bread away from starvation. The Vatican has over a thousand rooms and no fewer than twenty courtyards. I couldn't help wondering what percentage of my Marist college fees had been donated towards its upkeep. The ceiling of Michelangelo's Sistine Chapel defies description. We were there for two hours or so. In my opinion it needed at least that number of months to begin to take it all in. The amount of consummate nudity depicting both sexes, predominantly the ignudi at which the homosexual genius excelled himself, made me wonder how the Vatican clergy managed to remain celibate surrounded by so much raunchy painting and statuary. I also wondered how often the Pope prayed there.

I counted my own blessings. So much to see, to savour, to enrich lifelong memories. I mean how many young South Africans had ever seen the Pope, let alone spoken to him? OK, so maybe it was because the interpreter told him I had been a pupil at a Marist Brothers College that he beamed at me benevolently in Italian (or was it Latin?) - and blessed me. I grinned back, wondering if his beatific smile would have been quite as broad had he known I was Jewish. My thoughts turned to the Brothers at my College. I doubt if any of them had been to the Eternal City and I couldn't help wondering what they might have sacrificed to be where I was on that sunny winter's day in Italy. The resemblance between His Holiness Pope Pius XII and Cossack was so remarkable that they could have had the same mother except that the Pope had a gentler, far kinder demeanour. He then consecrated a boxful of medallions bearing his likeness and had his minions ensure that all 133 of us received one. I treasured mine until an elderly, staunch Catholic friend in Johannesburg contracted cancer. I gave her the Pope's medallion in the hope that it might help her - which it did - but unhappily it only improved her mental state.

Next stop Venice, Queen of the Adriatic - another wondrous city encompassing St Mark's Cathedral and its piazza, the Doges' Palace, the Bridge of Sighs and freezing gondola and ferry journeys on the Grand Canal.

The Swiss Alps were overwhelming for those of us who had neither seen nor experienced snow. Johannesburg winters had occasionally brought a few flakes with it but not all our comrades were from the Witwatersrand and the intense enthralment of seeing and handling it provided an exultant frenzy of fun.

We'd been booked in at Pontresina, a quaint winter sports village not far from its brasher famous neighbour San Moritz which it rivalled for both friendliness and facilities. Our hotel, the Engadinerhof, nestled alongside an open air ice rink and those of us who could skate helped our companions stay upright.

Skiing took a mere dozen falls before I got the hang of it on the nursery slopes where I qualified for two proficiency badges in the week we were there.

By far the utmost Pontresina thrill was the sled run, which I think had been designed for toboggans. I reconditeup the steep path to queue for repeat runs down this curved wall of compacted ice about six feet wide and hundreds of yards long with some sections angling downwards at forty-five degrees plus.

The sledger ran flat out towards the launch point hugging the wooden sledge (today made of metal and renamed the 'skeleton') and dived head first over the starting line with it. Goodness knows how fast it went. Estimates were over 70 mph for an exhilarating, hair-raising ride. It didn't take long to work out that the additional weight of extra passengers would increase the speed. We got round to experimenting with up to four of us on one sled. It didn't always work, as one Old Maristonian, Bokkie Livshitz, discovered when three of us leapt on top of him. We took it for granted that his yelling was of adrenaline jubilation but at the bottom of the run we found out that we'd lost the sled and had made the descent entirely on Bokkie's back by which time poor old Bokkie was almost frozen solid and had to be wrapped in blankets and assisted, as carefully as we could, trying to stifle our jocularity while escorting him to the hotel's roaring log fire. A stiff brandy seemed to buoy him up while he thawed during an examination by a doctor who found nothing more serious than bruises and minor grazes. He felt Bokkie was very lucky to have been let off quite so lightly.

Sleighs were a different matter. These horse drawn vehicles can carry three passengers. You're wrapped in fur against the weather and I was all prepared for a romantic snuggle with my NUSAS girlfriend until one of her plain friends spotted us and inveigled her way into the sleigh with us. I was the meat in the sandwich between the two and remain too much of a gentleman to relate what happened beneath the blankets as the horses jingle belled their way through the snow on the journey to St Moritz and back.

The hotel fancy dress evening was ruined for me by boils developed in my armpits by a new material marketed as 'genuine parachute nylon.' According to the advertising, it dried out almost immediately after washing and needed no ironing making it sound ideal for travelling so I'd taken a few along with me. The disadvantage with nylon was that it didn't 'breathe' like natural shirt materials and as soon as I replaced them with plain old fashioned cotton shirts my boils disappeared.

Thanks to overdoing the alcohol at the fancy dress party none of us remembered how we got from Pontresina to Holland where my grandfather David Naar was born and bred. Following the exertions of Switzerland's winter sports indoors and out, everyone needed an early night but our group determined to check out the sleazier side of Amsterdam's nightlife and at the end of an early evening reception given for us by the South African Ambassador we scurried out and managed to 'do' five clubs before succumbing to the Dutch beer and singing our boozy way back to the hotel.

In the morning our hangovers accompanied us to the Rijksmuseum to admire Rembrandt's *'The Night Watch'* - a giant painting about fourteen across by twelve feet high with life size characters. The use of light and shade is astonishing. We were also booked in at a concert featuring Eve Boswell, South Africa's favourite Hungarian singer performing her effervescent toe tapping repertoire.

Typo correction
Page 148 2nd sentence Line 2
Delete 'reconditedup'
Insert 'trudged up'

Amsterdam was very important to me. Here I visited Anne Frank's home. And after innumerable telephone calls, I traced and spoke to members of my grandfather David Naar's family who lived in Den Haag, The Hague. The tour itinerary did not allow time for a visit them but it was wonderful to know that a few of my Dutch forebears had survived the Holocaust.

Holland was where we were shocked to hear that King George VI of England had died on the 6th of February 1952 at the early age of 56. We dearly wanted to see him lying in State on our return to London a few days later. A number of us went to Westminster Hall but the thousands of mourners waiting in line put us off so that we never paid our personal respects to the Last Emperor of India; and the First Head of the British Commonwealth.

On the 14th of February 1952 our ship set sail for South Africa. Speaking personally I spent my first twelve hours at sea trying to digest my adventures but the time had not yet come for me to resist challenges like the drinking contest in which entrants each put a fiver into a kitty entrusted to a nominated non-contestant whose job it was to ensure fair play, to settle the drinks bill from the kitty and to pass the money left over to the winner, the last man standing. I'd underestimated my own capacity and was only the third or fourth runner-up out of twenty contestants.

Our ship, the Athlone Castle, was due to stop at Madeira that night but being behind schedule, only disembarking passengers went ashore. It seems that before I passed out I'd extracted a promise from mates to waken me as soon as the ship dropped anchor to allow me to buy my mother one of those fancy Madeira tablecloths that resemble a quantity of holes sewn together, from the vendors who boarded our ship from small launches.

On force-focusing my hung-over eyeballs next morning I found my cabin choked with piles of worthless junk. There were bunches of bananas, two toy guitars, a horrid wooden carving and a few sets of baby clothes. I wondered what had possessed my cabin mate to buy such a load of *drek*. I started to dress but couldn't find a shirt so I borrowed one of his and went to find out why the guys who'd promised to wake me hadn't done so. My cabin mate assured me that they had woken me. He told me I'd wandered round telling the vendors I had no money while bartering my shirts for the accumulated rubbish in my cabin. Fortunately, my good friend Ivan who knew how badly I wanted a cloth for my mother had bought me one in appreciation of his coming of age gift.

Two-Timer Or Was It Three?

At the Cape Town docks the ship's loudspeaker blared out an announcement that the person meeting me would be at the quayside ticket office. My heart sank. It had to be Jack. On reaching the office I saw no one I knew. Another of Jack's pranks? Then a voice greeted me with a big hello. There stood Arthur, my millionaire Uncle Harry's driver, who told me my blind uncle wanted to see me - sic! This was puzzling as my uncle wasn't exactly renowned for his sociability. Evidently my mother had mentioned I was returning from Europe and he told her he'd be in Cape Town at the same time and suggested that maybe he would meet me. To my astonishment he invited me to travel with him on the journey back to Johannesburg in his car. Having never before seen the famed Cape Garden Route I gladly accepted his unprecedented magnanimity.

He and I relaxed in the back of his plush American limo while his secretary/mistress, travelled up front with Arthur. Uncle Harry even paid my overnight hotel bill. On our return to Johannesburg, Arthur dropped him off and I went in to say hello to Aunt Minnie. Then Arthur drove me home and left with a big tip and a bagful of goodies from my Mom. I got on very well with Arthur, a man of mixed race, whose surname no one ever knew and who was always referred to as Arthur Vorenberg. His presence had swiftly jolted me back to the reality of the curse of apartheid when we stopped overnight at an hotel where Arthur was forced to sleep in the car because the hotel was not allowed to cater for non-whites. Indeed, it reminded me that there were no hotel facilities anywhere in the country for non-whites.

Arthur often brought my aunt to visit us and I occasionally gave him toys and books for his kids. Although he was required to be on call 24/7, he was very content with his lot as his boss rarely went out at night.

Uncle Harry must have taken a shine to me or maybe he felt he should get to know his first grandson's godfather slightly better and he invited me to call in at his business. I did and was ushered courteously into his office by his secretary who poured tea for us and left. Uncle Harry fumbled in his desk drawer for a tin of Benson and Hedges cigarettes, an expensive imported English brand. The distinctive red tin had only one cigarette in it and I wasn't going to take the last of a blind man's ciggies so I turned it down, lit one of my own and went round his desk to light his for him. He hadn't closed the drawer properly and there, inside, I glimpsed several unopened tins of Benson & Hedges. Vorenberg had become notorious for his ploy of producing a tin containing but a single fag secure in the knowledge that his first time visitors would decline, as I had, to take a blind man's last cigarette. The minute they left he'd replace a single fag in the empty tin in readiness for his next caller. No one could calculate how much his cigarette trick had contributed towards his first million.

I had always kept an open mind about him and his reported financial foibles until, years after I migrated to the UK. Vorenberg had bought the Eloff Street property block where Pop rented one of the shops. It was then that HWV's barefaced avarice surfaced. You see Polliack's, a major electrical goods store next door to Eddies wanted to expand and made Vorenberg a mouth-watering offer to rent Pop's shop to them. This led Vorenberg to increase Eddies' rental so colossally that my Pop was forced out of business.

Pursuant to so incredible a European journey my home town seemed even more humdrum than before. To further complicate matters; during my absence fate had taken a turn for the worse for me. Two turns in fact. You see, I suffered from this overweening superiority complex apropos women, considering myself to be the answer to every maiden's prayers - a failing I attribute to my mother whose ambition it was that I should meet and marry Princess Margaret, the only woman she regarded as sufficiently worthy of being number one in line of succession to the post of her son's wife.

Prior to NUSAS I had two girlfriends. Renee, who lived in Orange Grove, was a tall, slender, brunette with wonderfully expressive, dark, sparkling, doe eyes. This stunning young woman radiated poise and elegance but was definitely not the sharpest intellectual knife in the drawer, a petty imperfection which did not diminish my feelings towards her one iota.

Anita, the other lady in my life, lived in faraway Durban. She too was bewitching and indubitably the most cultured, intelligent young woman I knew. She had a dazzling smile blending beautifully with her warm, soft voice. If I'd had to choose between those two exquisite creatures I would have found it an impossible task.

Regrettably the problem resolved itself in a downright unforeseen manner thanks to my indulging in a highly devious act prior to my departure for Europe. I sent a request to Springbok Radio, the national commercial radio station, to broadcast a farewell message to 'The most wonderful girl in the world' then I told both ladies in my life to listen in for my personal greeting on that station.

What I didn't know was that Renee's brother had visited Durban on holiday and happened to meet yup, Anita. And yes, he mentioned that his sister's boyfriend happened to be in Europe and how thrilled she had been to hear a radio message from him to 'the most wonderful girl in the world!'

And yes again – back in Johannesburg Renee's brother naturally discussed the 'coincidence' with his sister, thereby effectively ending both relationships. Serves the blighter right I hear you say. And I agree you're damn well right!

It was just as well I spoke to Dave before calling Renee to tell her I was back. He had promised to look after her for me while I was in Europe and had taken her to the movies where a newsreel report filmed in Cape Town about the NUSAS tour was being screened. I wasn't on camera but the ship was and Renee jumped out of her seat, wild with excitement, loudly declaiming 'My cookie's on that boat...' That was of course before her brother returned from his holiday. The next time Dave telephoned Renee her mother picked up enquiring if he was a friend of mine and on his answering yes the instrument had been slammed down.

As if losing two girlfriends was an insufficient penalty to pay for my impropriety, my 'return to Joburg blues' were aggravated by a lady with whom I'd had a modest affair on tour. She came from an unusually affluent family and I found myself being patronized by her socialite friends, to wit, those at her private tennis club. But I didn't fully appreciate my situation until we went on a water- skiing outing to Vereeniging, on the Vaal River, where a pride of her brother's handsomely athletic male cronies demonstrated their expertise zigzagging along, jumping over wooden ramps and, in one case even somersaulting in mid-air - while displaying sparkling, pearly white glistening smiles befitting toothpaste ads - as they effortlessly glided through the huge sprays of water which their skis forced into the sky.

Being able to ski on snow in addition to a picayune amount of surfboarding in the Indian Ocean made me moderately sanguine about emulating their efforts. Hmm... I clutched the bar attached by a long rope to the speedboat. The rope tautened far sooner than anticipated as it jerked me away from the shallow water of the starting position. All the instructions I had been given by a guy I thought was being supercilious were immediately forgotten as I realised that I was travelling at high speed under the muddy brown water swallowing most of the foulest tasting river on earth. Fortunately I let go of the bar. I was nearly drowned by the time the boat returned to collect me. I was mortified by my pathetic performance. My morale was further diminished on being told that I had been coached by no less a personage than the South African water-skiing champion. The censorious look of opprobrium I received from my female companion finally convinced me that I was not the guy for her. She subsequently married one of the less intelligent old Maristonians and helped turn him into a billionaire hotelier. That's life innit?

On the NUSAS voyage home I realised that I could not, in all conscience, continue to sponge off my parents, wasting my father's hard-earned money. For once in my life I curbed my baser instincts and determined to take on a measure of adult responsibility.

The first step was to drop out from Wits and find employment. I dearly wanted to work in the film industry but the problem was there wasn't one to speak of in South Africa. The only film production company per se, African Films, produced a weekly newsreel called African Mirror in the mould of the po-faced, albeit worthy, Gaumont British News - i.e. moderately interesting but mostly monotonous. Ah yes, they also made 'Filmlets' the local name for cinema ads. Apart from a few supremely awful Afrikaans language 'musical comedies' featuring a local celebrity of Lebanese parentage called Al Debbo, indisputably the ugliest man in movies after Quasimodo, that was about it in terms of feature film production in South Africa. A man called Harry Stodel had entered into partnership with Isidore W Schlesinger the doyen of local movie producers and distributors. Between them they kept a firm grasp on the distribution monopoly they had established. Stodel was vaguely related to my mother but steadfastly refused to grant me an interview for a job at his studio at Killarney.

I was hunting for any sort of creative occupation, only these were thin on the ground and I lost count of the number of interviews I had and details of jobs I tried have evaporated except for a few highlights.

Monty's Uncle Morris owned a modest whites-only funfair which roamed the provinces with simple mechanical rides and a few sideshows. School vacations and public holidays were particularly busy times for Uncle Morris who gave me one of my first paid jobs by putting me in charge of the 'Tricolour Darts' gambling stall at one of the shows he held on the shores of the Johannesburg Zoo Lake over the long Easter weekend break.

At the far end of my oblong stall was a large board with coloured diagonal stripes. Red and blue stripes at even money were equally wide while white at half their width paid two to one. Punters laid bets on their chosen colour on a shelf at the throwing counter six or seven feet away from the target. One strapping *oke* placed a significant bet of maybe five shillings on white. His dart landed exactly between the blue and the white and, considering it to be more advantageous to Uncle Morris' finances, I called blue. A punter who had won on blue cheered, sparking off a heated shouting match between him and the brawny guy who unhesitatingly vaulted over the counter to examine the board for himself. He considered my call questionable and presented me with a punch up the bracket, thereby demolishing my career as a showman.

My B.A. Fine Arts year at Wits hadn't been a total waste as it provided me with credentials for a sortie into the art world as a commission-only dealer. I travelled through the bucolic backwaters of the Transvaal and the Orange Free State with a carload of oil paintings by young, up-and-coming South African artists whose names escape me but who displayed high regard for the Great South African Outdoors by expressing themselves with strong, stylish brush strokes and bold pigmentation befitting the austere vitality of the landscapes they captured on canvas.

To accommodate my paintings the rear seats of a company car were removed to allow as many as 25 framed paintings to be jammed in for me to take to tenebrific towns and villages dispersed in secluded out of the way locations dotted hither and yon. The idea was to approach the headmasters of rural schools for authority to exhibit 'important paintings' in the school hall if indeed the school boasted a hall! Country schools had limited space and the paintings were hung in classrooms and corridors. The deal was that the school would be paid a percentage of my sales. The children took invitations home in the hope that some parents would show up at my one night stands.

The head teacher, often the only teacher, in the small schools I visited, occasionally turned the evening into a social gathering by laying on tea or coffee with biscuits paid for by the parents. The head would introduce me and recommend that they should quiz me about the paintings and painters. The problem was that people who lived so far away from cities were mainly farmers who could ill afford the luxury of oil paintings so that sales were minimal. My Afrikaans improved but I can't say the same for my bank balance since my income barely covered my expenses. If those who bought them held on to them they are probably blessing the night they met me because the pictures will have appreciated a hundredfold or more. I wish I'd invested in a couple for myself.

Much of my employment among the quirky inhabitants of the Johannesburg business world proved decidedly peculiar. Take Mervis Brothers for instance, a manufacturing, wholesale jewellery business where, having frequently worked in Pop's shop on Saturdays during school holidays, I strove to emulate his admirable art of chatting up people. Well, women mainly. I regarded myself as a good salesman, as salesmen go and I was very polite to customers. Both my bosses approved of that. They were a strange pair of short, shy, stressed-out souls with sort of leathery, rubbery, permanently perturbed faces that looked as if they'd been sculpted by clumsy kids using plasticine trying to copy Grumpy from Disney's Snow White. Not that either of them was grumpy, they just appeared that way. One had a zookie eyeball so out of synch with its neighbour that having a conversation with him proved acutely disconcerting with one eye looking east while the other pointed north.

You may have gathered I had no interest whatever in the prospects of remaining in so dull a business with its lingering metallic pong from the grinding and polishing machines in the workshops next to the walk-in safe at the rear of the shop. As far as I was concerned, it was a time killer during my ceaseless quest for something challenging. Customers were infrequent, allowing me to spend a lot of time daydreaming. Since I had the least foreign sounding voice on the payroll, I was put in charge of the telephone until tedium tempted me to answer the telephone with the words 'Nervous Brothers, good morning.' The rascal in me dictated that I should continue to amuse myself by repeating the same phrase again. And again. And yet again. In fact every time I answered the phone. Not once did any of the callers catch on - nor did either of the brothers. It took weeks of innumerable incoming calls before a jolly lady co-worker cornered me and told me she knew what I'd been saying. She refused to accept my denials. From then on I listened carefully to what she said if she answered that blower before I got to it. If I was too far away to hear her conversation, the conspiratorial smile she shot me confirmed that she was at it as well.

I resigned from Nervous Brothers on good terms to join Forget-Me-Not Greetings Cards who paid me quite reasonably to call on shops to re-stock their display fittings. Oddly my sales were predominantly to chemist shops. My only other remembrance of that dead end job was a message from the office to ring a Mr. Skweppies. My detective work revealed that the call was from Schweppes the mineral water people.

The words Electronic Applications sounded as up-to-date as tomorrow except... the company turned out to be manufacturers of steel kitchen cupboard units, chrome plated chairs and Formica topped kitchen tables. Business was buoyant since conventional wooden kitchenware faced the hazard of insect infestation in a country where infestations of insects flourished whereas Formica and steel were impervious to *goggas* as well as being far easier to clean than wood. I got on so well with the director who interviewed me and vice versa that the Monday following my Friday interview found me reporting for duty at their factory near Germiston, just outside Johannesburg. My first assignment was to take charge of an aeroplane hangar at the disused Baragwanath airport where the company stored enormous quantities of hardboard (or was it chipboard?) backing for the Formica work tops and kitchen tables. The stock at the hangar had simply been dumped higgledy piggledy all over the place.

Having decided on how best to arrange the boards, I had a number of black guys help erect a ten foot high, stepped pile of boards in the centre of the hangar, affording me a bird's eye view of everything happening on the floor below. Then I had an old desk, a chair and my battered portable typewriter placed at the summit. That eyrie helped me along my writing path. It was there that I began my serious writing and where I completed my first play.

My staff respected me because if there was nothing to do I didn't devise useless tasks for them so they could relax and play cards or *umlabalaba* for which they had a more permanent board than the makeshift one at Eddies. Theirs was a square hardboard off-cut with markings made by indelible pencils. Remember them?

My boss was quite chuffed since my presence at the hangar ended a spate of pilfering. One day an unusually large consignment of boards arrived and I felt it incumbent upon me to help my black colleagues unload them. Such unaccustomed heavy work induced my second hernia. This time I knew about it the moment it occurred. I telephoned my boss who sent two drivers round - one to drive me home in my car and the other to take his colleague back to work. Two weeks later I was in hospital having my second herniorrhaphy.

155

Not long after my operation I unexpectedly met up with Jack Sholomir at a Hillbrow eatery where he subjected me to a lengthy monologue about the Flying Enterprise whose skipper, Captain Henrik Carlsen, had displayed intestinal fortitude above and beyond the call of duty by remaining on board his ill-fated, sinking ship in the Bay of Biscay until the very last minute. Carlsen deserved his standing ovation at a press conference at Falmouth after he'd been rescued, he remarked: '*I don't want a seaman's honest attempt to save his ship used for any commercial purpose or to get anything out of it.*'

I wondered why Jack chose to harp on about this. Although the NUSAS tour's *Winchester Castle* had sailed through the fag-end of Carlsen's storm long after Jack had debarked he felt an affinity towards Carlsen since he was convinced that coming close to almost sharing a storm with Carlsen was a sort of augury. He confided that he wanted to start an advertising agency to honour Captain Carlsen by naming the business Flying Enterprises. He was confident that people would recognize the cachet inherent in so legendary a name which, he maintained, would stick in the minds of future clients. He wanted me to join him in a business that, he confidently predicated, had limitless potential.

Having no compunction about dismissing Carlsen's noble philosophy and with nothing better on the horizon I entered into a partnership with Jack Sholomir. Neither of us had the remotest idea of how to run a business. Nor had we any capital but we did have ideas, the main one being to produce and market illustrated, framed mottoes for businesses to display prominently in their premises.

We shared a flair for concocting or modifying horrendously awful slogans such as 'The management is short sighted. Please do not remove its glasses.' Depending on the type of business, we would add a colour illustration of say, an ice cream parfait or a milkshake for milk bars and cafés. Garages took kindly to our awful guff. To quote but one example - '*We are not responsible for the loss of property left in cars, but we are responsible for top class service*' complemented with a full colour illustration of a gleaming state-of-the-art contemporary motor vehicle. Any marque would do. If Inspiration for quaint quips failed us, ardently scanning old *Readers Digests usually helped.*

Unable to afford an illustrator we utilised colour advertisements from glossy American magazines. We carefully cut these out; losing all printed matter, then pasted them neatly on to colour art card and had a sign writer add the customer's aphorism. All that remained was to frame them; a service carried out by Mr. Maroun, an uncle of a school friend. He not only did an excellent job but also gave us wholesale prices and allowed us a few weeks' credit.

The next stage was marketing them. Our products looked professional, were reasonably priced and business began to boom. Our primary problem was obtaining sufficient illustrations. In the early fifties colour magazines were in their infancy and we relied on the excellent ads culled from American film fan magazines and journals like *Good Housekeeping* and *Saturday Evening Post*. The estimable artwork on the covers of the latter, illustrated by geniuses such as Norman Rockwell, Steven Dohanos, George Hughes and John Falter to name but a few, provided profuse pleasure for persons aplenty but it was the quality of the ads featuring the latest automobiles and mouth-watering illustrations of ice cream sundaes, cakes, pies and what-have-you that we really appreciated since they were essential to our continuing success.

As most glossy magazines featured cars we concentrated our sales drive on garages, panel beaters, motor spares, tyre dealers and accessory shops. Colour illustrations dwindled rapidly. We could not afford to buy new magazines so we had to scrounge old 'uns. We worked from Fatti's Building in central Johannesburg in a rented office barely three or four times the size of the average booth in the average public lavatory. Our furniture comprised an ancient desk, and two rickety chairs.

The light of Jack's life was his motor car, a 500cc Baby Fiat. It was not so much a car, more a sky blue, four wheeled typewriter; a two-seater barely larger than the average fairground dodgem car and only marginally faster. To its slide-back opening roof Jack added a blue and white striped canvas canopy, the type of awning a fond mother might fit on to a child's baby carriage as protection against the sun. Hardly a vehicle to go unnoticed.

One fine morning after exercising at the YMCA gym near the office, Jack met a young lady he fancied and his gambit included the offer of a lift to wherever she might be going. At first she demurred but Jack could be very cunning if he put his mind to it, which he did, allaying her concern by telling her that as South Africa's most famous wrestler everyone knew him. His name, he added, was Liteseronovich, which, due to its length and the difficulty with its pronunciation, had been abbreviated by press and fans alike to whom he was 'Liteseron' or simply plain 'Lites'...

By the time she got into his car the streets of central Johannesburg were packed, as they always were on Saturday mornings, with heavy traffic and wall to wall shoppers. Jack's journey took him along Eloff Street the busiest street in Johannesburg's equivalent of Oxford Street in London or Fifth Avenue, New York. The lass didn't notice that Jack had turned on his car lights. In bright sunlight it's impossible to tell from inside a car if its lights are on but people in the milling crowds could hardly fail to notice them and waved at him. Jack waved back flamboyantly.

'Hey baas,' called black pedestrians in unison with other guys on bicycles, 'Boss lights are on!'

'Hi Koos! Hello Willem,' responded Jack.

'Lights!' yelled car drivers, flicking their own lights, 'Lights!'

By now Jack was behaving as if he'd won gold at the Olympics.

And on it went, people signaling, gesticulating, shouting 'Lights are on!' with Jack responding as if every waving wacko was a lifetime pal, so completely mesmerizing his passenger with the amazing popularity he seemingly enjoyed among the proletariat that she let him drive her all the way home and asked him in for a cold drink or tea and who knows what else?

Jack had an uncanny propensity for picking up and attaching himself to anyone who was in any way 'different'. He loved associating with kindred oddballs to whom he was drawn as a moth to a flame. One morning he arrived at the office with a ruddy faced man called John Phillips, a tall, well groomed, well built, trendily dressed Australian aged about forty who claimed he was visiting South Africa to beat the drum to find investors to finance a world bantamweight title boxing match between

South Africa's Vic Toweel and Jimmy Carruthers, the Australian champion. That will be the day, I thought.

Unlike Jack I had reservations about Phillips' story suspecting he was a con man and, in common with most men of that persuasion, he was suave and charming and showed a far deeper interest in what we were up to than one would expect from a big-time boxing promoter. The only flaw in his make-up was his top denture which had a habit of slipping now and then causing his speech to slur ever so slightly making him sound a trace intoxicated.

Jack had found John Phillips that morning during a workout at the gym where they had shared a barbell or two. Phillips invited Jack to share a carton of yogurt with him and Jack outlined what we were up to. Phillips stated the obvious by suggesting that we could increase our turnover if only we had a better supply of magazines. Why not employ black women - men would be too threatening in the racist South African society - to go from house to house in upper income suburbs of white Johannesburg collecting them on the pretext that they were for distribution to medical waiting rooms in deprived areas. Phillips issued each lady with an official looking, signed letter in case they were challenged by householders or the police. We tried his scheme for a week and the number of magazines collected by the women filled the office to such an extent that we stopped the collections and taught the ladies to cut and trim our illustrations, quickly building up a good picture library. Flying Enterprises was taking off and we began working full-time rather than as a temporary hobby while chasing personal rainbows.

Phillips' intentions soon became clear. While Fatti's Building was not exactly one of the crème-de-la-crème Johannesburg office addresses it did provide an inexpensive central base for Phillips. He agreed to pay half the rent which would boost Flying Enterprises' profitability the moment his bank drafts arrived from Oz. Oh yes?

Phillips was living in the mansion home of a famed Johannesburg theatrical and music impresario name of Yango John. 'Until my papers arrive... Well, you know how it is.'

Jack nodded.

'These people,' Phillips remarked, 'they're loaded. Big house, swimming pool, tennis court. They wouldn't take a penny from me.'

Jack understood.

'They've got everything money can buy. Even if my draft came through today I wouldn't know what to get him.'

Jack made a few suggestions.

'Hmm,' Phillips mused, 'what I really had in mind was a bench for the tennis court. You know the ones - with the multi-coloured slats - each one a different colour.'

'Yes,' responded Jack. 'I saw one the other day.'

'Well', continued Phillips, ignoring the interruption, 'I want to get them one of those.'

'How much are they?' asked Jack.

'Fifteen quid. Maybe twenty.'

Jack didn't have that sort of spending power and said so. 'My dear boy', smiled Phillips, 'even if you did, I wouldn't dream of taking money from you.'

Jack heaved a silent sigh of relief convinced that this sophisticate was not looking for a soft touch. Yet, Jack admitted years later, if he'd had the money he would probably have lent it to Phillips.

'As a matter of fact,' said Phillips, 'I know where I could pick one up. Any idea where I could get hold of a delivery van or a lorry for half a day?'

One of Jack's innumerable contacts owned a van, and arrangements were made to borrow it the next day. They convened at the YMCA for a workout, a shower and another yogurt before setting off to fetch the bench.

Phillips had reconnoitered Lower Houghton, earmarking a house with a multicoloured slatted bench near its tennis court. Knowing it was improbable that anyone other than the domestic staff would be home midmorning, Phillips and Jack, suitably attired in white dust coats, confidently knocked on the front door. They told the maid they were from Henwoods, a store specialising in garden furniture, and that the owner of the house wanted the bench to be repainted. The maid shrugged and closed the door. Within the hour that very bench graced the tennis court at a very grateful Yango John's palatial home a few blocks away from the source.

At the time Vic Toweel, a 24 year old wood carver from Benoni, was *the* national sports icon, being the first South African to become a world boxing champion.

'Bet your bottom dollar on Jimmy', Phillips stated passionately, 'he'll murder Toweel.' I scoffed at this. After all, 'our' Vic had lost only two fights in over 300 amateur bouts and had not yet been defeated professionally, so what chance did a gawky, virtually unknown Australian southpaw stand facing up to our Benoni Buzzsaw, a guy who fought with the tenacity of an attacking Rottweiler? We were soon to find out.

By the time Phillips was due to return to Oz Jack again felt the urge to yield to his wanderlust and I was in line for a full time salaried position. It was therefore mutually agreed that we scuttle Flying Enterprises and dispose of the 'assets' by throwing darts for them. Highest score would win first choice, next second and loser last. Jack won the most expensive item in our company's inventory - an antiquated portable typewriter. Phillips got the desk. The chairs were too far gone to be of any use other than fire wood so I went home with a well abused dart board and three bedraggled darts.

A month later Toweel signed to defend his title against Carruthers at Johannesburg's Rand Stadium in November 1952. It was an instant sell-out. No one spoke of much else. People scorned Phillips' forecast. Toweel had not been knocked off his feet in any of his previous bouts. And hey, Vic had featured on the front cover of *Ring* magazine, the sport's equivalent of *Time* magazine.

On fight night the stadium was packed to capacity. The moment the match began, Carruthers unleashed the first of 147, yes, one hundred and forty seven, bombshell blows in as many seconds, against Toweel's single retaliatory swipe which failed to find its target. Carruthers' team had accurately assessed that Toweel was a slow starter. Vic was stunned by Carruthers' blitzkrieg onslaught from the first bell. There was an unnatural silence in the Rand Stadium as the local hero hit the canvas in the first round, taking the full count to make Carruthers Australia's first world champion, a fact I lamented since I hadn't bet a penny on him. Toweel had spent more time walking to and from his dressing room into the ring than he had fighting in it.

I resisted the temptation to bet on Carruthers at the March '53 rematch as I considered that his first win had been a fluke. Toweel did slightly better this time. It took Carruthers ten rounds to knock him out.

We never saw nor heard from John Phillips again. Presumably he'd procured enough to place a sizable wager on his man, a wager which would have won him enough to repair his faulty denture and to take an early retirement with the balance.

Of the dozen or more jobs I'd tried so far, the one that held out the most creative potential was as a trainee sound recordist working for Henry Barzilay, a recent migrant from Britain.

He was under the illusion that his plummy, fruitcake voice placed him a cut above the local radio announcers whose pronunciation betrayed their South African origins no matter how hard they tried to lose the 'excent' at elocution classes, hey man. Bombastic Barzilay's patronizing attitude neither won him friends nor influenced his peers. Had his intelligence matched his solipsism he may have had an inkling that he was too thick-skinned to notice his own inadequacies.

He wasn't a big man height-wise but his flabby, rotund belly wobbled abdomenably er – abominably, ahead of him as he entered the room before the rest of his body caught up with it. The African caretaker christened him with a crude, unambiguous nickname - Mafuta, The Fat One.

Fatso's studio was located in Commissioner Street; close to the South African Broadcasting Corporation's headquarters. The SABC occasionally called on him to participate on broadcasts requiring a pukka cut-glass English voice. He also worked for Springbok Radio, the first commercial radio station in South Africa, set up by the SABC to compete for a share of the income from the commercials emanating from Lourenço Marques Radio aimed at South African listeners who preferred brighter, more imaginative fare than the stodgy output from the staid SABC.

Barzilay also produced demo discs for the music business. But the icing on his financial cake was devoted to flattering the vanity of well-heeled upper middle class people from the Jewish 'ghettoes' proliferating in Johannesburg's northern suburbs, by producing audio recordings of weddings, *Bar Mitzvahs* and occasional landmark birthday parties, twenty one, fifty, and so on.

Barzilay's staff were all freelancers working on a percentage basis. Playbacks were arranged in customers' homes where relatives and friends gathered to listen to the outcome and if the client bought the recording it was delivered in a presentation album of vinyl gramophone records. No sale? Well, tough on the recordist.

One of Barzilay's band of not very merry men included an old *oke* whose qualification was more freeloader than freelancer. He always took two suitcases with him on assignments. A medium size one held his equipment and t'other was empty for him to load with enough left- over sustenance to nourish him for a fortnight. He confided to me that his conscience didn't bother him in the least, arguing that the value of his nobbled nosh was higher than his earnings would be even if his recordings sold.

My responsibilities at the audio factory included checking forthcoming marriage and *Bar Mitzvah* announcements in the evening paper *The Star,* and the *Rand Daily Mail* in the morning in order to contact families for permission to record their function. Refusals were rare since there was no obligation to purchase and weekend Sundays could mean six or more bookings for Barzilay's services to Jewish family nostalgia.

My trainee's paltry pittance for transferring the sound onto discs tempted me to accept Mafuta's suggestion that I too should work as a recordist on weekends and busy periods. I soon got to look forward to the outside work thanks to the main perk, that of meeting comely young bridesmaids with whom to flirt. Even the ugly ones and boy, the Jewish community could lay claim to more than a fair share of prize uglies, were worth cultivating as they proved to be reliable informants on the subject of upcoming parties. I even accepted invitations to several of them.

The studio's disc-cutting machine produced significant quantities of purple vinyl swarf so highly flammable that it had to be stored in water until it could be disposed of. I decided to help Barzilay get rid of it. I knew that the swarf would be ideal for getting the imminent Guy Fawkes bonfire off to a flaming good start, so I took a pile home with me to test it.

At sunset Justin and a handful of his friends accompanied me to a wedge of wasteland where we unloaded shopping bags crammed full of dry, compacted swarf. After ensuring that the boys were a safe distance away I lit the swarf but it didn't burn: it exploded with the frightening hiss of a gargantuan flamethrower firing at the moon. Synchronously a vast column of fire scorched upwards which was bloody fortunate for me because had it gone in any other direction I would have been barbecued instantly instead of merely being singed. The youngsters fled in terror. I was too transfixed by the result to run away. Instead of disappearing into nothingness, as one would expect, a flicker of flames appeared to hover in mid-air. My heart beat ten times faster as it flashed through my thick skull just how narrowly I'd come to being incinerated. Next day I visited the scene of the crime where I was relieved to find that I hadn't imagined the residual flames in the sky. These had been caused by melting blobs of overhead telephone wires leading into nearby homes. I considered myself exceptionally lucky to have escaped the attention of the police. From then on the swarf remained in the studio water buckets until Barzilay dealt with it.

Personal sound recorders were unheard of in the early fifties. The bulky, clumsy machines of the period were prohibitively expensive imports from the USA. These employed extremely fine chrome plated steel wire, nearly as thin as human hair, onto which the sound was recorded. I didn't know it at the time but Barzilay's recorders were the last vestiges of an ancient technology about to be superseded by the thrilling introduction of coated magnetic tape and even weightier, more expensive recorders.

Sound equipment was disallowed in orthodox synagogues, but since weddings and *Bar Mitzvahs* both held lucullan receptions bursting with *brochas,* speeches and music, we were always busy on weekends.

As the selling price depended on length we taped everything, including the dance music. It was thanks to Barzilay that I first encountered the bathetic face of the Jewish community who were seriously susceptible to disingenuous blarney.

As a rule wedding receptions commenced with music from a live band to accompany the grand entrance of the bridal entourage into the hall. Once everyone was cosily settled the best man, or, if the budget permitted, a professional MC, would clink a knife against a glass to quieten the noisy chatter. He welcomed the guests and proposed the loyal toasts of which there were three in Jewish South Africa - '*God Save the King*' (South Africa was, after all, a British Dominion), *'Die Stem'* ('Uit Die Blou Van Onse Hemel' - Out Of The Blue Of Our Heaven, South Africa's national anthem) and '*Hatikvah*' -'The Hope' for Israel.

At more orthodox weddings rabbis intoned lengthy prayers while the guests *chalished* for the four or five course banquet awaiting them. As we all know there is no such thing as a free lunch - or wedding feast for that matter - and the high price paid by the guests, on top of their gifts, was the struggle to digest their meal in the face of banal speeches in praise of the bride, the groom, both sets of parents, the bridesmaids, the pole holders, the page boy(s), the flower girl(s), Uncle Tom Cobleyvitch and all, while we recordists monitored the sound level as we greedily calculated our income if perchance the whole *schmeer* was sold.

Weddings and *Bar Mitzvahs* always had a first waltz after the speeches. This was used as the background to a custom-made commentary that was added later if there was a sale. By custom-made, I mean the scripts were virtually identical for every function. Only the names and the fashions varied from *Bar Mitzvah* to *Bar Mitzvah* and wedding to wedding. At the subsequent home playbacks the recordists made detailed notes about the garments worn by the bride's mother, sister(s), bridesmaids, flower girls etcetera, sourced from the pedantic founts of all such knowledge - the mother of the bride or that of the *Bar Mitzvah* boy.

Barzilay personally wrote and voiced it in grovellingly unctuous prose delivered in the obsequious tones usually reserved for solemn occasions such as state funerals and coronations. Barzilay's sycophantic, saccharine, platitude polluted flumadiddle was closely similar to this ...

To the resounding applause of the privileged guests present in this delightful hall, superbly decorated in pink and white carnations, the bride and groom are taking the floor for the bridal waltz 'Paradise.'

(Pause. Enhance applause from guests. Establish music.)

Goldie looks radiant in her striking full length gown of white shantung silk embroidered with mother of pearl sequins edged with diamante reflecting the light from the glitter ball revolving above the dance floor creating a truly unforgettably romantic, grotto effect.

(Pause. Bring up music.)

As Goldie twirls gracefully in time to the music of Archie Silansky's orchestra we glimpse no less than six multi-layered petticoats edged with white satin trim.

Her gown's heart shaped neckline is offset by a flawless pearl necklace. Her long satin gloves match her delicate white diamante trimmed satin shoes. And to crown this loveliness is a Swan Lake tiara supporting a short net veil edged with more mother of pearl sequins.

The facts that the orchestra was but a small band of maybe five musos and that Goldie was a plump Jewish Princess who could have been mistaken for Billy Bunter's twin sister, did not deter Barzilay's bilious burble. Occasionally he even resorted to appropriating poems from books of Ancient Rimes such as...

Her feet beneath her petticoat
Like little mice stole in and out,
As if they feared the light,
But oh, she dances such a way
No sun upon an Easter-day
Is half so fine a sight.

One wouldn't think it could worsen. Wrong!

163

As the bride's parents took the floor Barzilay's prattle continued …

The guests rise to applaud and honour our hosts, Bert and Zelda Fahrshtaitnit, our lovely bride's parents, join the bride and groom on the dance floor.

That preceded graphic details of the mother's outré outfit, down to the last infinitesimal detail. Skim through this as it's frightfully tiresome …

And to more applause from the guests the groom's parents Sarah and Jacob Essengut are taking the floor. Sarah looks luminous in her pastel pink blah, blah, blah. What a touching sight it makes watching the happy families circling the floor with such grace... And so it rambled on and on. And on.

It was always a vital rule at Jewish functions for the hosts to strive to avoid *farribels* (differences of opinion) of any sort, a family vendetta if you like, between any of the guests. *Farribels* were launched for any of a dozen or more momentous reasons real or assumed, such as why so-and-so's children hadn't been invited - or why Aunt Sadie, she of the asymmetrically penciled on eyebrows, had been seated at the same table as third cousin Maish to whom she had not spoken for twenty years because he once dated her daughter and did not marry her... It's interesting to note that in nearly 6,000 years of Jewish history not one single *farribel* free wedding has yet been recorded.

And finally, to stretch the running time we rounded up scores of guests to record congratulatory greetings from family and friends.

Oddly enough there was a general reluctance on the part of interviewees to agree to say something and if they did there was a invariably a superfluity of immortal lines such as;

'Dis is Uncle Gus. Mazeltov'.

'I hope your troubles are all little ones.' Followed by fifteen seconds of uncontrollable giggling.

'Milcie, vot shall I say again?'

'Hello mine darlingks, this is Milton, your father, speakingk. I vant you should alvays be so happy trewout your lives like you are tonight. Goodbye from Milton, your daddy. Oh and here's your mama who vants to say sometink.'

Slightly peeved voice off mike, sotto voce, 'Milton you know how I hate dese microscope things! Please to leave me alone. Besides, the kids already know how much ve love them...' Silence.

Several henpecked mahouts confided that for the first time ever their elephantine spouses had been lost for words, thanks to my microphone.

Once a sale was completed and a deposit paid, Barzilay recorded the commentary, and I transferred it and his smarmy voice-over on to vinyl discs, checked the discs for flaws, typed the labels, packed them into the sleeves of posh presentation albums and delivered them to the client and collected the shekels.

Barzilay was a greedy rodomont. As I mentioned, my pay was pitiful and the fact that he withheld my commission for at least a month after he'd been paid so that he could earn interest on it rankled me no end as did his lanky, vinegary, mean-minded, shrewishly arrogant English-Jewish wife. Here we had a domineering termagant who behaved as if she were royalty treating me, and everyone else with whom she came in contact, with despotic disdain, ordering me around imperiously, perhaps expecting me to kowtow as if I were her personal dogsbody. I put up with this until the day she instructed me to wipe down some shelves for her. Had her request been less belligerent I may well have done so without demur, but her arrogance offended my hackles and I told her politely but firmly that I was a trainee sound engineer not an office cleaner.

Barzilay was out at the time and next morning he affirmed I was fired for disobeying his wife. He listened carefully to my side of the story before pointing out, quite sympathetically, to give him his due, that he would prefer to get rid of her rather than me, but that was not an option and in order to placate her I had to leave immediately. I requested my wages and he told me he needed to calculate the amount and that he would mail me a cheque.

Clearly there was no point in continued argument so I left and went straight round to Pop at work to tell him what had happened. Pop was far from pleased to hear I'd not been paid and he sent me back to collect my wages. A surly Barzilay testily contended that since I had refused to carry out my 'duty' I was not entitled to any payment. I reported this to Pop who immediately contacted his solicitor who saw me right away. While I was there he dictated a letter to Barzilay demanding he pay my wages forthwith. Very little legal tender was involved but the matter dragged on and on. Mafuta only stumped up after receiving a court summons. His recalcitrance cost him substantially more than he had bargained for since my solicitor was awarded all legal costs, my back pay, two weeks' notice money plus interest on withheld payment.

A very positive outcome emerged from my dismissal. A message arrived from a Mr. Ivan Sackheim, owner of Universal Recordings, a company comparable to Barzilay's. The grapevine had brought the Barzilay contretemps to Sackheim's attention and he wanted to meet me. We liked each other on sight and he invited me to join him to do virtually the same work I'd done with Barzilay, and at a far better salary.

Sackheim was a very *frum* Orthodox Jew who observed the tenets of his religion so scrupulously that he once walked from Benoni to Johannesburg to be with his sister the day her baby was born which happened to fall on *Shabbat,* the Jewish Sabbath, a day on which driving is prohibited. The distance was about 25 miles but in the heat of the highveld summer it must have seemed more like 50. Darn nearly killed him.

His strong beliefs led to a lot of work from the Jewish Board of Deputies including the transfer from tape to disc of a series of dramatized American radio plays and documentaries entitled *The Eternal Light,* all concerned with aspects of Jewish interest.

As well as our love of quality sound, Sackheim and I shared this penchant for delightful damsels. Occasionally, with his knowledge, I invited girlfriends to visit the studio with me. Universal had moved from Troye Street in a grotty corner of Johannesburg's commercial sector to the top floor of a block of residential flats in Bertrams which wasn't that much less sleazy but more spacious, cheaper and more comfortable than Troye Street. The new studio was housed in the living room which the innovative Sackheim soundproofed by gluing those dimpled egg cartons over the walls and ceiling and fitting heavy drapes across the windows.

One Saturday night after taking in a movie, my date accompanied me to the studio to listen to selections from the productions I was working on. At the time I was transcribing episodes of a drama called *'The Warsaw Ghetto.'* More copies were still needed and I felt I might as well take the opportunity to transfer an episode to disk while she was there. I set it all up and began. As did another, far more interesting occupation when, abruptly, just as the story and I were on the verge of climax, the main lights went on and there stood my boss. He had the decency to lessen the embarrassment of catching us 'at it' by turning the light back off. He'd been driving home past the studio and noticing a burning light he'd come to turn it off. I told him I didn't think he'd be anywhere nearby especially since it was the Sabbath. He reminded me that it was now eleven at night and that *Shabbat* ended at sunset.

'Next time you want to work overtime, let me know in advance OK?' he commented as he left, chortling heartily. A moment later his head reappeared round the door. 'By the way,' he added, 'I want to commend you on combining business with pleasure. It's a technical skill I haven't mastered. Yet. Don't forget to turn off the lights when you leave! And hey, remind me to give you a raise.'

He left the flat thoroughly enjoying his pun. That night was the beginning of a lifelong friendship with soul mate Sackheim whose marriage gift to me was, yes, you guessed it, an audio recording of my wedding.

A decade later while working as a television producer in London I answered a phone call from a vaguely familiar voice which said, 'I'm Henry Barzilay. You may remember me from Johannesburg.' I remembered him all right and expressed my amazement that he had the audacity to phone me and asked what it was he wanted.

Seems he'd bought a camera in order to switch from radio to television production in South Africa. The Nationalist government hadn't taken kindly to a foreigner who sent video reports abroad showing them in a poor light and Barzilay was classified as 'undesirable' and advised to leave the country. Within ten days! As a result he was back in England seeking work in television. I asked him if he recalled the manner of our parting and reminded him that I had been forced to go to law to get what was due to me.

'Oh,' declared he, 'that was a very long time ago. Can we not let bygones be bygones?

'Absolutely,' I agreed. 'Bye, I'm gone.'

Johannesburg supported half a dozen amateur dramatic societies, one of which tried, unsuccessfully I'm afraid, to emulate Orson Welles' famed Mercury Players whose name they had appropriated. My girlfriend was a member and I played an enthusiastic role in their acted play readings and occasionally stage managed sundry mundane, dated, one-act productions.

Said lady showed sufficient acting promise to win a bit part in *The Love of Four Colonels* directed by Anthony Farmer at the Reps Theatre in Braamfontein. Hence I became a member of Raps, the Repertory Amateur Players as opposed to Reps, the Johannesburg Repertory Theatre. The amateur section was a shrewd idea which provided the theatre with supernumeraries from the Raps ranks, all of whom were thrilled to have the opportunity to participate in a professional production. This is how I came to appear as a junior barrister in Agatha Christie's Witness for the Prosecution, never dreaming that this would one day boost my prospect of becoming a full-time director in Britain.

The legal teams for both Defence and Prosecution were on stage throughout the performance. I hadn't reckoned on the monotony of a four week run, six nights a week and Saturday matinees. We barristers sat in two rows of benches, one at stage floor level with a second, slightly higher bench, behind it. I had a front row seat. A back row super and I had been directed to hand occasional notes to one another and we obliged by playing battleships, a paper and pencil game. We passed our notes intermittently until, soon after the opening, Anthony Farmer came to check on the play and told us we were very much over the top with the note business and we had to restrict them to ten per performance at most. We did that and I filled in the rest of my time looking busy while modifying passages of the play from drama to comedy sketches.

Stage managing was much to my liking. It enabled me to observe and compare how different directors tackled their work. When an annual South African one act play festival loomed ahead, I decided it was time to make my directorial debut. My play, *The Jest of Hahalaba*, a two hander by Lord Dunsany, was not the wisest choice. Although it received but a lukewarm reception, it led to a meeting with Basil Sloman, a versatile director, who agreed to read the play I'd written called *Shaft Seven*, a tale of three miners, one black and two white, trapped by a rock fall thousands of feet underground in a gold mine. They conclude that in the face of such extremity colour and creed are totally meaningless.

This play, written atop the pile of boards in Electronic Applications' aeroplane hangar, had been kindled by a visit I'd made down a very deep gold mine with a girlfriend and her father, a mining engineer. The cage we descended in was giddyingly fast. The oppressive suffocating heat so far beneath the earth made me marvel at the stamina and bravery of men carrying out strenuous physical labour down there for protracted periods. We had walked a long distance in the mine's eerie silence to reach an underground lake a good deal larger than about three Olympic size swimming pools. Much as I relished the experience, I was relieved to reach the surface and to breathe fresh open air once more.

I like to think my play conveyed a sense of being isolated deep in the bowels of the earth. It must have rung a bell with Basil Sloman who appreciated it sufficiently to ask if he could direct it. I agreed without the slightest hesitation. Observing its evolution from read-through to rehearsals and on into its first and only, public performance was an invaluable, edifying experience which further whetted my aspiration to direct.

The theatre brought me into contact with Ray Matuson, a man who actuated one of the top ten of my life's most memorable moments. Ray was a leading light in the Mercury Players and other amateur dramatic societies.

He earned his living as a scrap dealer. His business, located deep in the heart of Vrededorp (meaning Peace Village and pronounced Freda Dorp) while not the most disreputable Johannesburg suburb, was certainly in line for the runner-up title. No white person in his right mind would risk strolling too far from the main drag where stood Ray's junk emporium.

It was as stage manager for an imminent Mercury Players production that I made my first journey there in search of props. Ray proudly gave me a conducted tour round his premises which overflowed with every kind of junk that springs to mind. To name but a few examples - ancient impaired artefacts, battered bent, brollies, broom handles and bicycles, chipped crockery, damaged desks, ersatz earphones, fusty filing cabinets... When you have absolutely nothing better to do compile your alliterative list of detritus that springs to mind and you'll only have scratched the surface relating to Ray's monumental stock inventory which, incidentally, also included a gross assortment of stuffed animals, birds, reptiles and framed butterflies. Not to mention unclaimed dry cleaning, recyclable lavatory bowls, lead piping (doubtless nicked by local *tsotsis)*, all lined up outside in serried rows beneath corrugated iron shelters in the enormous back yard.

My conclusion was that he should have named it The One Stop Prop Shop. It was a veritable Aladdin's Cave of the junk world with Ray its Sesame. The set dresser on the Mad Max movies might well have acquired all his props at Ray's place. Name almost any product under the early 1950's sun and provided you were prepared to overlook a bit of dirt, assorted dents, or a soupçon of rust here and there, whatever you wanted could be found at Raymond's. He obtained his merchandise from anywhere, from anyone who had anything to sell, preferably in bulk. Ray's association with the Mercury Players first began when, in return for free props, they presented him with tickets. It wasn't only to relieve the tedium of his day job, or to be a star that he had joined. Oh no, he had signed up, as I had, for the opportunity to meet young wannabe actresses.

Ray was annoyingly confident that everything he stocked, no matter how wacky or tacky, would find buyers. It was a place that car boot sales junkies of the 21st century would drool over and even die for.

The interior was not far removed from *Steptoe and Son's* home base in the classic BBC television series, except that Ray had substantially more junk than the Steptoes inside and outside the decrepit old house. I procured my first antique there - one of those old candlestick telephones and after I got to know him better he relished reminding me I'd spent more on that single phone than he'd paid for 25 of them.

Ray reserved the highlight of my tour for last. A surprisingly damp-free room contained a mountainous treasure trove of thousands of books stacked willy-nilly on arrival from auction rooms, deceased estates, publishers' remainders, and lending library clearances. They appeared to have remained undisturbed for months, perhaps years. Sifting through them was hazardous due to the possibility of being buried alive under a literary avalanche. The wisdom of ages filled that room. Here and there one glimpsed bound copies of *'Punch - or London Charavari'* stretching as far back as the 1920's, nestling cheek by jowl alongside mouldering, leather-bound, incomplete sets of *Encyclopaedia Britannica*.

Ray was geniality personified and always glad to see me and no matter how busy he was he'd immediately pour me a cracked mug of the excellent tea he constantly kept on the brew. The tea and the books made me a regular customer and good friend. One day he pointed to a large jute sack on the floor in front of the well-worn wooden counter on which stood a rococo brass cash register with levered buttons to display the amount of each sale. A handle at the side opened the machine with an agreeable pinging sound. If it felt like working that is.

Ray invited me to guess what was inside that sack by touch alone. After his sworn assurance that it did not conceal an exotic live critter or any offensive substance, I played along with him and gingerly inserted my hand into the sack. The contents felt soft and powdery but I hadn't a clue what it was in there until Ray told me to remove a handful from the sack. I was staggered by what emerged - a fistful of dry prophylactics. There were thousands of them in that sack. A hundredweight or more, according to Ray. I managed to stop chuckling long enough to ask where on earth he'd found them. They were rejects from a condom factory Ray told me before he went into detail about how they were made.

In case you're ever unfortunate enough to appear on one of those mindless television game shows, and suppose the subject crops up of how to test condoms, you'll possibly win a point or two. Well… at least you'll be able to relate Ray Matuson's version, which may even be accurate.

According to him, after the shaped condoms emerge from the machine which spawns them, they land in a sort of sieve of vibrating talcum powder which coats them thoroughly after which they are shaken onto conveyor belts which pass in front of teams of women who pick them up individually and fit them onto an inverted ice cream cone shaped piece of smooth metal with holes through which a foot-operated pedal forces compressed air into the condom, inflating it to the size of a rugby ball. A light behind the condom enables the operator to ascertain whether or not there are any flaws in the rubber. If there was the slightest doubt the condom was rejected.

'And here', proclaimed Ray, 'are last year's rejects!'

'Who the hell wants reject frenchies?' I asked.

'Dunno,' he answered, 'but someone will.'

It never crossed my mind that it would be me. I bought a small selection of books, went home to immerse myself in my acquisitions and forgot about the condoms - for the time being anyway.

Now my cousin Ivan and I had always been close friends and he invited me to be best man at his forthcoming wedding to his childhood sweetheart Marlene. Of course I accepted but it wasn't until planning his stag night that Ray's condoms sprang to mind motivating an unprecedented plot.

When I asked Ray if I could buy his sack of condoms, he disclosed that they were selling well at a penny apiece but, since I was a friend, I could have them at a quarter of his regular asking price - four for a penny. I told him that what I had in mind was to hire the entire sackful. It was his turn to register bewilderment and after a session of hilariously nonsensical negotiations we reached a deal whereby I rented them for a weekend, pledging to pay half a crown per pound for any that went astray. On the morning of the bachelor bash my brother and I collected the condoms which weighed in at about 98 lbs. which meant that Ray had sold about 2 lbs. worth.

'Who actually bought them?' I wanted to know.

'Almost all my black customers,' he said, 'and I'll let you in on a secret - even if they use them there's going to be a population explosion in Vrededorp nine months from now, you mark my words...' He chortled all the way as he helped me lug the jute sack into the voluminous boot of my father's Oldsmobile.

The party, held at my cousin's in-laws' home in Yeoville, was filling up with staid old blood uncles and presumptive uncles-in-law who, I feared, might take our complot amiss. How wrong I was.

The soiree officially commenced at eight in the evening. An hour or so later everyone, including the uncles, had mellowed on Castle or Lion beer and/or prodigious quantities of Chateau or Oude Meester brandy-and-coke, the 'in' drink of the period, the party began to swing. The outbreak of dirty anecdotes and the singing of filthy rugby songs made it clear when the time was exactly ripe for the highlight of the night. We persuaded my somewhat inebriated cousin to sit blindfolded on the floor in the middle of the front room. Two guests were shanghaied to help us haul the sack inside and to empty its contents over the bridegroom.

Within seconds my cousin was submerged beneath a cataract of condoms. I had no conception, if you'll forgive the pun, that there were quite so many condoms in that sack, but if anyone really wants to check on the number, by all means weigh a dry condom and work it out or take my word for it that there were sufficient to reach my cousin's armpits.

No one, other than my brother and I knew what was in the sack and at first no one had any idea of what was engulfing Ivan. It should be emphasized that the condoms weren't the flashy Technicolor, ribbed, flavoured, lubricated sexual playthings of today, but simple, old fashioned, gimmick free johnnies covered in white talc (which purportedly slowed down the perishing process of the rubber) so that his hair, his face and his clothes, were all a spectral shade of white chalk.

Seconds later, the collective pennies dropped and precipitated a chorus of 'Oh-my-gods!' and miscellaneous gasps of incredulity all round. Doubtful guests needed to feel the condoms to check that they weren't hallucinating and once they had confirmed that their suspicions were correct, the shrieks of elation and applause could be heard a block away. No one present, previously or since, to my knowledge, had ever seen such quantities of condoms in their natural state in one place.

My cousin's annoyance quickly metamorphosed into mirth once he twigged what had turned him into a snowman. Everyone was verging on hysterics. I don't think the risibility diminished for hours except for brief pauses to top up liquor levels. Inhibitions went down the drain as guests started to experiment with the condoms. It was simple to start with. The condoms were merely blown up and used as balloons to be bounced off the ceiling or punched back and forth to the accompaniment of small explosions as they burst, thereby inspiring a contest to see who could inflate his the largest before it burst.

Inventiveness burgeoned. Someone inflated a condom then released it allowing the escaping air to propel it phrrrrrriping noisily across the room. A flurry of gambling ensued, with wagers on whose air filled condom would jet furthest away from its release point. The decibels increased in direct proportion to the silliness of the participants, such as rolling a condom onto every digit to form a glove that might conceivably be worn by mad scientists in horror movies. It was not only the young guys like us in our early twenties but even Ivan's older uncles who joined in the condommery with zeal.

We all strove to outdo one another. Resourceful revellers blew into them and twisted the balloons into bizarre shapes. One guy filled condoms with brandy and coke which he put in the refrigerator to make brandy and coke ice lollies.

Another bloke strung them together to wear as a sweatband. Yet another came up with a Roman style laurel crown. A Jack Horner sat in a corner industriously fashioning a party streamer which he hung from a picture rail to the light fitting in the centre of the ceiling. Others swiftly emulated that and in no time at all the ceiling was festooned with a rubber decoration not unlike the pattern of Britain's Union Jack. An artistic accountant made French letter leis to hang round the necks of other people. Two old guys sharing a pile of prophylactics on the coffee table in front of the couch carefully fitted a condom over each ear. Something like this may well have been the inspiration - years later - for the 'Vulcan' ears worn by Mr. Spock in the *Star Trek* television and movie series.

Others tried to fit condoms onto peeled bananas without damaging the fruit.

A catapult was soon devised to shoot balls of knotted rubbers. Soon it seemed everyone was similarly armed.

A conga began. It moved out of the house into the street and back inside, then migrated into the garden and thence into the street again. The small front garden, a narrow patch of grass between the edge of the *stoep* and the garden fence, contained a hose tap which led to the zaniest contest of the evening - water bombs. Guests lined up for a turn at filling their rubbers with water before lobbing them about every which way.

By now any vestiges of decorum or dignity had been expunged from all the participants' mental hard drives and the words 'bedlam' and 'pandemonium' sprang to mind to describe the most rambunctious thrash ever held in the history of the (formerly) quiet, peaceful, middle class suburb of Yeoville.

When it dawned on them that with lesser amounts of water in the condoms they could be knotted, twirled and then hurled, David versus Goliath style, with varying degrees of accuracy, at passing cars. Motorists were too sensible to stop to curse the adult delinquents. However the outdoor condomania came to an abrupt end when one landed squarely on the windscreen of a swiftly moving car which screeched to a halt narrowly missing vehicles parked at the kerb. Talk about Goliath! An enormous enraged Goliath clone of a driver emerged shaking his fist and yelling profanities containing explicit descriptions of our resemblance to intimate body parts and what he was going to do to ours.

The multitude wisely retired to the safety of the house to find towels to dry themselves. Miraculously no one summoned the police even though the raucous horseplay continued into the small hours. The only thing those condoms weren't used for that alcoholic evening, as far as I know, was the purpose for which they had been designed.

Early in the morning, nursing formidable hangovers, my brother and I gathered up the remnants of the condoms to return them to Ray who weighed the sack and announced that it was 25 lbs. lighter. I happily paid for them and Ray had earned another tidy profit. But it had bought a priceless occurrence which, even today, over 50 years later, is still spoken of in hushed tones of awe and respect by all who were there.

Days later Ivan's future mother-in-law discovered numerous oddly shaped alcohol based ice lollies in the freezer. For months tired condoms continued to lurk in or under her sofa cushions, down the sides of armchairs and even inside electric light fittings.

The final prophylactic postscript came months later after my father had a puncture. He summoned James to fit the spare wheel while he 'supervised.' I can only imagine his reaction to what he saw under the spare as it emerged from its curved nesting space in the boot (trunk to my American reader) to reveal a hoard of shrivelled, perished, yellowed condoms. There could be but one malefactor - me! (My brother was too young at the time to have a driving license). All Pop said on his return home was 'I had a puncture today and discovered a collection of interesting goods belonging to you under the spare.'

It didn't matter much that I couldn't borrow Pop's car again because by then I had my own banger, but after what had happened prior to my NUSAS departure I suspect that perhaps my parents assumed that they had spawned a sex maniac. Well, not quite, but close. I doubt my mother ever told my father about her NUSAS discovery and Pop was too much of a gentleman to share such information with her.

Hillbrow, straddling one of Joburg's highest *koppies*, was reputedly the most densely populated square mile in the British Empire, outnumbering even Hong Kong and Calcutta. Cafés and clubs, poofs and pimps, tearooms and tarts, restaurants and rogues, drugs and doughnuts. You want it, you name it, Hillbrow had it. And supplied it if you could afford it. Gambling casinos were the exception - not that they didn't exist, they just took a modicum of effort to unearth and a lot of effort to gain admission. Not even apartheid's execrable shadow could diminish the sheer voluptuousness of Hillbrow in the late forties and early fifties. Provided you were white.

Hillbrow was where all the Johannesburg action was and hence an automatic choice of where most upwardly mobile young white Joburgers of the era aspired to reside on leaving the family nest. I moved into flat 303, Bentley Place, Van Der Merwe Street, just off Clarendon Circle.

'Flat' sounds posh I know, for in reality it was really a furnished bed-sitter with a divan doubling as both bed and sofa. British estate agents would have described it as a 'studio flat.' Mine was moderately upmarket with a separate bathroom and a modest kitchen. Just the sort of place a young bachelor could handle without a regular maid to help with cleaning and laundry which didn't matter much as I usually took my laundry home and paid my parents' maid to iron my shirts and sheets. Cooking was not a problem as I frequently dined with my family and in any case there was a profusion of good, relatively inexpensive eating places in Hillbrow.

One of my neighbours, Peter Lotis, proved to be as amiable a companion as one could wish for. He had an encyclopedic knowledge of jazz and a covetable collection of gramophone records. He and I spent frequent relaxed evenings downing Chateau brandy laced with Coca-Cola while listening to or discussing jazz. Peter was to become a celebrity on the South African music scene. His brother Dennis made inroads into British show biz singing with the Ted Heath Band. I didn't meet Dennis until years later when I booked him for a television show I was producing in the UK. He was one of the early 'rock brigade' with a singing style similar to Sinatra's. Dennis and Peter were astonishingly alike in terms of both talent and friendliness.

My circle of friends used to congregate at The Oasis or preferably, if you could squeeze in, The Golden Ray Café where a juicy steak the size of a small cow was served with lashings of chips, two eggs (sunny side up of course), an unlimited supply of buttered toast with a coke or hot drink at a cost of less than a quid between seven in the morning and midnight. Or you could opt for a steak liberally garnished with monkey gland sauce - a singular, fiery, piquant sauce relying heavily on garlic, Tabasco and Worcestershire sauce and seemingly, exclusively concocted by South Africans. If you're squeamish, you'll be pleased to hear it has nothing to do with either glands or monkeys and its name is accredited to numerous silly sources.

The clatter of state-of-the-art sound effects and discordant music from pinball machines coining in money hand over fist and cliques of argumentative guys hovering about waiting to play as soon as a machine became available, turned Saturday night at The Golden Ray into noisy chaos. But we were part of it and the camaraderie was one of the reasons we went there. Another was to gather the latest intelligence on the party front. In the unlikely event of there being no crashworthy weekend parties, we relaxed over a quiet, relatively cheap drink in the swish kitsch of the Skyline Hotel or took ourselves to one of Hillbrow's two bioscopes, the Clarendon or the Curzon.

At this stage of my life I made frequent journeys south to the city's ice rink in Turffontein where, as a bonus to the exercise and fun of skating, the rink was frequented by young women who were not often averse to spending the night at my flat for the modest price of a hamburger and a soft drink at the Doll House. The dual snags relating to skating outings lay in the possibility of encountering a troll-like boyfriend come to collect his *meisie* after an evening he'd spent downing beer in bars with his mates in preference to the sissy pastime of ice skating. The other was having to drive them home in the small hours of Sunday morning, risking the wrath of irate male parents.

On Saturdays, quiet Sundays, or indeed any day of the week, you could visit the Florian Café with its open first floor balcony facing onto Twist Street. From this vantage point you could observe the passing show of electric tramcars and pedestrians. It was considered the acme of sophistication to sit there dunking anchovy toast in your Russian tea. If you were flush or in poseur mode you'd light a black Balkan Sobranie cigarette. You know the ones: they had gold tips and also came in varicoloured pastel shades - light green, pale pink, and sky blue, all eagerly pounced upon by the tiny minority of females who smoked in public in those days. You always hoped your new date was a non-smoker as those Sobranies were bloody expensive.

Much as I enjoyed working with Sackheim he couldn't afford to employ me full-time so I continued to fit in occasional recordings for him on evenings and weekends while searching for an interesting, well paid permanent post. As luck would have it, Neville's mother had joined the newly established South African branch of Rothmans of Pall Mall and recommended me for a public relations vacancy job with them. My interview was merely a formality and the following Monday I reported for work starting with a paid month's familiarization course.

During this period I befriended Roger, another Rothmans rookie, and we planned to motor to Lourenço Marques in my car for the long Easter holiday weekend. He wanted time off away from Johannesburg with his girlfriend and my motive was to increase my ever growing collection of miniature liquor bottles, aka liqueurs, a recent collecting craze in South Africa because the government banned their sale on the grounds that availability would encourage the natives to drink. The price of the miniatures mostly containing less than a single tot was three times higher than the same quantity of alcohol bought in a bar or a bottle store. Anyhow apartheid law disallowed black people from entering white bars and liquor stores. Hey man, they got their own beer halls... In a nutshell the no-brain legislation transformed those miniature bottles into an obsession resulting in their changing hands at black market prices of up to ten times their original cost.

The visit to L M was fun. Not that I saw much of Roger, who spent almost the entire weekend in bed with his girlfriend while I combed the shops for exotic offbeat miniature bottles. I unearthed a number of beauts such as an oily German liqueur with gold flakes floating inside a transparent blown-glass dachshund. Another find was a yellow Dutch liqueur in a splendid blown-glass tulip. One distiller marketed ten differently coloured liqueurs in bottles shaped like dumpy artillery shells. All in all I acquired a glorious selection for inclusion in my mother's tall kidney shaped showcase which was exclusively devoted to my collection.

On the return journey every inch of space in my Anglia was filled with them. The spare tyre, the interiors of the doors, under the seats, behind the dashboard, in the glove compartment; even the windscreen washer water receptacle was utilised. We had no reason to be concerned until we reached the exceptionally lengthy queues of cars lining the road in front of us at the Komatipoort customs post.

'*Goeie namiddag meneer.* Anything to declare?' enquired the customs man in both official white languages.

Of course the answer was no.

'Yus bring in yaw luggidge,' said he.

We did as instructed and they ignored our inexpensive, allowable souvenirs. There was nothing untoward about our baggage.

'Yew,' he looked at me, 'yew the drarver?

I nodded.

'Yus take yaw core roun' there,' he ordered.

'Roun there' was behind the customs shed, where two customs men literally took the car apart extracting contraband from every nook and cranny in the Anglia, including the windscreen washer water container. Those industrious officials found every last one of the 50 or so bottles I'd bought. These were taken into the shed.

'Well meneer,' asked the customs guy in a measured, deliberate tone, 'wot have yew got to say about orl this hey?'

If you're caught red-handed, as I had been, there's not a lot one can say, so I simply shook my head.

'Yew realize we is confirskating the bottles.'

That thought had crossed my mind. I nodded again.

The man began writing in his pad. Then he glanced up at me and said, 'The excise jewty comes to...' and he mentioned a figure which was more than five times the total cost of all my miniatures. I felt the blood draining from my face. But he wasn't finished.

Now I was in Hades for sure!

'In cases of attempted smugelling, the jewty payable is dubbelled.'

I thought I was going to die. But worse was yet to come.

'Now,' stated he, 'thereza question ovva fine. In yaw case arm gonna be gen'rous an' limit it to £25 or yew could go to court if yew prefer but ar think yew'll find it wull cost yew a lot more. An' don't forget the legal costs.'

I knew I was going to die. £25 was a huge amount, probably a month's wages. I couldn't speak. The suspense persisted.

'One thing maw,' he continued, 'in cases lark 'is we's entartled to confirskate the vehickel carrying the contraband.'

He paused to allow me time to digest that.

Johannesburg was nigh on 300 miles away. Hesitatingly I asked him how we would get home without a car.

'That's not mar problem,' my tormentor answered. 'But I tell yew wot. Seeing as how yew're a narse parlite oke arll let chew off with the core.'

I resisted the urge to yell with relief at that. Nevertheless I had to pay the fine there and then. Credit cards were still science fiction. By a stroke of good fortune Roger had his cheque book with him and we handed over all the cash we had with us and settled the balance by cheque.

I asked the customs guy why he'd stopped us. He lifted a counter flap, tilting his head as a silent invitation to join him behind the counter and to follow him into the room behind it. The twenty square feet of this room had no furniture other than a small table. Almost the entire floor was taken up by impounded miniature bottles. My jaw dropped. It felt as if my eyes were popping out on snail-like eye stalks.

'It's lark thus ev'ry weekend man. The public think we's *mamparas*, specially the Teejays.'

(All South African car number plates had a prefix before the numbers – T for Transvaal, J for Johannesburg. Durban was ND – N for Natal, D for Durban and so on throughout the Union).

'The Teejays,' he continued, 'orl come yere onna weekends mainly to pick up those minichewers but we look in every damn core. Can yew believe we even find them wrapped in dirty nappies? Ja man, snot us that's the blerry *mamparas* hey?'

So pleased was he at his own brilliant turn of phrase that he burst into gales of self-congratulatory guttural guffaws.

As we *mamparas* drove away Coleridge's immortal words rang in my head…

He went like one that hath been stunned,
And is of sense forlorn:
A sadder and a wiser man
He rose the morrow morn.

Not long before my Rothmans stint I met my first wife at another girlfriend Zelma's 18th birthday party in Doornfontein. In those days guests pooled gramophone records all of which had the owners' names on the labels. I was in charge of the music and while choosing my playlist, I found a small pile labelled 'Ostrofsky.' While trying to pronounce it out loud, to myself in fact, a voice behind me said, 'Oss-stroff-skee - the name's Ostrofsky.' The girl possessing this tongue twister suggested that if I repeated it three times I was bound to remember it. Which proved true. To top it, her floricultural first names were Myrtle Iris, a quotidian combination.

My first encounter with her father was on the night of our first date. Seems she was not to be trusted with a key and Ostrofsky opened the front door for her. She said, 'Daddy, this is Eddie.'

I said 'Good evening.' He looked at his watch. It was about ten past his turning into a pumpkin.

'Good evening?' he growled, 'It's more like bloody good morning!' He turned his back on me and went inside.

I was not invited in.

I felt an instant antipathy towards him and how accurate I was we shall see. Mind you, I believe the feelings were mutual and in this respect I can't blame him.

Around this time I had decided to acquire a long deferred self-indulgence - a bush baby. I had always wanted to own one of these *nagapies* (night monkeys), the Afrikaans name for the enchanting wee primates whose tails - which help their balance as they leap about energetically like tiny Olympic gymnasts - are longer than their opened-hand-size bodies. They are gregarious animals who seem to relish the company of humans. They are easy to maintain as they eat almost every kind of fruit and nut and if there are a lot of insects around, as there are in Africa, they are in their element plucking them out of thin air with their soft, padded fingers to enrich their dining pleasure.

The downside of keeping them as pets is that they are creatures of the night whose exquisite, large, amber eyes allow them to see in the dark so that they are most active nocturnally. The main drawback is their deplorable habit of marking their territory with pee and a tendency to regard your home as 'theirs'. That's easily forgiven when they're really tame and hop around imitating miniscule kangaroos, chattering to themselves (or to you?) with a variety of sounds some of which, had they been louder, could easily have been attributed to humans. It is said that their English name derives from the similarity of their calls to the cry of human babies.

To my delight the Lopis Pet Shop in downtown Johannesburg had one of my furry fantasy friends in stock and it was love at first sight, for me anyway, and I took this beguiling little animal home and spent all my spare time getting to know him. The moment I returned home from work, he would leap onto my shoulder excitedly imparting his day's news while foraging in my pockets to check if they held any treats such as nuts, raisins or biscuits. I did not let him down. He too became a jazz aficionado and delighted in those evenings with Peter as much as I did.

'Daddy' Ostrofsky had reluctantly accepted me as part of his daughter's life and on Sundays I normally lunched at their flat. In time I considered my bush baby tame enough to meet them, but Myrtle's mother firmly made it abundantly clear that he was not a welcome guest in their compact abode in a block named Champs-Élyseés by someone with a flair for irony.

The only interesting thing about the nondescript block was that it housed the Isaacs family whose daughter Mareon was a very sexy young dancer. Her brother Johnny was a bodybuilder I'd met at Ash Kallos's place way back during our schooldays. One afternoon I was staggered to see Johnny get out of a car with a Herculean human who I recognized immediately as the Englishman who not only put bodybuilding on the world map but also influenced the early career of no less a personage than Arnold Schwarzenegger. He was Reg Park the famous Mr. Universe, who starred in a number of peplum movies, but it was hard to believe he was actually going into the same building as I was. Johnny greeted me saying 'Ed, this is Reg, my sister's fiancée!' Reg smiled 'Hello Ed,' he said as he shook my hand. I muttered something unintelligible and walked with them into Champs-Élyseés. 'See you around Ed,' said Reg. The exhilaration of meeting an international celebrity left me unable to speak, and I could only wave goodbye to him. I was greatly impressed by his handshake which was firm only without the hurtful crocodile jaw squeeze common to Ash Kallos's muscular mates.

The Ostrofsky home on the ground floor of the block was marginally bigger than the average dolls house and decorated accordingly.

The living room, all gold coloured bobbles with matching trimming, was barely large enough to swing a kitten without damaging it against a radiogram cabinet occupying far more than its fair share of space. The mini kitchen doubled as a dining area except on occasions such as Sunday lunch, at which time the folding table in the narrow corridor was opened to accommodate six cramped people. If you sat against the wall or furthest from the kitchen and were suddenly caught short, everyone had to move twice, once to let you out and again to allow you back. At meal times the black maid was summoned from the kitchen, about ten paces away, by ringing one of those twee china hand bells.

The flat's bathroom was three paces from Myrtle's bedroom door. In there was a handmade play area allowing Billy Boy, their pet budgerigar, to exchange pleasantries with its reflection in the medicine cabinet mirror while keeping Ostrofsky company when he was shaving beside the lavatory seat covered with fluorescent green Day-Glo faux fur. *Très chic oui?* On the windowsill, a genuine hand-knitted toilet roll holder contained three, yes *three* spare rolls of toilet paper awaiting their turn to address the user's needs. On the cistern pipe itself a printed notice, protected by waterproof celluloid, bore the timeless truism "Stand closer, it's shorter than you think."

The reason for detailing this seemingly useless information will soon become clear. I hope. Space in both minute bedrooms was scarce. The master bedroom contained a double bed, a wardrobe and a stool facing a Dolly Varden kidney shaped dressing table. Myrtle's seriously incommodious bedroom also sported a similar glass-topped dressing table, a built-in cupboard and minimal squeeze-by space around its single bed. Both bedroom windows faced out onto the driveway at the side of the building. Champs-Élyseés was located on Louis Botha Avenue, the main arterial road to Pretoria and no parking was allowed on the street so I habitually parked my car in the building's driveway just outside the Ostrofsky flat's bedroom windows.

One Sunday Myrtle's parents asked if we wanted to accompany them on a visit to relatives in Benoni, a place whose only claim to fame, you may remember, was as the home town of the famous fighting Toweels.

I had previously met the branch of the Ostrofsky family who lived there. They were above averagely tiresome, addicted to picayunish, parochial prattle about even more uninteresting family members, so I felt it hardly worth wasting a fine sunny Sunday afternoon with them, and politely declined the invitation. Benoni was almost an hour's drive away from the Ostrofsky flat.

Ten minutes after her parents departed we decided to take the opportunity to catch up on a bit of how's-your-father. Less than five minutes from the off we heard a car tooting outside the bedroom window. It was customary for guests to take cakes to Sunday tea parties and the Ostrofskys had forgotten theirs in the refrigerator. On their return to collect it they knew we were home since my car was still parked in its usual spot in the driveway. Ostrofsky left his engine running and within seconds the doorbell rang and he was calling, 'Hello, hello!' His key rattled in the front door lock. Bloody hell!

What to do next?

We were both naked, stark, staring butt naked and dressing as fast as panic allowed. There was barely enough time for me to pull on my underpants. In the nick of time I managed a Eureka Moment. I locked the bedroom door (which was all of two paces away from the front door) as quietly as possible and a micro second later Ostrofsky was turning the handle calling 'Let me in...' Rattle, rattle, rattle.

'Why's the door locked?' he demanded, 'Open up!'

'I can't,' I lied, 'the bush baby's out. We're trying to catch him.'

Silence.

'Lionel', I called, 'Do me a favour.'

'What?' he barked suspiciously.

'Can you please pass me a bath towel?'

'A bath towel? What for?'

'I want to try to throw it over the bush baby.'

'Christ,' he fulminated, 'if it pees in there Ray (his wife) will kill you!'

Seconds later he knocked again.

By now I had my shirt on and my pale faced girlfriend had pulled on her blouse and skirt - there was no time for bra or panties which were hurriedly stuffed under a pillow, but it didn't matter because I was one hundred per cent determined not to let Ostrofsky into the room under any circumstances.

I swiftly ran a comb through my hair before I opened the door ever so slightly to ensure, I hoped, that my shoeless foot would disallow his entry if he tried to push it open. I took the towel from him before relocking the door. Just in case, you understand.

'I'm off now,' he called, 'we left the cake behind.'

He closed the front door yelling petulantly, 'I hope for your sake that bloody rodent hasn't crapped anywhere.'

I still can't believe he fell for my story...

Apart from gossip, Mrs. Ostrofsky was pre-occupied with her blue budgerigar on which she and her husband doted. It accompanied them from home to work and back every day, sitting pretty on its personal perch fitted to the dashboard of their car. Billy Boy Ostrofsky (honest!) was transported to their shop in a portable travel cage and released into its budgerigarian Utopia which was part of Mrs. O's daytime realm behind a plate glass fronted cash desk facing the shop door from where she ruled the roost. She handled payments made through a strategically positioned hole in the glass. She also tended the accounts and kept an eagle eye out for thieves and undesirables. Within this glass case the budgie had free reign. Here, this colourful, fine feathered friend with clipped wings ceaselessly deposited its black and white calling cards everywhere. If it wasn't playing with its selection of plastic toys with wheels and bells, it pecked at paperclips and pins, chattering away merrily to itself all the livelong day. Mrs. O talked to it as if it were human and it tirelessly repeated immortal phrases such as *'I'm a little Jewish bird,'* and *'A gezunt in dein keppela'* the Yiddish for 'a blessing on your little head.' I professed I couldn't decipher a word of budgiespeak but secretly I was very impressed.

Mrs. O's other preoccupation was an on-going *affaire* with Ostrofsky's bachelor business partner Ernest Erling née Pffiferling (silent p), an émigré who had fled Germany when Hitler reared his hideous head. After the war he and Ostrofsky met while both were working as window dressers at an Eloff Street men's outfitters. They pooled their resources to open their own business and by dropping the *Pffif* from Ernest's silly sounding surname the shop became Erlings.

Ernest was quite an amiable, lonesome bachelor who accompanied the Ostrofskys everywhere they went - the cinema, meals in, meals out, the bowls club, family gatherings, whatever, wherever, he was there too. More often than not his English provided a source of mild amusement since his South African German Jewish accent approximated a poor imitation of that peerless film star Peter Lorre on an off day. Ernest yearned to be considered erudite and diligently worked on it by purloining puerile poems, junior jokes, odd epigrams and quaint quips from varied sources, primarily the *Readers Digest.* He tried to commit said witticisms to memory in the hope that, sooner or later, an occasion would arise to enable him to deliver one as if it were spontaneously his so that people might regard him as being ever so droll. Such opportunities were few and far between. And, as we shall see, didn't always work the way Ernest would have wished.

Two hours' drive north of Johannesburg in the Magaliesberg Mountains, the oldest mountain range in the world, a guest farm called The Wigwam had been established to cater to Joburgers wishing for weekend breaks years before Sun City was born. One long Easter holiday weekend the Ostrofsky ménage trekked there.

At breakfast the first morning, the hundred seater dining room hummed with conversation cum clicking cutlery on crockery. The waiter asked Ernest what he wanted and he ordered fried eggs, tomatoes and sausages. Then, to Ernest's delight, the waiter suggested he might also wish to have a side order of baked beans unknowingly presenting Ernest with a long awaited opportunity to give voice to an example of his *Reader's Digestives.* He'd been nursing one which went 'I don't like baked beans, they make me ffffffffff...' leading the listener to possibly anticipate the word 'fart' after all those effs. Then, when you heard *fat* instead, you might, just might, smile politely at such spontaneous brilliance. However, almost as if it had been pre-planned, a sudden lull occurred in the ambient noise and not a soul among the diners missed his words. 'I don't like baked beans,' declaimed Ernest fortissimo, 'they make me FFFFFAAAAART!' A stunned silence hung in the air at this apothegm until a small boy started to snicker. 'He said it daddy,' exclaimed the youngster elatedly, 'he said FART!' This brought the house down.

Being German, Ernest had joined the Johannesburg German Club. Another member was my girlfriend's singing teacher, Brunhilde, a bountifully busted Valkyrie lacking only a horned helmet and spear to augment her resemblance to the mythical heroine who was her namesake. She was accompanied by Shultz, her most improbable spouse, a good head shorter than she and about half her weight. One night we were Ernest's guests at a beer fest or whatever that particular German cultural convocation was called. We shared the same table as Brunhilde and her husband. Brunhilde and Ernest had much to talk about, allowing Shultz's wandering eye to focus upon a winsome, petite, young woman with whom he spent a lot of time on the dance floor. He eventually returned to the table where Brunhilde confronted him with Wagnerian intensity. 'Shultz!' she proclaimed lustily enough for everyone to hear. 'Shultz!' Maybe he had a first name, but apparently she never used it. 'Shultz! Don't sink you can vork up an appetite here unt zen come home to eat!'

On completing my Rothmans induction I drove eight hours to Port Elizabeth where I was to operate as a 'market researcher'. In reality I peddled cigarettes in a most insidious fashion. At that time Rothmans were introducing their king- size filter cigarettes to the South African market. An errant marketing guru had predicated that if each smoker influenced one other person to smoke his/her brand and then the new smoker influenced a third smoker and so on, their sales would increase exponentially. If the theory worked, the entire South African population would be inhaling Rothmans King- Size in next to no time.

Accordingly the main thrust of my 'public relations' duties involved visiting bars where I ingratiated myself with the barman by presenting him with a complimentary carton of 200 cigarettes ostensibly to ensure he stocked Rothmans and if not, the free fags helped nudge him to comply. Those freebies, according to the Rothmans think tank, afforded me the barman's tacit authority to introduce myself to smoking customers in order to proselytize among them. The first step was to strike up a conversation by asking if he (hardly any women other than those on the game ever visited South African bars) would help with market research. He'd then be offered a cigarette which customarily led to a discussion about his current brand. People invariably smoked the freebie and if they were positive about it, I'd give them a buckshee packet of twenty and try to arrange a meeting the following week to follow up and check if they had switched to Rothmans. If not, why not? Maybe a second free pack would help?

It was pleasant, cushy work which did not trouble my conscience in the least because in those days no one had seriously checked on just how lethal smoking was, resulting in the public being bombarded with advertising material such as:-

Chesterfield, to put a smile in your smoking.

According to repeated nationwide surveys more doctors smoke Camels than any other cigarette.

Doctors in every branch of medicine were asked 'what cigarette do you smoke?' The brand named most was Camels.

At Rothmans we coined our own pet slogan for Camels - *'From camel to consumer.'*

In retrospect I am repentant and embarrassed to admit that I had, albeit unwittingly, helped spread lung cancer and that the excuse 'I was only doing my job' doesn't really apply to my guilt. But then my influence was confined to confirmed chokers and no one has since established which brands were the worst. I mean, would it be possible to contract say Rothman's cancer, opposed to Camel cancer, or C to C cancer or even Springbok brand cigarette cancer?

My freebies gained me a distinct social standing among Port Elizabeth's puffers and I accumulated a substantial number of new friends and acquaintances all of whom knew where to find me thanks to my fire engine red Rothmans van parked outside or near bars. A conspicuous giant metal cigarette adorned its roof. I had personally modified it, Heath Robinson style, by drilling through the roof to connect a length of rubber tubing attached to a demijohn of water inside the van. Holes drilled through the front of the cigarette and dry ice actuated by the water made it 'smoke' quite effectively. Cognoscenti agreed on 'spectacularly' except for Rothmans' taciturn old office manager who reported me to headquarters for desecrating company property. But this backfired on him since my Johannesburg boss valued my initiative sufficiently to look into the possibility of fitting similar devices to all their vans.

Ben, another Wits dropout, who hailed from Port Elizabeth became my constant companion on non-business outings. P E was not exactly renowned as a swinging city and unless something more interesting cropped up he and I spent Saturday nights reconnoitering the Union Castle Line passenger ships which docked there en route to Cape Town or heading north to Durban. There were usually young women aboard and now and then we'd get lucky.

One Saturday night we drew a blank and headed back to Ben's house to listen to music. His parents were in the middle of a social evening and we were invited to join them for a drink.

Naturally I always carried a supply of Rothmans' cigarettes in my van and while enjoying a beer and Ben's mother's tasty canapés, I took advantage of the occasion to distribute a few packets among the guests. Every smoker in the room was soon cheerfully inhaling Rothman's King-Size freebies.

Ben became deeply engrossed in a confab with an uncle. One of the fringe benefits gained from visiting the ships was that we came away with free supplies of those handy book matches which, surprisingly, were not available in shops. The Union Castle matchbooks were almost exactly the same size and shape as the tins of Sheik condoms which could not be mistaken for anything other than what they were. Ben, unlit cigarette dangling from his lips, fumbled for his matches. Instead he pulled out a packet of Sheik from his pocket. I was sitting next to him but his head was turned away from me. Now Ben, given to gesticulating animatedly with his hands while talking, was so carried away with his discourse that he failed to notice what he was holding and flourishing for all to see.

The hum of party chatter diminished as every eye in the room was focused on his small orange tin. I could do nothing to interrupt his flow. Conversation died completely and Ben thought it was his oratorical excellence which had the guests hanging on his every syllable. The only thing I could think of to make him aware of his *faux pas* would be to light his cigarette for him so I took out what I thought was one of my matchbooks. Only it wasn't either...

Ben was a golf enthusiast and he and a couple of friends wanted to introduce me to the game in the hope of my becoming the final member of a regular foursome. A dramatic outing lay ahead. After receiving a few basic tips on which of my borrowed clubs did what, how best to hold a club, and how to hit the ball, it was all 'go!'

The first three holes were disastrous. I had no idea what 'par' was until they revealed I was about ten over par at each hole. They stressed the self-evident information that low scores were the aim of the game. The sixth tee overlooked a fairway fifteen feet below. I shut my eyes, took a swipe at my ball, hit it cleanly and lost sight of it against the sky. We searched for the ball for ten minutes while an impatient, irascible foursome behind us insisted on playing through but as they were about to tee off Ben shouted rapturously. He'd found my ball! No one was more aghast than me to see that it had landed six feet from the hole. None of them believed this was my first ever game of golf until it took me three more strokes to hole out recording two over par, my best hole of the day.

Only that was not the most memorable incident of the outing. One of my companions, by far the best golfer among us, sliced a powerful tee shot into a nearby tree trunk. The ball ricocheted and hit him precisely on the top of the bridge of his nose smack between his eyes, knocking him unconscious. We rushed him to hospital where he heard how incredibly lucky he was to have escaped with a badly broken nose and a lump the size of half a tennis ball. The doctor informed him that if the ball had connected a scintilla either way he'd have been blinded in one eye.

It was only when my girlfriend left Port Elizabeth after spending a fortnight's bonking holiday with me that I realised how much I missed my family, friends and the lifestyle in the Golden City but Rothmans could not offer me anything there so I resigned and returned home.

The only job readily available was as a part-time reporter and sports editor for a weekly newspaper which paid peanuts. Ostrofsky had a business crony, a jejune German called Kurt Bernstein whose sales agency handled a selection of products. Ostrofsky inveigled me into thinking there was a future for me in sales and that working for Bernstein would be a good career move. Career? What career? To end his badgering I reluctantly agreed to give it a go by again taking on a commission-only job handling a product that would transport me to another world - that of the Concession Store.

In South Africa in the early days mining companies auctioned concessions (equivalent to 21st century franchises) to people wishing to open stores catering to black mineworkers and the scattering of white mining and farming families who lived on or near the mine's land. These stores were mainly leased by Jewish immigrants from Lithuania, few of whom spoke English. Working hours were long and exhausting, making it difficult for traders to find young white South Africans prepared to live in the back of beyond for ridiculously frugal wages, leaving the concessionaires no option but to import adolescent family members from Europe. These 'greeners' (greenhorns) picked up *Fanagolo*, the *lingua franca* of black miners, long before they mastered English simply because there was no one around who spoke Shakespeare's tongue.

In the mid-1930's anti-Semitism reached its zenith in Europe terminating Jewish immigration to South Africa, compelling storekeepers to employ 'native' (black) shop assistants.

Undermanned stores endured expensive losses from shoplifting, with one exception. A trader who knew that black miners, conscripted from far-flung rural areas throughout Southern Africa, were deeply superstitious and that pilfering had reached its highest ever level, this man had a revelation involving his glass eye. One hectic Saturday afternoon when his store was awash with newly paid miners he climbed up onto his wooden counter, banging a metal plate with a spoon. This was so outlandish that the hubbub died down instantly. The man scooped out his glass eye with his forefinger to the accompaniment of awestruck exclamations from the natives whose own eyes were wide as saucers. Flourishing the eye above his head, the trader announced through an interpreter that from then on he was leaving his eye on a high shelf where it would see everything that happened anywhere in the store and he would know who was stealing from him. From then on his pilfer rate was eliminated. That shopkeeper had unwittingly foreshadowed CCTV by more than fifty years!

Concession Stores were the only place where the miners could congregate other than in the desolate accommodation of their barrack-like compounds which were no more or less than human filing cabinets in which they slept. The miners' cramped dormitories were far from conducive to social intercourse thereby presenting traders with golden opportunities to increase turnover by adding butcheries for customers to buy meat to cook personally or, if they preferred, dine in the other innovation - eating houses - where patrons had to provide their own enamel plates which, by the way, were also sold in the stores.

Nauseating, pungent cooking smells assailed your nostrils well in advance of reaching the store. At meal times the area resonated with roisterous exuberance emanating from the eating house where the Basuto-blanketed men sat on benches on both sides of long tables eating in much the same style depicted in Hollywood versions of mediaeval banquets. Knives? Forks? Hell no! We've been eating with our hands for centuries before forks were dreamt of.

The meat they consumed would not prove terribly popular in 21st century *haute cuisine table d'hote*, consisting, as it did, of sheep's heads, cattle cheeks, pigs' trotters, tripe and other offal - best sellers all.

Concession stores were known to sell chickens and livestock. Now and then you'd see a black buyer carrying a live sheep 'piggyback' style, with the animal's forelegs tied around the customer's neck and the back legs around his waist. Local tribesmen wearing similarly tethered sheep could be observed transporting trussed sheep home on squeaky, rusty bicycles.

Inside the stores the pervasive, cloying effluvium of greasy food from the dining area could not have been deadened by anything less than a mushroom cloud of disinfectant. Or maybe not, considering the omnipresent odour of goods like paraffin, cheap tobacco, snuff, and that blue and white speckled carbolic soap.

Top sellers included Primus stoves, candles, oil lamps, tin mugs, tin trunks, enamel goods, cheap blankets, dried goods, boiled sweets, canned goods, especially sweetened condensed milk, highly prized by black folk, and whites, who punctured two holes in the lid for ease of pouring into tea, spreading on bread or consuming it neat by sucking one of the holes.

The stores also stocked shoddy clothing and cheap shoes which included the product I was peddling - *takkies*. Only mine differed from the original tan soled variety. Indeed my *takkies'* soles were remarkable, state-of-the-art, grass green, rubber ones. I was reminded of my mother's distaste for that colour since the black miners shared her aversion to green, especially green soled *takkies* which dismally failed to catch on with black miners. They were cheap, compared to even the least expensive alternatives and the makers, D I Fram and Company, maintained that their most promising market was that of the black native population.

My territory embraced Concession Stores and outlying shops in distant *dorps* throughout the Transvaal. I had been briefed to ensure that all the stores were stocked up in all sizes at all times. I also had to remove and credit or replace old stock that had perished. The latter proved to be my main occupation and I usually returned to Johannesburg in an overloaded car piled high with decaying *takkies*. Maybe if they'd been manufactured in bright colours they'd have gained a foothold in the market, but *white* canvas? Nobody, it seemed, had ever bothered to conduct any market research among the black population. Had they done so they may have noticed that black folk outside the cities seldom wore shoes and even if they had, it didn't need a mastermind to deduce the colour they would turn to in the labyrinthine depths of the gold mines and coal mines. The result was that *takkies* were a disaster so far as putting any cash in my back pocket but the stores enriched my memory banks with an intimate insight into a parallel universe.

During my Concession Store era the aftermath of Myrtle's holiday in Port Elizabeth became evident. She was pregnant. This presented her father with a key role in my saga. Ostrofsky now knew with certitude, that I was what he'd always thought I was - a ne'er do well rapscallion and, worse still, one who'd knocked up his daughter.

Nevertheless he began to hint that I might care to join his business as a sales assistant. The vision of a future measuring male inside trouser legs scared the bejasus out of me. I had other ideas of how I wished to shape my life. Needless to say Ostrofsky was not best pleased with his daughter's condition but his unhappiness was not quite as great as mine, having to reimburse him in full for the cost of the abortion which he personally arranged. I considered that the responsibility for his daughter's pregnancy was partly his. As the man of the world he aspired, indeed affected, to be, he should have had the intelligence to foresee the consequences that might arise from allowing two young people in their sexual prime to be together in a secluded hotel for two weeks. Bluntly, he should have denied her permission to visit me in Port Elizabeth. Period. Up 'til then the word marriage had not troubled my thought patterns and it was only after placing a bun in her oven that I felt guilty and that I should marry her. A decision that complicated and profoundly transmuted my life.

In parenthesis, as it were, I had not intended that this narrative should include my vicissitudes after settling in Britain in 1957, had Ostrofsky's interference in my marital affairs not effectively severed the wonderful relationship I enjoyed with my children.

Thirteen years later my wife and I entered the closing chapter of our marriage prompting the old curmudgeon to emplane to London specifically to persuade me what I already knew which was that our marriage was incompossible and that the time had arrived for a trial separation to allow us to cogitate on the situation. Very reluctantly I agreed that this would be in the best interests of our children. What I didn't know was that Ostrofsky was fully cognizant of the fact that Myrtle had no intention of ever returning to England as she was grieving over her recently deceased London lover. In fact I was unaware of either the lover or his demise until decades after our inevitable divorce but the knowledge of her affair explained the total lack of conjugal rights between us in the dying years of our marriage.

My family and I had lived in Australia for the best part of a year. I was producing a film series there with Tony Hancock, Britain's preeminent comedy actor, while she became a minor celebrity playing her guitar and singing the news on a local television programme. She deeply resented having to return to the UK to revert to her role of wife and mother. My 20/20 hindsight strongly suggests that her affair had a devastatingly deleterious effect on our marriage. If I'd had the slightest inkling that the 'trial separation' might mean losing my cherished children, I would never have consented to Ostrofsky's proposal. I did not take kindly to this blatant scoundrel who lied to me in order to abduct my children to South Africa. I therefore have no compunction in writing about so hypocritical a son of Belial with candour.

Lionel Juel (pronounced 'jewel') Ostrofsky co-owned Erlings which was situated in Fox Street close to the busy financial heart of Johannesburg. Erling and the Ostrofskys believed their shop rivalled any on London's Savile Row. The store did provide excellent value since the partners took it in turns to undertake annual buying trips to New York during the closeout sales season, held annually by wholesalers and manufacturers to dispose of surplus stock in bulk at bargain basement prices.

Ostrofsky was a boorish, gruff, morose, egocentric whose bent, bulbous snout was underscored by a moth-eaten moustache that only served to underline and emphasize its size. This, combined with his follically disadvantaged pate, contributed to his striking resemblance to both Clement Attlee, one time prime minister of Britain, and Mahatma Gandhi - primarily the latter. Indeed Ostrofsky had once arrived at a fancy dress dinner-dance draped in a white bed sheet, his naturally sallow complexion disguised by an overdose of Leichner coffee brown on his skull, face, arms, hands, legs and sandaled feet. So convincing was his guise that he was summarily evicted by a conscientious doorman - no such thing as security guards in those days - who took him for an Indian waiter who had lost his way to a nearby curry restaurant. The fact that he was wielding a wooden broomstick handle to represent Gandhi's trademark staff didn't help Ostrofsky's argument and it was only after a scenette involving an exchange of colourful nautical language that Ostrofsky was finally admitted. The judges awarded him a certificate for his commendable representation of the Mahatma.

The asinine Mr.O wore a constant frown, understandably, considering his relationship with his wife, who, he once confided to his daughter, had forbidden him to kiss her lips, an experience which would doubtless have been tantamount to snogging a hairy ashtray. I could possibly have tolerated his incontinent mouth and a mind which spawned his hankering to compose prolix outré verse in flatulent, toe-curling doggerel at the drop of a cliché, had he not chosen deliberately and with malicious *schadenfreude,* to mock my mother to her face at a social gathering shortly after my brother's marriage to a non-Jewish woman. Ostrofsky smirked as he loudly called out to her, 'I hear your other son married a *shiksa!'* (A derogatory, highly insulting name for a non-Jewish woman). My mother was mortified. Years later this loathsome, sanctimonious panjandrum met his nemesis in spades thanks to his only child, my ex-wife, marrying an elderly, alcoholic *yock* (an equally contemptuous name for a male non-Jew) who was closer to Ostrofsky's age than his daughter's. Later in life his kidnapped granddaughters both married 'out of the faith' and his grandson moved in with a non-Jewish partner. Bless 'em all.

Ostrofsky had developed a super-inflated opinion of his own self-importance, no doubt to compensate for his lack of stature, by busying himself with innumerable committees on which no one else wanted to serve. He was out almost every evening and much of the weekend either at meetings or hiding himself away from reality in an elaborate workshop where he produced finicky woodwork in that curly bracket style of furniture - {- highly favoured among nouveau riche South African Jews.

Gerry, his nephew, in whose garage Ostrofsky's workshop was located, had a small son named Howie. The garage opened onto a concrete driveway where Ostrofsky parked his car during woodworking sessions. One day Howie wanted to ride his tricycle there and brazenly told Ostrofsky to move his car. Ostrofsky derided the kid, aged about four, who responded, 'If you don't move your car I'll wee on it.' Ostrofsky warned him he'd smack him if he did, whereupon Howie lisped, 'Ith too late, I weed already' before he dashed for cover. I loved that kid.

In common with scores of other vertically challenged men Ostrofsky strove to camouflage his inferiority by emulating Lewis Carroll's White Rabbit skittering about as if his arse was on fire. Whenever his preposterous, peripatetic progress slowed down sufficiently for him to catch his breath, you knew he was close by thanks to the obnoxious odour of fetid tobacco which followed him around like a stray puppy dog. He was inevitably accompanied by his other constant companion, a pipe, which, he believed, afforded him dignity and gravitas. He bristled about with self-importance, a trait not uncommon among men harbouring a Napoleon complex, indulging in a recondite ritual of persistently poking a metal implement into the dottle in his pipe bowl which gurgled incessantly and disgustingly from the condensation of steam and not a little spittle in the bottom of the bowl. Imagine the din and the acrid reek of an asthmatic steam engine misfiring on all cylinders merged with a plentiful portion of *parfum* nicotine, and you may appreciate why his wife disallowed mouth to mouth affection and began an affair with Ernest, his business partner who, come to think of it, was a non-smoker who merely suffered from terminal halitosis capable of withering plants at five paces.

My future father-in-law was wont to express inane banalities. One unfortunate example was aired, so to speak, every time he broke wind. 'It's a poor arse,' he'd declaim, 'that can't rejoice.'

Mr. O even turned his fallacious literary skills to writing, seemingly determined that his dipsy doggerel should outdo that of the redoubtable William Topaz McGonagall, a Scot renowned as the world's worst ever poet. Ostrofsky would compose for any occasion: hatches, matches, dispatches, it didn't much matter. He'd write and deliver absurd ditties for anyone who asked, and many who didn't, subjecting guests at various functions to extreme boredom by regurgitating his lengthy, excruciatingly vomitus verse which displayed zero recognition of basic scansion, a trait, incidentally, passed genetically to his daughter who set her own rhymes to music which she sang to the accompaniment of her acoustic guitar. All in the key of 'C'.

Ostrofsky continued to sublimate his sexual frustrations by indulging in phillumeny, a pastime he'd adopted during WWII in preference to the beer bottle labels collected by his military comrades who, he repeatedly told us, humped their bottles around African deserts until they found sufficient water to soak the labels off the bottles. Matchbox labels were easier to cope with. When he discovered that his arcane avocation made him a 'phillumenist' he frequently employed the word as if it was an accolade he had won. I guess that sounded better than being known as a 'brothel keeper', an army assignment which kept him busy in Mogadishu, capital city of Italian Somaliland (today's Somalia), where he was based after the country fell to British forces in 1941.

Ostrofsky was not only short in stature but in personality as well. He grimaced his way through clouds of putrid pipe smoke as if emulating Chicken Little waiting for the sky to fall in. Mr. O became Grand Pooh-Bah at the local Jewish Reform synagogue where, as far as I could make out, he was in charge of everything, from conducting square dancing classes, through organizing camping holidays in Natal somewhere for children (hmm) to hiring and firing rabbis. Why he held his Orthodox co-religionists in contempt was a mystery. I'd witnessed an example of his paranoiac antagonism in that respect at a wedding reception in Sydenham, a predominantly Jewish suburb, where the Orthodox rabbi's witty speech likened the Reform movement to the 'ham' in Sydenham. This harmless jibe evoked much derisive cachinnation whereupon Ostrofsky leapt up out of his seat, stridently berating the rabbi at the top of his voice about the 'insult.' It took three male guests to quieten him down and persuade him to bugger off.

He and I had umpteen differences of opinion, chiefly about apartheid. It was from him that I first heard a detestable, untenable axiom that bigots who supported the Nationalist ideology were prone to use when logic fled. 'My uniform is my skin!' he'd proclaim defiantly... I found it particularly paradoxical that a business owned by racists owed much of its success to its black customers who were fleetingly accorded the same courtesy extended to whites except that black guys were never addressed as 'sir.' Egalitarian was a word neither Ostrofsky nor partner Pffiferling, had ever heard of and even if they had, as die-hard dogmatists they would never have subscribed to so radical a doctrine.

All his activities and absences from home left his mini missus masses of time to herself. Other than visiting the partner's flat for a spot of who knows, who cares, she constantly re-tidied her already tidy, miniscule flat with its tasselled lamp shades and reproduction classic furniture. She was addicted to collecting souvenirs from her international journeys. These items were, not to put too fine a point on it, of such awfulness that they can only be described as *tzatzkas,* a Yiddish word which loses everything in translation into any other language but if you choose to work it out for yourself, think of the nadir of tacky trash people acquire abroad such as those wooden, donkey shaped dispensers which, when the head was pressed downwards, delivered your cigarette via its anus.

The apartment was basically a knick-knackatory chock-full of other tawdry travel trinkets. Favourites took pride of place on Ostrofsky's masterwork, a 'whatnot' I think he called it, featuring more curly fronted shelves, made from the appositely named stinkwood, connected by chromium pipes all resting on top of an electric fireplace fashioned from faux stone.

On this 'Shit Shelf', so dubbed by one of his grandchildren, knelt a metal Mohammedan on a magic carpet keeping company with the Statue of Liberty, the Leaning Tower of Pisa and the Eiffel Tower, all jostling for pole position between a Manikin Pis, a Japanese Geisha Girl, a doll's house size Limoges porcelain tea set and a dreadful gold plastic Mr. and Mrs. Planters' Peanuts among assorted other monstrosities. If there'd been a contest for the Most Odious Object Ever Conceived By Man it would doubtless have been awarded to the metal statuette of a red nosed drunk brandishing a bottle with one hand while clinging on to a bent lamp post with the other. But the vulgarity didn't end there - oh no - the lamp post bore a street sign reading 'Rue de la Paix' and the amen was a tiny clock above that which had given up the ghost on its journey to Joburg.

Mrs. Ostrofsky, Ray to her friends and family, *kukkela* to her husband, Mrs. O to the shop staff, and Lady Poomshtoch to non-friends, was, in reality, Queen of the Quidnuncs. She was paranoid about cleanliness and I used to speculate as to whether or not she wiped her backside wearing rubber gloves. Only divine intervention could help the dressing down the black maid would suffer if there was a speck of dust anywhere or if each and every *tzatzka* was not replaced less than one hair's breadth away from its carefully calculated distance from its neighbours.

Thanks to her tiny feet she attained real popularity with little children. Her discarded size two shoes were treasured dressing up appurtenances among small girls (and boys even) and on her travels overseas (abroad in UK parlance) she spent most of her time sniffing out high heeled shoes that might fit her. Mind you, she was always impeccably turned out wherever she went. Even to bed, only *haute couture* would do. Her concrete textured, blue rinsed, candy floss look coiffure was capable of withstanding gale force winds without disturbing a solitary hair. Her lacquered head was permanently preserved that way by her clockwork weekly rendezvous with her hairdresser. She looked as if she had stepped out of a Vogue magazine feature on grooming for trainee *yentas* as sponsored by, say, Max Factor. Or maybe she thought Karsh of Ottawa or Lord Snowdon would someday glide into her orbit to preserve her on film for posterity.

To digress momentarily, 'hairdresser' is a word that often brings to mind Mrs. Ostrofsky's dumpy sister Anne who once accompanied us on an Italian holiday. Auntie Anne owned two wigs to conceal her alopecia. On my way to the beach I passed an outdoor hairdresser's establishment and noticed Auntie Anne seated under a dryer. I later suggested to her that she could probably save a lot of time by leaving her spare wig to be washed and set in her absence. She enthusiastically approved of my idea and followed my advice but that didn't work out too well for her as the wig was passed to an unsupervised apprentice who set it back to front. I remained unforgiven for the rest of her life.

Not a man to be knowingly outshone by anyone, especially his business partner, Ostrofsky chose to follow Erling's example by memorising quotations of humorous origin and from Shakespeare and the bible. Since he'd seen fewer than two Shakespeare plays in his life he never fully understood the subtlety of the bard's work but so many of his acquaintances were parvenus anyway it didn't much matter.

Ostrofsky acquired the first portion of his just deserts when his *kukkela* and Ernest turned him into a cuckold. One can only speculate on the motives that enabled the blustering hypocrite to carry on working with Erling while pretending that nothing was going on despite the fact that he and the rest of Johannesburg were aware of the affair. Any slight doubts I may have harboured were confirmed years later by my discovery of trite 'romantic' correspondence between Mrs. O and Ernest inadvertently left behind in my home in Britain after one or the other had visited us.

Ostrofsky wangled himself a reputation among the Reform Jews of Johannesburg for his good works among less fortunate co-religionists. He utilised his knowledge to great financial advantage as a shill for an orthodox Jewish property racketeer who preyed on victims earmarked by Ostrofsky. This finagling heralded the second serving of his desert when his fortune was wiped out by the racketeer who turned nasty and took him to the brink of bankruptcy.

Unbelievably, on turning 83, the shardborn wittol celebrated a second *Bar Mitzvah* because, as he confided in anyone who would listen, he had enjoyed thirteen years more the time on earth than is biblically allocated to mankind.

P.S. Numerous noses were later put well out of joint by Ernest's marriage to his mistress's late brother's widow.

My numerous distractions failed to dispel thoughts of the plight of my black countrymen, thoughts which concerned me deeply. Apartheid's ugliness was approaching monstrous proportions. Most of the whites of South Africa still lived high on the hog believing that everything in the garden was coming up roses. They were fully aware that they possessed the highest standard of living in Africa yet they ignored the fact that the immoral tsunami of terror being inflicted by the Nationalist 'master race' upon their disadvantaged black compatriots continued to escalate as did the savagery with which the police enforced the punitive rules.

Bids to engage whites in discussions on the subject were met with raised eyebrows, disapproving looks and responses such as 'So what are you up to next weekend?' or 'How's Bobby Locke doing in the Open?' In essence it was a collective case of letting sleeping dogs lie and I had to regularly control my urge to yell at these numbskulls that the Shangri-La they believed they lived in was doomed to end in radical change or bloody conflict. I for one wanted no part of the brewing storm and my thoughts of leaving South Africa were escalating.

After quitting Rothmans to return to Johannesburg, I obtained a measure of creative satisfaction from sports reporting for an ethnic minority newspaper. Well OK, I was covering sport for a Jewish weekly with marginally more readers than there were Jewish sportsmen of newsworthy stature. My lineage based pay tempted me to waffle on until my editor, Henry Katzew, forced me to write economically either by rejecting my drawn-out purple prose (such as this book!) or by sharpening his blue pencil whenever I handed in a story about characters such as Raphael Halpern the 'Rasslin Rabbi' (honest!). Halpern was an Israeli who refused to fight on the Sabbath. So firm were his beliefs that he went on to devise a credit card that was inoperable on Saturdays. He was matched against local hero Willie Liebenberg who was immortalised in Jeremy Taylor's famed song *Ag Pleez Deddy*.

Ag Pleez Deddy.won't you take us to the wrestling
We wanna see an ou called Sky High Lee
When he fights Willie Liebenberg
There's gonna be a murder
'Cos Willie's gonna donner that blerrie Yankee.

The notoriously thin air on the Witwatersrand, 5,750 ft. above sea level, had Halpern breathing hard to cope with the altitude yet he won the bout after Liebenberg, having twice been warned by the ref about strangling, took umbrage at the third warning and summarily threw the ref out of the ring, a tactic that ensured his instant disqualification. Great stuff!

Other journalistic perks included invitations to events I would have probably have paid to visit even if I hadn't been reporting them. Few members of the public would have had the pleasure and privilege of attending a buffet reception in honour of the manager and members of Britain's celebrated Wolverhampton Wanderers Football Club who hardly broke sweat thrashing South Africa's national team with a resounding four goals to one win. If Soccer is your bag, my mouldering old programme lists the team as Booth, Broadbent who scored a hat trick - i.e. three

193

goals - Clamp, Deeley - one goal, Finlayson, Flowers, Harris, Hooper, Mullen, Murray, Showell and Stuart,

Then there were cricket tests, ice shows, and an international rugby league exhibition match between England and France. That sport didn't stand a snowball in hell's hope of diminishing the public's obsession with South Africa's hallowed national sport - rugby union.

An outstanding highlight was the world bantamweight title fight between Vic Toweel's younger brother Willie Toweel and the title holder, Algerian born Jewish Frenchman Robert Cohen. This fight proved unique in the annals of world title clashes. As soon as the bell clanged they went at it hammer and tongs, both men looking to finish it swiftly. The second round saw Cohen drop Toweel three times. Everyone thought it was over but Toweel bravely managed to stay on his feet for the full fifteen rounds. The referee could not have anticipated the uproar he created by holding both boxers' hands aloft, signalling a draw!

I took an interest in stock car racing, a sport new to South Africa. This feral phenomenon originated in the USA from whence it spread globally like wildfire eventually making its debut on the speedway track of Johannesburg's Wembley Stadium in the 1950's. The inaugural meet had over 40 garishly painted, reinforced old rust-bucket bangers manufactured between 1930 and 1940, displaying weird names such as Cement Mixer, Crash Flash, The Creeping Paw-paw and Mad Pongo. Ten cars raced in each of four heats round a circuit barely wide enough to take two cars alongside one another. In order to overtake the car in front it was necessary to bash it, dodgem style, from behind or amidships to try to ram it off the track to force a way through. Mostly the cars were driven by insane idiots hell bent on reducing their opponents' vehicles to absolute scrap. To call such activity crazy is an understatement. It was mechanized mayhem which became known as Demolition Derbies, the primary objective being to demolish all other competing cars, the winner being the only remaining car still running. A sort of motorised *bok-bok* which remains alive and well in various countries.

Dick Campbell, one of the star drivers, let me try out his car at the end of the meet. Without traffic on the track I'd managed a top lap speed of 45 mph. Then Dick took me round as his passenger. Seeing the corners coming at me at 60 mph didn't really scare me but the thought of having another nine cars on the track all seemingly heading directly at me wasn't my idea of a Sunday afternoon jaunt.

On the non-sporting front I signed up for a Dale Carnegie Course 'How to win friends and influence people' – bulging with American hype and reminiscent of a Charles Atlas course aimed at mind power instead of muscle power.

Now and then I had an occasional feature accepted by magazines paying chicken feed but drip-feeding my incentive to keep on writing. I also revived one of my hobbies - assembling and painting old classic cars from kits. I had befriended the owner of a car spares shop in downtown Joburg who I asked to sell my models on a percentage basis. His agreement transformed me into a mogul model maker. Perchance he looked on me as a potential brother-in-law for his pleasantly plain sister as he sold a number of cars for me refusing to take any commission. The problem was that this source of income hardly kept me in cigarettes.

Then I came across a newspaper ad…

Kismet launched itself in 1955 when the Sunday Times, a Johannesburg newspaper, featured an advertisement headlined:

'ACCOMPANY THE GREATEST FILM SAFARI TO CENTRAL AFRICA'
('Well I'm damned,' thought I, 'this is for me!')
It read:-
'Leaving Johannesburg early July.
Visiting Victoria Falls, Kilimanjaro, Serengeti. Ngonongoro Crater, Murchison Falls, Mountains of the Moon, Pygmies, Gorillas and Active Virunga Volcanoes...'
(Wow!)
'...and take part in all crowd scenes for this magnificent documentary TV Film. See unusual places not normally visited by safari and experience first class camping facilities'.

ALL THIS FOR ONLY £175

It sounded too good to be true. Surely, I reasoned, this is opportunity come a-knocking. It might even provide the first rung of the filmmaking ladder I wanted to climb. Could this safari offer me that key to my future?

The telephone number in the ad connected me to a Mr. Bruno Crone (pronounced Crow-ner). I told him I'd be interested in writing an article about his safari. He asked when I would like to meet him. I said any time to suit him.

'Now?' he replied.

An hour later I pressed the doorbell of Crone's home near Northcliff on the outskirts of Johannesburg. It was a large, unprepossessing bungalow set in the middle of a bleak neglected field. From outside I could hear the sound of a piano playing Brahms. I supposed the occupants had probably spent all their money on a top quality radio or record player. Hardly had my finger left the bell push than the music stopped and the door was opened by a decorous, peroxide blonde with nary a hair out of place. I was not expecting to find so glamorous a lady, wearing at least a month's supply of make-up, in such pedestrian surroundings. Wanting to test her sense of humour I asked if her father was home. She chuckled and called out 'Bruno, Bruno, your guest is here,' in one of the few German voices I ever found appealing. To me she said, 'Good morningk, I am Helga Crone. Police come in.'

I followed her wiggle into a generous lounge commodious enough to house an immaculately shiny black concert grand piano with enough space left over to accommodate a small audience. Could it have been her playing Brahms?

My reverie was interrupted by Bruno Crone's entry. He was a Teutonic version of Benito Mussolini. His chunky build, short haircut and quiet sibilant voice delivered with the confidence and self-assurance bordering on arrogance typical of the race which had brought the world to the brink of extinction. A gold right incisor gleamed prosperously at me in the bright room. He spoke reasonably good English apart from a few peculiarities now and then such as his w's expressed as v's. Over an excellent cup of freshly percolated coffee Crone related how he'd spent decades of his life as a farmer and white hunter in Tanganyika. Ven ze var - sorry - when the war broke out his coffee plantation had been confiscated by the British who interned him, disregarding his protestations that he had no Nazi sympathies. Nor had he set foot in Germany for decades. At the end of the war he was sent to Rhodesia to await deportation to Germany. Except Crone had other ideas and escaped to spend five weeks living off the land, travelling at night to avoid the patrols hunting him. His extensive knowledge of the outdoors and his natural hardiness enabled him to reach and to swim across the crocodile-infested Zambezi River into South Africa where he worked as a manual labourer under an assumed name until the Malan Government took over the reins of state and granted pardons to all illegal white immigrants.

Crone outlined his plans. 'I vant to establish a regular overland safari business betveen Johannesburg unt Shermany but before ve begin ve need a preliminary safari for sree reasons. To gain experience unt to make a propaganda film for American teewee.' He stood up.

'I tell you ze sird I outside. Come,' he said, 'come look at zis.' He beckoned me to follow him.

'Zis' was a huge, blue, six wheeled, open Dodge truck of a type unknown to me.

'Get in,' said Crone. More an order than an invitation. He started the engine as I settled on the double passenger seat to the right of the steering wheel, Zis being a left hand drive. We headed for a marshy open field sloping downwards into a *sloot*.

I shuddered as he drove the lumbering vehicle into it. The mud reached more than halfway up the wheels.

'How the fuck,' I wondered, 'am I going to get out of this thing without ruining my good suit and shoes?'

Crone had doubtless previously performed such a demo and was well aware of my concern. He stopped the truck in the middle of the gully and turned off the engine. It's all right for you, I felt, dressed in your old khaki gardening outfit and *veldskoene*...

'Vatch,' he said as he restarted it, engaged one of the gears and let out the clutch. The truck began to inch slowly but surely up the side of the muddy hole at an angle of something like 40 degrees. He read my doubtful face, smiled and told me it could negotiate any incline up to 60 degrees.

I ventured the opinion that perhaps a Jeep would be more suitable on a safari. He patiently detailed how much more the truck could carry by way of tents, baggage, spare fuel, oil, tyres and water than a Jeep.

'In any case,' he added, 'just sink of ze publicity ve'd attract if ve could drive to the top of Kilimanjaro viz it!'

'If you could do that, you'd make a fortune,' I remarked.

'Exactly,' he replied, leaning back smugly contemplating his mirage of a Fort Knox sized mound of U S dollars.

Safely back in his house without a speck of mud between us he provided more data about the truck, a former USA army vehicle used to haul very heavy items such as broken down tanks and anti-aircraft guns to and from inaccessible places.

It had, he explained, three differentials working its six wheel drive. He told me he had lived in the shade of Kilimanjaro, the highest mountain in Africa, on whose slopes he'd worked as a white hunter for over twenty years taking time off from his plantation to conduct shooting parties for German business magnates. He knew of a route to the summit where the angle was nowhere greater than 30 degrees.

'Ve vill reach ze top vizout difficulty. Of zat I am convinced. No vehicle has ever done zat. It vill be ze motorised equivalent of climbing Everest.'

Soon afterwards Crone called to say he'd been thinking of my interest in filming and invited me to direct and write the script for the safari film. This was far and away the most irresistible job offer I'd ever received and I hurried round to see him to discuss terms. Neither my family nor my close friends were a smidgeon as enthusiastic as I. My future father-in-law remained unimpressed with the information that American television had offered ten U S dollars a foot for the completed film. That fortune was earmarked to fund Crone's highly ambitious business schemes.

Ostrofsky's concern hinged on the potential embarrassment he might suffer if I resigned from the lacklustre labour he'd persuaded me to undertake. But nothing he could have said or done would have changed my mind and the day I left that sales job, the one with the *takkies*, was, for me, a day of vivifying freedom. What I didn't tell him or my parents was that I'd been offered a free safari trip and a share in the proceeds.

So what was the catch? Well, Crone had hoped for at least 25 paying tourists but only ten had materialized. He was therefore short of working capital and offered me a partnership of one third of the profits in return for an investment of £500 repayable as soon as the film was sold. I accepted and preparations began in earnest. Two film cameramen, Beatty and Jeorge were enlisted and a deal was struck with Charles, a well-to-do Swiss student turned playboy who owned a 16 mm Paillard Bolex camera and a Studebaker car. He bartered the use of these as well as his work as our third cameraman in lieu of payment. My £500 came from the sale of my car.

One chilly July morning (in the Southern Hemisphere July is mid-winter) a convoy of four vehicles containing a cosmopolitan cargo of fifteen people departed from Johannesburg, heading north. We were almost as mixed a bunch as the variety of animals we planned to film. There were four Swiss, two Germans, one South West African, a Belgian, an Australian, a Dutchman and five South Africans.

Occupations were equally varied. Our contingent comprised a brace of photographers, a university student, a concert pianist, a farmer, a teacher, a mechanic, a printer, an engineer, a sheet metal worker, a housewife, a professional spinster, a schoolgirl and Charles, whose Studebaker was far and away the most comfortable car. Its passenger seats were reserved by Crone for himself (unless he was driving the Dodge) and his wife Helga and Mrs. Dinger, a Swiss paying tourist, whose first name no one knew, nor cared to find out, was the other regular passenger. This American vehicle's bullet nosed design made it difficult to tell the back from the front until it moved. Charles once confided that he happened to be the black sheep of his family who had intimated that he might like to return home to Switzerland, whereupon his father bought him the car and paid him handsomely to remain in South Africa.

Eric Katz, a paying tourist, was a Wits student. He and I travelled mostly in the truck with Smit, an Afrikaner hailing from South West Africa who shared driving Zis with Crone.

Tourists Bert Long, his wife Mildred and their overindulged teenage daughter Fay from Durban, were passengers in Frans' Peugeot. Frans, a Belgian, was another non-payer in exchange for the use of his car.

The same deal applied to Hans Horst, a Dutchman, whose Swiss companion Trudi was more than somewhat neurotic. His Volkswagen passengers were Beatty, a professional Australian cameraman, and Jeorge, once a member of the Swiss army, had recently turned his hand to film camerawork.

A tarred highway accompanied us north through the flat, uninteresting bushveld of the Northern Transvaal until we reached a signpost indicating that we were entering the Tropic of Capricorn. Almost immediately the landscape became dominated by a proliferation of menacing Daliesque trees whose sombre, surreal trunks resembled bloated, charcoal grey, greasy pig flesh, their misshapen branches, incestuously distorting themselves every which way. The natives believed the devil had created baobabs while in playful mood by upending trees and replanting them with their roots in the air. These trees can live for centuries. In fact one recently carbon dated specimen was 6,000 years old.

The locals utilise these astonishing trees for the water stored within their trunks; for their edible leaves and seeds and for their fibrous bark for making rope and cloth, while hollowed out trunks are sometimes inhabited. Others have become shrines or tombs among heterogeneous tribes. Even the roots are used for their medicinal properties. Baobabs are known to have grown to gigantic dimensions of up to 70 ft. tall. One awesome specimen with a diameter of 50 ft. housed a drinking den accommodating innumerable contented boozers.

Notwithstanding the benefits, filming them precipitated a strange sense of ominous foreboding that the cynic in me couldn't shake off. I wasn't the only one among my companions who had misgivings about them and the legend of ill-luck attributed to these grotesque trees seemed to trigger a series of odd events during which the devil's mood changed from mischief to malevolence, and from then on we experienced devilish trouble with vehicle breakdowns dogging us on a daily basis. That, and drivers getting lost for hours on end, wasted precious filming time doubling back to find the laggards, which factor caused significant frustration throughout our 7,000 mile journey. But we only encountered the full infernal baobab influence on our return to Johannesburg.

Mind, the blame for our tribulations didn't all lie at the devil's doorstep since Crone's leadership skills would have seen him drummed out of the Hitler youth movement, and at times, it seemed as if our safari was being run by the Mad Hatter wearing Crone's pith helmet with a card on its hatband reading 10/6d.

The fact was that the drivers seemed incapable of following his simple instructions regarding departure times and since the slow, cumbersome Dodge truck dictated the speed of the convoy Crone felt it necessary for the other vehicles to keep it in sight at all times. Of course the lamentable state of the road north of the South African border further complicated matters. Other than the truck, our vehicles had not been designed for the punishment being inflicted on them by the predominantly inimical roads not far removed from dried out rocky riverbeds.

En route to Bulawayo in Southern Rhodesia (now Zimbabwe) through drab bush country two of our drivers raced impatiently ahead to the next village for a cooked meal, the joy of a hot bath and a good kip in a comfy hotel bed in preference to the mosquito ridden discomfort of sleeping in tents on stretcher beds in rundown rest houses where the myth of glamorous tropic nights was dispelled. Thankfully the nights we had to sleep out in the bush were, few and far between and only came about when vehicle problems were too complex to repair in the dark. Now and then Helga Crone entertained us with the piano accordion she'd brought along. She quickly picked up tunes which we hummed to her and Afrikaans songs like *Sarie Marais, Suiker Bos* (Sugar Bush) and *Daar Kom Die Alabama* (There Comes the Alabama) drowned out the sounds of irritating insects and antisocial animal noises of the night. Jeorge occasionally accompanied her on his guitar. I cherish memories of those sing-songs around blazing camp fires and the camaraderie that evolved from them under canopies of trees and the wondrously crystal clear tent of stars in the heavens above Africa.

Sometimes all three cars vanished. The undulating nature of the terrain meant it was often quite a while before those on the truck became aware that a car had detached itself from the convoy necessitating unwelcome U-turns to find it.

The Dodge was the first vehicle to have suffered a puncture. It was so overloaded that its jack was unable to lift it making it necessary to unload much of the paraphernalia. We started with the heaviest single item - a 44 gallon oil drum containing emergency gasoline. Three of us tried to move it but couldn't budge it a fly's eyelash. Smit, a Herculean South West Afrikaner, built like the proverbial brick shithouse with outsize hands to match, cackled away watching us *sukkel*.

'*Pasop* (mind out) you nincompoops,' he demanded, climbing aboard. We did. Smit put his arms round the drum. Guessing that he intended to move it on his own we sceptically surveyed his unsuccessful attempts until he tried a different grip and manoeuvred it to the back of the truck where he leapt off and heaved the drum to the ground.

Phew! We were gobsmacked, man. None of us nincompoops uttered a word. We simply gawked in disbelief at the strength of this man who quickly set about fitting the jack, changing the tyre and returning the oil drum to its original position. Unaided. No one knew how much fluid the drum held but there was no doubt whatever that Smit was at least three times stronger than we three nincompoops combined.

One day when the Volkswagen punctured a tyre, its jack had gone missing. Smit couldn't be bothered to ferret out the spare from behind other items on Zis so he loosened the wheel nuts while informing us he'd raise the rear of the Volksie and that we were to remove the punctured tyre and position the spare immediately. Raise the Volkswagen? Yes, oh yes! He turned his back on the vehicle, hooked his mammoth digits under the top of the mudguard and with hippopotamus snorts of effort not altogether dissimilar to those generated by Achille Kallos at work on his weights, Smit raised it high enough off the ground to allow us to fit the fresh wheel.

Strong as he was, Smitty graphically demonstrated just how many loose screws he'd lost on the day he tried to catch a giraffe. Fortunately for him the animal's speed of over 30 mph was greater than any world athlete and if Smit had caught the world's tallest animal it would probably have kicked him to death.

Our first major film location was the Victoria Falls. We were running late on a moonless night with no illumination other than our headlights cutting through the blackness. The distant roar of 300,000 gallons of water plummeting down 360 ft. per minute heralded that Victoria Falls was nearby, well ahead of our reaching it, but it was impossible to gauge its immensity in the dark.

We were up before dawn to start filming at sunrise. The sights that awaited us beggared description. The breath-taking spectacle of so mind-boggling an amount of water hurtling over the 5,600 ft. wide lip of the stupendous Zambezi River makes it one of the seven wonders of the natural world. Victoria is our planet's largest curtain of falling water. Twice as high as Niagara it provides a humbling experience. Drinking in such Olympian grandeur instilled in me a feeling of how insignificant we mortals really are and I could hear the background music composing itself on my soul with cadences of indescribable emotion. The Falls overpower the senses producing a vista that no words, no prose nor poetry nor song, no photograph, no film will ever adequately capture. It simply has to be seen to be fully appreciated.

Aeons before David Livingstone came across it in 1855 the natives called it Mosi-oa-Tunya - the smoke that thunders. Its plumes of coruscating spray rising heavenwards 1,300 ft. during the rainy season can be seen 30 miles away. The falls and surrounding rain forest are adorned with exquisite jewels of rainbows dancing nymph-like in and out of the mist. Livingstone himself had a go at describing the falls which he renamed in obeisance to his queen and came up with *'scenes so lovely must have been gazed upon by angels in their flight.'* Aaaaahhhh. But then one would expect no less from a missionary.

At the Eastern Cataract Smit decided it was time for a dip. He stripped to his underwear and fearlessly leapt from rock to slippery rock revelling in the constant shower of spray. Then he chose to dive in for a swim less than 50 ft. from the lip of the precipice where, fortunately for him, the full strength of the current was reduced by numerous rock islets jutting upwards at the very edge. He was damned lucky not to have been swept into the turbulence of the maelstrom below fittingly named The Boiling Pot.

That day's problem was keeping the cameras dry. Despite the damp we exposed a substantial amount of film shooting the Knife Edge, the Palm Grove, Danger Point, the rain forest, and the bridge linking the two Rhodesias. We then moved on to a nearby game park teeming with antelope, warthogs, ostrich, giraffe and zebra including one bold enough to stick its head into car windows hoping to receive a tasty titbit. Heady stuff. For reasons which will be revealed later, this intensive 'shoot' turned out to be the saviour of our motion picture.

We continued northwards on dirt tracks that made the river bed roads, as already touched on fleetingly, seem like expressways. Vacuum cleaner manufacturers would have been thrilled to have their products behave as effectively as our vehicles which sucked in such vast quantities of fine dust that we had to stop frequently to breathe a little clean fresh air. Aside from exacerbating human breathing problems the dust seemed to trigger extra mechanical breakdowns.

Overnight stops were generally spent in hotels, motels and government sponsored hostels that fell far below our expectations in terms of comfort and cleanliness and the best that can be said of them is that they were marginally preferable to sleeping in the open. So much for Crone's Sunday Times advertisement 'First class camping facilities...' The sites we visited were mainly managed by as aberrant a selection of people as you could find outside a cartload of chimpanzees.

One 'rest house' offered a unique early morning wakeup call which proved to be a startlingly effective method of not only awakening us but also all the dead in nearby cemeteries. The manager had casually mentioned to Jeorge that he used a bugle and an incredulous Jeorge couldn't believe his luck. You see he'd been a bugler in the army and unbeknown to any of us he took his faithful battered army bugle everywhere he went so he volunteered to 'do the honours' for the manager but failed to tell any of us about it. The manager's bugle station happened to be at his home five minutes' walk away from us only he forgot to tell Jeorge that; with the result we were all scared shitless to hear reveille played out of tune within spitting distance from our lugholes. Subsequently Jeorge went potty trying to find his mouthpiece which mysteriously went missing soon afterwards. For the sake of everyone's safari sanity I had Eric nick it and hide it away until we returned to Johannesburg.

Near a town called Mpika I nearly demolished a filling station whose solitary hand-operated petrol pump only dispensed complete gallons. There was no way to stop any overspill if you misjudged the capacity as I did. The black guy working the pump under the supervision of the owner's pretty daughter yelled out a warning and I immediately blew out the match I was using to light the girl's cigarette and threw it away. Only it wasn't out. There was this frightening WHOOSH as the spilt gasoline ignited. Two of our vehicles stood alongside the pump - the truck and the Studebaker. I had visions of both of them plus the pump going up in flames. I yelled at Charles to reverse. He panicked and put the Stud into first gear instead as the flames started licking his tyres. Until then I had never seen anyone literally leap into action but the pump attendant did just that and managed to douse the flames by scooping up dirt and frantically hurling it at the tyres. Another guy appeared from nowhere and, using the same technique, he managed to extinguish the burning gasoline. Understandably, Charles ranted at my stupidity. I had learned another invaluable lesson and quit flirting at filling stations.

At Mbeya Crone recruited four black guys to help with menial work like lugging stuff on and off the truck; keeping it and the other vehicles clean; erecting and dismantling tents and attending to our every need in much the same way as the servants of South Africa. John was the majordomo. His assistants were Kenneth, Alan and Andomeli who was a *'pishi'* the East African name for a cook.

These guys had a rough time travelling on the truck atop piles of lumpy luggage. They and the gear were sheltered by a large tarpaulin tied over a removable metal framework that kept the driver's cab and the goods section dry and sheltered from the sun but there was no protection from the dust and whenever we stopped all that was visible of their faces were red eyes squinting through masks of powdery dust. I was soon to experience their discomfort at first hand.

In Tanganyika (now Tanzania) the roads were even worse than those of Northern Rhodesia (today's Zambia) but we were consoled by the attractive terrain that was far more interesting than the dreary Rhodesian bush.

The walls of the bar at one hotel we visited were decorated with the skins of colobus monkeys, rare creatures whose gorgeous, silky black fur with snow white mantles was in great demand by interior decorators of the era. It was sickening to think that these magical monkeys were threatened with extinction on a daily basis by avaricious humans who paid serious boodle for the skins to decorate their dwellings.

This was but one example of heinous criminality towards wild life. Stories of animal massacres abounded including the dastardly deeds of trigger-happy British soldiers who used automatic weapons to mow down herds of animals for target practice during both World Wars.

We were able to corroborate another particularly terrible act of human atrocity against animals near a village called Ol Tukai where a party of *askaris* were manhandling several huge elephant tusks, each one over five feet long, to a government office run by a white major. At first he declined to talk about the tusks insisting that they were evidence and therefore could not be photographed. A little liquid persuasion later he relented and during our filming he told us that the chief offender, a white poacher, had been caught with the ivory. He and his gang had used motor vehicles to chase a herd of elephants into a corner of dense vegetation from where they could not escape. The bastards then set fire to the tinder dry bush burning the trapped animals to death. All that remained were charred carcasses. The tusks, worth a king's ransom, had been skillfully removed suggesting that professional criminals were involved. Unfortunately the gang had escaped and the major was deeply upset and felt that people of that ilk deserved to be hung. The story of another horrendous animal massacre vied with this one as we later discovered at the Ngorongoro Crater.

During the next leg I took Smitty's place in the Volkswagen because the Dodge was becoming ever dodgier - a truculent truck you might say - and was suffering constant problems, so Crone chose to drive Zis personally and needed Smitty, a deft mechanic, at his side. What with Eric and the black guys riding on Zis I headed off in the Volkswagen with Hans and Trudi. Little did I guess what lay ahead.

The road sinuated up superb foothills, passing terraced farms whose crops presented a symphony of green. We admired picturesque huts with their stately owners posing aristocratically in colourful robes as if modelling for those elongated East African wooden carvings so popular among tourists.

Then we reached the real mountains and what a nightmarish ride that proved to be. I kept my eyes closed most of the time not simply from fright - and boy was I petrified by Hans' driving - but because the billowing dust both inside and outside the car seemingly came through the floor as well as the closed windows.

Hans drove like a rally driver without the aptitude so to do but that did not in the least deter him from slaloming the Volksie through squiggly S-bends at anything up to 40 mph, wrestling the car around imagining, I guess, that the sandy road would keep it on an even keel. The fact that we stayed alive remains a source of amazement to me. I was being subjected to the scariest event of my life thus far and fully expecting it to be my last journey on earth, I took out my notebook in an attempt to leave my last thoughts to posterity. I wanted people to know how I had shuffled off my mortal coil. Trudi on the other hand seemed quite accustomed to the frenzied driver in the front seat next to her, prompting my suspicion that the roll-your-own cigarettes she smoked continuously were laced with *dagga* which probably accounted for the sort of glazed Stan Laurel look she always wore.

As we began the descent from the highest point of the mountains, we passed a signpost indicating that we were 30 miles from an unnamed destination. By now my head was aching numbly from repeated contact with the car's roof every time we went over the unavoidable bumps in the road. It was well beyond a joke and my begging Hans to take it easy resulted in his slowing down to 25 mph but even at that speed the dust continued to swirl inside the car. My hopes of respite were again shattered when Hans got it into his head that he could evade the demon dust by picking up speed again so that the jolting, bumping, stomach-churning swerving down the mountain did not abate in the least as Hans continued to abuse the steering wheel as if he nursed a grudge against the car. He zipped along at life-threatening speeds, cutting corners and sliding all over the road. I vowed then and there that if I survived I would never again ride with him at the wheel.

Touch wood only one car headed towards us and, as fate would have it, this was on one of the rare flat sections otherwise I doubt if this narrative would have been written since all that hit us when the other car whizzed past us was its dust cloud which shot angrily into the air enveloping the Volksie. Still Hans kept his leaden foot down hard against the gas pedal disregarding any possibility that the huge amount of dust stirred up by two cars would obscure any vehicle behind the one that had just gone by. Even if he had thought of it Hans was not in the least deterred by such a minor consideration and drove into the dust cloud with as much concern as an airplane pilot flying through fluffy cumulus.

He utterly ignored all twists and turns of the mountain contours, accelerating without the slightest intention of braking should an emergency arise. None did, which was providential as braking at that speed would have forced the car over the edge of the road into a valley far below.

My prayers were now for a puncture or a mechanical problem or at least for steeper gradients where low gears may have slowed us down.

We reached the comparative safety of the foothills but neither the dust nor the speed nor the danger diminished in the slightest. We now encountered dips, ridges and occasional shallow fords which all seemed invisible until you were upon them. Car seat belts had not yet been introduced. Hans at least had the steering wheel to hold on to as he zoomed through the hazards without a second thought. To my horror he continued at breakneck speed by which time my head became immune, well almost immune, from frequent contact with the roof. My spine however, was nearly dislocated.

The next sign post indicated there were only ten more miles to our unidentified destination. The road now changed from radically dangerous curves to radically dangerous straights. At last fate came to my aid - a spark plug failed, reducing our speed to a maximum of 30 mph.

'You know,' said Hans turning round in the driver's seat to face me, 'I think we've been running on three cylinders all the time.'

I thanked my lucky stars for that mercy. Four working cylinders would have had us airborne. I'm convinced that a broken spark plug preserved my life as Hans had driven the car at its absolute maximum so that the fortuitous loss of performance made the difference between a grave in Tanganyika and recording these notes years later in the safety of my home.

My agony was finally relieved by our arrival at Chimala where I tottered out of the car with an impulse to kiss the ground and bless having not come into contact with it six feet below its surface. There I learned we had passed over the Mporoto Ridge. I was not sorry.

On reaching Dodoma, mosquito capital of the world, we experienced the same extremes of weather that my father had endured during World War 1. Dodoma was a dull, melancholy dump. The only good thing about our stopover was that we were able to sleep beneath mosquito netting Crone had brought along to protect us against the dreaded malaria.

Dodoma marked the start of the Maasai Steppe, an immense area skirting the edge of the mighty Serengeti Plain. Mighty is itself an inappropriate word to describe this tremendous savannah which, combined with its northern continuation into Kenya, extends over 12,000 square miles along the edge of the 3,700 mile Great African Rift Valley. The region boasts numerous game parks and we headed for the Amboseli reserve where two major movies were filmed - 'The Snows of Kilimanjaro' starring Gregory Peck, Susan Hayward and Ava Gardner and 'Where No Vultures Fly' with Anthony Steel and Dinah Sheridan. Here we were lucky enough to spot a pair of rhino. Those of us on the open back of the truck filmed them secure in the knowledge that if the animals, notorious for charging full tilt at motor vehicles, went for the Dodge we were perfectly safe. However we all suffered second thoughts and anxious moments when the larger animal, an overprotective, antagonistic mother of a 2,000 pound calf stared at us shortsightedly until her 'baby' lumbered off happily into the thick thorn bush.

In Amboseli we met the most impressive animal that any of us, including former big game hunter Crone, had ever seen. Our *askari* guide jubilantly called out 'Simba, simba, bwana!' It was always goose-pimplingly exciting to see lions in the wild. Crone checked this one out with his binoculars. 'It's a *swart-maanhare*,' he gasped, 'ze biggest I haf ever seen.' I'd heard of this animal, a black-maned lion, fabled throughout Africa and seldom, if ever, glimpsed by tourists. As Zis neared it, I realised why this iconic animal was held in such awe. It was huge. It weighed, said Crone, in excess of 500 lbs. It was elegant. It was the king of the kings of the jungle. No, wait a mo, the Emperor of all animals would be more appropriate. His imperial majesty promenaded along regally, as befitted so magnificent a monarch. The dense black hair covering his head, shoulders and neck resembled a black beard flowing down to his tawny knees. As he padded past us his ineffable, impeccably groomed mane rippled almost imperceptibly making it easy to imagine that he had just emerged from a jungle hair salon. He ignored us completely although he was fully aware that we were there. While we gawked at him, he turned his back on us and urinated... Prodigiously.

The Maasai word Serengeti means 'endless plain'. It sustains innumerable species, particularly immense herds of wildebeest. We're talking nigh on 1.5 million of them. Every year seasonal weather patterns dictate that these animals migrate north to the Maasai Mara accompanied by perhaps quarter of a million zebra all aiming for fresh grazing and plentiful water. This is by far the largest seasonal animal migration in the world.

The Serengeti was virtually devoid of people making it an animal paradise sustaining countless beasts which live as contentedly undisturbed as they had prior to the invasion of human predators.

Adorning the parlous dirt track on which we were driving was a group of about twenty Maasai women dressed in leather skirts and red shawls around their shoulders. Zulu style bead necklaces and beaded earrings dangled from multiple holes in their ear lobes which had been stretched almost down to their shoulders.

We stopped to photograph the barefoot belles but our cameras startled them, scattering them like frightened gazelles. Crone had an *indaba* with their leader to negotiate a filming fee and, when that was agreed, the ladies reconvened and began to perform for us like veteran thespians. To our delight they also removed their shawls and obliged us with a topless song and dance routine involving strange shrugging movements of heads and shoulders. Soon the Studebaker drew up and when Helga Crone emerged the Maasai women were as fascinated by her blonde hair as she was at her first sight of them. They stared long and hard at each other until one bold Maasai girl pulled belligerently at Helga's yellow sweater indicating that she wanted to check what it concealed. The others laughingly followed suit, flaunting their bare breasts, plainly wanting Helga to get her gear off, but despite their babbled insistence Helga remained adamant and the women had to settle for protracted stroking of her hair. Then, to the enthusiastic applause of all, Helga joined them in one of their dancing sing-songs.

Our diet in the bush was more than monotonous. Shooting permits were restricted to a minimal number of antelope for the pot forcing us to rely on chicken much of the time - tough, backyard birds obtained by barter from the local natives. The chickens were, however, an improvement on the bill of fare of the Maasai tribe. As with South African Zulus their status is measured by the number of cattle they own. These nomadic people travel epic distances to ensure that their livestock are well fed. The Maasai seldom kill their animals for meat, they simply puncture a convenient vein, let off a serving of fresh blood and lace it with milk. Maybe that's why we never saw a plump Maasai warrior.

We encountered a Maasai hunting party whose cloaks matched the colour worn by the women we filmed. Their faces were painted with ochre and their long hair was plaited in braids and elaborately decorated with ostrich feathers. They were reluctant to allow us to film them so our footage had to be shot surreptitiously at a distance.

These proud, fearless warriors, none shorter than six feet, each carried an impressive double edged spear slightly longer than a broomstick with a stabbing spike at one end connected by a hardwood shaft to a fearsome, hand-forged cutting blade at the other. I wanted one of these unusual weapons as a souvenir and asked Crone to negotiate a deal for me. He refused point blank, revealing that Maasai warriors would die rather than part with their weapons. They are often buried with them. They had been known to kill Europeans for trying to acquire their spears. I later met a game warden who had confiscated a spear from a murderer and was happy to sell it to me, warning me to keep it well hidden until we left the country.

We arrived at the Kibo Hotel at dusk on a Saturday night. Nestling 6,000 ft. up Kilimanjaro's sloping profile, the snug little establishment with sponge rubber mattresses and silky soft rock-rabbit karosses on the beds afforded us a welcome hot meal, and a warm restful night.

Morning dawned bright and clear with a decided nip in the air. At seven am the six of us who were participating in Crone's assault on Kilimanjaro climbed aboard the Dodge. While waiting for him to make a final vehicle check I reread a leaflet containing mind-boggling statistics about the world's largest free-standing mountain. It is a gigantic extinct volcano covering an area of about 290 square miles and at 19,340 ft. high, one of Africa's supreme sights.

Well satisfied with his inspection Crone turned the ignition key of our ungainly vehicle which burst into song sweetly as if to reassure us that all was well. The rest of our party came out to wish us *bon courage* and wave us goodbye. Charles filmed our departure then raced ahead in his car to the first stop, a nearby petrol pump where we collected our chief guide Yohan with his two assistants and their meagre blankets. The trio was lean, fit, and totally acclimatised to the altitude with the strength to carry heavy kit up the mountain for tourists on the climbing route.

A group of young boys gathered round the truck discussing it enthusiastically repeating the words 'Land Rover'. In fluent Swahili Crone let them know that our Dodge truck had 'tatu' (three) differentials at which they became very excited. A pair of them even crawled underneath to inspect so impressive a mechanical wonder. One English speaking tyke, aged about nine, told the others about our intentions, a statement they found highly hilarious and advised Crone about 'big stones' the importance of which we were soon to discover. It struck them as even funnier when Crone told them the Dodge would reach the summit of Kibo and we'd return in two days. The translator boy said, 'Bwana, a safari up to Kibo takes five days.' Even so we received enthusiastic, albeit it somewhat cheeky cheers - or were they jeers? - from them as we drove off up the conventional climbers' route which proved no more demanding than a pleasant Sunday morning uphill drive through verdant scenery until the track ended abruptly a mile or so from where we had left the children. Here stood an outcrop of formidable boulders the smallest being the size of an average motor car. These were the 'stones' the kids had warned us about. There was no way forward. Our route was totally blocked. Nature had won. Turning the truck to face downwards was terrifying and could only be achieved by manoeueuvring inches at a time.

Crone's acquaintance with the mountain was obviously not as precise as he'd led us to believe. After a lengthy discussion with Yohan, Crone adopted, or perhaps invented, not so much a 'Plan B' more a plan maybe which involved trying a different route. Zis headed for the main road towards Loitokitok, three hours' drive away.

On the way down a small party of climbers from our hotel greeted us with friendly waves. 'Hello', one called jovially, 'changed your minds?'

Further down we again encountered the kids to whom Crone had bragged. We received hoots of derision. The English speaking boy yelled, 'You going the wrong way bwana!'

The tarred road took us through lush forest, flamboyant with every hue of green that ever graced a master painter's palette.

All along the route the locals waved us by, shouting their *'jambos'*, saluting us, waving sticks and doffing hats at the sight of this strange vehicle loaded with its odd cargo of whites and blacks. Wherever the road slowed our progress we attracted escorts of small boys running beside us excitedly shouting their lungs out making it easy to appreciate how weary royalty must feel continually acknowledging the plaudits of the masses.

On reaching Loitokitok we found its singularly alliterative name failed to live up to the expectations we'd nursed of a rustic African village. It was merely a sad hugger-mugger of grubby mud huts surrounded by grubby, uninteresting buildings. Grubby children played in the equally grubby company of mongrel dogs and scraggy chickens foraging for food in garbage strewn gutters, while lazing adults cynically contemplated our intrusion into their hitherto peaceful environment.

For a change we had a stroke of good luck because one of Kilimanjaro's two lower peaks made a most unexpected appearance in the far distance. At 16,896 ft. high Mawenzi is known locally as 'the invisible mountain' since it is almost always obscured by heavy cloud formations. Naturally we stopped to film it. Not a lot of people know that Kili's third peak, Shira, a mere 13,000 ft. high, lurks somewhere on Kilimanjaro's huge footprint but we didn't have time to look for it.

Moving on we soon reached the entrance to a logging track which we followed upwards through newly dropped elephant dung accompanied by the sound of the unseen perpetrators trumpeting their relief in the far distance. Near the sawmill we encountered a Land Rover driven by a pink-turbaned Indian sporting a well-groomed beard and an impressive waxed handlebar moustache, its tips curving upwards presenting a stern visage which belied his real character. He was Mr. Singh, manager of the Loitokitok logging operations. He greeted us warmly in impeccable English. It was nearly sunset and he offered us the overnight use of a guesthouse, built by his loggers from the very timber of Kilimanjaro itself to accommodate visiting forestry officials. We were fortunate to have found so altruistic a man without whom we would have had to camp out in the damp jungle.

The lodge would not have been out of place in an English county village surrounded as it was by geraniums and climbing roses, growing in wild abundance.

Mr. Singh's pearly white teeth flashed smiles of pride at our reactions as he showed us round our manor which enjoyed electric light, two bedrooms, a living room, a bathroom, a kitchen and an outside toilet. He told us we were over 9,000 ft. up the mountain. Hence, Crone assured us, our first main objective, the saddle, the area between Kilimanjaro's two main peaks, was now within easy reach.

The sawmill's shrill whistle blew at precisely 6 am. Mr. Singh arrived almost simultaneously to say he was prepared to guide us into the forest as far as possible on the track used by his loggers. He jokingly offered us 50 British pounds if we reached the summit. 'But,' he added, 'my money's safe. The jungle is impenetrable. The trees are too dense for your truck. I know. I've climbed this mountain and I know.' Yet Kibo seemed to disagree with him. Its peak looked tantalisingly close. With a gobbet of luck our machine was destined to reach the highest point in all Africa.

We followed the Land Rover to the end of the loggers' road where we came face to face with the real Kilimanjaro forest, the rain forest, whose trees scraped the skin of the sky. Mr. Singh left his vehicle to join us on the truck where he kept repeating clichés like 'amazing' and 'remarkable' as Zis bulldozed its way over saplings and thick underwood, effortlessly mowing through tough undergrowth with its six wheeled power. Other than worrisome whining tyres spinning on the sodden compacted vegetation the Dodge's systems were all 'go'.

We had fitted our snow chains to give greater purchase to the tyres, but to further reduce weight we all had to walk alongside Zis. Everyone mucked in to help clear rotting tree stumps from the Dodge's path until we reached a section with deep gorges on both sides which put paid to manoeuvring past large trees, leaving us no option but to fell those Zis couldn't flatten, a tiring, time-consuming procedure which was justifiably criticized by the press back in Johannesburg.

The Dodge continued to behave itself, taking everything in its stride, running smoothly on the aviation fuel we'd filled it with. The engine was not even hot, but at that altitude, the exertion and thin air began to take effect on the human lungs and the only ones who weren't too badly off were Crone, our experienced guides and the Johannesburgers, Eric and me, both born and bred on the thin Witwatersrand air. The rest of our party suffered other symptoms of altitude sickness such as headache and fatigue which kept them groggy for days.

Mr. Singh was so impressed by the relentless way the Dodge inched its way upwards through such hostile terrain that he asked if we would order two similar trucks for him on our return to South Africa.

Here, dear reader, if you don't mind, are a few words of advice if you are considering the second expedition to try to scale Kilimanjaro in a vehicle. Take a six wheel drive, equip it with a winch and snow tyres; fit an oxygen supply to the carburetor, get hold of a petrol-operated chain saw and do not forget to include a tower of strength like Smitty, a human dynamo whose remarkable vigour helped us out of all the treacherous quagmires we encountered both physical and metaphorical. He chopped down trees, put his back into shoving Zis forward another fly's whisker, scouted ahead, cajoled us one moment and harried us the next. In short, he did everything one would expect from a man weaned on crude oil.

Suddenly the mist lifted. And HOORAY, we'd reached the saddle! At 15,000 ft. Singh assured us that this was easily the highest point ever reached by a motor vehicle on Kilimanjaro. We applauded our own success while Crone basked, hubristically conceited - his body language plainly proclaiming 'Oh ye of little faith, I told you we'd make it.' Exhausted from the strain of steering his metal monster he called a halt for a breather and a well-deserved cuppa and biscuits for himself and his crew.

Whilst relishing our hot refreshment we were once again treated to an unrestricted view of both Kilimanjaro's main peaks. In the distance Mawenzi's summit, only slightly lower than Kibo's, was also assaulted, this time by our clicking, whirring cameras while Kibo herself posed for us, magnificent in her shawl of pure white snow - and this less than three degrees latitude from the Equator. The Kibo summit looked close enough to reach in less than ten minutes. Although we were aware that distances on mountains can be deceptive, we remained optimistic about our chances of success. But suddenly the mist returned to obscure Kilimanjaro's peak like a coquettish woman teasing her lover. We piled eagerly back onto the truck singing '*We*'ll be comin' round the mountain when *we* come.' We were only into the third chorus before the mist thickened. With a vengeance.

We had enjoyed but a Pyrrhic victory. After waiting several chilly hours hoping for the mist to blow away, Crone, Singh and Yohan held a lengthy summit meeting at which their joint prognosis was that the mist would persist at least until the morrow and we'd best turn back before nightfall.

The descent was not as easy as we'd presumed. The idea was to simply retrace our upward tyre tracks. Finding those proved a pointless task because by then the mist had thickened enough to scoop up with a runcible spoon, forcing us to zigzag down at snail's pace. It was dark by the time we reached Singh's Land Rover. He was crestfallen to hear that we would not be returning to consummate our mission. We all shared his feelings and he understood and commiserated with us after Crone explained that we were now well behind schedule and were obligated to our paying tourists who were tetchy about the delays and wanted assurances that we would return them to South Africa on schedule without fail.

It wasn't until we returned to Johannesburg that Crone grudgingly admitted choosing the wrong time of year for the assault since between mid-December and March, the warmest months, the mountain would have been relatively free from clouds.

Inopportunely the very first issue of the Guinness Book of Records went to press at about the same time as we returned to Johannesburg or, had anyone thought of it, we may have qualified for two world records: as the first motorised vehicle to reach an altitude of 15,000 feet and having undertaking the first motorised vehicle to attempt to scale Mount Kilimanjaro. Ah well...

In Africa distances are so immense that if you ask locals how far you are away from your destination, the answer is almost inevitably given in days not miles or kilometers.

Africa is a continent of superlatives - the biggest this, the longest that, the tallest something else. The Ngorongoro Crater is no exception. It is our planet's largest caldera, nearly 12½ miles in diameter, with walls rising over 2,000 ft. above its 100 square mile floor which shelters astronomical numbers of animals living in comparative isolation from human interference. Statisticians claim between thirty and forty thousand creatures can be found in there at any given time. It is unquestionably the jewel in the crown of the incomparable East African Crater Highlands. The claim that Ngorongoro is the eighth wonder of the animal world is undisputed by no one who has been there.

Despite the depressing disappointment of defeat dealt to us by Kilimanjaro, this breathtaking crater provided spiritual balm to our badly bruised egos. Ngorongoro's inhabitants include 30 varieties of antelope, and game such as zebra, elephants, leopards, cheetahs, hyenas, jackals, hippos, buffalo, rhinos, baboons and monkeys as well as perhaps a hundred bird species. Although there are no giraffe, gorillas, okapi or crocodiles, you name a wild African creature and it's a fairly safe bet that Ngorongoro sustains it.

Once thought to be a natural pen for its beasts, the animals, who know a thing or two about their own environment, wander in and out whenever the urge is upon them. Within the crater varied mini ecosystems can be seen. Grassland, being the largest, supports huge herds of wildebeest. Other habitats encompass swamps, wetlands, small clumps of trees, forests, springs, lakes and a river meandering into a soda lake where flamingos gather in their thousands.

The crater lions are particularly content with their lot since they are so close to boundless fresh meals on the hoof with easy access to ample supplies of fresh water, allowing them to loll around all day in the shade of the flat topped acacia trees, waiting for a wildebeest to wander close enough for them to reach out and grab it almost as casually as we help ourselves to meat in supermarkets.

The Ngorongoro wildebeest were once severely endangered, not by four legged predators, but by two German brothers who built homes in the crater eight miles apart where they lounged about on their shady *stoeps* sipping *schnapps* while shooting wildebeest willy-nilly and canning their tongues for Germany's gourmets, leaving the carcasses to the best fed scavengers on the continent. These men, the Siedentopf brothers Friederich and Adolph were a law unto themselves, treating their black workers apartheid style, beating them up and abusing them at will. It was only when they summarily executed one for disobedience that the authorities took notice and dispatched a platoon of *askaris* to arrest the brothers who scoffed at the black soldiers telling them that if any arresting was to be done it would have to be by white men. The *askaris* slunk off, tails between their legs, leaving the Siedentopfs to carry on butchering wildebeest while amassing a tidy fortune until WW1 broke out and Siedentopf the elder returned to Germany where he qualified as a pilot before returning to Africa to scout for the German ground forces. This didn't affect the advance of the British towards Ngorongoro. The brothers vacated the crater after poisoning their cattle to prevent them from falling into enemy hands.

The precipitous road down the inner wall of the crater was both steep and narrow, severely taxing Crone's not inconsiderable driving skill to its limits. For sightseeing and filming forays, Zis's cargo was unloaded wherever we were overnighting to allow everyone to fit comfortably on what was, in effect, a mobile film and viewing platform. We were all captivated by the aesthetic wonder of this crater brimming as it was with the most densely packed wildlife population in all Africa. Again our cameras ran hot.

After seriously depleting our film stock and sating our eyeballs it was time to start the two hour return journey. Much to Crone's consternation Smitty announced his intention to walk home preferring a 30 minute climb to a tiresome, circuitous, two hour drive back up to our camping lodge. He left, followed by Eric, Jeorge and Hans. As they strolled away we spotted a small pride of lions about 200 feet away from them. We dared not shout a warning for fear of drawing the lions' attention to them. The deserters didn't even notice the animals. Propitiously those lions must have lunched well and simply ignored the quartet.

Not far from the top of the crater road Zis wheezed to a halt. Out of gas! No option but to walk. Then the sun set. In Central Africa there is no twilight. Exquisite sunsets are short and sharp and then it seems the switch is turned off. It was pretty damn scary with unseen creatures grunting and crashing around in the dark bush surrounding us, but as we had an armed *askari* with us we were fairly sanguine. Tired and hungry as we were, we reached the lodge safely. The warden was none too pleased and berated us for stupidly risking our lives on foot, reproaching us in no uncertain manner about African buffalo being responsible for more human deaths than any other animal in the world since they attack people for the hell of it.

When we told him we felt safe with the *askari* and his gun, he went ballistic with rage. 'You don't think we give those buggers bloody ammo do you?' he yelled, 'Those effing rifles are just for show...'

Not even Crone knew that.

Dotted throughout East Africa tsetse fly 'barriers' were established to inspect vehicles for any signs of the deadly insects which cause the dreaded sleeping sickness. The inconsiderate, dipterous little bastards willfully ignore notices reading 'No tsetse flies beyond this point' and dart straight past them. The flies rarely choose to hitch lifts thereby tempting the barrier minders to catch them dining on local cattle to prove their watchfulness and efficiency to the *bwana* in charge. Even so the interiors of our vehicles were liberally sprayed with a stirrup pump filled with a concoction whose nauseous stench lingered on for days.

Fortunately none of us caught any of Africa's other innumerable parasitic diseases such as malaria, bilharzia, yellow fever, tick bite fever and what not. In fact the only one to fall foul of *goggas* was our führer Herr Bruno Crone who encountered almost microscopic sand fleas which white people call the jigger, presumably a corruption of its African name 'chigoe.' The female of the species burrows under human toenails where it lays its eggs while obtaining its sustenance from the surrounding flesh. The egg sacs mature to the size of small peas and when the grubs hatch or if a sac bursts the infection can cause the loss of a leg. The only way to remove the sacs is by surgery but surgeons are somewhat thin on the ground in remote areas where one can travel hundreds of miles to the nearest town and even there the best one could hope for is a nurse. Providentially a miniscule number of Africans have become adept at removing the sacs and Crone was damn lucky that our *pishi* Andomeli was well versed in such matters.

We headed for a rest house which, fortunately, flaunted electricity.

Having survived a *bris* I was the only volunteer to help with an extirpation that required a rock steady hand and a very sharp, brand new, one sided safety razor blade. The minutest slip could have pierced the sacs but this guy knew his business and cut round them perfectly, enabling him to gently squeeze them out *in toto*. A couple of dabs of iodine and Crone's toes were good as new. This convinced me to never again walk barefoot in the great African outdoors.

We spent the night at that guest house. The 'bathroom' was nothing more than a small, shabby outbuilding containing a waist-high cold water tap. It was as well that I didn't try to test that tap because clinging to the downpipe inches above it lurked a vile black centipede which, I was told, might have fixed itself onto my arm by digging into my flesh by means of its poisonous claw-like legs. Brrr...

We killed it with a long stick but even in its death agonies it waved its menacing stingers about, feeling for something to fix them into before dying.

This part of the world was infamous for its multitudes of unfriendly flying or crawling pests and most of us were covered with bites, rashes and swollen body parts from who knows what repulsive vermin, giving credence to the aphorism 'No one walks beneath the palm unpunished.'

We were far behind schedule due to long hours of backtracking to find laggards; to haul cars out of deep mud caused by unexpected downpours, to getting hopelessly lost. The delays activated acrimonious arguments between Crone and the errant drivers about convoy discipline so he decided to take a ferry diagonally across Lake Victoria, the world's biggest freshwater lake. In fact if it were possible to drive round its entire shoreline you would have to travel 2,137 miles.

The idea was to sail from Musoma, Tanganyika, to Entebbe in Uganda bypassing Kenya to make up for much of the lost time. Except... no advance booking had been possible and there was no room on the vessel for all our vehicles so Crone had to settle for a much shorter short cut by means of a ferry plying from one side of Mara Bay to the other.

It was in Musoma that I saw my first leper. Initially I didn't realize what he was because at a distance he simply looked like a village idiot with wild unkempt hair wambling along the road in the contorted way Charles Laughton interpreted Quasimodo on film. Clad only in a filthy breechcloth, children playing in the street and passers-by gave him a wide berth. Even as I write this 60 years on, my mind's eye still conjures up his ghastly expression - that of a damned soul as might have been painted by William Blake in one of his highly horrendous phantasmagorical moods. Noticing my shocked reaction an Indian man told me I was staring at a leper. I asked him how lepers survived. He shook his head and admitted his ignorance saying he knew not since lepers were not allowed in shops to buy food with any coins they managed to beg. Nevertheless I threw coins towards the afflicted man and, I am ashamed to say, turned on my heels lest he follow me to try to thank me.

That night Frans and Trudi divulged that they wanted to return to the Union of South Africa. I helped Crone plan their route which left us with only four hours sleep. As shareholders in the venture Crone and I were delighted they were leaving because it not only saved us the cost of their gas, accommodation and food but also eliminated the frustration of having to find them after Frans got lost by dashing ahead of everyone else.

It was still dark when we reached the jetty at 6 am to board the ferry. The 65 foot Helen Lloyd pulled away from its moorings and by 6.45 the sun rose allowing us to glory at the grandeur of the graceful bay we were crossing where the only sounds were of gently lapping water and the almost imperceptible pulsation of the ferry engine. The rising sun flecked the surrounding hillside and clouds with stunning African orange. The sun was high as the ferry approached Kinesi where multi-coloured dhows rocked peacefully at anchor while au naturel natives busied themselves with their morning ablutions in the calm lee of the shore. The more modest ones fled from our gaze and hastily dressed as our vessel drew closer to them.

After breakfast we headed straight for the Kenyan border where the only formality was to record our vehicle registration numbers in a tattered book. An official alerted us to the possibility of encountering Mau Mau insurgents, but all we saw were well-disposed members of the Kikuyu nation going about their business. Whether or not they were involved in the bloody Kikuyu uprising to wrest independence from Britain can only be speculative and it was upsetting to think that such peaceful folk may have been dragged into a barbaric conflict of unrestrained horror.

Our journey on the western edge of Kenya led through lush, attractive scenery where there was no sign whatever of trouble and all the people we saw owned fat cattle and raised well-nourished, well-scrubbed children carrying water gourds or leading goats or calves on rope leashes. Zis' cacophonous passage caused young goats to bolt and we were greatly amused at the sight of animal kids dragging human kids into the roadside bush.

Our next overnight stop was at Kisumu ten miles south of the equator. Crone was in favour of my organizing a ceremony for those who hadn't yet crossed the Equator. After all why should such frolics be restricted to folk at sea? Finding suitable certificates to present to Bert Long, Fay, Eric and Smitty proved fruitless so I improvised with typewritten certificates embellished with Kenyan stamps, gummed hotel labels and Crone's signature. The only inhabited spot on the equator itself was the Maseno Mission School where, coincidentally, President Barack Obama's father was educated.

The school staff obligingly allowed us to stage our equatorial baptism frivolities in their grounds. They supplied warm water for us to mix into lather for the landlocked Neptune, played by our very own führer himself, to 'shave' them with a blunt axe while they were held fast by Neptune's four African assistants John, Kenneth, Alan and Andomeli. Thanks to his age, Long received far milder treatment than Eric and Smitty while young Fay was spared from the lathering. Then the victims had the residual suds washed off with buckets of water which thoroughly soaked everyone, including the spectators, to the skin. As I had hoped the merrymaking served to cool the tensions that had been festering among us, much to the amusement of the neatly uniformed boys from the mission school dressed in white shirts with red crosses on the pockets. Doubtless none had ever witnessed such surprisingly boisterous behaviour from the staid white people they were accustomed to.

Afterwards our party devoured a handsome picnic lunch prepared for us by the hotel at Musoma so that we were all in a good frame of mind and ready for the next long stretch of travel via Bugiri and Jinja towards Entebbe on roads made of a substance called murram which is rock hard when baked dry by the sun but murderously slippery when wet causing horrible corrugations. The dryer it gets the more the road surface develops treacherous potholes exposing sharp stones - a perfect combination for shredding and puncturing the toughest of tyres.

In this part of East Africa Arab influence is particularly evident since they were the first outsiders to exploit the country and were deeply involved in the slave trade. Their *dukas* and mosques are plenteous throughout Uganda.

At Kampala we checked in at the Imperial Hotel where the manager and staff were polite and helpful. Their cuisine would have passed muster in Europe itself. Miracle of unexpected miracles provided private bathrooms in each suite.

The best thing about Uganda was that there was no outward sign of apartheid and blacks, whites, Asians and Arabs mingled freely together, a sight which proved enlightening to the South Africans among us.

Kampala was a healthy city with an exhilaratingly temperate climate. It laid just claim to being 'The Garden City' of East Africa not only by virtue of its superbly laid out gardens but also because of the luxuriant natural foliage with which it is blessed. The profusion of lilies, hibiscus, bougainvillea, plumbago and other exotic plants such as wild fig, olive, banana and palm trees combined with the scent of jasmine everywhere making it a botanist's vision of heaven on earth.

The city was also rich in respect of beguiling buildings with selected hills serving as plinths for imposing structures such as the Rubaga Cathedral built on the site where the Palace of the Kabaka (king) once stood. Mengo Hill is adorned by the Luberi (royal enclosure) home to 'King Freddie' Mutesa II. On top of Kibuli Hill is a mosque straight out of an illustrated book of Scheherazade's 1001 Arabian Nights. I had to forego much of the sightseeing, hunting instead for tyres to replace those crippled by the murram. This was both boring and frustrating since the local stores only catered for British and Continental cars so we had to settle for re-treads for the American Stud and Zis.

We left Kampala en route to the Mountains of the Moon, well content with a highly enjoyable, relaxed stopover.

Smitty had the gumption to pack the truck in such a way as to allow space for those of us travelling in the truck to lay full length and sleep if we wanted to. Here I should mention that in Johannesburg the word bazaar meant only one thing - the OK Bazaar - the largest department store in the country. Facing onto Eloff Street and occupying an entire city block it specialized in cheaper merchandise than any other in the city. Mrs. Dinger's voluminous handbag was filled to bursting point with unlikely contents such as safety pins, adhesive plasters, aspirin, pencils, needle and thread, sun cream, screwdrivers, a rusted pen knife and even a pair of pliers along with other anomalous impedimenta.

When one of Smitty's rifles rattled loose from its rack it fell behind the pile of tightly packed luggage and Smitty was unable to haul it up with a wire coat hanger so he asked Mrs. Dinger if she had any string. She was in a waspish mood and snapped 'You don't think I'm a bazaar do you?'

Quick as a flash Eric retorted, 'No Mrs. Dinger but we do think you're OK.'

Two hundred miles west of Kampala lay Fort Portal, which held even less tourist interest than the average soporific South African dorp except for large herds of Ankole Longhorn cattle which thrive thereabouts. These splendid animals have amazing curved horns - some larger than mature elephant tusks. Ankole horns can grow as long as six feet from skull to the tip and up to twelve feet between one tip and t'other.

Fort Portal is the gateway to the immense Ruwenzori Mountains, 75 miles long and 40 miles wide, vaguely similar to Natal's Valley of a Thousand Hills except that the hills and valleys of the Ruwenzori are bigger, loftier and far more jumbled than its South African counterpart. In Uganda they are known by special names such as 'King of the Clouds', 'Rain Mountains' and, most evocatively, the Mountains of the Moon due to the erosion of volcanic craters forming the transcendent peaks that abound in the region. The unusual vegetation flourishing on the mineral rich soil completes the illusion of being on the moon as mankind may have imagined it before telescopes revealed the true moonscape.

Aristotle spoke of the Nile river *'rising in a silver mountain'* which may have led to another of the scores of legends associated with the Mountains, one of which maintains that somewhere in its aloof reaches lay the fabled King Solomon's mines as immortalsed by Rider Haggard.

The scenery is striking. Ruwenzori's magnificent peaks surge towards the sky; its fertile forests and vivid vegetation spring from the earth; incredibly exquisite lakes repose everywhere while myriad birds and beasts all conspired to challenge my attempts to capture them in words. In fact animals are so plenteous in this vibrant area that we took the daily sightings of galactic herds of buffalo for granted. Tropical birds are so profuse that a birdwatcher in the Ruwenzori can spot more species in one day than in a month of Sundays anywhere else in the world.

We stopped at the forbidding Semliki River. Sluggish and grey green it has the densest crocodile population on earth. We filmed a bask of more than twenty of these petrifying primeval predators fifteen feet long from nose to the tip of their ugly tails.

The Semliki flows through the Continent's first national park - the Albert National Park now renamed the Virunga National Park - said to be the largest game reserve in Africa stretching over 3,000 square miles from the Ruwenzori to the northern shores of Lake Kivu.

We drove over the Ruwenzori into our first Congo town, Beni, on the edge of the massive Ituri forest. Road builders had punctiliously cleared away the almost impregnable wall of trees lining both sides of the narrow road. In places the forest is so vitally alive that newly cleared undergrowth would be completely overgrown the next day - a tale we took with a pinch of salt. This posed the question of whether or not even snakes could wriggle their way through such harsh compacted vegetation where tenacious parasitic creepers endeavour to choke life from tall trees towering above us like pillars in a vast natural cathedral. Vines and monkey ladder lianas seemed to tether the trees to the ground as if trying to restrain the topmost branches from poking cherubs up their backsides.

Throughout this phase of the journey we were, as usual, dogged by breakdowns. Sporadically our vehicles were all buggered at the same time. Spare parts were not in plentiful supply in jungle regions and our search for spares necessitated lengthy journeys back and forth to the nearest town. Aware that buyers were in desperate need unscrupulous traders routinely demanded exorbitant prices generally accompanied by the seller's mantra about the item required being in short supply hereabouts. Zis was often stuck in outlandish places for days on end waiting for parts. This further frayed worn tempers and fresh dissent among us.

Our route skirted the western escarpment of the Great Rift Valley's formidable roads. There were few passing places among its thousands of convoluted twists and turns and the only way traffic could be assured of safe passage was by means of native drums generally fashioned from 44 gallon oil drums. No one could explain the language of the drums to us but thankfully they worked well and not once did we encounter a vehicle heading towards us and we seldom had to stop at a drummer's passing point on the single track road to make way for an oncoming vehicle. Whether or not this service was funded by local administration is not known but Crone ensured that drummers were rewarded both at the start and finish of every drum zone.

The okapi is among the rarest creature on earth. The only one we saw was stuffed and on display in the foyer of a Congolese guest house. It was an odd beast vaguely resembling a hyena with a large neck. Stripes on its haunches gave rise to the mind-boggling premise that it is a cross between a zebra and a giraffe but in fact it is a cousin to the giraffe.

Not many humans have seen those shy, elusive creatures in the wild apart from another rare species, the Mbuti pygmies, with whom they share the equatorial rain forest's 24,300 square miles.

These Lilliputian pygmies, the tallest measuring only four feet high, were not nearly as unsophisticated as we'd been led to expect. Indeed they proved adroit at negotiating filming rights with us via a sort of agent in Beni on the edge of the forest. He was a pathetic wee man with a withered arm who had to be lifted aboard the truck to guide us to the pygmies.

Eventually the jungle trail became too dense for Zis to continue so we had to get off and walk towards their encampment. Along the way we were met by a band of tiny people who'd come to greet us. It was quite literally a band. They plucked crude bowlike instruments, blew into miniature flutes, banged their wee drums and danced and sang spiritedly while escorting us to their clearing in the forest. The men, who wore only loincloths, were well proportioned but the mature women all had saggy breasts, tattooed bums and belly buttons comparable to beer barrel bungs conjuring up the concept that if they could suddenly be unplugged the little women would spurt through the jungle like those deflating stag party condom balloons.

The men demonstrated their archery expertise with bows fashioned from sticks rammed into deboned monkey tails. They fired their poison tipped arrows extremely rapidly, at about a second per shot. Their prey, monkeys, deer, birds and fish each had its own specific arrowhead. The Mbuti relied entirely on the forest for food, drink, shelter and clothing and venerated its bounty to the extent that they proudly professed to be 'Children of the Forest.' They had no use for coinage and our fees were paid, in advance, with cigarettes. They weren't as possessive of their weapons as the Maasai and gladly bartered them with us for cigarettes.

It's hard to say who enjoyed themselves more, the pygmies or us. Our cameramen were shooting as if there was to be no tomorrow. The females had seldom seen a white woman, let alone one with peroxided hair. All the pygmies, men included, wanted to touch Helga Crone's golden locks and she graciously allowed them to do so. They were far less belligerent than the Maasai but equally impressed by her patience and would have happily have stroked her hair all day if she'd let them.

While this obeisance was at its height I borrowed a tiny baby from one of the throng of women surrounding Helga. Its naked rear fitted comfortably in the palm of my cupped hand. Smitty took the infant from me and sat it in his inverted pith sun helmet - the kind with an air ventilation button at the top. No sooner had I started to warn him that the baby might have a natural urge, than four small streams of amber liquid trickled through the vent button. I don't think I'd seen or heard so many people hoot so loudly or so long since Cousin Ivan's stag night.

The journey from the smallest humans on earth to the tallest was less than 90 miles as the crow flies from Beni to Ruanda-Urundi only the winding escarpment road probably doubled that distance. Would you believe we were again behind schedule and were greatly distressed that this prevented us from exploring Virunga to film the mountain gorillas.

When we reached the realm of the lofty Tutsis, we discovered that their male height averaged seven feet. Their origins are lost in time and their imperturbably regal bearing lent itself to the disproved theory that they were descended from the Pharaohs of Egypt. The Tutsi Mwami (king) ruled malevolently over the country's Hutu people, numbering about 85% of the population, mimicking the practices of South Africa's minority apartheid regime.

The Hutu deeply resented their feudal masters until, in 1994, they turned on them in a three month killing spree. Africa's holocaust involved the horrifying massacre of nigh on a million Tutsis.

But in 1952 everything seemed blessedly tranquil in the land which had to be the blueprint for the Garden of Eden, on the shores of Lake Kivu, 5,000 ft. above the ocean and arguably the most sensationally beautiful lake in existence.

Once filming fees had been levied we were allowed to shoot a Tutsi dance display. Clad in tribal battle array, the dancers wore bright red calf length trousers held in place by crisscross bands of white beads Sam Browne belt style across their bare chests. Their white apron overskirts were emblazoned with black open hand patterns and their headdresses were fashioned from long white banana tree fibre. Their feet were bare save for leather anklets each having twelve small bells sewn on them. Dancers in today's clubs would sell their souls to be able to achieve the sheer athleticism and effortless movements performed by the Tutsis to the accompaniment of extraordinary sounds created by sixteen musicians wearing simple red saris with circular blue patterns. The unusual instruments included unique flutes and drums of differing tones found only in that region.

Another touch of magic in this enchanted land came shortly after sunset when a few of us swam beneath the crystal clear stars reflected in Kivu's crocodile and hippo free volcanic water illuminated by the fiery exuberance of a distant active volcano.

Years later when Ruanda-Urundi became an abattoir it appalled me to think that such a magnificently ravishing corner of our planet was transformed into bloodstained killing fields on an industrial scale greater than Europe's genocide.

As we progressed through the Congo, the tyre woes and breakdowns escalated, compelling our party to camp out for several days within the confines of a very basic native village while Charles, Smitty and I left in the Studebaker, the only remaining roadworthy vehicle, in another quest for tyres and spare parts. If it had been possible to map our route the pattern would have resembled the haphazard peregrinations of an alcoholic ant. Local people directed us to various *dukas* and villages but on arrival we'd be advised that we'd either taken the wrong route or no, they had no idea where we should be but suggested possible sources of tyres and parts and - hell, multiply that by ten and you will know why, over six decades later, I am unable to retrace the route we took on our fruitless task. Meanwhile, back at the village with no name our colleagues were not having a very congenial time either. No toilets, no fresh water, no meat, and the canned food aboard Zis was rapidly dwindling. However they weren't terribly badly off. There was fruit and vegetables galore and fresh - though scrawny - chickens and their eggs but no one had the stomach for their hosts' home brew.

Nevertheless Crone had suffered unrelenting grumbling from Dinger and the Long family due to boredom and the theft of small belongings.

The search for tyres and parts continued. Time was running short, as were tempers among us. We chanced upon a signboard in French stating that traffic on a nearby side road was absolutely forbidden. A party of natives moseyed towards us and told us 'Plenty white bwanas and soldiers down road.' It took a great deal of persuasion from me to get Charles to travel on it because he feared that the road led to a uranium mine where we'd be arrested and his car confiscated. I argued that if we explained what dire straits we were in we would not be spurned. He ultimately acquiesced to take his car in with the proviso that I would take full responsibility for the fate of his car. Naturally I agreed.

At the end of that road we reached a settlement of modern bungalows housing white miners. An engineer offered me a ride to Albertville (today's Kalemie) in his Ford station wagon driven by a very nervy Congolese. Before we reached the town we were stopped at a police road block set up because of a smallpox epidemic in Albertville. I had all my documents with me except, would you believe, my inoculation certificate. Fortunately the Belgian I was with assured them that my certificate was on its way in another car and we were grudgingly allowed to proceed.

None of the town's spare part dealers were able to help and as the mine driver had returned to the mine I had no alternative but to hang about waiting for the Stud in the hotel bar where I got talking to a man who suggested that perhaps the army could help. At last we hit the jackpot. The army had received a supply of tyres which did not fit any of their vehicles. These were passed to the local Public Works Department in case they could find a use for them. The tyres were, miraculously, the right size for Zis and the PWD was quite pleased to sell them to us at a bargain basement figure.

I found a transport company belonging to one Victor Nduma 'transporteur' to take me, Smitty and the tyres back to the truck. Charles sped off for the 'base village' where Crone prevailed upon him to drive the whinging Long family back to South Africa in his Studebaker.

Once Zis and the Volkswagen were repaired and re-tyred we set off homewards not really wanting to undertake any more filming or sightseeing, only Crone insisted we had to shoot at one last location. And how right he was because two astonishing cherries lay ahead waiting to top off our safari's filming cake.

At Kiubo on the river Lufira half a mile off the main road in the middle of an arid area of sundried bush we gasped with pleasure at an 880 ft. wide waterfall pizzicato-ing down nearly 200 ft. of rocks analogous to a pile of huge, multiple tiered, curved jelly moulds cleverly designed as if it were a water garden feature at the annual Brobdingnag Flower Show.

Its nearby sibling on the same river is a smaller, narrower and arguably even more unusual waterfall which is equally breathtaking. Its water tinkles gracefully down geometric rock steps which look as if they too were man made. In spaces, between the countless little tributaries abundant small trees and plants had taken root in the waterfall itself presenting a wondrous sight well worthy of being named 'The Fairy Falls'.

Today, in my dotage, I reflect with deep sorrow that the shedding of the European colonial shackles that were inflicted on most of the natives of Africa evolved, into other equally despicable, kleptocratic systems of so-called self-governance stridently echoing the greed and ruthlessness of its European invaders.

In the Congo one man in particular, the conniving King Leopold II of Belgium, coveted this titanic territory, nearly 80 times larger than Belgium itself. He began acquiring land by having his agents barter bolts of cloth or inexpensive trinkets for land before he appointed the famed explorer-cum-conman Henry Morton Stanley as his representative. Stanley amassed enormous swathes of land on a breathtaking scale on behalf of his boss until the king personally owned the entire Congo which was mercilessly pillaged and raped by Stanley's so-called *Force Publique* from around 1885 until, in 1908, when international revulsion built up to such a crescendo that the Belgian parliament annexed the Congo Free State, renaming it the Belgian Congo, and paid their king two million pounds compensation for his 'personal losses', conveniently overlooking the disgusting, inhuman measures and acts of unspeakable violence perpetrated by Stanley's mercenary murderers against indigenous tribes throughout the country. These were so abhorrent that they make even the worst excesses of the Nazis almost fade into insignificance. Estimates of the number of people exterminated vary from 10 million to 30 million. Detailing the atrocities would make you retch which is the last thing I would want to happen to you, dear reader, but if curiosity overcomes you, by far the best concise reference was published in the UK's Independent newspaper in July 2006 entitled '*Forever in Chains. The tragic history of Congo*' by Paul Vallely. Well worth Googling if you have a strong stomach.

As I conclude this narrative, the terror and butchery in the former Belgian Congo continues inexorably as hundreds of thousands more Congolese are still being slaughtered and face extinction at the behest of corrupt, rapacious politicians of the so-called 'Democratic' Republic of Congo.'

The final stopover at Elizabethville (today's Lubumbashi) was the start of our last lap. In 1955 Elizabethville was a large, modern, well planned, continental city founded on bounteous copper deposits.

Except for nearly being arrested at the Congo border as suspected gun runners we reached Salisbury (now Harare) in good time and in good spirits. There was a modicum of press interest there which prompted Crone to ask me to fly home to arrange for the media to greet the Dodge and its passengers on arrival in Johannesburg, an assignment I accepted with alacrity.

The South African press did not exactly fall over one another for the 'scoop' and the handful who did publish the story of our eco-unfriendly stab at scaling Kilimanjaro drew accusations of vandalism. Looking at it positively we felt that the American television company would not be averse to a little controversy relating to our films.

But the unfulfilled curse of the baobabs lay in ambush waiting to shock us to the core. All our film stock was delivered to Irene Film Laboratories for processing and, as soon as it was ready, we drove excitedly from Johannesburg to Pretoria to view the results.

The first few reels were excellent. The heat and the dust had been kept at bay by careful packing. Then disaster. About two thirds of the film was ever so slightly out of focus, falling well below professional acceptability. This, we discovered, was caused by minor damage to the only range finder we had. Since its readings were taken as gospel by all three cameramen everything shot at infinity was in clear focus while much of the middle distance and crucial close-ups were not. I was nearly sick all over the viewing theatre.

Our hope of producing six half hour episodes was stone dead and there was barely enough material for a single 90 minute film which I named *Tent of Stars*. Once we had completed a rough cut (i.e. the first trial edit) and a draft commentary was in place it turned out appreciably better than we could have hoped for thanks mainly to the Victoria Falls game park footage which was all in sharp focus suggesting that the viewfinder must have been damaged after we left the falls.

The film still required music and snappy graphics but, being aimed at North American audiences, a Serth Effrikin accented commentary would have been totally unacceptable. I agreed with Crone that the USA would be the ideal place for completion. Crone said finances only allowed for two air fares and he and his wife were off to the USA with the film and he'd see me soon.

Months passed without a word from him. His telephone was disconnected so I visited his house in the hope of discovering what was going on. The occupants who were renting it referred me to the landlord who told me Crone had done a moonlight flit owing him a lot of back rent. The only sign of the Crones was the rusting, worthless Zis. Africa Convoys, the name Crone gave our enterprise was merely a name, not a company, so there were no assets.

It was only shortly before I was about to migrate to Britain that I learnt that Crone was back in South Africa again, trying to reinstate his original trans-African safari company which he had abandoned prior to my meeting him. Crone had then been involved with two other Germans - a Baron von Mellenthin and Oskar Koenig, a professional white hunter. The Baron, a former German General had settled in South Africa after the Allies released him from prison.

These men had again teamed up with Crone to form Africa Overland whose intention it was to take tourists from Johannesburg to Algiers. They published a glossy booklet *'Expedition Adventure – Africa Overland in 80 Days.'*

The Baron was chairman, Koenig safari manager and, so said the booklet, '*Mr. B Crone with his vast experience of jungle law* (sic) *will enable you to find and observe every species in their natural surroundings. You are in good hands. All set? Let's go!*'

The small print reserved to Africa Overland the '*right to cancel or alter any tour if force of circumstances demand such action.*'

That venture had failed to attract any customers. My safari had seemingly been Crone's opportunity to salvage something from the ashes and there he was having another go. My efforts to trace him were a waste of time and I never saw nor heard from Mr. and Mrs. Bruno Crone again. I'd been well and truly stitched up.

In the months prior to my marriage I returned to live with my parents in their stylish, newly purchased double storey home in Westcliff, a smart suburb a mere lion's roar away from the Johannesburg zoo. It was deeply depressing trying to fall asleep at night to the sound of those noble beasts vainly broadcasting their appeals for freedom from behind the bars that confined them. Sadly they had much in common with millions of their two legged co-inhabitants of the Union of South Africa, the non-white people inside or outside apartheid jails whose restraints were far worse than those of the zoo lions. The animals were at least well fed, well-watered and sheltered against the searing daily heat and bitter cold of Witwatersrand nights. Those lions strengthened my resolve to leave the land of apart hate for good.

The moment I became engaged to their daughter the Ostrofskys began to plan a big, fat, ostentatious Jewish wedding and preparations speedily engaged top gear. The prenuptial hoopla entailed no fewer than three receptions. In retrospect my situation was not far removed from the scenario for a possible sequel to the movie Four Weddings and a Funeral. Only the title for my version would have been Three *Parties* and a Funeral.

The first 'do' was exclusively for the family: the second was allotted to the congregation of Ostrofsky's synagogue and for good measure a third was chucked in for the members of Allenby, his lawn bowling club.

The wedding itself was not to be a mere reception. No sir! The Ostrofsky wedding was designated a *Dinner Dansant* which is the precise wording he had printed on the invitations. Pretentious? *Moi?* The function took place in the Temple David hall adjacent to the synagogue next to the Doll House drive-in. Oh yes, the funeral? Mine.

Ostrofsky was determined that *his* wedding would outshine anything ever previously staged in the Golden City. Yes sir - it was to be full fig Dinner Jackets, Ball Gowns and other vulgarities all round, designed to ooze saccharine sentimentality to the *nth* degree.

Everyone they ever knew was invited. Not because they were friendly but to avoid the famous *'farribels'* touched upon earlier in this memoir. It all moved along unrelentingly without much consultation between me and my future in-laws. This wasn't a bad thing and I let them get on with it except to insist that my brother would be both best man and MC and that the speeches be kept to an absolute minimum. Secure in the knowledge that Ernest's pronunciation, his spoonerisms and his deadly malapropisms would enliven the proceedings with large lumps of levity, I agreed that he should propose the toast to the parents.

Nor did he let me down. Whilst extolling my bride's virtues, he mentioned her musical ability. She owned an early foldaway electric piano (since the Ostrofsky flat could not have accommodated a real piano, not even a wee upright). The brand name of the instrument was Univox. 'Myrdle,' declared Erling, pronouncing her name as always, with a 'd' instead of a 't', 'Myrdle sings in the choir and I always loved to watch her playing with her Uniworks.'

Nonetheless Erling's oleaginous panegyric left a sour taste in my mouth as he sycophantically showered praise on his mistress and his cuckolded business partner, somehow 'forgetting' to mention my parents. I remedied this pettiness by adding a touch of extemporisation to my prepared speech as I suspected that his oversight was not accidental but Ostrofsky motivated.

I would have preferred a percentage of the cost of the wedding as a dowry instead of having to endure all those freaky receptions on which a disgustingly profligate amount of money was squandered. I couldn't help speculating that a small portion of it could have saved a number of starving South African black folk. Instead I bit my tongue and kept *shtum* not wanting the Ostrofskys to get the slightest whiff of my objective to make our honeymoon visit to England a permanent one.

My strategy, substantially reinforced by NUSAS and the safari, was to escape South Africa's racist policies and inhuman mores and to seek work in the entertainment industry. In order to throw the in-laws further off the scent, I had asked, and was granted, Ostrofsky's authority to store my personal effects in the basement of his shop 'pending our return.'

My wedding was pretty much indistinguishable from those described earlier in these pages except I wasn't really a bridegroom, more a bridal accessory.

It only remains to record that my friend Sackheim was a guest. His gift? Yes, an audio album of my wedding, the perfect aide-memoire for my chapter on the Ghosts of Weddings Past.

I now look to the cockalorum Lionel Ostrofsky, to have the final say with the immortal verse he composed and had printed on the menus placed in front of every guest at my marriage *Dinner Dansant:-*

We've tried to do the best we're able
To see you're happy at your table.
And if there's one you do not know,
Extend your hand, "My name is Joe,
I've seen you someplace else, I think,
But last time 'twas without your mink!"
This no doubt will break the ice
The atmosphere will then be nice.
Pleasant company always tends
To make you folks the best of friends.
A good beginning from the start
Makes friends of strangers when they part.
Tonight dear people, we're intent
To see that you are all content
So go ahead and have your fun
And thanks for coming everyone

Oy vey!

As the good ship RMS Capetown Castle throbbed its way northwards my thoughts were of the large and loving family I was leaving behind. I had evanescent visions of the way life may have evolved for us had we remained in South Africa's repellent atmosphere of hate that I had been sheltered from by my parents and my school. I was very lucky indeed to have emerged relatively unscarred by the horrors of apartheid and anti-Semitism.

Fortune had favoured my family. Had my paternal grandparents remained in Lithuania they would doubtless have perished in the pogroms or the holocaust together with my great uncle Labe Joffe and his family so that I owe a profound debt of gratitude to Donald Currie without whom I would not exist.

My maternal family's migration to South Africa was due to the effect of the awful British climate on my grandfather David Naar's health. It amuses me to speculate that had he remained in England I may have been a Cockney instead of a Joburger.

I was leaving behind my closest boyhood friends and those with whom I'd bonded after leaving school. The pangs of parting were painful but the fact that I was leaving the miasma of apartheid made the unsullied sea air taste like the nectar of freedom. My heart soared at the thought that if I had children they would not be exposed to the trauma of living with a barbaric regime in a land of hatred and oppression. But fate decreed otherwise.

I never had doubts about succeeding in my adopted country where I was privileged to live but I had no idea that I would meet and work with such quantities of wonderful people ranging from the unemployed, through gamblers and jailbirds, prime ministers, prima donna politicians and copious quantities of thespians, abundant authors, famed painters and a major dollop of Who's Who celebrities in UK show business. And getting paid handsomely to do so.

But that's another story.

Apartheid. Afrikaans. (Pronounced Aparrrt Hate. Don't forget to roll the r's). 'Separate racial development.' Segregation.

Arbeit Macht Frei. German. Work makes free. Slogan found at Nazi death camps.

Askari. Swahili / Arabic. East and Central African term for a soldier but frequently used in relation to uniformed men, such as police and security guards.

Bar Mitzvah. Hebrew. Bar = Son, Mitzvah = Covenant. Although it is not obligatory, most Jewish boys read a portion of the Law in a synagogue usually followed by a party to celebrate his coming of age in the sense that he is now held responsible for his actions.

Beth Din. Jewish Ecclesiastical Court.

Bioscope. An early 20th Century motion picture projector. South Africans adopted the name in preference to cinema.

Blerry. South African pronunciation of bloody.

Bob. SA Slang for a shilling.

Boep. Afrikaans for belly, especially an obese one.

Bris. Circumcision.

Brochas. Hebrew blessings acknowledging the Almighty as the source of all blessings.

Broederbond. Afrikaans. Band of brothers. Brotherhood.

Bugger up. To give - or take - a hiding.

Bundu. SA Slang for remote uninhabited area. Used by city dwellers in relation to anywhere outside municipal boundaries. Far from town. To hell and gone.

Bwana. Swahili. A respectful form of address.

Caffie. Johannesburg pronunciation of café.

Challah. Yiddish. Braided egg bread similar to *brioche.*

Chalish. Yiddish. To faint from hunger. Yearning for food with watering mouth. (Pronounce as if clearing your throat - a hard, throaty 'ch' as in loch.)

Chrain. Yiddish. Grated horseradish dyed with beetroot juice. As with *chalish.*

Chutzpah. Yiddish. Damn cheek. Effrontery. Unbelievable gall. Pronounce 'ch' again as with *chalish.*

Coloured. Insulting apartheid term for people of mixed race.

Dagga. South African cannabis.

Daydog. Non boarding pupil.

Doek. Afrikaans for cloth. Generally used to describe a headscarf.

Donga. Zulu. A deep gully caused by serious soil erosion.

Donner. Afrikaans. To beat up. To give a blerry good hiding.

Doppies. Used cartridge cases. Source unknown.

Drek. Yiddish. Crap. Faeces.

Duka. Swahili. Shop.

Fanagolo. Mainly Zulu with modified English and Afrikaans words thrown in for leavening.

Farribel. Yiddish. Differences of opinion lasting forever.

Feldman. 'Cocky'- the 'Pocket Hercules'. Eight times South African champion jockey. He rode more than 1,500 winners, had the build of a boxer and dropped dead at the age of 35. Pop backed every horse ridden by him only to return his winnings to the bookies by betting on horses with less talented jockeys.

Fray. Afrikaans. Heavy petting.

Frum. Yiddish. (Pronounced froom.) Very religious Jew.

Gillygaloo. Mythical Australian bird that lays square eggs.

Goeie namiddag meneer. Afrikaans. Good afternoon sir. (Clearing throat 'g').

Goon. A large glass marble.

Guinea. Once a British gold coin valued at 21 shillings. It is a term still used in some UK horse racing circles.

Halfcrown. A coin worth two shillings and six pence in old British (and South African) currency.

Hau. Zulu. Expression of wonderment or bewilderment. Pronounced how!

Indaba. Zulu. A discussion.

Ironie. A steel ball bearing used when playing marlies.

Jambo. Swahili. Hello.

JLS. Acronym for Jack the Lad Swing, a British boy band. Winners of a UK television talent show.

Jol. Afrikaans. To play or enjoy. Often both.

Jong. (Pronounced 'yong') Afrikaans for 'youth'. South Africans are wont to over use the phrase 'hey man'. When addressing kids or good friends it often becomes 'hey jong.'

Kak. Afrikaans. Excrement.

Kakies. Afrikaans corruption of khaki. Kak is also the Afrikaans word for turds.

Kaross. Animal hide blanket with the hair left on.

Kashrut. Jewish dietary laws.

Keppel. Yiddish. Skull cap.

Kippa. Another word for Keppel.

Kosher. Clean or fit to eat in accordance to dietary laws laid down in the bible forbidding Jews to consume food to which they are spiritually allergic.

Kraken. An enormous mythical sea monster popularised by John Wyndham's novel *The Kraken Wakes.* See Google.

Kukella. Yiddish term of endearment. Cookie (?)

Lobola. Zulu and other tribal languages. Money or cattle paid to the bride's family.

Locke, Bobby. South Africa's first international golfer. Four time winner of the British Open Championship.

Mafuta. Zulu. Fat person.

Mahatma. Hindu holy person.

Mampara. Sotho. Idiot, simpleton.

Mamzer. Yiddish. An illegitimate person. Colloquially, a right bastard.

Marlies. Marbles.

Matriculation. In South Africa this marks the end of secondary schooling and qualifies the recipient to enter university provided the student has reached a sufficiently high standard such as a distinction, a first class pass or a very good second class.

Mazel Tov. Yiddish. Good luck.

Megillah. Yiddish. A tedious account.

Meisie. Afrikaans. A girl.

Melktert. Afrikaans. Milk tart.

Moenie. Afrikaans. Do not. Usually with the Afrikaans double negative - 'moenie dit doen nie.' Literally, do not do it not.

Mohel. Hebrew. He who snips. The circumciser.

Nats. Abbreviation for the Afrikaner Nationalist Party.

Oke. Slang. A bloke. Seemingly confined to describe South African males. He's a nice / lousy oke. You okes coming with us?

Ossewabrandwag. Afrikaans. Ox Wagon Fire Watch.

Oy vey. Yiddish. Woe is me.

Petomane. Joseph Pujol. Starred in the Moulin Rouge in 1892 outselling Sarah Bernhardt. His talents could not only reproduce sound effects with a rubber tube up his rectum, but could also play a tune on a flute connected to the tube. The climax to his act was to blow out a candle from a distance. I yearned to emulate him. Became a role model for schoolboys.

Poegaai. Afrikaans. Intoxicated. Drunk as a skunk. Pronounce 'g' as 'ch'. Can also mean overtired, exhausted.

Poomshtoch. Origin uncertain, thought to be derived from Yiddish. Uncomplimentary equivalent to British slang 'Lady Muck.'

Pujol. See Petomane above.

PUTCO. Acronym for Public Utility Transport Company. A blacks only bus service.

Randlord. Local word for rich property owners.

Riempies. Afrikaans. Leather thongs.

Schmeer. Yiddish. The entire package.

Shebeen. Irish. Drinking place. Usually illegal.

Shikker. Yiddish. Inebriated.

Shiksa. Yiddish. Non Jewish woman. Highly uncomplimentary.

Shmaltz. Yiddish. Chicken fat.

Shtetl. Yiddish. A Jewish community in a small town or village.

Shtum. Yiddish. Silent.

Sjambok. A rhinoceros hide bullwhip some six feet long. Originally used to drive cattle but evolved into a weapon of fear extensively employed by apartheid era police against black people.

Sloot. Afrikaans. A small stream or a ditch with water in it.

Smous. Afrikaans. Hawker.

Steptoe & Son. Popular BBC Television comedy series broadcast in the 1960's and 70's about two rag and bone men.

Stoep. Afrikaans. Veranda. Porch.

Sukkel. Afrikaans. To struggle unsuccessfully.

Swart maanhare. Afrikaans. Black mane hair.

Tickey. A very small silver coin. A threepenny piece or bit.

Tsotsis. Sotho. Gangsters, mainly teenagers but not confined to age.

Tzatzka. Yiddish. Kitsch junk.

Uitlander. Dutch / Afrikaans. A foreigner. Any non-Afrikaner.

Veldskoene. Afrikaans. Literally 'field shoes' of untanned leather.

Voortrekkers. Dutch / Afrikaans. Those who travel in advance of others. Pioneers.

Wheaties. 'The Breakfast of Champions'. A famous cereal heavily advertised at the time.

Yarmulke. Yiddish. Skull cap. Also known as a kippa.

Yentas. Yiddish. Elderly Jewish women. Generally overdressed and inveterate gossips often with a predisposition to matchmaking.

Yirra. Afrikaans. An expression of awe sounding as if it has extra r's. Yirrrrra!

Yock. Yiddish. A non-Jewish man. Not complimentary.

Zac. Slang. A silver sixpenny piece.

Zis. Dodge Brothers Model WC62, a 6 x 6 weapons carrier. Length 5.47 m. Height (covered) 2.17 m, without cover 1.57 m. Width 2.1 m. Weight 3120 kg. Payload fifteen kg (1.5 tons).

£sd. English. Pronounced LSD. Abbreviation for Britain's and South African currency of pounds, shillings and pence.

-o0o-

Bibliography

ARNOLD Millard, Editor THE TESTIMONY OF STEVE BIKO. First published by Random House USA 1978 and as a Panther book by Granada Publishing Limited UK 1979.

BIKO Steve. As above.

DAILY ADVERTISER. Port Elizabeth newspaper.

DURLACHER Barbara. Blank verse published on the web.

DUROS-FISH Bruce and Becky. CONGO - Exploration, Reform & a Brutal Legacy. Chelsea House Publishers, Philadelphia 2001

GATTI Ellen and Attilio. HERE IS AFRICA. Charles Scribner's Sons, New York 1943.

GOOGLE. In appreciation... How did anyone manage to do research B G (Before Google)?

HARRISON David. WHITE TRIBE OF AFRICA. Ariel Books the British Broadcasting Corporation, London 1981.

ISSROFF Dr. Saul. Numerous riveting papers accessed on the web - http/tinyurl.com/ SAJewishgenealogy & www.jewishgen.org/s.africa.

JOFFE Lord Joel. THE STATE vs NELSON MANDELA by one of the author's school friends who joined Mandela's defence team which saved the president-to-be from the death penalty. Madiba described him as *a man of rare courage and real devotion to the cause of justice.* This vividly explicit book is a must-read for anyone interested in the ridiculous senselessness of apartheid fanaticism. Oneworld Publications 2007.

KATZEW Henry. SOLUTION FOR SOUTH AFRICA. Nasionale Boekhandel Beperk 1956.

LAPPING Brian. APARTHEID A HISTORY in association with Granada Television. A definitive examination of a doctrine that incensed most of the world. A remarkably well researched work which followed the brilliant landmark television series produced by Mr. Lapping. These should be enshrined in the world television documentary Hall of Fame if ever one is established. Grafton Books a division of the Collins Publishing Group, London 1986.

LUTHULI Albert. LET MY PEOPLE GO. Fontana Books 1962.

MATHABANI Mark. KAFFIR BOY. A seminal work about his childhood and youth in Alexandra Township an appalling black ghetto of Johannesburg less than two miles away from the beautiful homes in which the author lived. Unmissable. Macmillan USA, The Bodley Head Great Britain – both 1986 and Pan Books 1987.

NEWMAN Professor Aubrey N. TRAINS & SHELTERS & SHIPS and UNION CASTLE LINE & EMIGRATION FROM EASTERN EUROPE TO SOUTH AFRICA. Published on the web.

PATON Alan. CRY, THE BELOVED COUNTRY published by Cape 1944 and Penguin Books 1958.

PORTER Andrew. VICTORIAN SHIPPING, BUSINESS & IMPERIAL POLICY. The Royal Historical Society, The Boydell Press Woodbridge, St Martin's Press New York 1986.

RAND DAILY MAIL. Johannesburg morning newspaper.

RUBIN Margot. THE JEWISH COMMUNITY OF JOHANNESBURG. A dissertation. Accessed on the internet 2009.

SAKS David Y. JEWS ON COMMANDO. Jewishgen internet 2005.

SHAIN Professor Milton. THE ROOTS OF ANTI-SEMITISM IN SOUTH AFRICA. University Press of Virginia 1994.

SMUTS J. C. JAN CHRISTIAAN SMUTS by his son. My boyhood idol General 'Oom Jannie' Smuts turned out to have feet of clay as the man who introduced the word 'apartheid' to the world. Cassell & Company Ltd. London 1952.

SOUTH AFRICAN DEPARTMENT OF DEFENCE Documentation Centre.

STAR THE. Johannesburg evening newspaper.

STRYDOM Hans. Co-author THE SUPER AFRIKANERS. See Wilkins below.

SUNDAY TIMES. National South African newspaper.

SYNONYMS360.com website.

TAYLOR Jeremy. Composer of *Ag Pleeze Deddy* an amusing popular song which was far from appreciated by the South African Nationalist government of the time.

TFD. The Farlex Free Dictionary website. Invaluable.

VAN RENSBURG Patrick. GUILTY LAND. This keenly observed insight into the psyche of the Afrikaners was banned by the apartheid regime. It makes a fascinating read. Penguin Special S205 1962. In 1957 Patrick resigned from the South African Diplomatic Service. In 1960 he went into exile in the UK where he worked as the Director of the South African boycott within the anti-apartheid movement based in London.

WEINER Rebecca. SOUTH AFRICAN JUDAISM. Paper published by The Jewish Virtual Library on the internet. Accessed 2008.

WIKIPEDIA. Where else could one go to verify esoteric words and facts? An indispensable reference tool for any writer,

WILKINS Ivor & STRYDOM Hans. THE SUPERAFRIKANERS. An extraordinary exposé of the macabre, clandestine, secret society, the Broederbond. Jonathan Ball Publishers, Johannesburg 1978.WOODS Donald. ASKING FOR TROUBLE. Once a supporter of apartheid Woods, a journalist and editor, was in his thirties before he realised quite how horrendous the South African regime was becoming. He was forced to flee South Africa after publishing his book about the murdered Steve Biko. Victor Gollancz Ltd, London 1980.

-oOo-

Lightning Source UK Ltd.
Milton Keynes UK
UKOW02f1238091215

264360UK00001B/130/P